TRUE CRIMES

# DEADLY INTENT

igloo

igloo

This edition published in 2010
by Igloo Books Ltd
Cottage Farm
Sywell
NN6 0BJ

www.igloo-books.com



A copy of the British Library Cataloguing-in-Publication Data is available from the British Library.

10 9 8 7 6 5 4 3 2 1

ISBN 978-0-85734-395-6

Printed and Manufactured in China

# Contents

# Ted Bundy

**The total number will never be known, but at least 30 and as many as 100 unfortunate women and girls were victims of Ted Bundy during his four-year killing spree. That such a savage slayer seemed on the surface to be a handsome, dapper and charming man makes his case all the more compelling. So when did this all-American boy turn into a depraved monster?**

## Charmer With Movie Star Looks Was Merciless Manic

**The answer may be earlier** than anyone thought. When he was three years of age, Ted's 15-year-old aunt awoke one night to find that Ted had lifted the bedclothes and had placing butcher's knives around her body. 'He just stood there and grinned,' she recalled. 'I shooed him out of the room and took the knives back to the kitchen. I remember thinking at the time that it was a very strange thing for a little kid to do.'

Young Theodore Robert was living with his grandparents at the time. Born on November 24, 1946, to an unmarried teenage mother in Philadelphia, he took on the name Bundy when she moved to Washington State in 1950 and wed hospital cook Johnnie Bundy. The bridegroom adopted Ted as his own son and he grew up with them in their Tacoma home in apparent domestic harmony.

Young Bundy became the all-American boy, joining the Boy Scouts, having a paper round and doing backyard clearance and mowing jobs for pocket money. His school grades were good and he was a high school athlete, then a student at the University of Washington. He became a campaign worker both for the Republican Party and for the Crime Commission in Washington State, where former colleagues believed he could have ended up a leading lawyer, a top politician, perhaps even a Senator.

But further clues to his character had arisen. His student reports spoke of a volatile temper. And although his undeniable charm and movie star looks won him no shortage of dates, some girlfriends recalled him as a sadistic lover who acted out weird bondage fantasies. Nevertheless, in 1971 he applied for voluntary work at a Seattle rape crisis center and, after being screened for

**LEFT:** The many faces of prolific American serial killer, Ted Bundy—all of them evil.

**ABOVE:** Bundy at one of many court appearances. During one, in Aspen, Colorado, he leapt from a window and escaped.

'maturity and balance', he was accepted as a counsellor.

It was this innocent image that Bundy played up to when he finally faced his accusers in a series of court appearances starting in 1975, during which the smiling, smooth-talker tried to charm jurors into believing he had no need to kidnap and kill. As he boasted: 'Why should I want to attack women? I had all the female companionship I wanted. I must have slept with dozens and all of them went to bed with me willingly.'

Even today, the mystery remains as to the total number of murders Bundy committed: the nine murders with which he was officially attributed, the 20 to 30 to which he had confessed or the 100-plus with which some investigators credit him, the general estimate being 35.

The manner of these deaths was not gentle. Typically, Bundy would bludgeon his victims, then strangle them to death. He also engaged in rape and necrophilia. His first known victim was law student Lynda Ann Healy, 21, who vanished from her Seattle apartment on the morning of January 31, 1974, leaving only a bloodstain on her pillow as a clue to her kidnapping and murder. Over the next three months, three more students, all teenagers, and two other women had been abducted and killed.

By mid-1974, Bundy, then aged 28, had become sufficiently emboldened to operate by daylight and even to give his real name, introducing himself with: 'Hi, I'm Ted.' In July, the killer, with his arm in a sling, wandered among a crowd of 40,000 who were swimming and sunbathing at Lake Sammamish State Park, near Seattle, approaching young girls and asking if they would help with his sailboat. One who declined nevertheless watched as the man—'really friendly, very polite, very sincere, with a nice smile'—lured another girl to his distinctive VW Beetle car. He killed two women that day, their naked bodies found in woodland months later, along with those of three other women, one a known missing person and two unidentifiable.

**ABOVE:** Bundy stalled his execution for 10 years, but eventually went to the electric chair in February 1989.

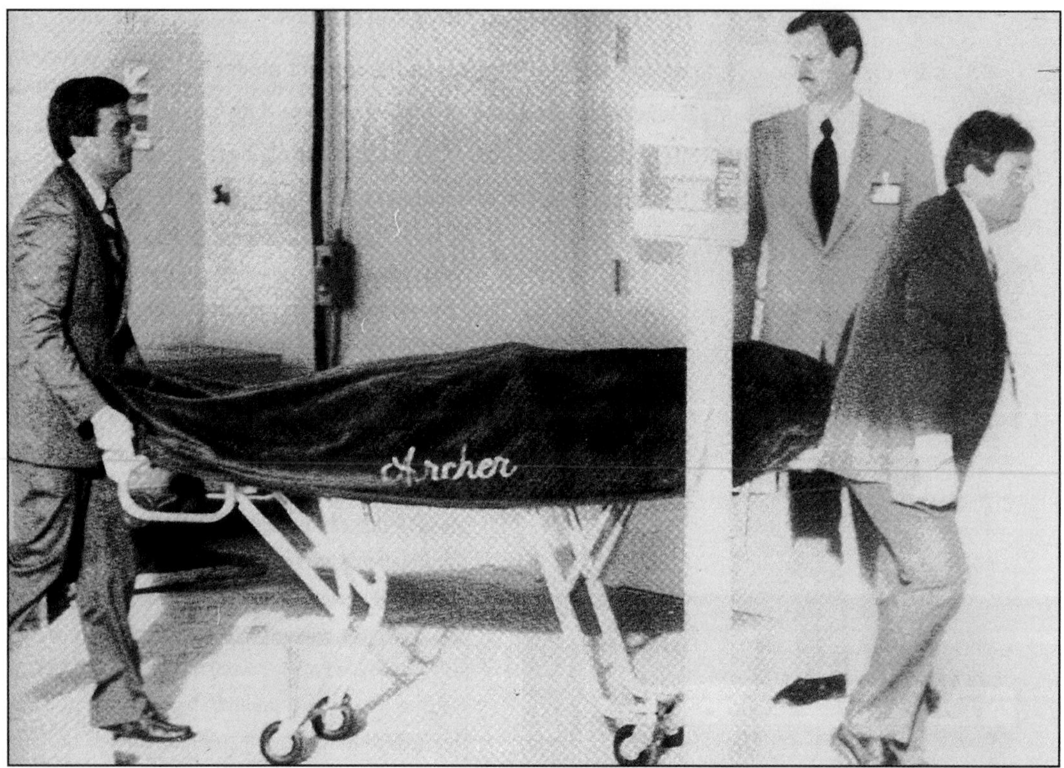


**ABOVE:** The body of Ted Bundy is wheeled away after he was executed in the electric chair at Starke Prison, Florida, on January 24, 1989.

But the trail in Washington went cold when Bundy moved state, enrolling at the University of Utah law school in Salt Lake City. There, in October and November, four girls aged between 16 and 18 were abducted, battered, raped, and strangled. The slaughter spread from Utah to Colorado, where between January and April 1975 at least five women went missing.

Police finally nabbed Bundy in Salt Lake City one night in August 1975—but initially only for a traffic violation. He was driving his VW with no lights when stopped and found to be in possession of a pair of handcuffs, a crowbar, a ski mask, and a nylon stocking. Charged with possessing tools for burglary, he was put in an identity line-up and was picked out by one of his would-be victims, 18-year-old Carol Da Ronch. She'd had a lucky escape when Bundy, posing as a police officer, had handcuffed her and dragged her into his VW, from which she rolled out as it slowed at a bend.

Bundy was charged with kidnapping but after months of legal argument—during much of which, incredibly, he was allowed out on bail—he was found guilty and sentenced to between one and 15 years. He was then moved to Colorado to stand trial for the murder of a 23-year-old student, abducted from a ski resort in January.

During a break in the court hearing at Aspen, Bundy leaped from a window and was free for eight days before recapture. He escaped a second time by cutting through a ceiling panel of his cell and stealing a police car. Driving first to Chicago, then traveling south to

Florida, Bundy rented a room near the University of Florida, Tallahassee, and again went on the rampage. On January 15, 1978, he crept into a dormitory at the university and viciously battered four students, strangling two of them to death before taking bites out of the buttocks of one of them.

Bundy's last victim was his youngest. On February 8, in Lake City, Florida, 12-year-old Kimberly Leach was strangled and sexually violated. A week later, when a Pensacola policeman stopped him for driving a stolen car, the killer tried to escape but was clubbed unconscious. He was brought to trial in Miami and convicted of the Tallahassee student murders and subsequently, in 1980, of the murder of young Kimberly Leach.

Bundy stalled his execution for almost 10 years with a string of appeals but finally confessed to 30 murders, including attacks in California, Michigan, Pennsylvania, Idaho, and Vermont. He went to the electric chair in Florida's Starke Prison in January 1989.

# John Bunting and accomplices

**On May 21, 1999, Adelaide police reopened a missing persons investigation that led them to a disused bank vault in rural Snowtown, South Australia. What they found there was a chamber of horrors that would stun the nation. Six acid-filled plastic barrels contained the grisly, mummified remains of eight dismembered bodies. Three days later, two further bodies were found buried in a backyard in a suburb north of Adelaide. A day later, four men were arrested, and the search for justice began.**

## Dismembered Bodies In Chamber Of Horrors

**Former abattoir worker** John Justin Bunting, born in Queensland in 1966, was the ringleader of a dysfunctional group of victims of child sex abuse and incest who shared an overriding hatred for homosexuals and pedophiles. Bunting, a psychopathic killer, and himself a victim of childhood sexual abuse, enlisted the help of friends (Robert Wagner and Mark Haydon, Bunting's second wife Elizabeth Harvey and stepson James Vlassakis) to partake in various acts of abduction, torture, and disposal of bodies.

Usually based on flimsy evidence or rumor, victims were murdered if suspected of being pedophiles. Others were killed because they were obese, illiterate, mentally disabled, gay or drug addicted. Most of the victims were friends, acquaintances or family members of at least one of the group.

Although not the motive for the killings, the murderers took on the identity of their victims to claim their welfare benefits, forging their signatures to pocket $95,000 and in some cases 'inheriting' their cars.

Bunting's killing spree began in August 1992. Clinton Trezise, 22, was struck about the head with a hammer several times in Bunting's living room after being invited round for a social visit.

For the next seven years, Bunting and his accomplices took the lives of various men and women—using torture methods such as electric clamps, pliers, cigarettes, and lit sparklers inserted in the penis in order to 'cure' their victims of their crimes. The victims were forced to call their torturers 'God', 'Master', 'Chief Inspector', and 'Lord Sir'.

Among the death toll was Suzanne Allen, 47, a friend of Bunting; Elizabeth Haydon, 37, wife of one of Bunting's co-conspirators; and Thomas Trevilyan, 18, who had helped murder one victim but was later killed after discussing the crime with others. In September 1998, Bunting's stepson, James Vlassakis, was persuaded to participate in the murder of his own half-brother

Troy Youde, just 21, who was killed in his house after being dragged from his bed while asleep.

David Johnson, 24, was the last to be murdered, in May 1999. He was lured to the disused bank with the promise of a low-price computer. There he was handcuffed and made to give his bank details. Two of the killers left to confirm the details were correct and Bunting strangled Johnson before they returned.

In the final stages of a complex, year-long missing persons investigation, police entered the former Snowtown branch of the State Bank of South Australia after a tip-off from neighbors. The discovery there of the eight dismembered bodies horrified hardened cops. Days later, two more bodies were uncovered at Bunting's former house and were linked to the same killers. Bunting, Haydon, Wagner, and Vlassakis were arrested and charged with murder.

After 11 months of shocking evidence in South Australia's longest and most complex criminal trial, the jury returned a guilty verdict against John Bunting and Robert Wagner. The jury found Bunting killed 11 people while his accomplice, Wagner, a bisexual muscleman, murdered seven. They were each sentenced to life imprisonment on each count, to be served cumulatively. The presiding judge, Justice Brian Martin, said the men were 'in the business of killing for pleasure' and were 'incapable of true rehabilitation'.

In a separate trial in the Adelaide Supreme Court, 22-year-old James Vlassakis, pleaded guilty to four counts of murder and was handed a life sentence with a 26-year non-parole period.

The proceedings against Mark Haydon continued into September 2005, when murder charges against him were dropped in return for guilty pleas to charges of assisting in the killings, including that of his wife, Elizabeth.

The convictions proved what South Australians first gathered four years previously: that a group of sadistic killers had operated unchecked in their midst for most of the previous decade. Finally, their reign of terror had been brought to an end.

# Angelo Buono and Kenneth Bianchi

**Kenneth Bianchi, born to an alcoholic prostitute who gave him up at birth, was deeply troubled from a young age. His adoptive mother described him as 'a compulsive liar who had risen from the cradle dissembling'. After a brief marriage to his high school sweetheart, he drifted from New York State to California, where in 1977 he teamed up with his older cousin Angelo Buono Jr.—and together they became known as the Hillside Stranglers.**

## Raped, Tortured, And Slain By The 'Hillside Stranglers'

**Buono was an ugly man,** both physically and mentally. He was coarse, ignorant, and sadistic but, incredibly, was popular with women and gave himself the nickname 'Italian Stallion'. Also from Rochester, New York, he had moved to California with his divorced mother and, like Bianchi, he briefly married a young girlfriend before walking out on her and their baby.

Between brief spells in jail for theft, Buono again wed and fathered several further children in and out of wedlock before his wife divorced him after he handcuffed her, put a gun to her stomach and threatened to kill her.

Buono worked as a car upholsterer, carrying out his business from his home at Glendale, in the San Fernando Valley. It was there that younger cousin Bianchi joined him and the couple, then aged 42 and 26, regularly invited prostitutes to the house. It would be these who would become their first victims.

**ABOVE:** Kenneth Bianchi and his older cousin stripped, raped, and sometimes sodomized their victims.

The body of a 21-year-old Hollywood girl was found on a hillside on Chevy Chase Drive on October 6, 1977. Twelve days later, the body of a 19-year-old was dumped near the Forest Lawn Cemetery. And on October 31, a girl aged just 15 was found dead on a hillside in Glendale.

A pattern had emerged. The girls had been stripped naked, violently raped, and sometimes sodomized. They were then carefully cleaned by the killers so as to leave no clues. Finally they were dumped by roadsides where they were certain to be discovered, often displayed in lascivious postures.

After the third murder, police knew that two men had been involved. The evidence was sperm samples taken from the teenager's body. As further corpses turned up, police also realized that the killers were experimenting with forms of torture. After being abused by both men, the girls would be strangled. But other methods of killing, such as lethal injection, electric shock, and carbon monoxide poisoning, were also tried by the killers.

During one week in November, Bianchi and Buono disposed of five bodies, the youngest being of

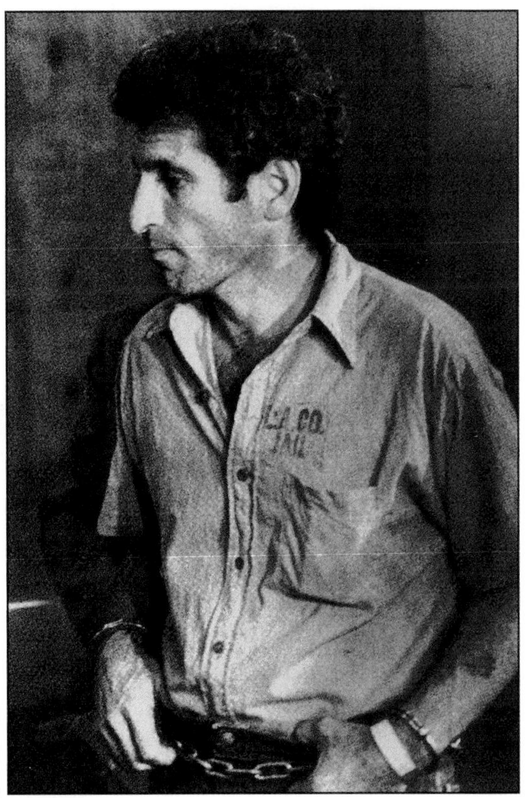

**ABOVE:** The self styled 'Italian Stallion', Angelo Buono committed his first murder in October 1977.

**ABOVE:** Bianchi takes the stand during his trial. His claim of insanity saved him from the death penalty.

schoolgirls aged 12 and 14. Two more teenagers and another woman were killed before the end of the year, and a 20-year-old died the following February.

The deadly duo lured their victims by cruising around Los Angeles in Buono's car pretending to be plain-clothes cops, stopping to flash fake badges at unsuspecting victims. Ordered into their 'unmarked police car', the girls were driven to Buono's home to be tortured and murdered. But in the spring of 1978, to the bafflement of Los Angeles police, the killings suddenly stopped.

The reason was that the killers had fallen out, and Bianchi had left California to live with his girlfriend and baby son in Bellingham, Washington State. There, Bianchi took a job as a security guard, and in January 1979 he lured two girl students into a house he was guarding and strangled them. But without the aid of his partner, he left many clues and police arrested him the next day. The nature of the crime and several documents in his possession linked him with the Hillside Strangler cases.

At his trial for the two Bellingham murders, Bianchi pleaded insanity, claiming that he suffered from 'multi personality disorder', and the evidence of six Washington State psychiatrists saved him from the death penalty. With a life sentence, he was moved to California to give evidence against Buono for the Los Angeles killings.

The inadmissibility of 'insane' Bianchi's testimony delayed the start of Buono's trial until November 1981 and, along with the lack of forensic evidence, caused it to last nearly two years. Buono denied all charges and blamed the murders on his cousin. On October 31, 1983, he was found guilty on two counts—but the jury's recommendation meant that he too evaded the death sentence in favor of life in prison, where he died of a heart condition in 2002.

At the close of his trial, it became clear that Judge Ronald George would have preferred Buono's death to have been administered more swiftly. He complained to the jury: 'Angelo Buono and Kenneth Bianchi subjected various of their murder victims to the administration of lethal gas, electrocution, strangulation by rope, and lethal hypodermic injection. Yet the two defendants are destined to spend their lives in prison, housed, fed, and clothed at taxpayer expense, better cared for than some of the destitute law-abiding members of our community.'

# William Burke and William Hare

**In the early 19th century, the frontiers of medicine were advancing at an inexorable rate. Yet there was one vital ingredient lacking in this exploration of the human body—and that was a supply of the bodies themselves. At that time, it was unheard of for anyone to donate their body for research, so a supply of corpses had to be provided for dissection and the fresher the better. William Burke and William Hare were the men to fulfill this service, and by their nefarious trade became Scotland's most celebrated and gruesome serial murderers.**

## Unholy Duo Who Went Into The 'Body Business'

**The Irish-born pair came together** when Burke, who had deserted his wife and young family, came to stay at Hare's cheap Edinburgh lodging house in 1827. They went into the 'body business' together soon afterward upon the death of a boarder known as Old Donald, who succumbed to a long illness, owing £4 in rent. To recoup his loss, landlord Hare hit upon the plan of selling the corpse to one of the city's doctors. They removed Old Donald's body from the coffin that lay in the backyard, wrapped it in sacking and presented themselves at the door of Number 10 Surgeons' Square, the Edinburgh establishment of the brilliant anatomist Dr Robert Knox. The price was struck at seven pounds and 10 shillings, and all sides left well satisfied with the night's work.

It was easy money but the pair realized they would have difficulty in continually restocking the merchandise they required for their new unholy trade. Churchyards were now well guarded at night because of previous raids by grave robbers, and many tombs even had iron bars around them. The only solution was to 'create' new corpses.

The first of a further 16 victims was an old man called Joe the Mumper, who fell ill of a high fever and was too weak to offer resistance as Burke and Hare laid a pillow over his face and held him down until he suffocated. His body fetched £10 at Surgeons' Square. The second victim was dispatched in what became the hallmark of Burke and Hare's murder technique. A boarder, whose name they did not even know, was confined to his bed with jaundice. While the man was asleep, Burke held his mouth and nose until there was no sign of breathing.

Third to die was an old woman tramp whom Hare met in a city bar, lured to the lodging house and suffocated. In the spring of 1828, the killers saw off two more boarders, both destitute women. Then came the murder of a prostitute, Mary Paterson. The sight of her naked body, barely six hours into death, aroused great excitement among the medical students, one of whom claimed to recognize her. Mary's shapely figure and good looks were even remarked upon in the popular newspapers. Dr Knox gladly reveled in the publicity and, rather than take the body straight onto the dissecting table, he had it preserved in whiskey for three months, allowing it to become almost a tourist attraction.

Burke and Hare became increasingly audacious. On one occasion, Burke encountered a drunken woman being escorted along the street by a policeman. He intervened, convinced the officer that he was a Good Samaritan and had the hapless wretch released into his care. Not surprisingly, she was delivered to Surgeons' Square that very night.

In June 1828, the partners committed their vilest crime. Burke was stopped in the street and asked for directions by a woman leading by the hand a young boy who was deaf and dumb. Burke led her to his home where he and Hare killed her before also disposing of her son. Burke took the boy over his knee and, as he later told police, 'broke his back' while the terrified youngster stared piteously into his face. The two victims were then stuffed into a barrel and sold for £16 the pair.

In the end, Burke and Hare were trapped by their over-confidence and carelessness. In October 1828, a female boarder turned up the corner of her straw mattress and was horrified to discover the body of a

**ABOVE LEFT:** Notorious Scottish murderer William Burke, as he appeared in court. Burke, with his accomplice William Hare, murdered nine people, selling the bodies to medical schools for dissection.

**ABOVE RIGHT:** William Hare was an accomplice of William Burke and Robert Knox. Burke was hanged for his crimes but Hare gave evidence and was released with Robert Knox.

**ABOVE:** An angry mob pursues Helen MacDougal, mistress of serial killer William Burke, through the streets of Edinburgh, circa 1829.

**ABOVE:** Crowds gather to watch the execution of William Burke at the Lawnmarket, Edinburgh, on January 28, 1829.

naked crone, her face horribly bloodstained. She went to the police and the killers were arrested. Hare, given an offer of immunity by turning King's Evidence, immediately denounced his former partner.

The trial of William Burke began on Christmas Eve 1828 and continued without pause until the last guilty verdict was returned on Christmas morning. The court's sentence was that he be hanged and his body be used for medical science. A crowd of thousands, among them the poet Walter Scott, watched him die on the gallows on January 28, 1829.

Burke's body was then removed to the medical rooms, where guests were admitted in batches of 50 to watch it being dissected. The following day, the general public was admitted, thousands of curious strangers filing past his remains. The body was then salted and put into barrels for use in future experiments.

Only Burke suffered the full weight of the law but the other players in the vile pantomime did not enjoy their freedom. The infamous Dr Knox continued to deny complicity in the crimes but found his medical career in ruins. He died in disgrace in December 1862. The wives of Burke and Hare, who assisted the pair in their vile trade, suffered public hatred wherever they went. And Hare himself, having turned against his accomplice to obtain his own freedom, moved away from Edinburgh and lived out a miserable existence in the slums of London, eventually dying a poverty-stricken blind beggar.

# David Carpenter

**The so-called 'Trailside Killings' in the San Francisco Bay Area began in August 1979 with the murder of 44-year-old Edda Kane, who had been hiking in Mount Tamalpais State Park. She was raped and then shot through the back of the head while kneeling.**

## Stuttering Psycho Known As The 'Trailside Killer'

**Seven months later,** 23-year-old Barbara Schwartz was stabbed while on her knees. Then came Anne Alderson, a 26-year-old jogger, found dead in the park with three bullets in her head. She, too, had been in the kneeling position at the time of her death.

**ABOVE:** Mount Tamalpais State Park, where David Carpenter carried out the 'Trailside Killings'.

The killer went into overdrive in late 1980. Hiker Shawna May, 25, was shot and placed in a shallow grave in Point Reyes Park. Nearby was the body of another missing person, Diane O'Connell, 22, also shot in the head. On the same day, November 29, two more bodies were found in Point Reyes: Cynthia Moreland, 18, and Richard Towers, 19, had been killed on the same October weekend as Alderson.

The discovery of four bodies in one day caused a howl of outrage in the media and spread fear across the Bay Area, where jogging, hiking, and other healthy outdoor activities were a way of life. However, police had few leads to follow. No one had seen the mysterious 'Trailside Killer' and survived.

Then, in March 1981, hitch-hikers Ellen Hansen and Gene Blake were threatened at gunpoint in a park near Santa Cruz. She was shot dead, but her boyfriend managed to crawl away, bleeding profusely from his wounds. Blake's description allowed police to release a composite picture of the killer.

The net was closing in on the 'Trailside Killer'—but not before he had claimed a final victim. In May, Heather Skaggs, 20, was found dead in Big Basin Redwood State Park. Bullets used to kill her matched those fired at Gene Blake and Ellen Hansen. But now there were further clues. Heather had worked in the same print store as a known sex offender, David Carpenter, she had last been seen near his home—and work colleagues said they believed Carpenter had tried to date her.

The trail clearly led to the man who should have been a suspect from the start. Carpenter was a psycho with a pronounced stutter who, in 1960 at the age of 30, had been arrested and sentenced to 14 years in prison for attacking a woman with a hammer and knife. Freed early, he re-offended in 1970 and spent seven years in jail for kidnapping. In between his two prison terms, he had been a principal suspect in California's mysterious 'Zodiac murders' (see page 219) but was ultimately cleared.

Indeed, one other murder victim may have preceded the uproar over the 'Trailside Killings'. Anna Menjivas, who had been a friend of Carpenter's, disappeared from her home in 1979 and was found dead in Mount Tamalpais Park, the area of the next three murders. Yet police failed to link her death to Carpenter until after his arrest.

On July 6, 1984, Carpenter was found guilty in Los Angeles of the murders of Heather Scaggs and Ellen Hansen. He was sentenced to death in the gas chamber of San Quentin. At a second trial in San Diego, Carpenter was convicted of five more murders and two rapes and again sentenced to death, but a string of appeals meant he languished indefinitely on Death Row.

# Andrei Chikatilo

**Crazed cannibal Andrei Chikatilo was questioned several times during his 12 years of slaughter and released on every occasion. The mild-mannered former schoolteacher convinced detectives that he was a faithful husband, proud father, and studious academic.**

# 'Rostov Ripper' Killed And Ate More Than 50

**A university graduate,** Chikatilo completed his military service and in 1963, at the age of 27, he met and married Fayina, a pit worker's daughter. They had a son and a daughter as Chikatilo continued his home studies, gaining a degree in literature and taking a job as a teacher. For reasons no one then guessed, he gave up the post in 1981 and started work as a supply clerk, a humble job but one that involved much travel.

This gave him greater scope for his perverted pleasures, for Chikatilo was already a killer. Although living in an apartment in Rostov-on-Don, Russia, he had also bought a dilapidated shack outside the town, to which he regularly brought back prostitutes for sex. In December 1978, he lured a nine-year-old girl there and, following a failed attempt at rape, brutally stabbed her to death.

It transpired from his wife's later evidence that Chikatilo could not have sex in any normal way. He needed to instil terror before he could perform adequately. He would rape his victims only after working himself into a frenzy as he stabbed and mutilated them.

He went on to kill at least 53 people around Rostov and as far afield as St Petersburg and Tashkent, Uzbekistan. He would hang around bus stops and railroad stations, stalking his victims, mainly targeting prostitutes, tramps or runaways, whom he lured with the promise of gifts or a meal.

Most of his victims were raped after death and then mutilated, with various organs cut out or bitten off. He would often consume their flesh. His oldest victim was a 44-year-old prostitute and his youngest a seven-year-old boy. There was also a mother and her 11-year-old daughter, who vanished after he took them on a picnic.

'I paid no attention to age or sex,' he later told police, adding: 'Eating my victims is the ultimate sacrifice they can make for me. They are literally giving themselves to me.'

Chikatilo avoided capture because of police blunders. He was arrested after his very first murder when neighbors reported strange happenings at his shack. During the 12-year hunt for the so-called 'Rostov Ripper', he was questioned by police on at least eight further occasions, on one of them being kept in custody for 10 days. They even closed the case briefly when inquiries switched to another suspect—who, bizarrely, confessed to murder and was executed.

**ABOVE:** Andrei Chikatilo behind the bars of an iron cage during his trial in Rostov in 1992.

The killings did in fact cease for three months. That was because Chikatilo had been sent to prison, not for any violent crime but on an old charge of stealing linoleum. After his release, he slaughtered eight people in a single month.

Chikatilo was finally arrested outside a cafe in November 1990. He admitted murdering 11 boys and 42 girls but police believe there may have been more. He went on trial chained in an iron cage within the Rostov courtroom where, in October 1992, he was sentenced to death. He was executed with a bullet in the back of the neck on February 14, 1994.

ABOVE: Chikatilo relished cannibalism. He once said that eating his victims is 'the ultimate sacrifice they can make for me'.

# John Reginald Christie

In the annals of British crime, few addresses are more enduringly spine-chilling than 10 Rillington Place, in London's Notting Hill district. Now trendily upgraded, the area was, in the postwar years, distinctly shabby and seedy. It is a description that could equally have applied to one of the occupants: the balding, bespectacled John Reginald Halliday Christie.

## The Chilling Secret of 10 Rillington Place

Christie committed at least six and possibly eight murders in his rented ground-floor apartment there, hiding the corpses around the house as a gruesome legacy for the next tenant to find. One body was of a woman for whose death her husband was wrongly sent to the gallows.

Born in Halifax, Yorkshire, in 1898, Christie was a weakly youth who nevertheless enlisted in World War One and suffered eye and throat injuries in a mustard gas attack. He returned home with a small disability pension, married a local girl and went to work for the Post Office.

This was where his life of crime began, for he was caught stealing postal orders and was sent to jail, the first of several spells behind bars for what were, at first, petty offenses. When wife Ethel discovered he was also visiting prostitutes, Christie moved alone to London, where he served three further jail terms for theft and attacking a woman.

**ABOVE:** John Christie was first jailed for stealing postal orders, but his criminal activities soon escalated to murder by strangulation.

**BELOW:** Austrian refugee Ruth Fuerst, who was murdered by Christie in 1943 and buried in his backyard.

After a nine-year separation, he wrote to Ethel seeking a reconciliation, and in 1938 they moved into 10 Rillington Place. Extraordinarily, World War Two saw him back into uniform as a police special constable, no checks having been made for previous convictions. Under that guise of authority and respectability, he began murdering women.

In 1943, he picked up a 17-year-old Austrian refugee, took her back to Rillington Place while his wife was absent and strangled her with a rope. Under cover of darkness, he buried her body in the small communal backyard, where it lay undisturbed for a decade.

After losing his police post the following year, Christie worked at various clerking jobs, in one of which he chatted up a 31-year-old co-worker and invited her to his home. There, he raped and strangled her with a stocking and buried her alongside his first victim.

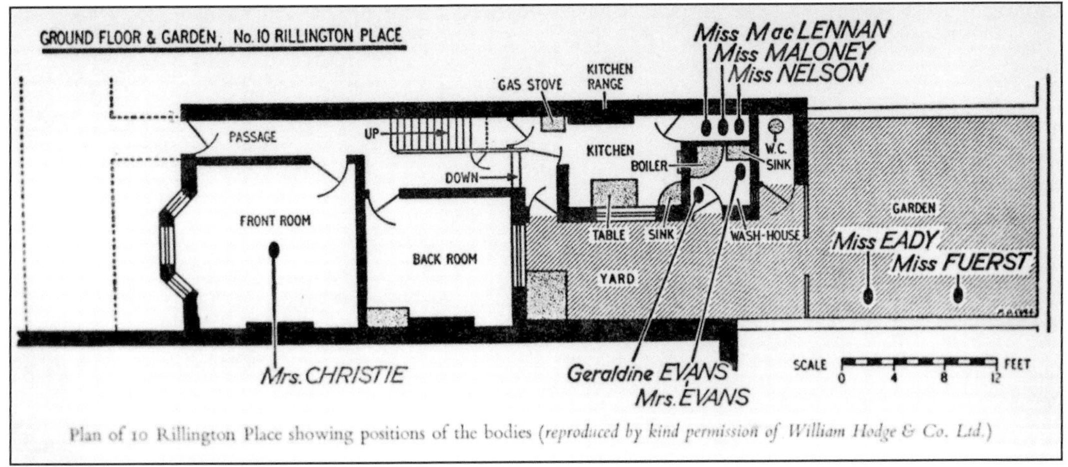


Plan of 10 Rillington Place showing positions of the bodies (*reproduced by kind permission of William Hodge & Co. Ltd.*)

**ABOVE:** A plan of Christie's apartment of evil, showing the locations in which his victims were buried.

**BELOW:** Christie's 'murder room', situated at the rear of his ground-floor apartment.

ABOVE: Christie pictured in a Black Maria on his way to court to answer for his crimes on April 29, 1953.

In 1948 truck driver Timothy Evans, his wife Beryl, and their baby Geraldine moved into the apartment above Christie's. A year later, Beryl and 14-month-old Geraldine were murdered. Inexplicably, Evans, who was of subnormal intelligence, went to the police to confess to killing his wife—but when they raided the house and also found his daughter's body, he changed his story, blaming his neighbor. Christie gave evidence against Evans, sealing his fate. He was hanged on March 9, 1950.

Christie's next victim was his wife. In 1952 he strangled Ethel in bed and buried her under the floorboards. That left him free to bring prostitutes to the apartment, three of whom he murdered and stuffed

LEFT: The bones of Christie's fifth victim are removed from 10 Rillington Place by police.

into cupboards. In March 1953, he moved out of Rillington Place and lived rough. Within days he was arrested after the apartment's next tenant discovered the grisly cause of the stench that permeated the house.

At London's Old Bailey, Christie's plea of insanity was rejected and on July 15, 1953, he was hanged for four of the murders, including that of Ethel. But who killed Beryl Evans? Christie finally confessed to her murder but two subsequent tribunals failed to overturn the verdict against Timothy Evans. In 1966, however, the lingering doubts earned Evans a long-overdue posthumous royal pardon.

# Douglas Clark and Carol Bundy

**Douglas Clark, the 'Sunset Strip Slayer', had a particularly gruesome fetish. He killed prostitutes, one of whom he decapitated and had sex with her head. His girlfriend Carol Bundy indulged this perversion by applying make-up to the head. Clark kept this grisly memento in his freezer for a few days, taking it out from time to time for the purpose of oral sex.**

## Hideous Habits Of The 'Sunset Strip Slayer'

**Clark, handsome son of a former admiral** in the US Navy, was 31 when, in 1980, he met Bundy, a dumpy 37-year-old mother of two, who worked as a vocational nurse in Los Angeles. He moved into her apartment in Burbank and made her his willing sex slave. He brought women and girls, as young as 11, home for sex while she watched and photographed them.

Then, in June 1980, the bodies of stepsisters aged 15 and 16 were found beside a highway. They had been snatched by Clark from Huntington Beach and forced to perform sex acts before being shot in the head. Although Bundy may not have been involved in that crime, she was an active participant in those that followed.

She and Clark would regularly drive along Sunset Boulevard to pick up a prostitute. Once parked in a quiet street, Clark would force her to perform oral sex on him while Bundy watched. As he climaxed, Clark would shoot the girl in the head.

Their murderously kinky games resulted in the bodies of prostitutes aged 17, 20, and 24 turning up during their June killing spree. Each had been disposed of in the same manner—except that in the case of the 20-year-old, her head was missing. It was found three days later in a box in the driveway of a house in Hollywood.

According to Bundy's later testimony, Clark had taken the head home with him so he could engage in oral sex with it at his leisure. She said that while her two children were out, Clark had produced the head from the freezer, ordered her to comb the hair and apply make-up to it. 'We had a lot of fun with her,' she told police. 'I was making her up like a Barbie.'

Clark's next victim was never identified. Her dismembered body turned up in Malibu in July. The final murder victim died the following month at the hands of Bundy herself. He was a former boyfriend, barman John Murray, who had foolishly confided to her that he suspected her new lover might be the 'Sunset Strip Slayer'. Bundy set up a meeting at which she shot and stabbed him, then decapitated him. His torso was discovered in his van but his head was never found.

Bundy may have been trying to prove to Clark her equal ability to kill but she could not carry it off. The overweight, mentally disturbed nurse broke down and confessed to a colleague. Police were tipped off and the killers were arrested. After initially blaming each other, Bundy confessed her involvement in the crimes, pleading guilty to the murder of Murray. Sentenced to

**ABOVE:** Sunset Strip in Los Angeles, the hunting ground of Douglas Clark and Carol Bundy during the summer of 1980.

life imprisonment, she became key witness against her boyfriend at his 1983 trial.

Clark was found guilty on six counts of murder and was sentenced to death. The Californian Supreme Court affirmed the sentence in 1992, leaving the 'Sunset Strip Slayer' lingering on Death Row—surviving his partner Bundy, who died in prison of heart failure in December 2003.

# Adolfo Constanzo

**Adolfo de Jesus Constanzo was a practitioner of voodoo for the power it gave him over others. He was also a devotee of the strange religion because it allowed him to satiate his bloodlust with regular human sacrifices.**

## Human Sacrifices Of The Voodoo Cult

**Born in Miami** of Cuban extraction in 1962, Constanzo studied the black magic arts of Palo Mayombe, a violent sect imported from the Congo. The cult believes the spirits of the dead exist in limbo and can be harnessed if the gods are regularly appeased with the fresh blood of human sacrifices. Constanzo would keep a cauldron constantly filled with blood and, most importantly, the skull of a human who had died a violent death.

At the age of 21, Constanzo moved to Mexico City where in 1983 he launched himself as a Palo Mayombe priest. Superstitious drugs family godfathers turned to him for magical protection at $50,000 a spell. As a consequence, his cauldron needed constant replenishment with fresh blood and skulls, and decapitated corpses were regularly fished out of rivers and lakes by police. On one occasion, the mutilated bodies of five members of the same household were discovered.

Constanzo's method of sacrifice was to have the victim beaten, then dragged to the sacred cauldron. It was essential to the success of the ceremony that there should be as much pain as possible and the victim should die screaming. So Constanzo would cut off the nose, ears, fingers, toes, and genitals of the hapless wretch

**ABOVE:** Adolfo Constanzo's obsession with the black magic arts of Palo Mayombe drove him to make many human sacrifices.

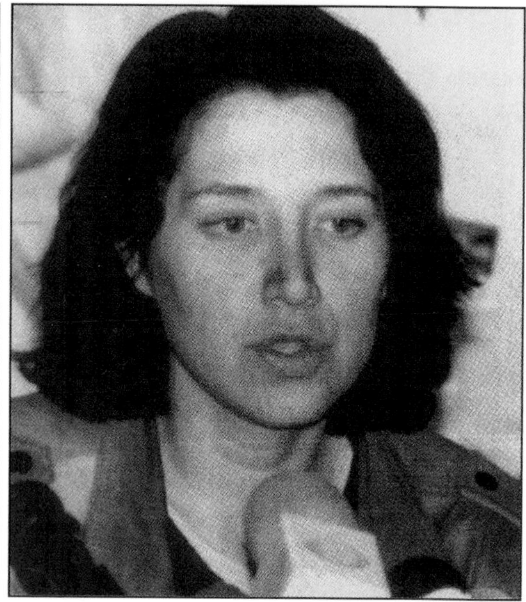

**ABOVE:** Sara Aldrete, a member of Constanzo's evil cult, was sentenced to 62 years without parole in 1994.

and partially flay him before sodomizing him. Only then would there be a merciful release through death.

Constanzo moved his voodoo circle to Matamoros, near the Texan border, where between May 1988 and March 1989 the gang ritually sacrificed at least 13 people. They were often rival drug dealers but also included strangers picked up at random.

Mark Kilroy was just such a victim. The 21-year-old medical student had crossed the border with friends to celebrate the end of their university term. When he became separated from them, he was bundled into the back of a truck and driven to Constanzo's remote Santa Elena ranch, where he was butchered and his brains tipped into the cauldron.

Kilroy's worried parents agitated for a properly conducted police investigation, and success was swift. Mexican police set up a road block near Matamoros, and one of Constanzo's gang drove straight through it—having been told by his leader that he was invisible! The cops simply followed him to the ranch, where they unearthed human remains including those of Mark Kilroy.

Constanzo was not there. He and his favored inner circle were spotted by chance in Mexico City, where an armed siege of their apartment ensued. Out of ammunition, Constanzo huddled in a closet with a male lover and ordered another gang member to shoot them both. 'Don't worry, I'll be back,' were his last words.

The rest were taken alive. In all, 14 cultists were given lengthy jail terms on charges from multiple murder to drug running. Oddest among them was Sara Aldrete, an all-American ex-college student from Brownsville, Texas, who had thrown away a glittering future as an athlete to join the cult. Sentenced in 1994 to 62 years without parole, she was asked why she had followed Constanzo. 'I could not leave him,' she said, 'because he threatened to use witchcraft on my family.'

# Eric Cooke

**To say that Eric Edgar Cooke had a bad start in life would be an understatement. Born in February 1931 in Perth, Western Australia, he suffered in childhood from his father's alcohol fueled beatings. Ostracized because of his harelip and cleft palate and resulting speech defect, Cooke grew up an angry, brooding loner.**

## Sad Childhood Of The Random Slayer

**He took a succession** of semi-skilled jobs, while committing a string of crimes in his neighborhood. After the accident-prone youth suffered several traumas to his head at work, he attempted to get his life together by enlisting in the military in 1952. He was discharged three months later when it was discovered that he had failed to declare a series of convictions for theft, breaking and entering, and arson of a church.

A year later, aged 22, Cooke again attempted to settle down by marrying Sarah Lavin, a 19-year-old waitress, and fathering seven children. Family life failed to calm him, however, and he continued to roam the streets by night, being arrested for minor offenses including voyeurism.

What turned Cooke from petty crime to serial killer is unclear but, in February 1959, he repeatedly and fatally stabbed an innocent woman while she was sleeping in her Perth apartment. Ten months later, armed with a knife and hatchet, he broke into the home of a 22-year-old woman, hacking at her face after he delivered lethal stab wounds. The police discounted sex and robbery as motives, as the girls had not been raped and nothing had been stolen.

Cooke's subsequent killing spree involved a series of seemingly unrelated hit-and-runs, stabbings, stranglings, and shootings which held Perth in a grip of terror. This was a strangely inconsistent serial killer whose methods seemed as random as his choice of victims.

Victims had been shot with a variety of different rifles, stabbed with knives, scissors, and hit with an ax. One victim was shot dead after answering a knock on his door, several were killed upon waking while Cooke was robbing their homes. Two were shot while sleeping without their homes being disturbed. After stabbing one victim, he got lemonade from the refrigerator and sat on the porch drinking it.

In August 1963, an elderly couple gathering wildflowers near the Canning River found a rifle lying in the brush and called the police. Ballistics tests confirmed it was the weapon used to kill a babysitter a week earlier. The rifle was impounded, replaced with a lookalike, and detectives staked out the scene. They waited 15 days before Cooke arrived to claim the weapon, and he was taken into custody without a struggle.

Apart from the eight or more murders of which he was suspected, Cooke admitted having committed more than 200 thefts, five hit-and-run offenses against young women, and two murders for which other men had already been wrongly imprisoned. Evidence indeed pointed to Cooke being the killer of the two women, and the convictions against Darryl Beamish and John Button were quashed—but not before they had served a total of 20 years between them.

Despite Cooke's defense citing his disturbed childhood, head injuries, and spells in an asylum, the court rejected the claim that he suffered from schizophrenia. The state permitted no other psychiatric specialist to examine him and, in November 1963, he was convicted of wilful murder after a three-day trial in the Supreme Court of Western Australia.

Cooke was sentenced to death by hanging. He ordered his lawyers not to appeal, conceding that he deserved to pay for what he had done. Aged 33, Eric Cooke became the last person to be hanged at Fremantle Prison, on October 26, 1964.

# Dean Corll

**Dean Corll was known as 'The Candy Man' because of the years he had spent working at home with his mother, making candies and selling them in a small store attached to their house in Houston, Texas. He had always sought the company of young men but, during a spell in the US Army, he realized he was gay—and that his sexual urges could only be satisfied by inflicting pain.**

## The 'Candy Man' Who Hired Kids To Kill Kids

**Released from service** at the age of 25 in 1964, Corll returned to his job at the confectionary factory and tried to befriend boys by giving them sweets. At roughly the same time as complaints about his sexual advances became public, his mother closed the company and retired.

Her son moved to the suburb of Pasadena and became a trainee electrician for the Houston Lighting and Power Company. He was well liked by colleagues but some of them thought it strange that he spent his free time mixing only with young teenagers. Two of them became his particular friends: Elmer Henley and David Brooks, both of whom dropped out of high school to spend more time with Corll.

In fact, what they had embarked on was not merely a homosexual relationship with the older man but a murder spree of shocking savagery.

Corll had met Brooks when the schoolboy was only 12. The older man at first paid the boy for sexual favors but then enlisted him as an accomplice. Henley, by contrast, had originally been earmarked as one of Corll's victims but avoided death by his willingness to plumb any immoral depth—and that included delivering his best friends into Corll's clutches.

The mission of these two Houston youths was to cruise the area seeking boys with whom Corll could forcibly have sex. Operating mainly in the rundown Heights area, they found they had no problem persuading young drug addicts to go to Corll's home with the promise of wild parties. There they would suffer prolonged torture at the hands of Corll before being murdered. 'He killed them because he wanted to have sex and they didn't', Brooks later told police.

All the victims were young males between 13 and 20 years old. Corll's first known victim was 18-year-old Jeffrey Konen, a student of the University of Texas who vanished in September 1970 while hitch-hiking to his parents' Houston home.

Tragically, most of those who followed were even younger. Typical was Billy Ray Lawrence, a 15-year-old friend of Henley, who was kept alive by Corll for four days before he was killed. By that August 1973, when 13-year-old James Dreymala became Corll's last confirmed victim, the tally had reached at least 27, most of them procured by Brooks and Henley, who had graduated from simply supplying the victims to helping commit the occasional murder themselves.

The official list of Corll's victims is likely to be underestimated. Forty-two boys had vanished within the Houston area since 1970 but, despite the anxiety of parents over their missing sons, police had failed to come anywhere close to solving the mystery. To the frustration of the families, many of the disappearances were written down as 'runaways'.

The breakthrough, when it came, was not due to police diligence. At 3am on August 8, 1973, Henley turned up at Corll's home with one of his friends, Tim Kerley, who had been happy to accept an invitation to a glue sniffing party but was in fact the next intended victim. Henley had also brought along his girlfriend, 15-year-old Rhonda Williams.

Corll objected to the girl's presence and, while Henley and Williams were in a drug-induced stupor, handcuffed and bound them. The 17-year-old pleaded with Corll to untie him, promising to continue helping him carry out the night's planned murder. But as soon as his hands were freed, he grabbed his captor's gun and shot him six times at point-blank range. The reign of the 33-year-old mass killer was instantly ended.

Henley called the police who found that one of the bedrooms had been turned into a 'torture room'. The centerpiece was a thick board with shackles for hands and feet. Various instruments of torture, including an assortment of dildos, were in evidence. Police also noticed that many wall and floor surfaces were covered with plastic sheeting—the better to contain the bloodstains that nevertheless spattered some of the walls.

Forced to confess his part in procuring Corll's victims, Henley led police to a boatshed where 17 decomposing bodies of boys lay in shallow graves. Corll had spread lime around them to disguise the stench of decomposition. Next stop was a local tourist spot, Lake Sam Rayburn, where more naked corpses were unearthed.

Many of the bodies recovered showed signs of mutilation and torture. It appeared that one of Corll's perverted practices was to insert a glass rod into the urethra of a victim and break it. The total body count came to 27 but police believe the higher figure of 42 was more realistic.

Henley and Brooks were tried in 1974 at San Antonio, where their pleas of insanity were rejected. Henley was found guilty of nine murders and sentenced to 594 years in prison. Brooks got life after being found guilty of one murder.

# Juan Corona

**Juan Vallejo Corona was at one time labeled the worst and most notorious mass murderer in United States history. Sadly, his tally of 25, killed during just a few months of 1971, did not remain a record for long. The other tragedy was that, by the nature of his crimes, many of the victims were barely missed. They were mostly Mexican migrants, largely itinerant fruit pickers, who hardly mixed with the local rural populations of California's Sutter County and of Feather River, where most of the killings took place.**

## Killer Dug Graves To Await Victims

**Corona, born in 1933,** had been an itinerant himself, having crossed the border into California as a 16-year-old in 1950. Despite his lack of schooling, he steadily worked his way up to become a successful businessman, a licensed labor contractor in charge of hiring fellow migrant workers to pick the fruit crops of the Yuba City area.

His book-keeping was meticulous—as police discovered when they followed up an anonymous tip and raided his farmhouse, near Feather River, in 1971. There they found 25 names carefully listed in a ledger. They corresponded with Mexican migrants and other itinerants all of whom had disappeared in the previous few months. Their bodies had been secreted around the farmstead after being hacked to death with knives and machetes.

The alarm had been raised on May 19, when a local rancher noticed that a hole, the size of a grave, had been dug in his peach orchard. Returning there the next day, he saw that it had been filled in with freshly dug earth. When police investigated, they unearthed the body of Kenneth Whitacre, a 40-year-old vagrant, who had been sodomized, stabbed to death, and his head almost severed with a machete.

The gruesome discovery sparked off the hunt for more buried bodies, with 25 eventually being found, although police maintained there must have been many more. The victims had all been murdered during a period of six weeks; an average of one death every 40 hours.

One grave alone yielded nine bodies. All had been subjected to homosexual rape before being stabbed and viciously slashed around the head. Corona had buried them face up, with their arms stretched above their heads and their shirts pulled up over their faces. Some had their pants pulled down.

When police searched Corona's farmhouse, they found—in addition to the notebook—a machete, a pistol, two butcher's knives, and bloodstained clothes. It became obvious that he had carefully planned the killings—digging a fresh grave in advance of each attack.

At his trial in 1973, his lawyers argued that all 25 charges of murder should be dismissed on the grounds of their client's mental instability. He had twice been treated at a psychiatric hospital where he had been diagnosed with paranoid schizophrenia, they argued. But their pleas were ignored and Corona was given 25 life sentences.

The killer lodged further failed legal appeals over the years, once telling a prison doctor: 'Yes, I did it but I'm a sick man and can't be judged by the standards of other men.'

During a parole bid in 2003, by which time he was 69, he said: 'The victims were all people who didn't have a family and they were ready to go to the next world.'

# Mary Ann Cotton

**Unlike most serial killers, Mary Ann Cotton was on intimate terms with all of her victims. The reason was clear, for all were members of her immediate family. It is not known exactly how many people she murdered but the candidates include her mother, three of her four husbands (one of them being bigamous), a lover, her best friend, plus 15 children, including 10 from among her own brood of 12.**

## Churchgoer Commits Multiple Murders With Arsenic

**That was a British serial-killing record** that has survived well over a century—and all the more remarkable since Mary Ann was a churchgoing girl born in 1832 far from the lure of any big city. Raised by strict Methodist parents in the County Durham mining village of Low Moorsley, Mary Ann was married in 1852 at the age of 20 to William Mowbray. They had eight children but the family appeared to be

**ABOVE:** Mary Ann Cotton, the churchgoer who claimed around 20 victims through arsenic poisoning in the 19th century.

plagued by health problems. One by one, the brothers, sisters, and their father William himself all died of gastric fevers. In fact she had poisoned them. Only one among the family survived, a daughter named Isabella who had been sent away to live with her grandmother.

Following the death of her poor husband, Mary Ann married George Ward. Yet after only 13 months he too was dead. The widow even murdered her own mother, who became ill at the same time as her third husband, James Robinson, asked Mary Ann to marry him. Conveniently, mother was dead within 10 days. Mary Ann herself became mother to James Robinson's five children, taking with her the surviving daughter Isabella. Within a few short months Isabella and four of the Robinson children had died from supposed natural causes. Robinson left his wife, taking with him his remaining child, and in doing so became the only husband to survive.

Mary Ann did not stay single for long, however. Even though she was still legally married, she next wed Frederick Cotton, who had two children from a previous marriage. Mary Ann soon fell pregnant and had another child but a year into the marriage, Frederick Cotton was also dead. Gastric fever was blamed.

At this juncture in her killing spree, Mary Ann met up with a former lover, Joseph Nattrass. The resumed romance was ill-fated, however, as the greedy widow found yet another way of improving her lifestyle. This time her heart was set on a customs officer by the name of Mr Quick-Manning and poor Joseph Nattrass was suddenly dispensable. Mary Ann killed him, along with her stepsons from her bigamous marriage to Cotton: 10-year-old Frederick junior and 14-month-old baby Charlie.

It was this final murder that doomed Mary Ann Cotton. Little Charlie had been fine one day and dead the next. His tiny body was subjected to an autopsy, which revealed not only the cause of his early demise—arsenic poisoning—but also the probable cause of all the other family deaths.

The suspicion was confirmed when the bodies of other family members were exhumed, and 40-year-old Mary Ann Cotton was tried for murder at Durham Assizes on March 5, 1873. Justice was swift and two weeks later she walked from her cell to the gallows.

# Thomas Cream

**Dr Thomas Neill Cream stood with a hood over his head and a noose around his neck on the scaffold at London's Newgate Prison in 1892 and, so the story goes, declared: 'I am Jack the...' He was cut short when the trap door burst open beneath his feet and he was hanged.**

# Last Boast Of The 'Lambeth Poisoner'

**Cream, tagged the 'Lambeth Poisoner',** had initially been a suspect in the search for Jack the Ripper, the killer of five women in London at the close of the 19th century (see page 95). But since he could prove that he was in jail in America at the time the Ripper was operating, his cry was judged a final attempt at a dramatic exit.

Cream was born in Glasgow in May 1850 to parents who emigrated to Canada, where the studious young Thomas qualified as a doctor. In 1876 he married Flora Brooks in a shotgun wedding—after her parents discovered he had carried out a bungled abortion on her that left her seriously ill. The day after the nuptials, however, Cream abandoned his wife, who later died—possibly at Cream's hands.

**ABOVE:** Strychnine was the method of execution favored by the 'Lambeth Poisoner', Dr Thomas Cream.

The callous doctor fled to Britain where he continued his medical studies in London and Edinburgh before returning to Canada and setting up a practice in London, Ontario. Soon afterward, in August 1879, the body of a woman was found in an alley near his surgery. She had earlier visited Cream to seek an abortion.

Under suspicion, Cream moved to Chicago, where he specialized in offering abortions to prostitutes. When one of his patients died in August 1880, he was taken into custody but released for lack of evidence.

Cream was again arrested a year later when the husband of one of his patients died of strychnine poisoning. There was firm evidence that Cream had supplied the wife with the poison, but when she turned state's evidence, the doctor was left to face a murder charge alone. He was sentenced to life in November 1881.

With remission, Cream was released a decade later and, with an inheritance left him by his father, returned to England and settled in Lambeth, a working-class area of Victorian London rife with crime and prostitution. In October 1891, he picked up two prostitutes, aged 19 and 27, both of whom died of strychnine poisoning.

The following April, he offered a girl some pills that he said would help clear a rash on her face. Suspicious because of her client's insistence that she swallow them all, she merely pretended to do so, thereby saving herself from the 'Lambeth Poisoner'.

But two other prostitutes hired by Cream a week later were not so fortunate. The girls, aged 18 and 21, were offered drinks the killer had brought with him and both died in agony. At last, suspicion fell on the local doctor, who was arrested at his home in June 1892. Police found seven bottles of strychnine in his rooms.

At the Old Bailey, Cream's pleas of innocence were rejected, the jury taking just 10 minutes to decide he was guilty. Seeming surprised at the verdict, he strutted from the dock, defiantly stating: 'They shall never hang me.' He was proved wrong on the morning of November 15, 1892.

# Alexander Pichushkin

Alexander Yuryevich Pichushkin lured his victims to Moscow's vast, wooded Bitsevsky Park with the promise of a bottle of beer or a shot of vodka. Occasionally, he would suggest a game of chess. And after bludgeoning each victim to death, he would place a coin or vodka bottle stopper on one more square on the chessboard in his apartment. That is the way the notorious serial killer recorded his grisly crimes, attaching a number to another square of the board every time he struck. By the time he was caught, Pichushkin had filled in 62 of the 64 squares.

## Woodland Victims Drowned In A Pit Of Filth

**The 'Chessboard Killer',** as Pichushkin came to be known, first struck in 1992 when he was just 18 years old, murdering the boyfriend of a neighbor he had fallen in love with. He later killed the girl, whose body

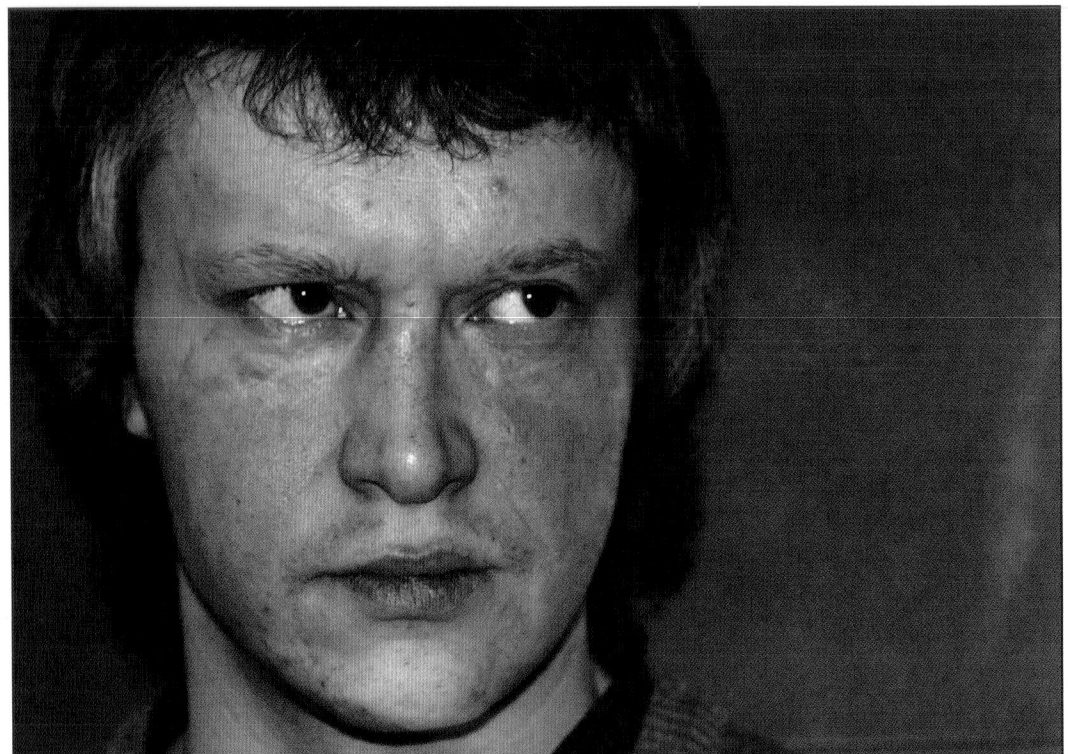

**ABOVE:** At one point during 2005, Alexander Pichushkin, 'The Chessboard Killer', was committing one murder a week.

was found in Bitsevsky Park, near to the apartment block where Pichushkin lived with his aged mother.

Subsequent murders were sporadic but in 2005 the supermarket shelf-stacker embarked on a killing spree. At one stage, police were uncovering one body every week—all having the serial killer's hallmark of a smashed skull, with the neck of a vodka bottle thrust into the gaping wound.

Most of his victims were homeless drifters or drunks. Those who were not killed instantly ended their agonies by drowning after Pichushkin threw them into the sewers that ran beneath the park. Others were strangled or killed with a blow to the skull from a hammer or blunt object. He would always attack from behind in order to stop blood from soaking his clothes, and finally he would stick the neck of a vodka bottle into his victims' skull, ensuring that they did not survive.

Three of his victims were women and one a child, a homeless nine-year-old boy. The body of one woman was found with tiny stakes hammered into her skull and around her eyes. His final victim, a female colleague from the supermarket where he worked, caused Pichushkin's capture. Before accompanying the killer to the park, she had left a note with her son telling her who she was meeting. CCTV cameras also caught them strolling toward the park shortly before she was murdered there in June 2006.

Under arrest, 32-year-old Pichushkin confessed: 'I liked to watch their agony. For me, a life without murder is like a life without food for anyone else. I felt like the father of all these people, since it was I who opened the door for them to another world.'

A psychologist who analyzed the killer prior to his trial in September 2007 reported that his love of chess, which ironically he couldn't play, was a clue to his character. Pichushkin, it was said, 'is detached from human beings, who are no more than wooden dolls—like chess pieces to him'.

At his trial, the prosecution claimed that Pichushkin 'dreamed of going down in history by surpassing Andrei Chikatilo'—the so-called 'Rostov Ripper' who was Russia's previously most notorious serial killer, executed in 1994 for murdering 52 women and children (see page 43). Pichushkin wished to confess to 62 slayings but there was sufficient evidence for only 48 charges of murder. With the death penalty no longer in force, he was jailed for life, with the first 15 years in solitary confinement.

**ABOVE:** The 'Bitsevsky Maniac' is escorted into the Moscow City Court on August 13, 2007.

# Jerry Brudos

**A detective asked Jerry Brudos a simple question: 'Do you feel some remorse, Jerry? Do you feel sorry for your victims, for the girls who died?' Brudos picked up a piece of paper, screwed it up and threw it on the floor. 'That much,' he said. 'I care about those girls as much as that piece of wadded up paper...'**

## Fetish Fiend Dressed Dead Bodies Like Dolls

**Jerome Henry Brudos was a murdering rapist** with a fetish for women's clothes and shoes. He first came to police attention when, as a 17-year-old, he forced a woman to pose for naked pictures at knifepoint. He was confined to a mental hospital for nine months with a personality disorder.

After his release, he continued stealing underwear from washing lines. By the time he was 28 and committed his first murder, Brudos had accumulated a large collection of women's attire.

That first victim was a 19-year-old encyclopedia saleswoman, Linda Slawson, who knocked on the door of the Brudos home in Portland, Oregon, one day in January 1968. With his wife and two children upstairs, Brudos, then aged 28, knocked the young woman unconscious.

He took Linda to the garage where he strangled her and abused the corpse. Brudos then sent his family out for hamburgers so he could play with her body. He dressed her up like a doll in the clothes he had been collecting over the years and photographed his handiwork. Finally, he chopped off the left foot and, with a newly fitted shoe, put it in his refrigerator. The body was disposed of in the Willamette River.

Three other murders followed. Jan Whitney, 23, was picked up at the roadside in November 1968 when her car broke down. He took her home and raped the corpse. After dressing her up, he decided to keep her and hung her from a hook in the garage ceiling. Several days later he consigned her body to the river, but not before slicing off her right breast.

**ABOVE:** The Willamette River in Portland, Oregon, where Jerry Brudos dumped the bodies of most of his victims.

Student Karen Sprinkler, 19, was abducted from a department store car park in March 1969 and taken to his home, where she was forced to pose for him. She was then hanged and her body similarly abused. This time, both breasts were removed before her corpse was dumped, this time in the Long Tom River.

Linda Salee, 23, died a month later. Brudos had flashed a fake police badge at her and 'arrested' her for shoplifting. He took her back to the garage where he strangled and raped her as she expired. He kept the body for a day, violating the corpse before she too ended up in the river.

After quizzing fellow students of Karen Sprinkler, police discovered several girls had received phone calls from a man asking to meet them. A trap was set with one of the girls arranging a date with Brudos and he was arrested.

He pleaded insanity at his trial but psychiatric reports declared him sane. He was sentenced to life imprisonment at Oregon State Penitentiary.

# Peter Sutcliffe

The hunt for the 'Yorkshire Ripper' began with the grisly discovery of the half-naked and viciously stabbed body of 28-year-old prostitute Wilma McCann on a Leeds playing field on the morning of October 30, 1975. The manhunt, dogged by blunders and slip-ups, lasted five years until, 13 murders and seven attempted murders later, Peter William Sutcliffe was finally caught in a routine motoring check. In his car, he had the luckiest prostitute in Yorkshire, along with a Phillips screwdriver and a ball-peen hammer.

## Police Blunders Left 'Yorkshire Ripper' Free To Kill

**Following the Wilma McCann killing,** Sutcliffe's next target was prostitute Emily Jackson, 42, whose body was found in the Chapeltown red-light district of

**ABOVE:** A phototfit image of the man Yorkshire police failed to capture for five years.

**ABOVE:** Peter Sutcliffe on his wedding day in August 1974. He began murdering women a year later.

**ABOVE:** Six of the Yorkshire Ripper's victims. Top left to right; Vera Millward, Jayne MacDonald, and Josephine Whittaker. Bottom left to right; Jean Royle, Helga Rytka, and Barbara Leach.

Leeds. Her post-mortem revealed more than 50 stab wounds inflicted with a Phillips screwdriver, the imprint of a size-seven Dunlop boot on her thigh and two heavy blows with a hammer to her head, the cause of her death.

Prostitute Number Three was also attacked with a hammer and, having masturbated over her semi-conscious body, Sutcliffe left her with £5 and a warning not to tell. Her description was found to be very accurate but, in a series of police errors, was largely ignored.

His next three victims in 1977 all bore similar horrific injuries: bodies face down, hammer blows to the skull, and frenzied stabbing to the stomach. Victim Number Seven in July that year survived the Ripper's attack and, following emergency surgery, was able to give a poor description.

The Ripper knew the police were scouring Leeds and Bradford and so found new hunting grounds. In October he murdered Jean Jordan, a 21-year-old prostitute in Manchester. Her body lay undetected for over a week, but he left a vital clue: a brand new £5 note, which had been issued to only 6,000 employees,

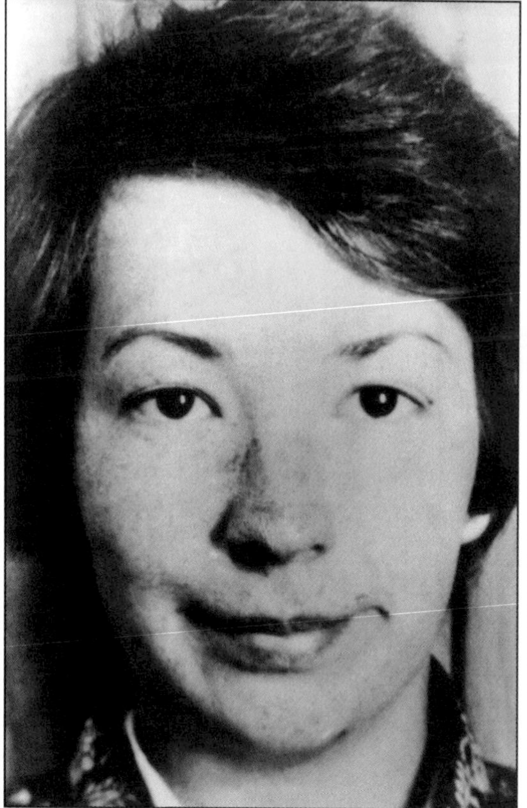

ABOVE: Student Jacqueline Hill, 20, was the Ripper's 13th and final victim, murdered in Leeds in November 1980.

ABOVE: The bus stop outside the Arndale shopping center in Leeds, where Jacqueline Hill was last seen alive.

among them those of the firm that employed Sutcliffe as a lorry driver. He was interviewed but police failed to pick up on his criminal record, which recorded his arrest in 1969 for 'going equipped for theft' with a hammer.

Following his next attack, in December that year—during which he screamed, 'You dirty prostitute' at his surviving victim—Sutcliffe killed again twice in 10 days. He hammered and stabbed Yvonne Pearson to death in January 1978, returning to her body before its discovery some two months later to inflict more macabre wounds. His next victim, an 18-year-old, was the only one he had sex with. Three more killings followed that summer, all victims receiving similar horrific wounds, including savage hammer blows to the head and the slashing to the stomach.

**ABOVE:** Yorkshire police chiefs look satisfied with Sutcliffe's conviction. But for their blunders, he would have been stopped sooner.

Sutcliffe lay low for almost a year without any further murders. More than 250 officers were working full-time to try and catch him, their attempts plagued by hoaxes. The police concentrated on suspects with Geordie accents following an audio tape supposedly from the Ripper.

With his final two victims, Sutcliffe changed his modus operandi in a bid to throw police off the scent. The second of these was lucky; a passing police car

**LEFT:** Police hold back crowds outside Dewsbury court during an appearance by Sutcliffe on murder chages in January 1981.

disturbed Sutcliffe. A 20-year-old student from Leeds was not so lucky, however, and became his next murder victim in November 1980.

Up until the time of his capture, Sutcliffe had been interviewed five times by police. He was known to frequent red-light districts. He had a previous record for possession of a hammer. Yet, as he didn't have a Geordie accent, he was never marked as a prime suspect.

Following his confession, Sutcliffe was tried at the Old Bailey and, on May 22, 1981, was sentenced to life, with a recommendation that he serve at least 30 years. Since then, he has been held in Broadmoor Hospital for the criminally insane. The reason for his crimes? According to his brother Carl, Peter Sutcliffe felt he was just 'cleaning up the streets'.

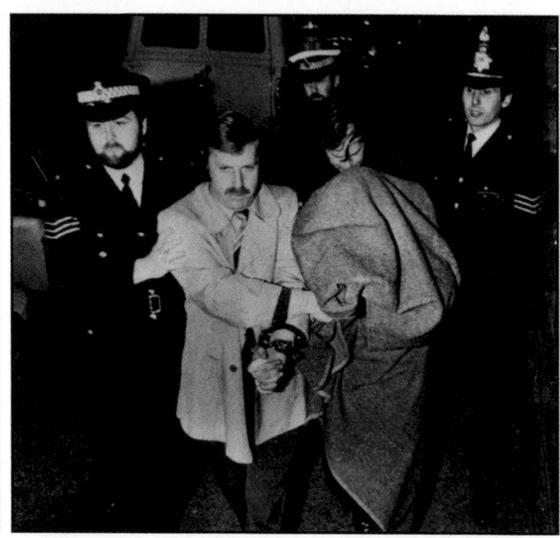

**RIGHT:** Multiple killer Peter Sutcliffe is bundled into Dewsbury court under a blanket on January 6, 1981.

# Joseph Swango

**Born Joseph Michael Swango, he shone at school, studying music and then biology before going on to Southern Illinois University where he graduated in medicine in 1983, at the age of 28, winning a year-long internship in general surgery at the Ohio State University Medical Center. But in January 1984, it was first noted that the former prize pupil was acting suspiciously. A nurse saw him checking on a patient and shortly afterward found the woman turning blue and suffocating. Emergency treatment managed to save her but a week later she was dead. Swango had been the last person to attend to her.**

## How Many Did The 'Doughnut Poisoner' Murder?

**Similar occurrences rang alarm bells** with anxious nurses who, comparing notes, discovered that at least six other patients, all evidently making good progress, had suddenly died. Their ages ranged from 19 to 47. Swango had been the duty intern at the time each of them had succumbed. Incredibly, although an investigation was carried out, none of the nurses who had raised the alarm were interviewed.

The high number of deaths whenever Swango was around continued, however, and the hospital terminated his employment. Swango returned to his hometown of Quincy, Illinois, where he joined the Adams County Ambulance Corps. On one occasion, an entire paramedic crew became ill after eating doughnuts bought in by Swango. His colleagues decided to investigate the newcomer a little further—and found arsenic in his locker. When alerted, police searched the poisoner's apartment and discovered a hoard of phials, bottles, syringes, and a library of books on murder. There was also a selection of guns and knives.

Dubbed the 'Doughnut Poisoner', Swango was arrested and charged with seven counts of aggravated battery. In April 1985, a court sentenced him to five years' imprisonment. He was released for good behavior only two years later.

Happily for hospital staff and patients, Joseph Swango spent the next few years in various jobs away from medicine. He also had a girlfriend, Kirstin Kinney, a 26-year-old nurse who moved with him to South Dakota in 1992 when Swango accepted a position as emergency doctor at the Veterans Affairs Medical Center in Sioux Falls. Both he and Kirstin were considered dedicated staffers.

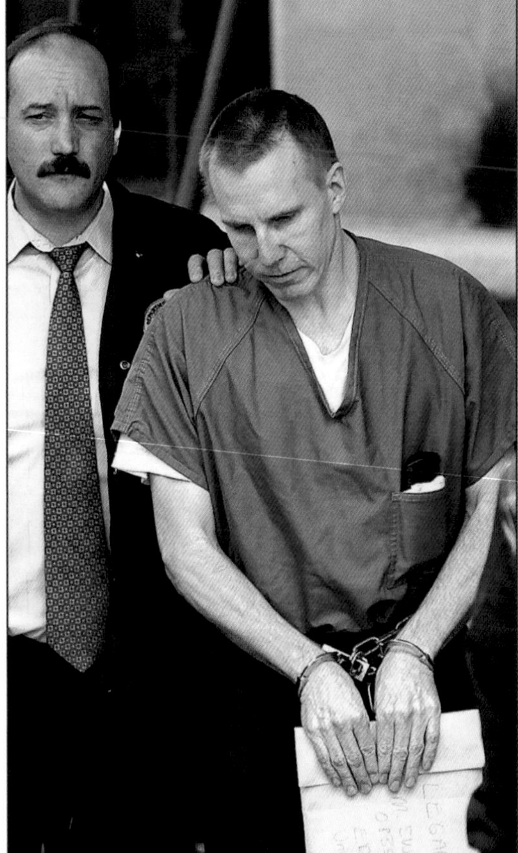

**ABOVE:** Justice finally caught up with Joseph Swango in July 2000 when he pleaded guilty to four murders.

The love affair ended, however, when a program about the notorious 'Doughnut Poisoner' was shown on television. Swango was dismissed. Kirstin, who realized the migraine headaches she now repeatedly suffered seemed to disappear whenever she was away from her boyfriend, fled home, wrote a note to her parents and shot herself.

With the fake references that he had become expert in forging, Swango moved to New York State in 1993 and got a job at the Internal Medicine Department at the Veterans Administration Headquarters, Northport, Long Island. His first patient died within hours of his arrival. Others were also to die in his 'care', all suffering heart failure in the dead of night.

It was not good police work or the vigilance of hospital authorities that finally halted Swango but Kirstin Kinney's parents, who could not forgive him for driving their daughter to suicide. They alerted the Long Island hospital and he was fired, the hospital authorities writing to every medical school in America warning them about him.

Swango disappeared, surfacing again in Zimbabwe at the Mnene Lutheran Outpost Hospital—where patients started to die with alarming regularity. A police investigation was launched and Swango fled to neighboring Zambia, and finally back to America. He was arrested the moment he landed at Chicago's O'Hare Airport in June 1997. He was finally charged with four counts of murder, pleaded guilty and, in July 2000, was sentenced to life imprisonment without parole.

Although only ever convicted of four murders, Swango is suspected of many more, estimates ranging from 35 to 60 in the United States—and perhaps hundreds overseas. A statement issued at the time by the mass poisoner's *alma mater*, Southern Illinois University, read: 'If Swango is legally connected to all the suspicious deaths of patients under his care since he began his residency with Ohio State University's medical program in 1983, it would make him the most prolific serial killer in history'.

# Johann Unterweger

**The most extraordinary thing about Johann 'Jack' Unterweger was that anyone believed him. When he was arrested for the murder of a teenaged girl, he seemed to be just another one-off killer. By the time he had reinvented himself as a 'reformed' celebrity ex-criminal, he had killed at least 11.**

## The Killer Who Became A TV Celebrity

**Unterweger was born in Styria,** southeastern Austria, in 1951 to a local prostitute and an American soldier he never knew. He was raised in the company of streetwalkers, their pimps and assorted petty thieves. He spent most of his late teens and early 20s in prison. By the age of 25, he had notched up 15 convictions, including burglary, rape, and pimping. So when, in 1975, he was convicted of strangling an 18-year-old girl with her own bra, the life sentence he received should have removed him from public harm forever.

While inside, however, he wrote poetry, a novel, and an autobiography titled *Fegefeuer* (Purgatory), which became a bestseller. His writing was unexpectedly proficient, and he achieved celebrity status, with a clutch of literary awards. Suddenly infamy turned to fame, and a petition organized by influential Austrians in the literary world helped him gain early release from prison in October 1990.

Unterweger was feted at glitterati events and on TV chat shows. He became a journalist, presenting himself as a reformed character and explaining away his violent past and rehabilitated future: 'I was no longer a youth. I was a beast, a devil, a child grown old before his time who enjoyed being evil. But that life is now over. Let's get on with the new.'

But Unterweger had fooled an entire nation. Within months of his release, he started killing again. During his first year of freedom, he is reckoned to have strangled at least six prostitutes. As more bodies turned up, it was only natural for the media to seek an expert on the subject—and, bizarrely, Unterweger found himself being asked for his opinions and advice on the latest deaths for which he alone was responsible. The killer basked in the spotlight while watching his books rise up the bestsellers list.

The only people not fooled were the police. They were suspicious of the publicity-seeking ex-jailbird and began linking the new slayings to Unterweger's movements. The killing spree spread across the Austrian countryside and into neighboring Czechoslovakia. Unterweger killed six women in the spring of 1991, the bodies of four victims who had vanished from the streets of Vienna being found during April and May alone.

The killings stopped in Austria shortly afterward—and began in Los Angeles. That was because Unterweger had been commissioned by a Vienna magazine to write an article on crime in Southern California. There, while asking the LA police to assist him with his research, he committed three murders in June and July, all of prostitutes whom he strangled with their own bras, afterward violating their battered bodies with sticks and other objects.

Unterweger was arrested in February 1992 in Florida, where he was traveling with his 18-year-old girlfriend. After a legal battle over whether he should be tried in the United States or Europe, he was extradited to Austria where he finally stood trial in April 1994. A psychologist described him in court as: 'A sexually sadistic psychopath with narcissistic and histrionic tendencies, prone to fits of rage and anger. He is an incorrigible perpetrator.'

Accused of 11 murder charges, including the three American cases, Unterweger was convicted of nine of them, two bodies being too decomposed for cause of death to be determined. On June 29, 1994, he was sentenced to life without parole and was taken to Graz prison where, just 12 hours later, he hanged himself in his cell using his own clothes as a noose—exactly as he had killed most of his victims.

# John Haigh

**John Haigh relished the title bestowed on him by the press: 'The Acid Bath Murderer'. He used industrial acid to dissolve away evidence of his crimes and, but for one careless oversight, would almost certainly have gone on to claim the lives of many more victims. It was his mistaken belief that a corpse could be completely disposed of by chemicals that led him to the gallows in 1949.**

## Deadly Charm Of The 'Acid Bath Murderer'

**ABOVE:** Dr Archibald Henderson and his wife Rose on holiday in 1944. They were both killed by the Acid Bath Murderer.

**John George Haigh** was a charmer. Born in 1909 and raised in a Yorkshire village by parents who were strict followers of the Plymouth Brethren sect, he grew up a bright scholarship pupil and choirboy. But when, at the age of 21, he was fired from an early job for

**ABOVE:** Haigh arrives at Horsham Magistrates Court handcuffed to a policeman, on April 1, 1949.

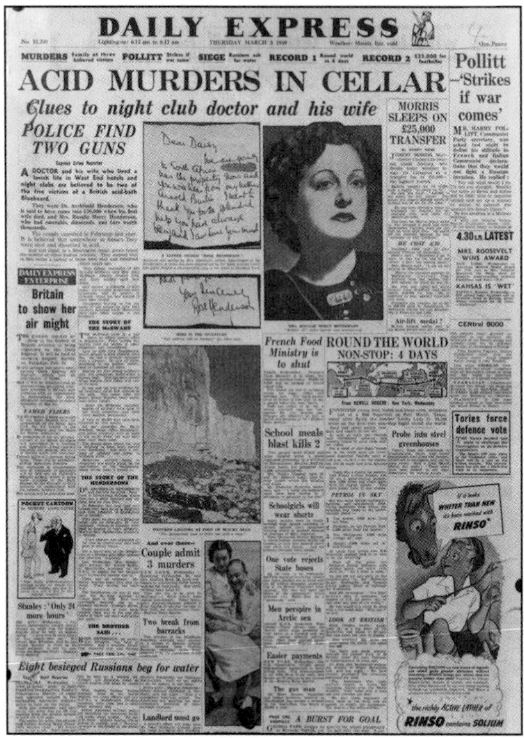

DAILY EXPRESS

THURSDAY MARCH 3 1949

MURDERS POLLITT SIEGE RECORD 1 RECORD 2

# ACID MURDERS IN CELLAR

*Clues to night club doctor and his wife*

*POLICE FIND TWO GUNS*

Express Crime Reporter

A DOCTOR and his wife who lived a lavish life in West End hotels and night clubs are believed to be two of the five victims of a British acid-bath Bluebeard.

Pollitt—'Strikes if war comes'

MORRIS SLEEPS ON £25,000 TRANSFER

4.30 a.m. LATEST

MRS. ROOSEVELT WINS AWARD

KANSAS IS 'WET'

Air-lift medal?

CENtral 8000

DAILY EXPRESS ENTERPRISE

Britain to show her air might

THE STORY OF THE McSWANS

FAMED FLIERS

*French Food Ministry is to shut*

ROUND THE WORLD NON-STOP: 4 DAYS

School meals blast kills 2

Probe into steel greenhouses

Tories force defence vote

THE STORY OF THE HENDERSONS

POCKET CARTOON

PETROL IN SKY

Schoolgirls will wear shorts

And over there—

Couple admit 3 murders

One vote rejects State buses

Stanley: 'Only 24 more hours'

THE BROTHER SAID . . .

Two break from barracks

Men perspire in Arctic sea

LOOK AT BRITISH

Easier payments

*Eight besieged Russians beg for water*

The gas man

Landlord must go

*A BURST FOR GOAL*

*If it looks WHITER THAN NEW it's been washed with RINSO*

*the richly ACTIVE LATHER of* RINSO *contains SOLIUM*

**ABOVE:** Haigh's vile crimes make the front page of the *Daily Express* newspaper on March 3, 1949.

stealing cash, he turned his hand to forgery and fraud, specializing in selling cars he didn't own. As the cash rolled in, Haigh acquired a gleaming sports car and a pretty wife. He lost both when he was jailed for fraud in 1934 and again in 1938.

Incarcerated in bleak Dartmoor prison, Haigh studied chemistry and worked in the tinsmith's store where he had access to sulphuric acid. The idea of dissolving bodies in acid began to take shape. He experimented on small animals brought in as pets by prisoners on outside work parties. He made careful notes about the time taken for acid to dissolve flesh and bone.

Freed in 1944, Haigh moved to the capital and set up his own business repairing pin-tables in basement rooms in London's Gloucester Road. His first murder victim, a draft dodger named Donald McSwann, was killed there in September 1944, Haigh smashing his skull with a pin-table leg and dissolving his body in a 40-gallon (180 liters) water butt filled with sulphuric acid. The little that was left of McSwann was then poured down a drain.

Haigh contacted the young man's parents, wealthy

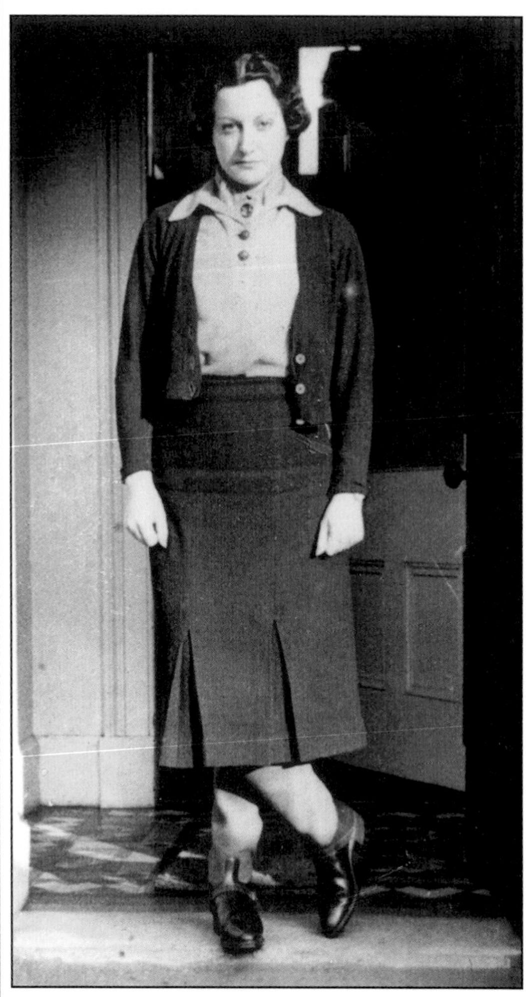

**ABOVE:** Rose Henderson in 1945. After murdering Rose and her husband, Haigh used forged papers to embezzle £7,000.

businessman William and wife Amy, with a message that their son had gone into hiding to avoid his call-up papers. When they turned up to learn more, they too were murdered and their remains swilled down the drain. Using forged papers, Haigh seized control of £4,000 of their assets and moved into the nearby Onslow Court Hotel. With money came a passion for gambling, however, and Haigh's debts mounted. He decided that new victims were needed.

The killer had moved his repair workshop to Crawley, Sussex, where, in February 1948, he lured London doctor Archibald Henderson and his wife Rose, murdered them and consigned their bodies to the acid vat. After forging letters giving him authority over their assets, he embezzled £7,000.

Haigh's final victim was a fellow resident of the Onslow Court Hotel, 69-year-old colonel's widow Olive Durand-Deacon. Lured to Crawley in February 1949, she was shot in the back and heaved into the acid vat. The resultant gunge was then poured onto the earth at the back of the workshop. Haigh had been too hasty, however. When police arrived, at the behest of a friend of the victim who knew of her appointment with Haigh, they found bone and false teeth which the acid had failed to dissolve.

Although police suspected Haigh of up to 15 murders, he confessed to just six. A jury at Lewes Assizes took just 17 minutes to declare him guilty. The deadly charming con-man was hanged at London's Wandsworth prison on August 10, 1949.

**ABOVE:** A crowd gathers outside Wandsworth prison in anticipation of news of Haigh's hanging.

# Henri Landru

Henri Landru was born in 1869 to a poor but honest hardworking couple. They gave him the middle name Desiré, meaning much desired. And indeed, despite his small stature, Landru would in time prove to be a magnet for the opposite sex. Given the nickname 'Bluebeard', he preyed on the women of Paris during World War One while their menfolk were away fighting—and it cost at least 11 of the ladies their lives.

## French 'Bluebeard' Was A Ladykiller

**ABOVE:** Henri Landru pleads his innocence from the witness box during his trial in November 1921.

**Landru married in 1893** and had three children but he gave up his job as an architect's clerk to lead a life of petty crime. On the run from the law, he started advertising for a new wife, even though he was still married. A widow aged 39, Jeanne Cuchet answered him and was greatly impressed by 'the widower Monsieur Diard', as Landru was calling himself. In December 1914, she gave up her apartment and, with her son, moved in with 'Diard' at his rented villa outside Paris.

Mme Cuchet and her son then vanished without trace, leaving Landru in possession of 15,000 francs worth of jewels, furniture, and securities. Over the next five years, Landru entertained scores of other women, at least 10 of whom never returned home. They ranged from a 19-year-old serving girl to a 44-year-old widow pretending to be aged 29.

Alarmed relatives began contacting the local mayor seeking help in tracing their loved ones. When he put

**ABOVE:** Two guards stand next to the oven in which Landru burned the bodies of his many victims.

**ABOVE:** 'Bluebeard', the murderous womanizer and nine of the victims he killed for money.

them in touch with one another, the families realized that the common factor in the disappearances was the bearded charmer, now confusingly going under the various names 'Fremyet', 'Cuchet', 'Guillet', 'Dupont', and 'Diard'.

**ABOVE:** The courtroom at Seine-et-Oise during Landru's trial. He was found guilty and sentenced to death in November 1921.

An arrest warrant was issued and, in April 1919, Landru was spotted strolling down a Paris street arm in arm with his proposed next victim. Police searched his city lodgings and recovered a handwritten book meticulously recording the women he had met through his advertisements, together with an account of their riches. A search of his country villa revealed the cause of thick, black, oily smoke that neighbors had noticed emitting from the chimney. Almost 300 fragments of bones and teeth were recovered from the stove where Landru had burned the dismembered bodies.

**ABOVE:** Landru burned the bodies of his victims in a stove in this house, pictured here in 1921.

Landru vehemently denied all charges, so there was never an answer to the question of how many victims he had claimed—many more than the 11 known about, it was suspected. At his trial at Seine-et-Oise court in November 1921, he was found guilty and, to hysterical scenes inside and outside the courtroom, was sentenced to die.

He faced his death, at Versailles prison in February 1922, like the gentleman he pretended to be. He refused the priest's offer of a confession, and instead wrote a note to the chief prosecutor at his trial: 'Farewell Monsieur. Our common history will doubtless die tomorrow. I will die with an innocent and quiet mind. I hope, respectfully, that you may do the same.' The next morning, after persuading the warders not to shave off his beard, Landru's shirt was ripped open and his neck laid on the guillotine. His last words were: 'I shall be brave'.

**ABOVE:** An artist sketches the scene of one of Landru's murders, in 1921.

# Bobby Joe Long

**Who knows what goes on in a brain as severely traumatized as that of Bobby Joe Long? He could not understand the forces that drove him to rape more than 50 women; neither could he control them. He was utterly disgusted with what he was doing but could not stop. And when his sexual obsession turned to murder, he knew that he just had to get himself caught.**

## The Serial Rapist Who Wanted To Get Caught

**Robert Joe Long, born 1953** in Kenova, West Virginia, was the product of a broken home and was completely dominated by his mother, who was constantly on the move seeking new jobs and new partners. At the age of 11, he was struck by a congenital disorder which caused his glands to produce extra oestrogen, making him grow breasts. Surgeons had to remove tissue from his chest but, although the physical abnormality was largely fixed, he was mentally scarred by the experience.

At 19, Long enlisted in the Army and six months later married his childhood sweetheart, who by all accounts was as dominant as his mother. At 20, he suffered a fractured skull in a motorcycle crash that left him in a coma for weeks. When he came round, he found that the least annoyance would make him erupt in violence. It was also, he said, when his uncontrollable sexual fixations began.

He demanded sex from his wife at least twice a day and masturbated obsessively. As a result, she divorced him and left with their two children. Sex also dominated his working day. He was a hospital X-ray technician but was fired from several posts for propositioning female patients, for showing a young girl pornographic pictures, and for ordering women to undress unnecessarily.

In 1976, he began raping regularly. Operating in and around Miami, Fort Lauderdale, and Ocala, Florida, he earned the nickname 'The Classified Ad Rapist' by ringing numbers from newspaper adverts and making appointments with housewives alone during daytime. Having gained entry to their homes, he would pull a knife, tie the victim up, and rape her.

From 1983, Long began murdering the women he abducted. At first in Jacksonville and then in the Tampa Bay area, he would cruise around looking for prostitutes or pick them up in seedy bars. He would take them to his apartment, bind them with rope and neck ligatures, then strangle them, bludgeon them or cut their throats. The bodies would be dumped, displayed in crude postures. During an eight-month period, he murdered at least nine women in the Tampa Bay area alone.

Long finally allowed himself to be caught by freeing one of his last victims, a 17-year-old girl whom he pounced on in November 1984 as she cycled home from her night-shift job at a bakery. He drove around with her blindfolded in his car for 26 hours and, although he raped her, he did not kill her. 'I knew when I let her go that it would only be a matter of time,' he said later. 'I just didn't care any more. I wanted to stop. I was sick inside.'

Nevertheless, two days later he struck again, strangling his final victim and driving around with her naked body but, on this one occasion, failing to rape her. Four days later, police identified him from the evidence of the freed 17-year-old. The following year, Long was found guilty of nine murders and given 32 life sentences and one death sentence.

He stalled all of the state's efforts to send him to Florida's electric chair, however, successfully gaining two new trials in one of the killings, though he was found guilty and re-sentenced to death both times. He was still sitting on Death Row two decades after his arrest.

A clue as to what made Bobby Joe Long tick came in a prison interview he gave. Talking of a stripper who accosted him up in a bar, he said he killed her because he was revolted by her. 'She picked me up,' he said. 'I didn't go after her. She was a whore. She manipulated men and she wanted to manipulate me. Once I had her in the car, I tied her up and raped her. Then I dumped her body along the highway. Next morning I couldn't believe what I had done. I was sick. Then I met another girl…and it happened all over again.'

# Pedro López

**Pedro López explained his murderous ways to police thus: 'I lost my innocence at the age of eight—so I decided to do the same to as many young girls as I could.' Born to a penniless prostitute in Tolmia, Colombia, in 1949, Pedro was one of 13 children. When the eight-year-old was caught sexually molesting one of his sisters, his mother threw him out of the house.**

## Did 'Monster Of The Andes' Kill 300?

**Left to beg and steal on the streets,** López was himself molested by a man who pretended to befriend him. At 18, he was jailed for auto theft and, on his second day in jail was gang-raped by fellow inmates. He got his revenge by murdering three of them with a knife he had fashioned—a revenge that cost him another two years behind bars after he pleaded that he had acted in self defense.

By the time he was finally freed, López was a hardened criminal and a killer beyond compare in South American criminal history. He earned himself the title 'Monster of the Andes', eventually confessing

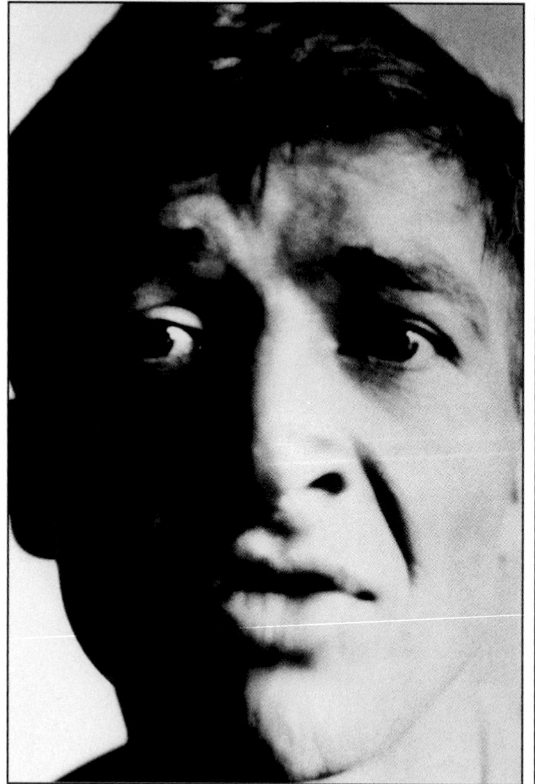

**ABOVE:** Vile Pedro López liked to see his victims' faces as they were murdered, so he always operated during daylight hours.

to the murder of 300 girls and, for a while, winning notoriety as the world's worst serial killer.

Roaming the impoverished countryside, his early victims were members of the native Indian tribes living on either side of the borders with neighboring Peru and Ecuador. López would stalk his young victims, sometimes for days, before approaching them with a supposed message from their mothers. López would then lead the girls to the outskirts of town where he would rape and kill them. He never worked at night because, as he later explained, he wanted to see his victim's face as she was murdered.

The hunt for a mass murderer began in earnest in April 1980 when a flash flood near Ambato, Ecuador, almost 10,000ft (3,000m) up in the Andes, unearthed the remains of some of his victims. Days later, López was caught by townspeople while trying to abduct a 12-year-old girl from a marketplace. Under arrest, he refused to answer questions, so police used an old ploy to trick him. They placed a priest in the same cell posing as a prisoner. The ruse worked almost too well. López confessed to such revolting acts of sadistic violence that the priest asked to be removed.

Confronted with the evidence, López finally cracked. He told of his five years as the 'Monster of the Andes', relating countless abductions of young girls, whom he would rape and then strangle while staring eagerly into their eyes. He said watching their death throes gave him heightened sexual pleasure.

López confessed to killing as many as 110 girls in Ecuador, 100 in Colombia, and 'many more than 100' in Peru. His story was only fully believed when he led police to his 'killing fields'. Near Ambato, mass graves held 53 girls aged between eight and 12. Police unearthed 28 other graveyards, although in many cases they had already been disturbed by wild animals.

Lopez was given a life sentence, segregated from other prisoners at Ambato prison following threats to castrate him and burn him alive. Prison director Major Victor Lascano said: 'We may never know how many young girls Lopez killed. His estimate of 300 may even be too low.'

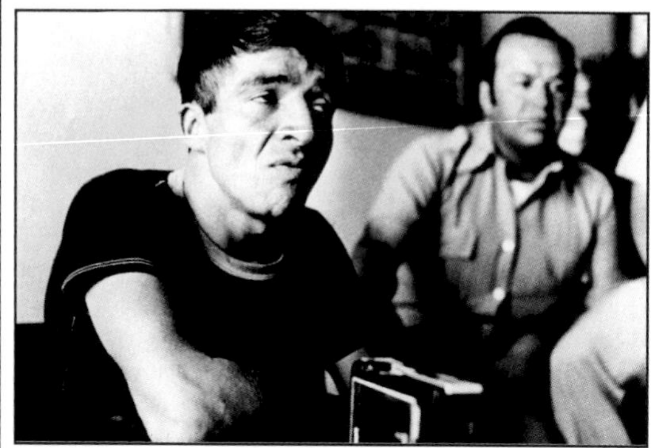

**ABOVE:** López during police interrogation in April 1980. He eventually confessed all to a priest, who was posing as a prisoner.

# Charles Manson

By the age of 32, Charles Manson was so institutionalized, having spent most of his life in prison, that he pleaded to stay in jail. If only the authorities had granted his wish. Two years later he had gathered a cult of impressionable devotees who were willing to kill to stay in his evil sect, which they referred to as 'The Family'.

## Bloody Massacre By Manson And His 'Angels Of Death'

**Manson was born in Cincinnati** in 1934 to Kathleen Maddox, a 16-year-old prostitute. The name on his birth certificate was No Name Maddox. He never knew who his father was and grew up in an environment of violence and drugs, spending long periods of his adolescence in juvenile institutions. At one detention center, Manson held a blade to a fellow inmate's throat as he violently raped him.

Although mainly homosexual during his teens, Manson married Rosalie Jean Willis, a 17-year-old waitress, in 1954. She was pregnant when he was next sentenced to three years in prison for auto theft. She visited him regularly at the start, bringing Charles Manson Jr. with her, but eventually met someone else and the visits stopped. Manson was never to see his son again. He remarried between jail sentences and had another son, also named Charles Manson Jr., but that marriage also failed.

In 1967 Manson found himself in San Francisco in the heyday of 'flower power' and drug-taking. He had a magnetism that seemed to attract drop-outs and middle-class young women alike. He formed a sect and settled in California's Santa Susana mountains, at Spahn Ranch, a one-time movie set.

Manson was convinced that an uprising between American blacks and whites was coming. He heard messages in the lyrics of Beatles tracks. He prophesied that only his disciples and the 'Chosen Blacks' would survive the mass slaughter and go on to take over the world. His followers, he believed, must rise up and strike out at the white establishment.

**BELOW:** In his warped mind, Manson foresaw a mass uprising of American blacks and whites which his 'Family' would survive.

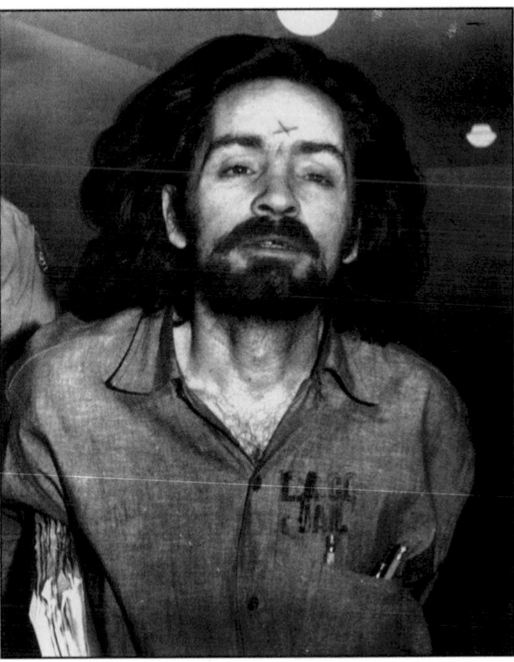

He called his devastating plan 'Helter Skelter' and on the night of August 9, 1969, sent four of his disciples—Susan Atkins, Patricia Krenwinkel, Linda Kasabian, and Charles Watson—to 10050 Cielo Drive, Benedict Canyon, Los Angeles, to begin the horrific slaughter. Movie producer, Roman Polanski and his pregnant wife, Sharon Tate, were renting the property. Polanski was

**ABOVE:** Polish film director Roman Polanski and American actress Sharon Tate at their wedding in 1968.

away filming but Sharon and friends were partying at the house when the self-styled 'Angels of Death' broke in.

They showed no mercy in their frenzied attack. Watson is said to have chanted 'I am the devil come to do the devil's work' as he battered Voytek Frykowski, a Polish movie director, who was then stabbed by Atkins. Jay Sebring a hairdresser, was stabbed and shot.

The most shocking murder was that of heavily pregnant Sharon Tate and her unborn son, who was stabbed 16 times. They tied a nylon rope around her neck, looped it over a ceiling beam and tied the other end around the hooded head of Sebring. Eighteen-year-old Steven Parent, a friend of the Polanskis' caretaker, was shot as he drove from the house. Abigail Folger, a coffee heiress, was slashed to pieces trying to escape the massacre. 'Pigs' was written in blood on the door of the mansion.

There is a theory that Manson's gang had killed the wrong people. The house in Cielo Drive had once been rented by record company boss Terry Melcher, Doris Day's son. He had apparently shunned Manson's attempts at breaking into the recording business. However, it is also believed that Frykowski and Sebring were drug dealers, whose business Manson coveted.

Displeased with the previous night's messy events at the Tate residence, Manson led the next 'Helter Skelter' mission on August 10. The four Tate murderers were again summoned, along with Steve Grogan and Leslie Van Houten, a former college queen and youngest member of the cult. They cruised the better neighborhoods of Los Angeles in search of potential victims before settling on the home of Leno and Rosemary LaBianca, who owned a small chain of supermarkets. Manson burst into their Waverly Drive mansion, tied them up and left them to the mercy of three of his cult slaves, Watson, Krenwinkel, and Van Houten.

The LaBiancas were subjected to horrific injuries, inflicted with a sword, knives, and forks. 'War' was carved on Leno's stomach and a fork was protruding from his body. He had been stabbed 26 times and, with a blood-soaked pillowcase acting as a hood, symbolically hung. Rosemary also had multiple stab wounds in her back and buttocks, was inscribed with 'War', hooded, and hung. The walls were covered with slogans written in their blood. They had misspelled 'Healter Skelter' on the fridge.

**ABOVE:** Manson shadowed by police officers in 1970. The spell he managed to cast over his followers was incredible.

**ABOVE:** A police mugshot of a crazed-looking Manson after his arrest in 1969.

Los Angeles police did not initially connect the two raids, and it was only the arrest of Susan Atkins in another investigation that brought the evil cult to justice. She was picked up in connection with the slaying of drug dealer Gary Hinman at his Topanga Canyon home 10 days before the mass murders. Atkins could not help boasting about her role in the Tate raid, describing her feelings of sexual satisfaction when stabbing the actress and hearing her scream for mercy. She even claimed she drank Tate's blood.

The police arrested the Manson 'Family' and, after a sensational trial that lasted 38 weeks, on March 29, 1971, they were all found guilty and sentenced to be executed—commuted to life imprisonment the following year when California quashed the death penalty.

**ABOVE:** Manson, as he appears today, the swastika tattoo on his forehead a reminder of his sickening past.

Leslie Van Houten succeeded in gaining two retrials in the late 1960s because her lawyer had disappeared during her initial trial. His remains were found later in the mountains, and members of the Manson cult were suspected of his murder. Van Houten failed to win her freedom and was again sentenced to life imprisonment.

America relived the horrific deaths in 1994, when a 'Free Susan Atkins Campaign' was launched. Her supporters felt she was now rehabilitated. However, after hearing evidence from Sharon Tate's sister, Patti, who was only 11 at the time of the murders, her appeal was refused. Patti told of her mother's distress each time a member of the murdering gang applied for parole and of the indifference of the gang as they left behind the sickening murder scene at Cielo Drive and moved on to the massacre at the LaBianca home. Atkins remained in custody, as does Manson, who admits he will kill again if he ever gets his freedom.

**ABOVE:** Manson during his trial in 1970. He was vowed to kill again if he is ever released from prison.

# Peter Manuel

**Peter Manuel turned to crime at an early age. When only 11, he was caught breaking into stores. At 15, he attacked a woman with a hammer. As a consequence, he spent a large part of his teen years in an approved school and in Borstal—all of which helped make him a hardened villain ready to turn to violence to obtain either money or sexual satisfaction.**

## Families Shot Dead By Gun-Toting Burglar

**On his release from Borstal** in 1946, the 19-year-old Manuel moved to Glasgow, where his Scots-born parents had settled after their Coventry home was destroyed in a German bombing raid. Within weeks, he was arrested for housebreaking and, while awaiting trial, he raped an expectant mother and indecently assaulted two other women. He was sentenced to eight years in jail and was released in 1953.

Three years later, Manuel graduated to murder. His first victim was 17-year-old Annie Knielands, whom he killed in January 1956, and whose body he left on the fifth fairway of a golf course at East Kilbride, near Glasgow. Manuel was questioned and released for lack of evidence. In September 1956, while free on bail over a burglary charge, he broke into a house in Burnside, Glasgow, and shot dead housewife Marion Watt, her sister Margaret, and Marion's 16-year-old daughter Vivienne. Again Manuel was arrested, quizzed and, although he was given 18 months' jail for the earlier burglary, there was insufficient evidence to pin the murders on him.

On his release, Manuel visited Newcastle Upon Tyne for a job interview in early December 1957, where he shot and killed taxi driver Sydney Dunn. Back in

**ABOVE:** Scottish mass-murderer Peter Manuel smiling during his trial in Glasgow on May 29, 1958.

Glasgow, he struck again on December 27. Isabelle Cooke, aged 17, left her home in Mount Vernon to go to a dance but never returned. Even as police searched for her, three bodies were found in a house just 10 minutes' walk away from Manuel's home. Peter Smart, his wife Doris, and their 11-year-old son Michael had all been shot through the head at close range.

Peter Manuel was arrested on January 14, 1958, and charged with the murder of the Smarts. His father was charged with receiving stolen goods from various burglaries, which, in an attempt to shield his son, he claimed to have bought at a market. Showing remorse for the first time, Manuel offered a full confession in return for his father's release. He led police to the spot where he had thrown two guns into a river and showed them where he had buried Isabelle Cooke.

At his trial, which began in May 1958, Manuel was found guilty of seven murders—although Glasgow police believe he may have killed up to 15 people. The judge commented that 'a man may be very bad without being mad' before sentencing him to death. On July 11, 1958, Peter Manuel was allowed to hear Mass and take Holy Communion before making his final, short walk to the gallows at Glasgow's Barlinnie Jail.

**ABOVE:** Manuel is led away by police following his arrest for murder on January 17, 1958.

# Robert Maudsley

**Robert Maudsley may not be Britain's most prolific serial killer but the jailbird is certainly judged the most dangerous. He committed 'only' four murders—three of them while in prison on a life sentence for the first. His most sickening claim to infamy was taunting jail warders by eating the brains of one of his victims.**

## Cannibal Killer Ate Prisoner's Brains

**Robert John Maudsley** was born in Liverpool in 1953, one of 12 children of a violent father. He spent his early years in an orphanage run by nuns. As a teenager, he moved to London and became a rent boy to pay for his drug addiction. In 1974, he attacked a laborer who had picked him up for sex, stabbing him, smashing him over the head with a hammer, and garrotting him. He explained that he had become angry when the man showed him pictures of children he had sexually abused.

Maudsley was given a life sentence and sent to Broadmoor hospital for the criminally insane. There, in February 1977, he and another prisoner, David Cheeseman, dragged convicted pedophile David Francis into a room on their ward, barricaded the door, tied him up with flex from a record player and held him hostage. For 10 hours, staff listened to his screams as he was tortured. Eventually the pair came out, holding the garrotted corpse above their heads as a trophy.

Following this Maudsley was sent to Wakefield Prison, in Yorkshire, where, despite the high security, Prisoner 467637's killing spree continued. In July 1978, Maudsley fashioned a knife from a soup spoon and waited for sex offender Salney Darwood to enter his cell. Maudsley plunged the knife into his back and head, then expertly garrotted him. He stuffed the body under a bunk and went in search of another victim.

Next to die was William Roberts, who was lying face down on his bunk. Maudsley stabbed him then smashed his head against the wall. He is then said to have used his homemade knife to prise open the skull 'like a boiled egg' to scoop out the brains. Afterward, Maudsley strode up to the officer in charge and said: 'There'll be two short on the roll call.'

The incident earned Maudsley the media nickname 'Hannibal the Cannibal', although his fellow inmates referred to him simply as 'Spoons'. Deemed too dangerous for a normal cell, he was placed in solitary confinement in a purpose-built Perspex cage with cardboard furniture and concrete bed beneath Wakefield Prison's F-Wing. Over the next quarter century, he allowed his hair to grow long and his fingernails to 'look more like a vulture's talons', according to one newspaper report.

Maudsley, who enjoys poetry, classical music, and art and has a genius-level IQ, once described life in his 10ft (3m) square cell as 'like being buried alive in a coffin'. He wrote: 'I am left to stagnate; vegetate; and to regress; left to confront my solitary head-on, with people who have eyes but don't see, ears but don't hear, mouths but don't speak; consequently I too am left with no voice, nowhere to turn to but inward.'

# Ivan Milat

**In September 1992, ramblers in the Belanglo State Forest, New South Wales, Australia, discovered a corpse. The following day, police discovered a second body nearby. The corpses were those of two British girls, 21-year-old Caroline Clarke and 22-year-old Joanne Walters, who had been missing since hitch-hiking from Sydney.**

## Hitch-Hikers Executed By The 'Backpack Killer'

**Caroline had been stabbed** and shot in the head several times, the angle of the bullets' entry suggesting to forensic scientists that the killer had used her for target practice. Joanne had been stabbed in the heart and lungs, one cut penetrating her spine and probably paralyzing her before the wounds that finally killed her.

The discoveries sparked a hunt for one of Australia's most notorious and evil serial killers: Ivan Robert Marko Milat. Born in 1945, one of 14 children of a Croat immigrant, he became known as the 'Backpack Killer' because of the way he targeted young hikers. Belanglo State Forest seemed to be his favorite 'killing field'.

Other corpses began turning up in the forest. In October 1993, a walker discovered the remains of James Gibson, and his girlfriend Deborah Everist, both 19 and from Victoria, who had disappeared while hitch-hiking in December 1989. Forensics later confirmed that James had suffered the killer's 'trademark' knife wound through the spine, paralyzing him before he was killed.

The same fate had been suffered by Simone Schmidl, 21, whose body was found the following month. The German girl, missing since January 1991, had been sexually assaulted. Clothing found at the scene was not Schmidl's, however, but matched that of another missing backpacker, 20-year-old Anja Habschied. What was left of Anja and 21-year-old boyfriend Gabor Neuebauer was discovered a few days later. Her head was missing, together with two of her vertebrae. She had been decapitated with a sword while alive and in a kneeling position, Gabor had been gagged and strangled. His skull showed six bullet entries.

It was now clear that a ritualistic serial killer was on the prowl. Police received hundreds of calls from worried parents around the world who wanted assurance that their backpacking children were safe.

**ABOVE:** The house of the 'Backpack Killer', Ivan Milat, raided by Australian police in 1994.

**ABOVE:** The scene outside Campbelltown Local Court in May 1994 as Ivan Milat is charged in relation to the Paul Onions case.

But news of the killing spree also brought the first clue as to the identity of the perpetrator.

British student Paul Onions, 20, had been picked up by a driver in southern New South Wales in January 1990. The man acted so peculiarly that Paul fled and, with his pursuer chasing him gun in hand, Paul flagged down another passing vehicle and escaped. He reported the attack but was told by police that, without the license plate number, there was little chance of tracing the gunman.

Tragically for other, less lucky victims, that proved to be the case. But when Paul Onions repeated his story four years later, police had a description of the 'Backpack Killer'. And when Ivan Milat was subsequently fingered as the prime suspect, Paul was shown a photograph of Milat and was able to identify him straight away.

The final breakthrough came when a woman called to say that her boyfriend worked at a ready-mixed concrete company with a man called Ivan Milat who lived near the forest and was a gun fanatic. Detectives established that Milat had been absent from work on the probable dates of murders, and they pounced on him at his home in Eaglevale while he lay in bed with his girlfriend.

Milat vehemently denied knowledge of the slayings but a search of his house produced items of property belonging to his victims, along with cartridges that matched those found near the backpackers' bodies.

Charged with the seven murders, Milat was finally found guilty on all counts and, in June 1995, was sentenced to life imprisonment. He was taken to a high-security jail in Maitland, southwest of Sydney, bragging that he would one day escape. He made one failed escape attempt in July 1995.

Six years later, a closely-guarded Milat was brought from prison to appear at a reopened inquest into the deaths of three girls who had disappeared in 1978 and 1979 in similar circumstances to those surrounding Milat's other victims. The killer refused to cooperate, and the deaths of the girls, aged 20, 17, and 14, remained unattributed. However, Milat is still suspected of being responsible for many other murders.

Over the years, Milat continued to raise appeals against his conviction. Several times, he injured himself in prison, swallowing razor blades, staples, and other metal objects. In January 2009, he cut off his little finger with a plastic knife, planning to mail it to the High Court.

**ABOVE:** The prison van used to transport Milat to court to face various charges in May 1994.

# Herman Mudgett

**Herman Webster Mudgett arrived in Chicago in 1886 with two wives, no money, a fake university degree, and a mission: to get very rich very quickly. He had charm, style, wit, and a way about him that women found irresistible—more often than not, to their cost. Mudgett realized that, in this booming, anything-goes, crime-ridden city preparing to host the World's Fair, he had found the ideal environment in which to carry out his nefarious projects. In so doing, he became America's first identified serial killer.**

## Secret Gas Chambers In Torturer's Castle

**Born in 1860 into a prominent family** in Gilmanton, New Hampshire, mustachioed Mudgett was intelligent, handsome, and charming. Kicked out of medical school for stealing cadavers, with which he planned to defraud insurance companies, his knowledge of medicine nevertheless enabled him to pass himself off as a qualified physician, 'Dr Henry Howard Holmes', once he had settled in Chicago.

His first job in that city had been more modest. He took a job as a prescription clerk at a drug store in the Englewood district. After a few months, his employer, a widow, and her young daughter disappeared, Mudgett telling any curious customers that they had moved to California after selling him the store. In fact, Mudgett had killed them.

From his newly acquired base, Mudgett launched a series of dodgy ventures. He bottled tap water as an all-purpose 'miracle cure'. He sold a 'sure-fire cure for alcoholism' at $50 a bottle. And he claimed to have invented a device for turning water into domestic gas that won him a research contract from a utility company. As the money rolled in, he purchased a large plot of land across the road at 701 and 703 Sixty-third Street. It was to be the site of what later became known infamously as Holmes Castle, a three-storey labyrinthine edifice of 100 rooms, with secret passageways, false walls, and mysterious trap-doors.

Mudgett completed his mansion in 1888, when he

LEFT: Herman Mudgett confessed to 27 murders at Holmes Castle, but the true figure may have been as high as 200.

was aged just 28. Over the years, he lured scores of young women to Holmes Castle with the promise of non-existent jobs. There, he would murder his visitors by leaving them in one of the several rooms that were sealed and fed by mysterious pipes. These were his gas chambers. He would then dispose of the bodies in one of two ways—either in his 6ft (2m) wide stove or in barrels of acid.

Mudgett got away with mass murder until September 1894 when he killed a small-time Philadelphia criminal to claim life insurance. A sharp-eyed insurance investigator cast doubt on the claim, and detectives

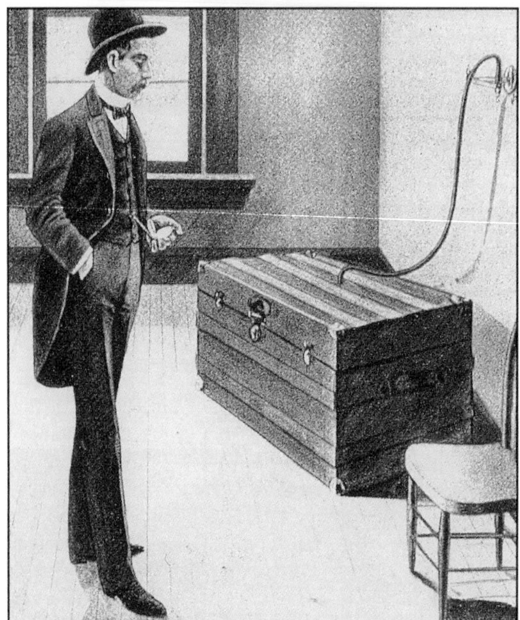

**ABOVE:** A contemporary print of a detective looking at a trunk fed by a gas pipe—the 'execution chamber' of some of Mudgett's victims.

**ABOVE:** An ink sketch published at the time of his arrest showing how the 'Torture Castle' killer disposed of his younger victims.

visited the address to where the money was to have been sent: Holmes Castle. What they discovered there is related in a report of the time which describes ordinary bedrooms used for seduction, alongside windowless rooms fed by gas pipes. More horrifically, police believed that in one asbestos-lined chamber he had devised a means of introducing fire, so that the gas pipe became a blow-torch. The basement contained a medieval-style torture rack—and several women's skeletons from which the flesh had been carefully stripped.

Mudgett went on the run but was traced to Boston, where he was arrested in November 1894 planning to flee the country. He was put on trial in Philadelphia for the murder of the petty criminal, although by then it was known that he had also killed the man's three children. After his conviction but while awaiting sentence, he sold his story for $7,500 to Hearst newspapers, in which he confessed to 27 murders in Chicago, Indianapolis, and Toronto.

Although estimates of the number of his victims range up to 200, the true count will never be known. Herman Mudgett was hanged at Philadelphia's Moyamensing Prison on May 7, 1896. He took almost 15 minutes to die.

# Dennis Nilsen

**Dennis Nilsen was a prolific serial killer, preying on men throughout London in the 1970s and 80s. Insisting he had no control of his actions, he claimed to be in a trance throughout and would 'wake up' to find a dead man in his home. While he argued that his murders were the fault of a personality disorder, the sheer ruthlessness of his killings and disposal of the bodies demonstrated a deadly instinct. Nilsen's own efforts to end his rampage would prove to be his downfall.**

## Killer Boiled Human Head In A Cookpot

**Nilsen killed for the first time** in 1978. He picked up a stranger in a pub and they slept together. As dawn broke he realized that he could not bear this newfound bedfellow to leave. He used a tie to strangle the sleeping man, then finished him off by plunging his head into a bucket of water.

Nilsen was at first shocked by his own barbarity but he soon overcame any qualms. His compulsion to kill led to bodies being stored beneath the floorboards of his apartment at Melrose Avenue, Willesden. One nameless victim was so physically appealing to Nilsen that it was a week before the body was put underneath the floor. The killer kept him in the room, returning from work to 'chat' with him and have sex with the corpse.

**ABOVE:** Dennis Nilsen developed a fascination with corpses, aged five, following the death of his grandfather.

**ABOVE:** Nilsen at Highgate Magistrates Court, London, during his trial for murder.

Another of his many victims had the misfortune to suffer an epileptic fit outside Nilsen's home. Nilsen tended him and, when the man returned the next day to thank him, he was murdered. Nilsen eventually disposed of his stash of corpses by chopping them up and burning them in backyard bonfires.

When Nilsen moved to an apartment at Cranley Gardens, Muswell Hill, he no longer had access to a garden, so he was forced to dissect corpses more fully, flushing the skin and bone down the toilet. Eventually the plumbing failed and kindly neighbors posted warning signs on his door. Nilsen knew he had to work fast—for if plumbers entered his apartment, they might find the malodorous body of a 20-year-old man killed the previous week and hidden in his wardrobe.

Nilsen laid plastic sheets across the floor of his front room and, with a kitchen knife, dismembered the body and severed the head, placing it in a large cooking pot simmering on the stove. The body parts, including the boiled head, were put into black plastic bags. Nilsen had no time to dispose of them, however, because neighbors had decided to resolve the plumbing problems by calling in industrial drain clearers.

When an engineer removed a manhole cover, he found decomposing matter was still evident. Police were called and a forensic scientist confirmed that it was human flesh.

When Nilsen returned home from work on February 9, 1983, detectives were waiting for him. He confessed, showing them the bags containing body parts stored in his wardrobe. He went on to relate a macabre series of murderous crimes committed by one of the most unlikely looking villains ever.

For Nilsen just did not look the part of a serial killer. He seemed just too 'ordinary'. Yet it transpired that his

**ABOVE:** Nilsen's apartment in Melrose Avenue. Victims were murdered and their bodies stored under floorboards.

fascination with human corpses had been spawned in him when he was very young…

Dennis Andrew Nilsen was born in November 1945 in Fraserburgh, Scotland, the second son of Olav Nilsen, a Norwegian serviceman. Dennis grew up without his father but received enough love and attention from his grandfather, Andrew Whyte, with whom he and his mother lived. When the old man died of a heart attack at the age of 62, he was laid out at home. And it was noted then that little Dennis, just five years old, was fascinated by the corpse. He later admitted that the powerful image of death loomed large in his mind for years.

Aged 16, Nilsen enlisted in the Army, serving as a butcher in the Catering Corps, learning the skills that served him so well during his five-year killing spree. On leaving the Army in 1972, he took up police training but resigned and went on to become a recruitment interviewer. In 1975, he moved into the Melrose Road apartment with another man, although the latter denied it was a homosexual relationship. Their friendship lasted two years but when the man left, Nilsen's life began a downward spiral into alcohol and loneliness that culminated in the first murder 18 months later. Nilsen resolved that nobody would walk out on him again—and, for many visitors, that really did mean 'never'.

**ABOVE:** Nilsen during his spell in the Army in the 1960s. He worked as a butcher in the Catering Corps.

**ABOVE:** The lack of outside space at Nilsen's apartment in Cranley Gardens led him to flush his victims' remains down the toilet.

One visitor who did live to tell the tale was a male model who, during the wave of publicity following Nilsen's arrest in February 1983, told police that he had narrowly escaped death at the hands of the mass killer after meeting Nilsen in a bar and returning with him to his apartment in Cranley Gardens. The model had later awoken gasping for breath, with a swollen tongue and burn marks around his neck. Nilsen had not only tried to strangle him but had also thrust his head into a bucket of water. The would-be victim sought hospital treatment but did not go to the police.

In court, Nilsen's defense counsel tried to persuade the jury that the killer was mad. Thanks in part to the male model's evidence, the panel at the Old Bailey did not believe it. He was found guilty of six murders and two attempted murders. The full tally was reckoned to be at least 15. On November 4, 1983, still showing not a shred of remorse, Dennis Nilsen was jailed for life.

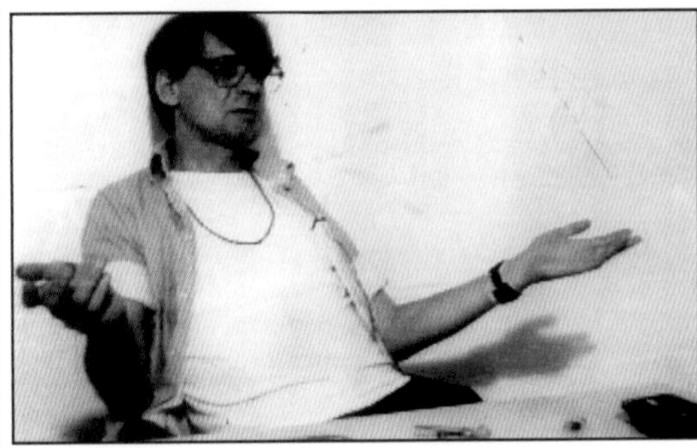

**ABOVE:** Nilsen during a police interview. He was found guilty of six murders and two attempted murders and jailed for life.

# Paul Ogorzow

**In 1940, as German tanks rolled across Europe, a few more acts of savagery would hardly be an issue for the Nazi hierarchy—or so one would have thought. But a few seemingly isolated events in the German capital gave more concern to the authorities than their actual numbers might have otherwise warranted.**

## Hushed-Up Shame Of Nazi Era Cops

**Over the summer months,** three women had been stabbed and two others assaulted in the eastern districts of Berlin. Now, as winter approached, women's bodies began turning up. In October, a 20-year-old mother of two was stabbed in the neck and strangled. A month later, a 30-year-old was thrown unconscious from a moving train but survived. In December, a 26-year-old nurse was beaten to death and thrown from a train. On the same day, and only 550 yards (500m) away, a 19-year-old girl had her skull smashed and was raped.

Just before Christmas, a 30-year-old woman was found with a fractured skull. The next victim, a 46-year-old with similar injuries, was found a week later. Another body, of a woman aged 28, turned up in January 1941. Police believed all or most of the victims had been attacked on a train or near a rail track.

The attacker, now labeled 'the S-Bahn (City Railroad) Murderer', brought terror to the capital. While the world recoiled at the mounting death toll of World War Two, Berliners concentrated on the slaughter of innocents closer to home. Not that they had much information to go on…

The Nazi propaganda machine, under Joseph Goebbels, wanted only 'good' news, so the murders were only publicized in brief detail for fear of causing public panic. Other factors hampered Berlin's serious crime force, the Kriminalpolizei, in their hunt for the serial killer. A blackout was being enforced in the city and this had proved a dream for criminals and a nightmare for the police. The blackout also caused numerous travel accidents, with an average of one fatality every day on the railroad system. It was initially difficult to distinguish between an accident and a homicide.

The result of these drawbacks was that there were two more victims. The body of a 39-year-old woman was found in February beside the railroad line, evidently having been thrown from a train, and in early

July, the body of a woman of 35 was discovered with similar injuries on waste ground.

Despite the problems caused by wartime restrictions, the Kriminalpolizei had been tardy in identifying the killer. All evidence had pointed to a railroad employee, yet it took several preventable deaths before detectives finally arrested an S-Bahn signalman, Paul Ogorzow, 28, who lived with his wife and two children close to where four of his victims were found.

Shamefully, the police realized that they had already questioned their suspect after a tip-off but had let him go, and on another occasion when challenged by Kriminalpolizei officers, he had simply fled into the night. The tip-off had come from the killer's railroad colleagues, who had long suspected him because of his loudly voiced hatred of women and his habit of vanishing for long spells while on duty.

Ogorzow was charged with eight murders, six cases of attempted murder, and a further 31 cases of assault. In court, he declared himself a family man, loyal Nazi Party member, and an active street fighter with the SA. But the judge agreed he was 'a killer of a completely cold and calculating nature, with depraved sexual urges'. He was executed by guillotine in Plötzensee Prison.

# Anatoly Onoprienko

**When police seized Anatoly Onoprienko, otherwise known as 'The Terminator', they locked up the worst serial killer the Ukraine had ever known. Onoprienko, a 37-year-old former forestry student, sailor, and mental hospital outpatient, was arrested in April 1996 at his girlfriend's apartment, where police found a shotgun matching the one used in no fewer than 40 murders. The total number of his victims was 52.**

## Bloody Trail Of 'The Terminator'

**Onoprienko eventually confessed** to all 52 murders in a six-year killing spree, in which he claimed he was commanded by 'inner voices'. Onoprienko's rampage began in June 1989, when he and accomplice Serhiy Rogozin robbed and killed nine people. They first blasted a couple to death in their car, then wiped out of a family of five, including an 11-year-old girl.

Onoprienko spent six years traveling around Eastern Europe, where police believe he may have been responsible for other murders. Onoprienko resumed the known killings in late 1995, and they followed a set pattern. He would choose an isolated house, storm in at dawn, round up the family and shoot them all, including the children, at close range with a 12-gauge shotgun. Any witnesses would also be dispatched.

**ABOVE:** Anatoly Onoprienko, aka The Terminator, is Ukraine's worst ever serial killer, with a body count of 52.

He would hack off fingers to get at wedding rings and even pull out his victims' gold teeth. He would then loot the house before setting it on fire.

In November 1995, after stealing a shotgun, he began a killing spree that at one stage went into manic overdrive—in just one 20-week bloodbath, he killed and mutilated 43 people in the Lvov region, near the border of Poland. Victims ranged from a 70-year-old pensioner to a three-month-old baby. Panic was so widespread in two villages, Bratkovichi and Busk, that the army was sent in, personnel carriers patrolled the streets and police imposed a security cordon.

A manhunt involving 2,000 police and more than 3,000 troops failed to find 'The Terminator'. In the end, a tip-off about an unlicensed gun led detectives, on April 14, 1996, to an apartment in the garrison town of Yavoriv. Onoprienko was sleeping beside his girlfriend—to whom he had once proposed with a ring he had chopped from the finger of one of his victims only a few hours earlier. Ordered out of bed, Onoprienko furtively withdrew a gun from a cupboard, but handcuffs were clapped on him before he could pull the trigger.

In February 1999, a court in the city of Zhytomyr, 90 miles (140km) west of Kiev, ruled that Onoprienko was mentally competent to answer charges. The 39-year-old killer sat impassively in a metal cage as a woman screamed from the back of the court: 'Let us tear him apart. He should die a slow and agonizing death.' The judge commented: 'He doesn't care about anything—

**ABOVE:** During a prison interview, Onoprienko claimed: 'I have never felt sorry for those I killed. No love, no hatred, just blind indifference.'

only about himself. He is driven by extreme cruelty.' Onoprienko was sentenced to death, later commuted to life in prison.

Explaining his murderous drive, Onoprienko said in a prison interview: 'To me killing people is like ripping up a duvet. Women, old people, children, they are all the same. I have never felt sorry for those I killed. No love, no hatred, just blind indifference.'

# William Palmer

**Deep in debt and gambling wildly, Dr William Palmer cheered up somewhat when the friend he was accompanying to the races won more than £2,000—a small fortune in 1855. Palmer, aged 31, watched as the lucky winner, 28-year-old John Parsons Cooke, drained a celebratory brandy and gasped: 'Good God, there's something in it—it burns my throat.' Palmer himself nonchalantly knocked back the few remaining drops in the bottom of the glass. In front of a witness he declared: 'Nonsense, there is nothing in it.'**

## How Dr Palmer The Poisoner Gambled And Lost

In pain, Cooke left the racecourse at Shrewsbury, Shropshire, and traveled the 40 miles (64km) to the doctor's home town of Rugeley, Staffordshire, where he stayed at an inn, which Palmer's visited regularly to treat his patient. Strangely, the medicine and broths prescribed only seemed to make Cooke worse.

**ABOVE:** Dr William Palmer on the stand during his trial at the Central Criminal Court in London, in May 1856.

**ABOVE:** The high street in Rugeley, Staffordshire, where Palmer murdered his 'friend' John Parsons Cooke.

Only when the bookmakers had paid out Cooke's winnings, swiftly pocketed by Palmer, did the doctor finish him off. After suffering convulsions for several days, Cooke went rigid in spasms and finally suffocated—the symptoms of strychnine poisoning.

Cooke, it transpired, was far from being Palmer's first victim in a medical career that was disgracefully blighted. By the time he was 17, he had already been dismissed from two pharmacy apprenticeships, once for taking cash and the second time for running an illegal abortion service. He finally qualified as a doctor in London in 1846 and the following year married Anne

**LEFT:** A period sketch of Dr Palmer at the horse races. He was known as the 'Prince of Poisoners'.

Brookes, the heiress daughter of a wealthy widow.

Palmer paid little heed to his family or to his doctor's practice, instead spending his days at racecourses. As his debts mounted, however, a string of deaths occurred in his family. First, Palmer's rich mother-in-law died, followed by his wife, who had been heavily insured. Palmer's brother, four children, an uncle, and several more of his creditors met similar ends.

Palmer became both greedy and impatient. And it was his blatant poisoning of his friend Cooke in 1855 that ended his one-man crime wave. Arrested and brought to trial at London's Old Bailey, he heard medical evidence that only strychnine poisoning could have produced such symptoms—and that the day before his friend's death, the doctor had bought a bottle of strychnine from a local chemist.

The jury was out for only 100 minutes before returning a guilty verdict and Palmer was sentenced to be hanged at Stafford Prison. Interviewed there by the governor, the condemned man replied: 'I have nothing more to say than this—that I am quite easy in my conscience and happy in my mind.' To the very end, he refused to confess. He insisted he had been unjustly convicted of murder by strychnine—though lawyers believed this was his way of hinting that he had killed his friend by some other means. Indeed, his last remark made to the priest who visited him before his execution was: 'Cooke did not die from strychninia.'

Such was the sensational nature of the case that an estimated 25,000 people flocked to Stafford by road, rail, on horseback, and on foot to cheer the evil doctor's hanging at eight o'clock on the morning of June 14, 1856.

# Carl Panzram

**Carl Panzram wrote from his cell on Death Row in Leavenworth Prison, Kansas, in 1929: 'In my lifetime, I have murdered 21 human beings. I have committed thousands of burglaries, robberies, larcenies, arsons and, last but not least, I have committed sodomy on more than 100 male human beings. For all these things I am not in the least bit sorry.'**

## 'I Hate The Whole Damned Human Race'

**Born of Prussian immigrant parents** in Warren, Minnesota, in 1891, Panzram had been in trouble with police from the age of eight, when he was arrested for being drunk and disorderly! Three years later, a string of burglaries landed him in reform school—which he tried to burn down, with some success. Freed at the age of 13, he had already gained the knowledge he needed for his life of crime: 'how to steal, lie, hate, burn and kill,' as he later wrote in his autobiography.

Panzram joined the US Army at 16 but was so rebellious that he was court-martialed and jailed for three years—the first of several terms in prison. He went on to murder indiscriminately all over the world, but his principal areas of operation were West Africa, Mexico, California, Montana, and Washington DC.

His two most infamous crimes were committed in the 1920s. Panzram bought a yacht, the *John O'Leary* (which was also one of his aliases) and lured 10 crewmen aboard with the promise of unlimited bootleg liquor. The men were given alcohol until they were senseless, then were raped and murdered, their bodies thrown overboard. Later, in Portuguese West Africa, he hired 10 locals to accompany him on a crocodile hunt. He killed them all, sodomizing their corpses before feeding them to the crocs.

In 1928 he was jailed at Leavenworth for 20 years for another murder. He told the warden: 'I'll kill the first man who crosses me'—and carried out his threat by battering to death a civilian employee with an iron bar. He was sentenced to death, spurning attempts at a reprieve by telling liberal campaigners: 'I believe the only way to reform people is to kill them.'

He went to the gallows on September 5, 1930, berating his executioner: 'Hurry up, you bastard, I could hang a dozen men while you're fooling around.' The remorseless killer left behind an autobiography in which he summed up his philosophy in three defiant sentences: 'I don't believe in Man, God nor Devil'; 'I hate the whole damned human race, including myself', and 'I wish the whole world had but a single throat and I had my hands around it.'

# Elaine Parent

**Elaine Antoinette Parent traveled the world under at least 20 stolen identities and eluded investigators for 12 years. Although hunted by police for killing and mutilating one female victim, she is feared to have murdered and stolen the identities of many more.**

## The 'Chameleon' Who Stole Other People's Lives

**New York-born Parent,** nicknamed 'The Chameleon', was an expert con-artist; bisexual, beautiful, clever, and deadly. This is how she operated…

In early 1990, lonely bank employee Beverly McGowan, 34, placed a newspaper advertisement for someone to share her Miami condominium. A woman in her late 40s, calling herself 'Alice', answered the advert, and swiftly moved in. Beverly told her brother, Steve, about her charming new roommate and said she felt her life 'had turned around'. Indeed, it was about to.

Pretending to be an expert on numerology, and promising to predict a rosy future for her, the newcomer convinced Beverly to part with her date and time of birth and her credit card and driver's license numbers.

On July 8, someone using the name Beverly McGowan called her place of work to take a day off sick. A day later, brother Steve received a goodbye letter supposedly from Beverly, saying that she was leaving home for a while. Knowing this to be uncharacteristic behavior, he called at his sister's condo and, finding her missing, stopped her credit cards.

At about the same time that Steve arrived at her front door, however, a mutilated and decapitated corpse was being recovered from a remote canal bank in southern Florida. The female's head and hands had been hacked off at the wrists with a chainsaw to delay identification, a hole in her stomach had been gouged out to eradicate the identifying tattoo that lay there, and only five teeth and half a jaw remained. But the killer had missed the tattoo of a rose on the woman's ankle and police were able to identify the body as Beverly McGowan's.

A few days later, 'Alice' tried to use Beverly's canceled credit card to book a flight to London and rent a car. Nobody by the name of Alice or Beverly McGowan turned up at Heathrow Airport, and when the credit card transactions failed, the investigation became an international manhunt. 'Alice', however, disappeared.

Six years later, after reinvestigating the manifest for the 1990 flight to London, detectives concentrated on a passenger listed as 'Sylvia Ann Hodgkinson'. They found that Hodgkinson was a deceased British citizen and had three other identities linked to her: Charlotte Rae Cowan, Ann Tremont, and Elaine Antoinette Parent.

Inquiries back in Florida revealed that Parent, using the alias Ann Tremont, had befriended a woman in a bar in Orlando in 1989 and, using numerology to obtain vital information, had stolen her identity. A modus operandi was emerging that made Elaine Parent prime suspect for the murder of Beverly McGowan.

Forensic investigators now re-examined the writing pad supposedly used by Beverly in her 'goodbye' letter. Impressions on the pad revealed hidden correspondence in Parent's handwriting—the content being angry threats to an ex-lover living in London, where Parent had fled in 1990. The lover, a businesswoman, told police of Parent's violent mood swings. Another ex-lover revealed that she was sometimes so frightened of Parent that she would drive 80 miles (128km) to a friend's house to escape.

In April 2002, Parent, then aged 60, was finally tracked down to a house in Panama City, Florida, where she was using the name 'Darlene Thompson'. When police called to arrest her, she asked if she could change her clothes. She went back into the bedroom—and fired a shot through her heart with a .375 Magnum.

To this day, police still don't know how many identities Elaine Parent acquired, and they fear several more women suffered the same fate as Beverly McGowan. The full extent of secretive Parent's homicidal history may never be known.

# Leszek Pekalski

**When Leszek Pekalski confessed to 70 murders, he became infamous as Poland's most prolific serial killer. Whether he really did slaughter so many is unlikely, and the true figure may never be known, for Pekalski later retracted his confession. But police believe that a tally of 17 butchered and abused female victims is a sad certainty.**

## 'I'm Just A Weak Man' Claims Killer

**Born in 1966 at Osieki** near Bytów, Poland, Pekalski was deserted by his father and abused by his mother before she also abandoned him. Raised by nuns, he was never able to form a normal relationship and instead discovered that by attacking women, he could control them—beating, stabbing or strangling his victims in order to have sex with them.

Pekalski first killed when, at the age of only 16, he pounced on a 13-year-old girl playing in the countryside on a school outing. It launched him on a reign of terror lasting a dozen years as the misfit became a wanderer, traveling the length and breadth of his homeland.

A detective later said: 'We couldn't find his trail. He never followed a regular pattern. There was no typical victim or a repeated killing method. He would hit with a wooden cane or would strangle his victim with a belt.'

Yet a chance to stop Pekalski was lost in 1990 when he was arrested on suspicion of rape and positively identified by the victim. The investigating officers merely ordered that he attend a psychiatric examination. He was finally given a two-year suspended sentence—and the killing spree continued.

Now labeled the 'Vampire of Bytów', he went on to beat a 17-year-old girl to death with a metal post in woods near her home. The sick killer watched from a hideout as the girl's devastated father discovered the body. Pekalski spoke too openly about the killing, however, and in 1992 police interviewed him as a suspect. He made a handwritten confession, claiming he had committed 70 murders, but, by the time he appeared in court in the northern city of Slupsk, he had changed his mind.

He told the magistrate: 'I'm a gullible man and I was easily persuaded by what the officers had told me. I'm mentally weak and if somebody pushes me I break down. Then I admit to things I have never done. I have never killed anyone. I'm so scared.'

The accused man struck a pitiful pose in the dock and, to the anger of the dead women's families, the magistrate said he could not 'help feeling vaguely sorry for him'. The case faltered when DNA evidence was ruled to be 'contaminated'. However, police witnesses insisted that Pekalski's confession included details of crimes that no one but the killer could have known.

The trial dragged on for eight months. Victims' families were furious when, in 1994, the 17 murder charges against him resulted in only one conviction for a single killing. He was cleared of the others on the grounds of insufficient evidence. Pekalski was sentenced to 25 years in a psychiatric institute, where an initial report judged him, not unexpectedly, to have 'an abnormal sex drive'.

# Marcel Petiot

**When Dr Marcel Andre Felix Petiot became mayor of Villeneuve-sur-Yonne, in Burgundy, he seemed a paragon of respectability. Yet strange events began to occur in the French town. In 1928 the mayor's pregnant housekeeper vanished without trace. Two years later a woman patient was murdered. A friend who pointed the finger of blame at the doctor also mysteriously fell ill and died. Petiot signed the death certificate.**

## Treacherous Doctor Death Dies By The Guillotine

**How Petiot ever got to become mayor** in the first place is as astonishing as his becoming a doctor. Born in Auxerre, 100 miles (160km) south of Paris, in 1897, the young Marcel was expelled from school for circulating obscene photographs to other children. He also enjoyed torturing animals to death.

An early career of petty crime was foreshortened when, in January 1916, with World War One in progress, he was drafted into the French infantry. He was discharged in 1917 with the recommendation that he enter an asylum. Instead, he took advantage of an education program for war veterans, trained as a doctor and, amazingly, qualified.

Petiot began a practice in the town of Villeneuve-sur-Yonne, where he married, had a son and eventually became mayor. He stole from the townspeople,

**ABOVE:** Marcel Petiot speaks from the dock during his trial at the Palais de Justice in March 1946.

ABOVE: Petiot in the dock, with his lawyer Dr Fleuriot, in the foreground.

overcharged his patients, and cheated on his wife, having an affair with a young woman whose dismembered body was found in a river. When his housekeeper died in mysterious circumstances, Petiot was accused of her murder. The charges had to be dropped, however, when the case files disappeared.

Petiot and his family moved in 1933 to Paris, where he set himself up in a practice on the Rue Caumartin. He thrived by supplying drugs to addicts and carrying out illegal abortions until, charged with stealing from a dead patient, he pleaded insanity and was sent to a mental hospital.

Released in time for the outbreak of World War Two,

**RIGHT:** Charged with multiple counts of murder, crazed Petiot claimed he was in fact a hero of the French Reistance.

Petiot pretended to be a member of the French Resistance and offered to aid refugees, mainly Jewish, who were trapped in Paris when the Nazis took the city in 1940. Instead, he robbed and murdered them.

The bodies of dozens of these unfortunates were found in his cellar when firemen were called to his elegant house at Rue Lesueur, in the fashionable Etoile district, in March 1944. Neighbors had complained of thick, black, foul smelling smoke spewing from the chimney. Firemen soon discovered the cause—the flames of a coal burning furnace consuming human arms, legs, and torsos in every state of dismemberment. In an outhouse were several corpses covered with lime. Petiot fled and really did join the Resistance, using the name 'Henri Valery'. Finally arrested in October 1944, he put up an outraged defense, passing himself off as a hero of *La Liberation*. At his trial at the Palais de Justice in March 1946, the jury were initially sympathetic—until they heard how the doctor had injected an entire Jewish family 'for typhoid' then watched through a peephole as they died in agony.

Petiot admitted killing 19 of the 27 victims found at Rue Lesueur but denied any knowledge of a further 44 identified victims. Sentenced to death by guillotine, he cried out to his wife Georgette: 'You must avenge me.' Her appeals for presidential clemency failed, however, and the evil doctor's head was laid on the block of the guillotine early in the morning of May 25, 1946.

**ABOVE:** The jury at Petiot's trial learned how the evil doctor had administered lethal injections to an entire Jewish family.

# Waltraud Wagner and colleagues

A doctor was having a quiet after-work drink in a Vienna bar in February 1989 when he overheard parts of a conversation from an adjoining table. The bar was close to the city's Lainz General Hospital, and the table was occupied by a group of nursing aides who were employed there. The women were giggling over the death of an elderly patient—who had been treated to something they called the 'water cure' for refusing medication and calling one of the nurses, Waltraud Wagner, 'a common slut'.

## 'Water Cure' By The Angels Of Death

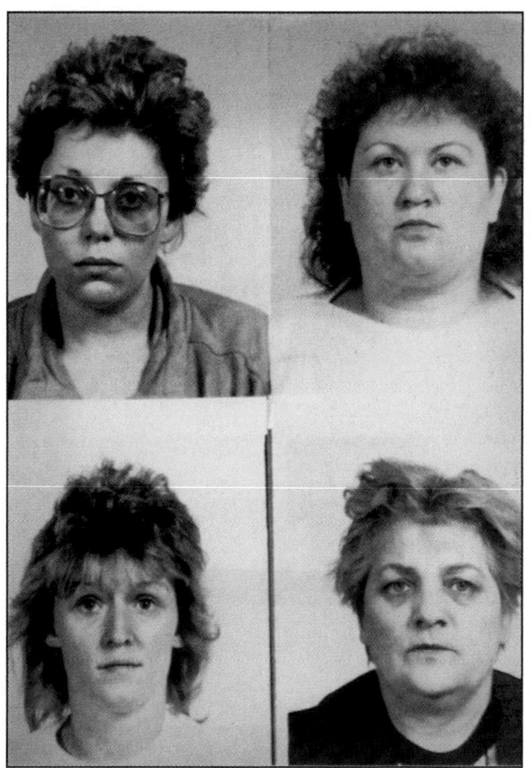

**ABOVE:** The 'Angels of Death', clockwise from top left: Waltraud Wagner, Maria Gruber, Stefanie Mayer, and Irene Leidolf.

The doctor seated nearby could pick up only snatches of the conversation but they were enough to shock him. He went to the police, who launched a six-week investigation that led to the arrest of Wagner and three other nurses. Together, they comprised one of the most unusual crime teams in 20th century Europe, and were subsequently proven to have murdered scores of patients in their care.

The ringleader, Wagner, had been 23 when she claimed her first victim in 1983. Disposing of a patient with an overdose of morphine, she discovered the thrill of wielding the power of life and death over her elderly charges. She recruited Maria Gruber, 19, Irene Leidolf, 21, and the senior member of the group, 43-year-old Stephanija Mayer.

For the next six years, the evil foursome gave death a helping hand at Lainz hospital, which specialized in geriatric cases. Officially, the body count would stand at 42, but many put the final tally at between 200 and 300 victims.

Since lethal injections failed to provide sufficient excitement, the 'Angels of Death' devised their own murder method. Usually working on the night shift, one would hold the victim's head and nose, while another would pour water into the victim's mouth, causing drowning. Since elderly patients were frequently found to have fluid in their lungs, it seemed an unprovable crime.

When arrested after their loose-tongued drinking session in 1989, Wagner was first to crack, confessing to 39 killings. She said: 'The ones who got on my nerves were dispatched to a free bed with the good Lord. They sometimes resisted but we were stronger. We could decide whether the old fools lived or died. Their ticket to God was long overdue anyway.'

**ABOVE:** Defendant Irene Leidolf testifies during her trial on March 4, 1991. She was convicted of five murders.

Although she later reduced her confession to only 10 cases of 'mercy killing', a court in March 1991 sentenced her to life for 15 murders and 17 attempted murders. Irene Leidolf also got a life sentence for five murders, Stephanija Mayer 15 years for manslaughter and seven attempted murders, and Maria Gruber 15 years for two attempted murders.

Austrian Chancellor Franz Vranitzky labeled the Lainz murder spree 'the most brutal and gruesome crime in our nation's history'.

# Frederick and Rose West

**In October 1996, Gloucester City Council demolished 25 Cromwell Street, crushing every brick so that no souvenirs could be taken of Britain's most infamous 'House of Horrors'. The house had been the site of such unspeakable depravity, cruelty, and torture that there could be no other course of action. Two years earlier, the mutilated bodies of nine of the victims of Frederick and Rosemary West had been discovered buried in the cellar or under the patio, ending a killing spree which had lasted for more than two decades, and resulted in Fred being charged with 12 murders, and Rose convicted of 10.**

# 'House Of Horrors' Couple Killed Their Own Kids

**Frederick and Rosemary met in 1969** when Rosemary was just 15 years old and already dabbling in prostitution. She was living with her mother Daisy and two younger brothers. They had escaped her violent and incestuous father, although Rosemary moved back in with him after becoming intimate with West and it is said that she still had sex with her father, with West's consent, even after their marriage.

In this respect, Frederick's childhood was very similar to Rose's. He was his mother's favorite of three sisters and two younger brothers and it is rumored that he was just 12 when she seduced him. His father treated his children as sexual playthings and Frederick grew up believing it natural to behave in this way. Indeed, when questioned by police in 1961 accused of child abuse by impregnating a 13-year-old, he commented: 'Doesn't everyone do it?'

By the time West became acquainted with Rose, he had already murdered at least once if not more. He was married at the time to Rena Costello, reputedly a prostitute, who already had a baby daughter, Charmaine. The couple soon had a child of their own, Anne-Marie, and a friend of Rena's, Ann McFall, moved in to help with childcare.

**ABOVE:** Evil Fred West grew up thinking that incest and rape was normal behavior. He committed suicide while awaiting trial in 1995.

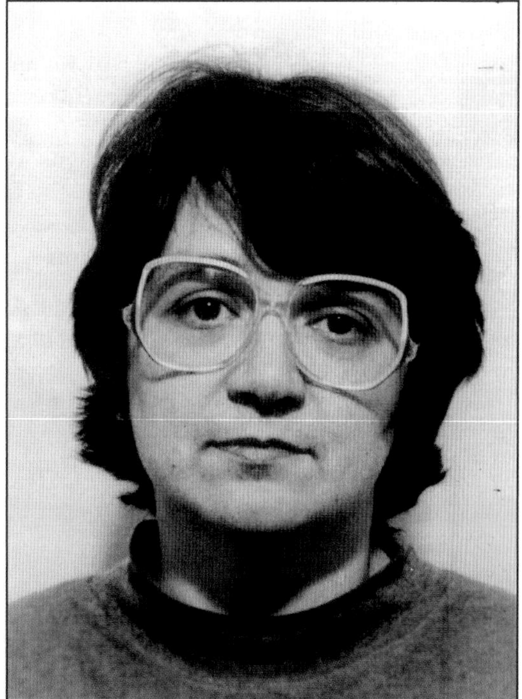

**ABOVE:** Rosemary West was convicted on 10 counts of murder, including those of her own children.

Ann became infatuated with Frederick, willingly taking part in his sadistic sex games, so Rena moved out, leaving the girls with their father. Ann, now heavily pregnant with West's baby, constantly urged West to divorce Rena but, unwilling to do so, he murdered Ann instead, removing her fingers and toes—later to become his signature mutilation—and burying her in a field in Kempley, Gloucestershire, along with the body of her unborn baby.

On moving in with West in 1969, Rose took the role of surrogate mother to Charmaine and Anne-Marie, and in October 1970 gave birth to her own daughter, Heather, thought to be her father's incestuous child. Poor little Charmaine had a pitiful existence, abused by the couple and subjected to regular beatings. It is believed that Rose murdered Charmaine during a savage attack while Fred was serving a short prison sentence for burglary in 1971, hiding her body until his release, when he removed her toes and fingers and buried her at 25 Midland Road, Gloucester, their home at the time. When Rena came to visit her daughter, West also murdered her and buried her in the field in Kempley.

Fred and Rose married in 1972 and had their second daughter, Mae, in June that year. They moved into the much larger 25 Cromwell Street, enabling them to take in boarders to help with the bills. Fred fitted the cellar

**ABOVE:** Heather West was murdered by her parents in June 1987 and her body buried under the patio.

**ABOVE:** Fred and Rose look the epitome of a normal loving couple in this photograph...yet they were anything but.

out as a torture chamber to enable him to engage in his sexual fantasies involving young girls, and Rose, still operating as a part-time prostitute, had a red light outside her bedroom so that the children knew not to enter when mummy was busy. Eight-year-old Anne-Marie became a regular victim of their sadistic games, held down by Rose while Fred violently raped her and threatened with more violence if she told anyone.

Rose was often pregnant, and gave birth to Tara in 1977, Louise in 1978, Barry in 1980, Rosemary Junior in 1982, and Lucyanna in 1983. Tara, Rosemary, and Lucyanna were not Fred's children. During this period, as the family expanded, so too did the Wests' insatiable perversions.

**ABOVE:** Fred West turned the cellar at his 25 Cromwell Street home into a torture chamber.

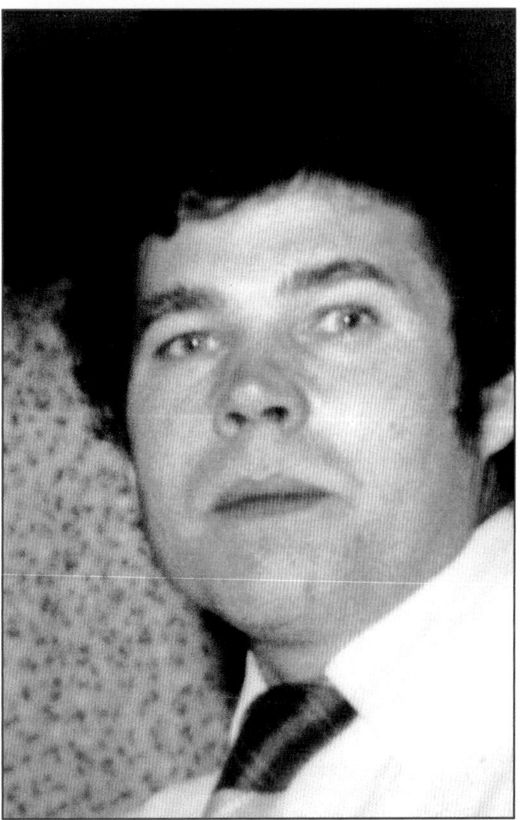

**ABOVE:** West buried the body of his first known victim, Ann McFall, in a field in Gloucestershire...minus her finger and toes.

In the space of five years, the couple's appetites for violence and sex games resulted in the brutal murders of eight young women, lured by the couple into their home either as boarders or picked-up hitch-hiking or at bus-stops and taken home to be used as sexual playthings. They all suffered horrendous torture and rape. Sometimes West would wrap their heads tightly in brown tape and insert breathing tubes into their nostrils while he subjected them to his sexual deviations involving whips and chains, rape, and bestiality. Once dead, they would be mutilated and buried under floorboards, in the cellar or under the patio.

One willing participant to their games was 18-year-old Shirley Robinson, who engaged in three-in-a-bed sex sessions with the couple. However, she fell in love with Fred and became pregnant with his child. Rose became jealous, despite the fact that she was pregnant at the time by a West Indian visitor. She put pressure on Fred, and Shirley vanished in May 1978. Her body was discovered in the garden on 25 Cromwell Street, along with that of her unborn child.

Their next victim was 16-year-old Alison Chambers, who moved in to become their nanny. She was last seen in August 1979 and was found underneath the lawn.

Fred's sexual interest in his own daughters did not wane and, after Anne-Marie moved out to live with a boyfriend, he switched his attentions to Heather and Mae. Despite violence and threats, Heather managed to resist his incestuous acts, confiding in a friend. She disappeared in June 1987. Her parents pretended she had run away. In fact, she was buried under the patio—a fate promised to the Wests' other children and joked about by them when later interviewed by police.

The Wests were arrested in 1992 following allegations of child abuse, and their five children under 16 were taken into care. The police found evidence of child abuse, including rape and buggery, but the case against them collapsed when two key witnesses refused to testify. However, Detective-Constable Hazel Savage of Gloucestershire Police was convinced something terrible was going on at 25 Cromwell Street. Investigating further and coaxing information from the West children, she persisted, despite the skepticism of senior officers, and obtained a search warrant in February 1994. The following day, the digging began—and Fred and Rosemary were arrested.

Fred escaped trial for the 12 murders, as he hung himself in his cell on New Year's Day 1995. Rosemary was brought to trial in October 1995 and found guilty of 10 murders, including those of her own children. She was sentenced to life, with the judge's recommendation that she should never be released.

Police believe that they may have murdered many more young girls, as there was an eight-year gap between the murder of Alison Chambers in 1979 and that of Heather in 1987. Without their bodies, the true number of their victims will never be known.

# Wayne Williams

**When Wayne Bertram Williams was arrested in 1981 as chief suspect in the 'Atlanta Child Murders', the killings that had caused two years of terror throughout the Georgia capital suddenly ended. And after his conviction the following year, Atlanta police declared 25 of the 30 murders solved.**

## Riddle Of Pudgy Geek And The 30 Child Murders

**On February 27, 1982,** Wayne Williams was led to the cells, tear-stained and still protesting his innocence, to serve a double sentence of life imprisonment. However, it did not end the debate over whether Williams should have borne the blame for the entire string of Georgian slayings.

Many black citizens, including some families of the victims, believed the state had manufactured much of the evidence to bring the case to a close. For although the crimes were labeled 'child murders', Williams was convicted of only two of the 30 homicides investigated—and those two murders were of adults.

The series of killings loosely (perhaps too loosely) tagged the 'Atlanta Child Murders' began in July 1979

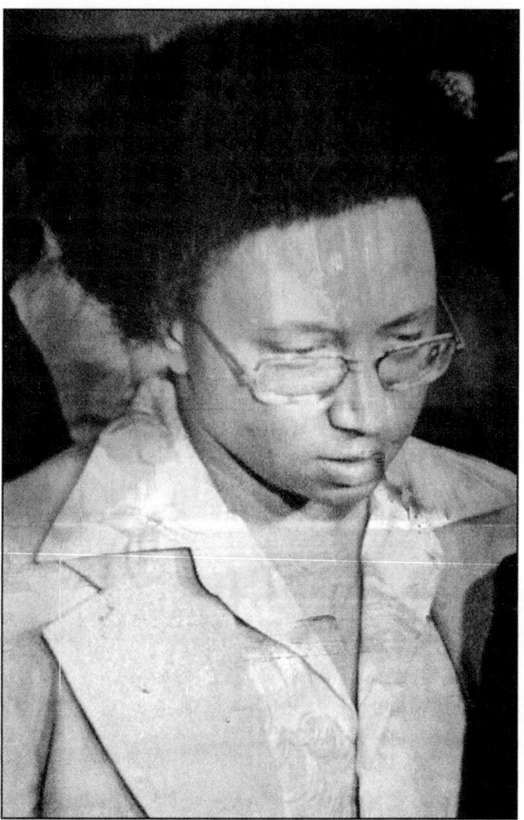

**ABOVE:** Wayne Williams was convicted of double homicide, but it is believed he was responsible for 24 other murders.

when the bodies of two black children, 13-year-old Alfred Evans and 14-year-old Edward Smith, were found in undergrowth. They had been strangled. Further young victims were discovered in September and November. The first female victim, a 12-year-old, was found tied to a tree with someone else's panties forced down her throat. She had been sexually abused before being strangled.

Within a year of the first attacks, victims were turning up at the rate of one per month. The dead were aged between seven and 14, and all but two were boys. When the number of unsolved deaths reached 26, the public were baying for justice. But months after the slaughter of the innocents started, Atlanta Police could find no pattern beyond the fact that the victims were mainly young black males. They had been stabbed, shot or strangled and their bodies were found dumped throughout the city in creeks, woods vacant lots, under floors, and in the Chattahoochee River.

On the night of May 22, 1981 teams of officers were monitoring cars using main routes around Atlanta. A police recruit on the Jackson Parkway bridge over the Chattahoochee heard a splash—and shortly afterward Williams's car was stopped as it crossed the bridge. Along with many other drivers, he was questioned, his name taken and was allowed to go.

Two days after that face-to-face encounter with a killer, the body of a 27-year-old petty thief was fished out of the river, followed two days later by the body of a 21-year-old. Both had been strangled. Police reviewed the names taken on the bridge earlier and came up with that of Wayne Bertram Williams.

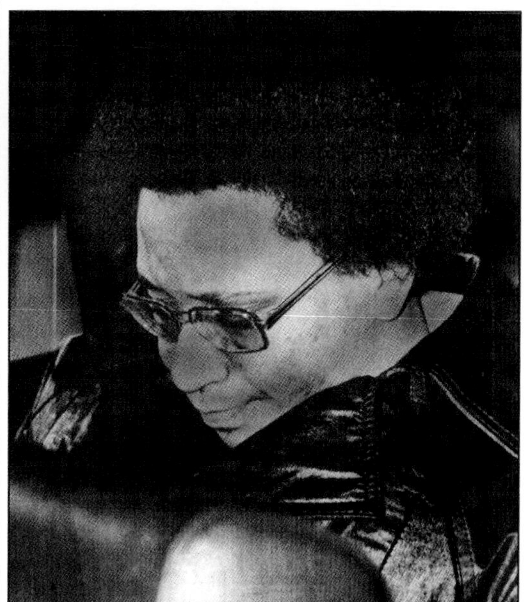

**ABOVE:** The prosecution in Williams's trial matched 19 different sources of fibers from around his home to a number of the victims.

**ABOVE:** Williams vehemently protested his innocence after his arrest in May 1981.

A surveillance team put a watch on the podgy 23-year-old, who lived with his parents, both teachers, in the Atlanta suburb of Dixie Hills, from where many of the victims came. A solitary figure, he was known as a 'scanner freak' because he spent hours tuned into short-wave radio to monitor police and ambulance activity. When an incident occurred, he would rush to the scene, photograph the action and try to sell the images to local newspapers and television stations.

Williams was arrested, still vehemently protesting his innocence. During his two-month trial, which began in January 1982, the prosecution matched 19 different sources of fibers from around his home to a number of the victims. Most significantly, dog hairs taken from the clothes of the thief found in the river on May 24 matched those in Williams's car. There was also eyewitness testimony placing Williams with different victims.

Williams was only ever charged with the murders of the two adults fished out of the Chattahoochee. But a crucial ruling by the judge allowed the prosecution to introduce evidence which linked him with other victims even though he was not accused of their murders. The prosecution, whose case had previously hung literally by a hair, were now able to paint Williams as a predatory homosexual, who they argued was guilty of all the murders.

On February 27, the jury deliberated for 10 hours before finding him guilty and he was sentenced to two consecutive terms of life imprisonment. Appeals for a retrial have consistently been rejected.

# Steve Wright

**The winter of 2006 saw Britain's biggest manhunt since the search for the Yorkshire Ripper (see page 197). It began with the discovery of the bodies of five murdered women in scattered locations near Ipswich, in Suffolk. All had been working as prostitutes in the town's red light district. Police immediately warned women off the streets and appealed for clues to the killer. More than 500 officers were drafted in to work on the case, and the number of calls received to the public information line reached 10,000.**

## The Killer Hooked On Hookers

**The murders took place** during November and December 2006. The bodies of the five women, aged between 19 and 29, were discovered naked but with no signs of sexual assault. Two of the victims had been asphyxiated but cause of death for the other three was not established. In a macabre twist, two of the women's bodies had been carefully arranged in a crucifix shape.

On December 19, police arrested a local man, Steve Wright, who lived within the red light district itself and whom they knew as a habitual user of prostitutes. Wright, born in the Norfolk village of Erpingham in 1958, had joined the merchant navy after leaving school, and followed that with jobs as a docker, a steward on the liner *QE2*, a lorry driver, a barman, and finally a fork-lift truck driver. He had two children, one from a nine-year marriage that ended in 1987, another out of wedlock in 1992. Wright was an inveterate gambler with large debts and had recently been declared bankrupt. He had twice tried to commit

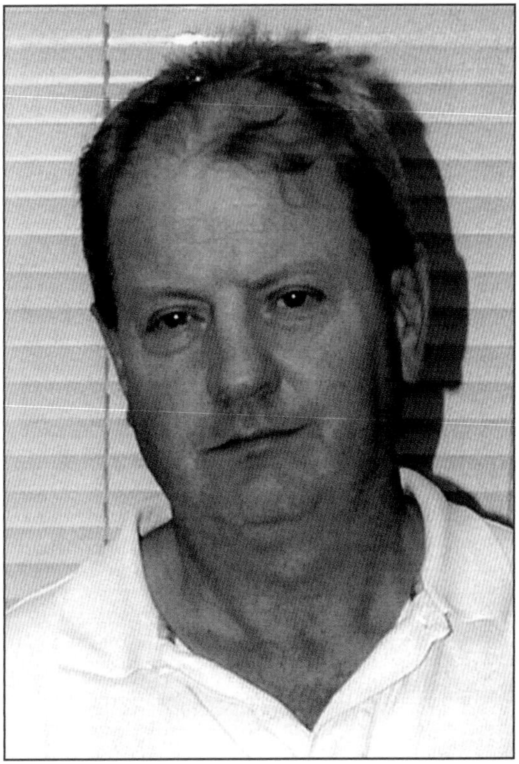

**RIGHT:** Fork-lift truck driver, Steve Wright, was a known user of prostitutes and lived in Ipswich's red light district.

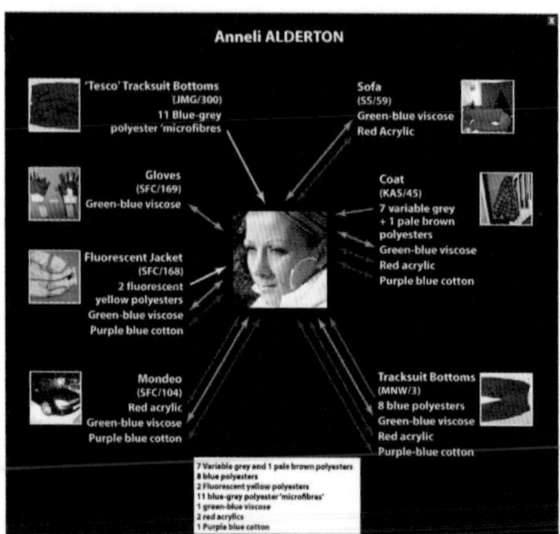


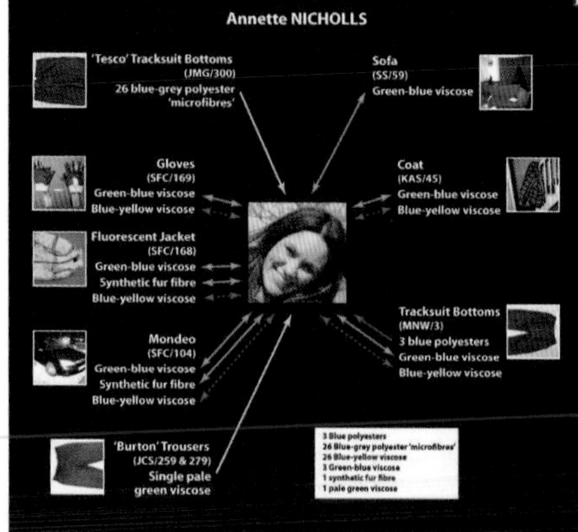


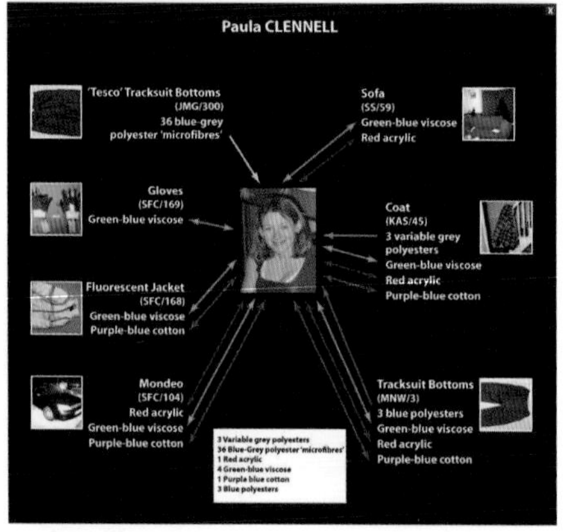


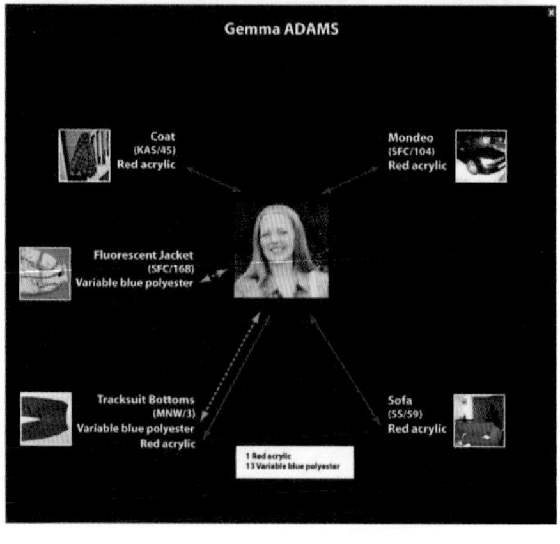


**ABOVE:** Top row left: Anneli Alderton, 24, was in the early stages of pregnancy when she disappeared on December 3. Top row right: The forensic evidence linking Wright to the murder of Annette Nichols—including tracksuit bottoms, gloves, fluorescent jacket, and samples found in his Ford Mondeo car. Bottom row left: Paula Clennell disappeared shortly after midnight on December 10. She worked as a prostitute to fund her drug addiction. Bottom row right: The body of 25-year-old Gemma Adams was found on December 2, in a river at Hintlesham.

suicide, the last attempt in 2000 with an overdose of pills.

At his trial, which began at Ipswich Crown Court in December 2007, Wright admitted hiring the girls for sex but denied any connection with their deaths. The prosecution produced DNA and fiber evidence that linked him to the victims. In a surprise move, it was also suggested that Wright may not have acted alone, as the remains of one girl was found some distance from the road but with no sign of her body being dragged there by a single person.

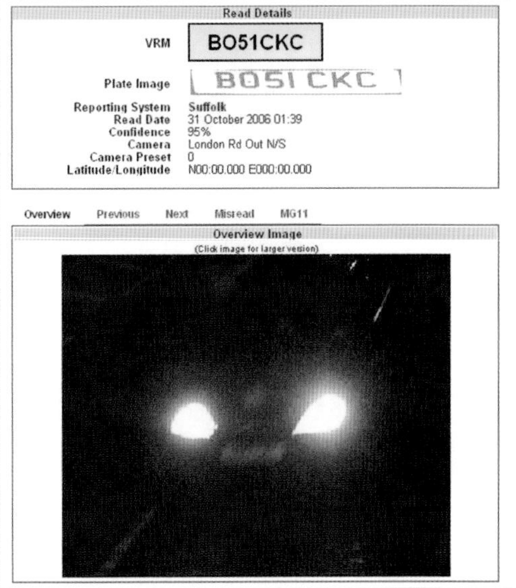


**ABOVE:** The jury in Steve Wright's trial visit Coddock Mill, Suffolk, where Tania Nicol's body was found.

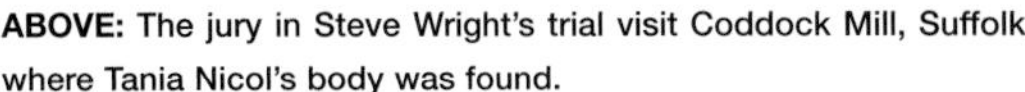

**ABOVE RIGHT:** An artist's impression of Steve Wright, appearing at Ipswich Crown Court on January 14, 2008.

**RIGHT:** Wright's car license plate captured on camera on a road near where one of the bodies was discovered.

In February 2008, Wright was found guilty of all five murders and was jailed for life, with the recommendation that he should never be considered for parole. Mr Justice Gross told him: 'Drugs and prostitution meant (the girls) were at risk, but neither drugs nor prostitution killed them. You did. You killed them, stripped them and left them... Why you did it may never be known.' The judge added: 'It is right you should spend your whole life in prison. This was a targeted campaign of murder (which entailed) a substantial degree of pre-meditation and planning.'

In view of the judge's wish that he should die behind bars, a suicide watch was put on Wright from the moment he entered Britain's highest security prison, Belmarsh, in southeast London. Meanwhile, police kept open the possibility that the 49-year-old killer may have been involved in other cases, including one of Britain's most notorious unsolved mysteries: the disappearance of estate agent Suzy Lamplugh in 1986. It emerged that Wright knew Miss Lamplugh after they worked together on the *QE2*.

**RIGHT:** Detective Superintendent Stewart Gull makes a statement to the media following Wright's conviction on February 21, 2008.

# Aileen Wuornos

**In the end, Aileen Wuornos chose death over Death Row. She effectively volunteered for her own execution. After dropping all appeals and dismissing the lawyers who were pleading her insanity, she petitioned the state for an early execution. She was described as being 'in a good mood' during her last hours. And at 9.47am on October 9, 2002, she got her wish when, at the age of 46, she was pronounced dead by lethal injection in Florida State Prison, near Starke.**

## Why I Hate Human Life, By The 'Damsel Of Death'

**Confessing to seven murders,** Wuornos was America's 'first female serial killer'—in the sense that she was the first female ever to fit the FBI profile of that normally exclusively male breed. Given her early upbringing, it would have been a miracle if her life had been anything but disturbed. Aileen was born in a Detroit suburb in 1956 to a mother who had married two years before at the age of 14 and a father she never met because he was in jail for raping a seven-year-old girl. When she was four, she was abandoned by her

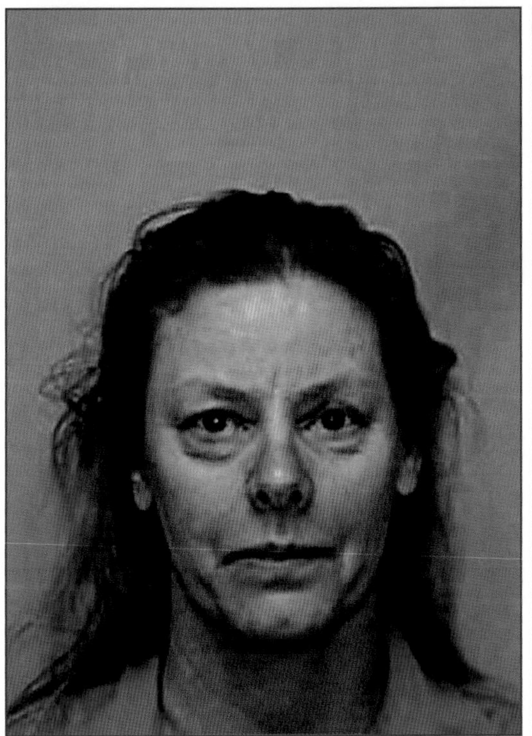

**ABOVE:** Aileen Wuornos was described by her own defense counsel as being 'the most disturbed individual I have ever represented'.

mother and was raised by her grandparents.

She endured a childhood of physical abuse at the hands of her grandfather and of sexual abuse by neighborhood boys. At 14, she was raped and became pregnant. At 15, her grandmother died and her grandfather threw her out of the house, calling her 'a whore'. She gave her son up for adoption at birth and began a life of petty crime and prostitution.

In 1976, Wuornos was picked up while hitch-hiking by a millionaire 50 years her senior and they married soon afterward. When her husband refused to give her money to fund her wild nights on the town, she beat him up. He successfully filed for divorce. Thus, at the age of 20, Aileen Wuornos was back on the road: a drunk, a drifter, a petty thief, and fraudster. She ended up in Florida where she had a longstanding lesbian relationship with a woman named Tyria Moore, surviving on the proceeds of Wuornos's prostitution.

Wuornos did not embark on her brief killing spree until November 1989, when she packed a pistol in her purse and flagged down a store owner near Daytona Beach. She robbed him and shot him dead. In May 1990, she shot a construction worker who stopped his pickup truck at a roadside near Gainesville. In June, another body turned up, this time near Tampa—naked and with nine bullet holes in it. The same month, a 65-year-old missionary was murdered near Jupiter. In August, a delivery driver was shot twice in the Ocala Forest. In September, a retired police chief was shot seven times and dumped in a vacant lot in Ocala. That same month, a truck driver was found shot through the head near Cross City.

The victims of Wuornos's two-year murder rampage were all middle-aged white men who had made the mistake of picking up the gun-toting hooker on the road. In each murder, Wuornos had followed the same pattern of flagging down men who were driving alone on or near Interstate 75.

Police finally caught up with Wuornos in a biker bar in January 1991. She confessed to the seven murders, claiming the men had tried to rape her and that she had killed them in self-defense. Now tagged the 'Damsel of Death', she was tried at Daytona Beach in January 1992 for only her first murder, of the store owner. Wuornos, who was distraught when her ex-lover Tyria Moore appeared as a witness for the prosecution, nevertheless showed no remorse as she was found guilty, with a jury recommendation for the death penalty. Her counsel afterward described her as 'the most disturbed individual I have represented'.

As other indictments were added, Wuornos told the Florida Supreme Court: 'I'm one who seriously hates human life and would kill again.' However, during her 10 years on Death Row, she became a born-again Christian and said she would welcome paying the ultimate penalty. Despite concerns about the execution of potentially mentally ill prisoners, Florida Governor Jeb Bush finally lifted his stay of execution after three state-appointed psychiatrists concluded that Wuornos was 'lucid and cognisant' and ready to die.

**ABOVE:** The hearse carrying Wuornos's body leaves the Florida State Prison following her execution by lethal injection on October 9, 2002.

# Graham Young

**Even as a schoolboy, Graham Young demonstrated a sinister bent. He developed a passion for poisons, reading up on infamous villains like the wife killer Dr William Palmer (see page 155). Young's father Fred inadvertently encouraged him by buying him a chemistry set.**

## Danger Signs Ignored Over 'Teacup Poisoner'

**Even at the age of 13,** Young's comprehensive knowledge of toxicology enabled him to convince a local pharmacist in St Albans, Hertfordshire, that he was 17, and he procured a dangerous quantity of the poisons antimony, digitalis, and arsenic and the heavy metal, thallium, for 'study' purposes. He began carrying a phial of the poison around with him at all times, referring to it as 'my little friend'.

Eager to put his knowledge to the test, his first victim, a school pal, became seriously ill after his sandwiches were laced with antimony but survived. In 1961, his elder sister was found to have been poisoned by belladonna but also survived. The following year, his stepmother was found by her husband writhing in agony in the back garden of their home, with Young looking on in fascination. She died in hospital and her body was cremated. Fred Young was next to suffer attacks of vomiting and excruciating cramps, and he was admitted to hospital where he was diagnosed with antimony poisoning.

It was Young's chemistry teacher who, suspecting his pupil's murderous intent, tipped off the police. Sessions with a police psychiatrist confirmed that he was a serial killer in the making but no murder charges could be brought against him because his stepmother's cremation had destroyed the evidence. Still only 15, he was committed to Broadmoor maximum-security hospital, the youngest inmate since 1885, for a minimum period of 15 years.

**ABOVE:** Graham Young's fascination with causing pain and death through the administering of poison began in childhood.

**ABOVE:** John Tilson, one of the surviving victims of serial poisoner Graham Young, outside St Albans Crown Court in June 1972.

Within weeks, a fellow inmate died of poisoning by cyanide, which Young claimed to have extracted from laurel bush leaves. The killer was not taken seriously and the death was recorded as 'suicide'. Another record on his file shows that in 1970, when recommended for early release, he told a psychiatric nurse that he planned to kill one person for every year he had been in Broadmoor.

Amazingly, he was still freed after nine years' incarceration and obtained a job with a company manufacturing photographic instruments. Within weeks, staff began to be struck down with a mystery disease. Of the 70 people affected, three died in four months. During a company investigation, Young could not resist revealing his knowledge of chemicals and Scotland Yard were contacted.

Young was accused of two murders, two attempted murders and two cases of administering poison. The case was clear-cut, and a single entry in his diary, relating to the death of one of his work colleagues, would have sealed his fate: 'I have administered a fatal dose of the special compound to F. and anticipate a report on his progress on Monday. I gave him three separate doses.'

He pleaded not guilty, relishing his moment of notoriety in the dock—although he was unhappy that the press had labeled him the 'Teacup Poisoner', believing that 'World Poisoner' would better fit his infamy. On June 29, 1972, the jury at St Albans Crown Court took less than an hour to find him guilty, and he was given four life sentences. In August 1990, warders at Parkhurst Prison found 42-year-old Young dead of a heart attack on the floor of his cell.

# Zodiac Killer

**Random and motiveless, they are the most difficult serial murder cases to solve. San Francisco endured a brief reign of terror in 1968 and 1969, during which time a ruthless killer slew five people and wounded two more. The killings were followed by detailed descriptions of the atrocities in letters to newspapers, signed by a cross placed on a circle: the symbol of the Zodiac.**

## Motiveless Crimes Grip San Francisco

cipher on your front page by Fry Afternoon Aug 1-69, If you do not do this I will go on a kill rampage Fry night that will last the whole weekend. I will cruse around and pick of all stray people or couples that are alone then move on to kill some more untill I have killed over a dozen people.

**The first murders firmly attributed** to the 'Zodiac Killer' were of a student couple, aged 16 and 17, who were shot in a quiet lane near Vallejo, near San Francisco, in December 1968. The pair had apparently

**BELOW:** One of the Zodiac Killer's coded messages which contained the hidden script: 'I like killing people'.

**LEFT:** One of the letters sent to a San Francisco newspaper by the Zodiac Killer, featuring his trademark signature.

**ABOVE:** Three of the Zodiac's victims. Left to right: cab driver Paul Stine, Cecilia Shepard, and Bryan Hartnell, who survived.

**BELOW:** Two homicide detectives inspect the clothes of a murder victim at a San Francisco morgue in March 1974.

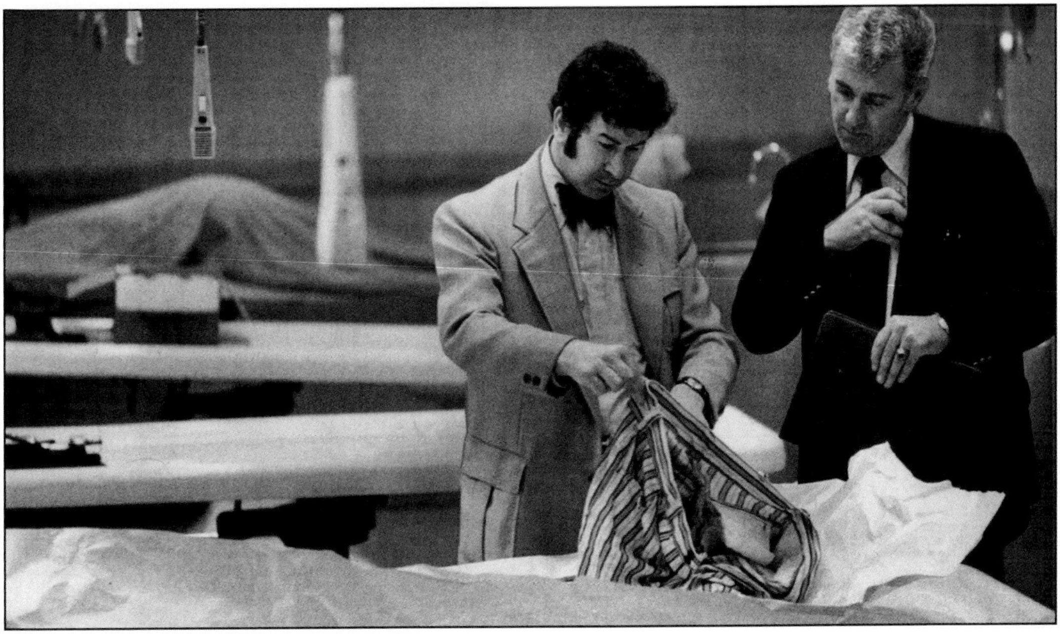

**ABOVE:** A card sent by the Zodiac Killer to Paul Avery, a reporter on the *San Francisco Chronicle*.

been fleeing from their car when gunned down, but there was no obvious motive for the crime.

A similar double shooting followed the next July. The gunman had driven up alongside a car and opened fire without warning, killing a 22-year-old girl and seriously injuring her 19-year-old boyfriend. Police were alerted to the crime by a call from a man, described as having a 'gruff voice', who boasted: 'I also killed those kids last year.'

Following this attack, three newspapers received coded notes which, when matched and decoded, provided a weird message from 'Zodiac' in which he said, 'I like killing people' and added that 'when I die I will be reborn in paradise and those I have killed will become my slaves'.

'Zodiac' fell silent again until September 1969 when the gruff voice at the end of the phone line directed police to the shore of Lake Berryessa, in the Napa Valley, where two students, a girl of 22 and her boyfriend aged 20, had been killed in a frenzied attack. The assailant had daubed the zodiac sign on the side of the couple's white car, along with the dates of the previous murders. The girl, who had been stabbed with a foot-long bayonet 24 times, died in hospital two days later; her boyfriend, with bayonet wounds in the back, survived. He described the attacker as wearing a black hood with slits for his mouth and eyes.

'Zodiac' moved onto the streets of San Francisco itself

**ABOVE:** Police arrest Heriberto Seda, a copycat killer from 1990. Seda planned to kill one person from each of the 12 astrological signs.

to strike again two weeks later, shooting a 29-year-old student and part-time taxi driver as he sat in a cab. The gunman, described by witnesses as short, in his 40s, with thick horn-rimmed glasses and crew-cut brown hair, fled into side-streets pursued by two patrolmen and escaped in the wooded military reservation known as The Presidio. The shooting was followed by letters to newspapers, this time enclosing a shred of bloodstained shirt torn from the victim—and claiming, not the five slayings attributed to him, but eight murders so far.

The 'Zodiac Killer' next struck in March 1970 when a 23-year-old woman was traveling toward Petaluma, northwest of San Francisco, when another driver flagged her down, told her that one of her rear wheels was wobbling and offered her a ride. Once in his car, he warned her: 'You know you're going to die—you know I'm going to kill you.' As he slowed, she leapt out and flagged down another car. Her description exactly fitted the taxi driver's killer.

Again, 'Zodiac' wrote to newspapers, acknowledging the kidnap attempt and upping his claimed victims to 37. The last letter was sent in April 1974. Since then, nothing…and the identity of the 'Zodiac Killer' has remained one of the greatest unsolved mysteries of modern crime.

# Hans Van Zom

**Hans Van Zon was a wastrel, a fantasist, a liar, and a cheat. But he had one asset that compensated for these deficiencies: he was absolutely charming. It won him admirers and lovers among both men and women, some of whom paid for this trust with their lives.**

## Fantasist Who Couldn't Take Failure

**Johannes Marinus (Hans) van Zon** was born of working-class parents in Utrecht, Holland, in April 1942. He was intelligent but there was no cash to advance his education and, at the age of 16, he turned to crime, first as a minor confidence trickster, then as a burglar.

Van Zon realized that he had homosexual tendencies but tried to hide them. In 1964 he dated Elly Hager-Segor but, after his first failed attempt at lovemaking, she called off the affair. Spurned, he strangled her before slitting her throat with a bread knife. His next love affair was with a homosexual movie director, Claude Berkeley, whom he met in Amsterdam in 1965. That relationship also failed and the man was similarly dispatched by his lover.

Shortly after the slaying, Van Zon married a chambermaid, Italian-born Caroline Gigli, 47, who supported both of them on her meager wages. After an attempt to kill her, his wife went to the police, who put him in jail for a month. But it was not his wife who was to be his next victim; Van Zon was keeping a 37-year-old mistress, Coby van der Voort—and was making money on the side by selling pornographic photographs of both his wife and girlfriend.

When Coby tried to end their affair in April 1967, Van Zon fed her barbiturates, pretending they were aphrodisiac pills, before smashing her skull with a lead pipe and finishing her off by slashing her throat with the familiar bread knife. He tried to fool police by making the murder look like a bungled burglary, stealing items of Coby's jewelry and handing them to Caroline.

Van Zon was now living in a total fantasy world. He claimed to be, variously, a fashion designer, private detective, movie star business tycoon, and a CIA spy. He could not help boasting about his killings to an ex-convict, Arnoldus Rietbergen, nicknamed 'Old Nol', who used the information to 'persuade' Van Zon to commit other murders for profit. Those known about are the death of a girl in May 1967 and of a farmer that same August.

Van Zon and Rietbergen were caught in December when blows from the lead piping failed to kill their final victim, an elderly lady. In March 1970, a Utrecht court sentenced Van Zon to life, with a minimum of 20 years, and his accomplice to seven years.

# Anna Zwanziger

**Poor Anna Schoenleben, born in Nuremberg, Germany, in 1760, did not have much going for her. A contemporary report described her as 'ugly, stunted, without attraction of face, figure, speech; a misshapen woman whom some people likened to a toad'. It would seem that she was lucky to have ever found a husband, but the marriage ended in misery. Herr Zwanziger, a successful lawyer, was a violent bully who spent her inheritance on drink.**

## Poisonous 'Toad' Dies By The Sword

**Anna was forced into prostitution** to support herself and two children, although she insisted to her friends that she only ever slept with 'gentlemen'. Upon the death of her husband through alcoholism, she advertised herself as a housekeeper and cook to the Bavarian judiciary and, from their elevated ranks, set about finding a new husband.

There was one flaw in her plan: each of the judges she went to work for was already married or engaged. Anna's solution was simple; she set about ridding herself of all rivals to her affections by poisoning two of the women, along with one of the judges, his guests, several servants, and a baby.

The widow's first potential husband was a judge named Glaser who, although separated, was still married. Anna engineered a reconciliation between the couple and, once the wife had returned to the marital home, fed her arsenic in her tea until she died. In the process, Anna also poisoned several of the judge's guests, although they survived.

Her next victim was another judge, named Grohmann, whom Anna killed when she discovered that he had wedding plans which did not involve her. He died an agonizing death after being served a bowl of soup. Anna also put arsenic in the drink of three servants who had upset her, although they survived.

Her third employer, Judge Gebhard, refused to believe his sickly wife's claims that food tasted strange since the arrival of their new housekeeper. It was only when he himself found a white sediment in his brandy glass that he became suspicious. It was too late. His wife died in convulsions. So did their baby after Anna fed the infant a biscuit dipped in arsenic-laced milk. Again, the servants were also poisoned but survived. Judge Gebhard had their food analyzed and traces of arsenic were found. By now, Anna had fled—but not before lacing every salt and sugar shaker in the house with arsenic.

Anna Zwanziger was arrested in October 1809 after police exhumed her victims' bodies and discovered traces of the poison. The poisoner had foolishly led them to her by writing letters to the Gebhard family asking if she could have her old job back. She eventually confessed, admitting: 'Yes, I killed them all and would have killed more if I had the chance.' She referred to arsenic as 'my truest friend' and said she 'trembled with pleasure' when handling it.

Before being beheaded by the sword in July 1811, she told her prison warders: 'It is perhaps better for the community that I should die, as it would be impossible for me to give up the practice of poisoning people.'

# Marquise De Brinvilliers

**Marie-Madeleine-Marguerite, Marquise de Brinvilliers was the eldest of five children in the French aristocratic 17th century family d'Aubray. The daughter of Viscount Antoine Dreux d'Aubray, a civil lieutenant of Paris, she was married in 1651 at the age of 21, to a married army officer, Antoine Gobelin de Brinvilliers, a gambling womanizer who paid her little attention. As a result, she took a lover, one Chevalier Jean-Baptiste de Sainte-Croix, an army captain and friend of her father.**

## Libertine Who Learned The Art Of Poison

**Outraged by his daughter's affair** with a trusted family friend, the old man forbade her from seeing Sainte-Croix, and in 1663 had him thrown into the Bastille. On his release, however, the lovers were reunited and plotted to take revenge on d'Aubray—and at the same time ensure her inheritance. In the Bastille, Sainte-Croix had learned the art of poisoning. With the assistance of one of the royal apothecaries to the court of King Louis XIV, he obtained tasteless but lethal potions, which Marie fed to her father, who in 1666 became her victim.

With her high-spending habits, Marie's share of Viscount d'Aubray's inheritance did not last long, and when the money ran out, she turned her attention to the rest of the family. Her elder brother died in 1670, followed by her younger brother and then her sister and sister-in-law. Former lovers suffered the same fate. Marie's husband survived but was prone to mysterious illnesses. Ruthlessly, Marie perfected her poison techniques on as many as 50 people during 'mercy missions' visiting the sick in a local hospital. The marquise was finally exposed when her lover Sainte-Croix died in 1672. He left instructions that a box should be delivered to his mistress, Marie, but his wife opened it and saw a variety of poisons and incriminating papers.

Marie went on the run but was arrested in Liege. Under interrogation, she threatened: 'Half the people of quality are involved in this sort of thing, and I could ruin them if I were to talk.' The once haughty libertine was brutally tortured, her jailers mainly employing what was known as 'the water cure'—in which she was forced to drink 16 pints (9 liters) of water. Tried in Paris in 1676 and found guilty, she was executed, her body and severed head being thrown onto a fire.

**ABOVE:** An artist's impression of jailers torturing the Marquise de Brinvilliers with the 'water cure'.

Many members of the French nobility breathed a sigh of relief at her death because, while confessing her own guilt, she had refused to name other aristocrats caught up in sex scandals. The dramatic and romantic mysteries surrounding the case have since inspired poet Robert Browning (*The Poisoner*) and several authors, including Alexandre Dumas (*The Marquise de Brinvilliers*) and Arthur Conan Doyle (*The Leather Funnel*).

# Richard Ramírez

**The spooky killer known as the 'Night Stalker' was an avowed Satanist who terrorized the streets of Los Angeles for 13 months from 1984–85. Richard Ramírez would creep into a house at night, shoot or strangle any adult males and then subject women and children to sadistic rape and mutilation. Occasionally he would leave his mark as the 'Devil's Disciple'—an inverted pentagram scrawled on a mirror or wall. He also used to draw occult signs on the victims' bodies.**

## Fan Mail Galore For The 'Night Stalker'

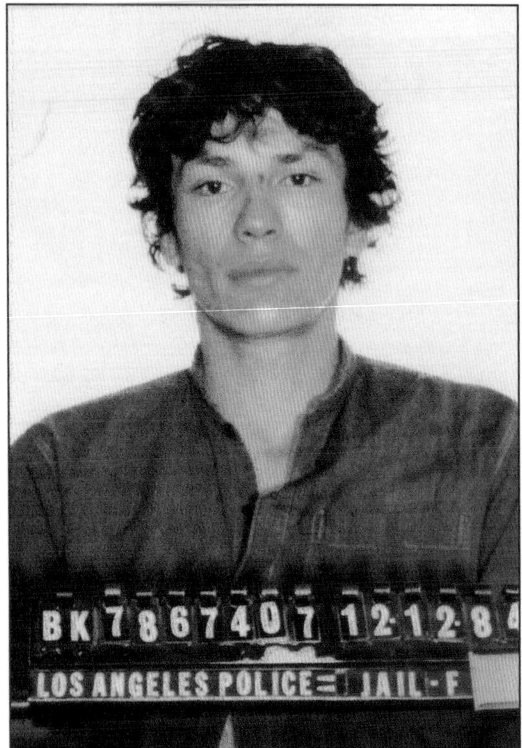


**ABOVE:** A police mugshot of Richard Ramírez. The Mexican was fascinated by death from an early age.

**Ricardo Múñoz Ramírez** was born in El Paso, Texas, the son of Mexican immigrants. At an early age, he was fascinated by death and would spend nights in cemeteries. At 12, he fell under the influence of a cousin, a Vietnam War veteran who told tales of killing and torturing civilian women. According to later testimony, the cousin murdered his own wife while Ramírez was in the same room.

**ABOVE:** Ramírez, appearing to revel in his notoriety, wears sunglasses during a court appearance.

**ABOVE:** After his conviction the killer proclaimed: 'I will be avenged. Lucifer dwells within all of us.'

In his teens, Ramírez turned to crime and drugs. A police profile described him as 'a confused, angry loner who sought refuge in thievery, drugs, the dark side of rock music, and finally murder and rape'.

Upon moving to Los Angeles, Ramírez committed his first 'Night Stalker' murder in June 1984 when, high on cocaine, he crept into the apartment of a 79-year-old woman, stabbed her repeatedly, almost decapitating her, then sexually assaulted her. He was responsible for at least 18 further killings, his victims' ages ranging from the early 30s to the 70s. The methods he used were varied but included shooting, bludgeoning, throat cutting, and battering to death. Although the attacks

**RIGHT:** Ramírez in court with one of his calling cards, an inverted pentagram, drawn on his left palm.

satisfied Ramírez's sadistic sexual urges, he also stole from those he killed.

Police finally got lucky in August 1985 when they found a fingerprint in a getaway car used for one of the attacks and matched it to Ramírez, then aged 25 and a known petty criminal. His photograph was circulated to the press—and had an instant result. Ramírez was recognized as he tried to drag a woman out of her car in a Los Angeles suburb. He was attacked by the woman's husband and by a gathering mob, who turned him over to the cops bruised and bleeding.

After one of the lengthiest murder trials in American history, Ramírez was found guilty in September 1989 of 13 murders, five attempted murders, 11 sexual assaults, and 14 burglaries. He was sentenced to death in California's gas chamber and, as he left the courtroom for San Quentin's Death Row, he snarled: 'You maggots make me sick. I will be avenged. Lucifer dwells within all of us.' Of the death sentence he joked: 'Big deal. Death comes with the territory. See you in Disneyland.'

Inexplicably, the 'Night Stalker' trial had generated an amazing amount of fan mail for Ramírez. One besotted woman, Doreen Lioy, who wrote him 75 letters, won a proposal of marriage. With California's death sentences seemingly permanently stalled, the couple were wed in San Quentin in 1996.

# David Parker Ray

**David Parker Ray is the serial killer who was never convicted of a single slaying, although his tally of female victims may be as high as 60; they died in the most horrific circumstances after kidnap, captivity, abuse, rape, and torture. Yet he escaped the full weight of justice, dying in 2002 of heart failure after just three years in prison on charges that all fell short of murder.**

## How Many Innocents Lured To 'Satan's Den'?

**Ray was a loner with four failed marriages** who built a torture chamber in a trailer at the back of his home. There, in what he referred to as his 'Satan's Den' or 'The Toy Box', his victims were drugged and chained to a gynecological chair fitted with straps and surrounded by an array of torture instruments and sex toys.

Ray's reign of terror ended in March 1999 when one of his victims, Cynthia Vigil, escaped from him and ran through the streets of Elephant Butte, New Mexico, naked, with a metal collar around her neck and trailing a chain. The sobbing 21-year-old had been held captive for three days and subjected to a terrifying ordeal of rape and torture.

Police arrested Ray, a 59-year-old park warden and mechanic, and searched his home and backyard den. A policeman said: 'There were sadistic pictures on the walls, straps and chains, a bar he'd labeled "ankle stretcher", sex toys attached to power drills, dildos with nails embedded in them. Everything in that trailer denoted pain.'

Officers found a tape recording in which Ray explained to his victims what he was about to do to them, saying that he had 'no qualms about slitting your throat' because 'you're a piece of meat to me'. On the tape, he talked of 37 previous abductions.

Police also examined videotapes containing footage of one of Ray's victims strapped to the chair. Apparently drugged, she could be identified only by an unusual tattoo on her leg. When the tattoo was shown on TV, a 25-year-old woman, Kelly Van Cleave, identified herself—but said she was confused because she had no memory of being held captive. It was only under police questioning that her memory partially returned and, horrified, she realized that the nightmares she had been suffering were of real events and that she had been drugged to prevent her from recalling the horrors of her captivity.

Police suspected that Ray may have slain as many as 60 women but, when a search of the area revealed not a single body, prosecutors decided a murder charge was impossible. Instead, Ray was charged with kidnapping, rape, and torture.

He almost escaped justice entirely, because the two principal witnesses were deemed potentially unreliable, Kelly Van Cleave still having only partial memories of her experience and Cynthia Vigil being a heroin-addicted prostitute. Moreover, at Ray's trial in July 2000, the judge ruled that the incriminating tape recording was inadmissible. The trial ended in a hung jury.

A retrial nine months later produced a different verdict. On April 16, 2001, the jury were unanimous.

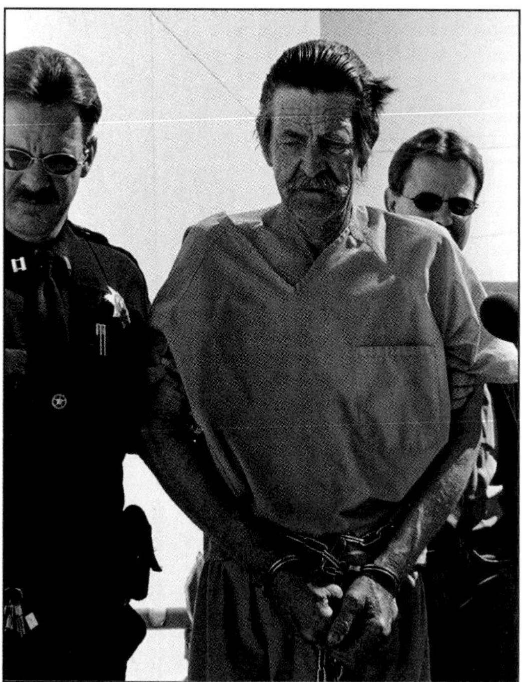

**ABOVE:** David Parker Ray, shackled by police officers after his arrest. He was later sentenced to 224 years in jail.

**ABOVE:** The smart appearance of Ray during his trial belied a man capable of remorseless evil.

David Parker Ray was jailed for 224 years, less the two and a half years he had already spent in prison. On May 28, 2002, just eight months into his sentence, David Parker Ray died of heart failure.

Earlier, in other trials, three of Ray's accomplices received lesser sentences after plea deals involving giving evidence against him. Dennis Roy Yancy confessed to strangling to death another kidnap victim, 22-year-old Marie Parker, whose body was never found, and was jailed for 20 years. Ray's live-in girlfriend Cynthia Hendy confessed to being an accessory and received 36 years. Ray's daughter Jessy was convicted of helping her father kidnap and torture Kelly Van Cleave but was released with five years' probation under a deal that her father forewent his right to appeal.

# Picture Credits

**Getty Images**
12 (both), 13, 14 Hulton Archive
15 Doug Pensinger
18 (left) Hulton Archive, (right) Keystone/ Hulton Archive
19 (top) BIPS/Hulton Archive, (bottom) Mitchell
20 (top) Keystone/Hulton Archive, (bottom) Nixon/Express
22 Robert Harding World Imagery
30 Maxim Marmur/AFP
31 Kostya Smirnov/AFP
33 (left) Keystone/Hulton Archive, (right) Express
34 Keystone
35 (left) Keystone/Hulton Archive, (right) Jack Hickes/Keystone/Hulton Archive
36 (top) Keystone, (bottom) Jack Hickes/Keystone/ Hulton Archive
37 Keystone
40 (both) Keystone/Hulton Archive
41 (left) Express, (right) Keystone
42 J. A. Hampton/Topical Press Agency
43 (left) Topical Press Agency/Hulton Archive, (right) Topical Press Agency
44 (top left, right) Hulton Archive, (bottom left) Topical Press Agency
45 Hulton Archive
49 (both) Evening Standard
50 (top left) Hulton Archive, (bottom right) California Department of Corrections and Rehabilitation,
51 (top) Michael Ochs Archives
52 (top left) Express Newspapers, (bottom right) Hulton Archive
54 (both), 55 Patrick Riviere
58 (bottom right), 59 (top right) Keystone/ Hulton Archive
63 Hulton Archive
64 (top) Illustrated London News/Hulton Archive, (bottom) Hulton Archive
68, 69 (top) Keystone, (bottom right) AFP
70 Keystone
83 Florida DOC
84 Chris Livingston
85 (both) Keystone/Hulton Archive

**iStock**
32 iStockphoto.com/cglow

**Press Association**
38, 47 (both), 61, 62, 71, 72, 79, 80 (all) Suffolk Police, 81 (left), (top right) Elizabeth Cook, (bottom right) ANPR, 82, 87 (both), 88 (both).



To Katie, Leonie and Mike
Who, in the interests of research, braved more gore and guts than any homicide detective would experience in a lifetime. My sincere thanks to them.

TRUE CRIMES

# SERIAL KILLERS

igloo

igloo

This edition published in 2010
by Igloo Books Ltd
Cottage Farm
Sywell
NN6 0BJ

www.igloo-books.com



A copy of the British Library Cataloguing-in-Publication
Data is available from the British Library.

10 9 8 7 6 5 4 3 2 1

ISBN 978-0-85734-394-9

Printed and Manufactured in China

# Contents

# Beverley Allitt

**Beverley Allitt suffered from the rare syndrome Münchausen's Disease by Proxy, a psychological disorder in which those affected feign illness or trauma to draw sympathy from others. She had visited doctors no fewer than 50 times since adolescence with phantom ailments, including pregnancy, a stomach ulcer, and a brain tumor. The freak Münchausen's condition can also have a much more perilous side effect—causing sufferers to harm others deliberately so they can care for them later. This was an especially dangerous trait in the case of Beverley Allitt—because she was a nurse.**

## Child-Killing Nurse Showed No Mercy, No Remorse

**Since childhood,** Allitt had always wanted to be an 'angel of mercy'. At the age of 17, she took a pre-nursing training course and got her first job at the Grantham and Kesteven General Hospital, Lincolnshire, as a trainee nurse on the pediatric ward, looking after sick children. But the children on Ward Four just got sicker and sicker.

Eight-week-old Liam Taylor was her first murder victim. He died of a massive heart attack on February 23, 1991, just two days after being admitted with a chest infection. Ten days later, Timothy Hardwick, a mentally and physically handicapped 11-year-old, died after being treated by Allitt for an epileptic fit, within three hours of being admitted. The following month, five-week-old Becky Phillips died after suffering convulsions at home hours after being released from hospital. She too had been under the care of Nurse Allitt on Ward Four. Finally, Claire Peck, aged just 15 months, died on April 22 after routine treatment for asthma.

Baby Claire was the last of Allitt's victims to die, although nine other children under Allitt's 'care' had contracted life-threatening conditions. Following Claire's death, the hospital authorities realized that the odds of so many children falling seriously ill on one ward was beyond coincidence and police were called in.

**ABOVE:** Mentally disturbed Beverley Allitt pretended to care for babies and young children, but she was in fact a callous murderer.

Their first convincing evidence that a killer was responsible came after tests on one of Ward Four's tiny survivors, frail five-month-old Paul Crampton, revealed that he had an abnormally high level of insulin in his blood. He could only have been injected with the drug while in hospital.

A lengthy police and medical investigation had at first failed to find the cause of the series of mystery deaths but, once blood tests had been carried out on other victims, a simple check of staff rotas showed that the common factor was Beverley Allitt. She had administered to the children lethal and near-lethal overdoses of both insulin and potassium chloride. She had also tried to suffocate some of them.

At her trial at Nottingham Crown Court in May 1993, a jury heard how, in her twisted mind, she believed she was doing no wrong in killing without mercy. The plain, overweight, frumpy 24-year-old was found guilty of murdering four children, attempting to murder another three and causing grievous bodily harm to a further six. For the families of the young victims, the jury's verdict ended two years of torment. However, Allitt herself showed not a shred of emotion as she was sentenced to serve life, four times over, in a prison for the criminally insane.

**RIGHT:** Allitt pictured at home. The nurse injected her multiple victims with lethal doses of insulin and potassium chloride.

# Nathaniel Bar-Jonah

**Although never charged with murder, 210lb (5.7kg) chef Nathaniel Bar-Jonah, a convicted felon and child sex attacker, was suspected of molesting, killing, and cannibalizing as many as 54 children. Born David Paul Brown in Worcester, Massachusetts, in February 1957, he might have been one of America's most notorious criminals—but it may never be known whether or not the frightening murder toll was real or the figment of his sick imagination.**

## A Sick Fantasy—Or Did He Kill 54?

In 1974, David Brown received one year of probation for impersonating a policeman and sexually assaulting an eight-year-old boy. In 1977, he was convicted of kidnapping and attempted murder by strangling two boys as they left a movie theater. He was sentenced to 20 years' imprisonment.

While incarcerated, he changed his name to Nathaniel Bar-Jonah, as he wished people to think he was Jewish—'so he could feel persecution', according to psychiatrists.

Shortly after his 1991 release, he was charged with assaulting another Massachusetts boy. A judge released him on the condition that he move in with his mother in Great Falls, Montana. Once there, he continued to prey on children, sexually assaulting a 14-year-old boy from Great Falls while hanging the boy's eight-year-old cousin from a kitchen ceiling. Both survived.

After more spells in prison and one in a mental institution, he was arrested again in 1999 for impersonating a police officer outside an elementary school and carrying a stun gun and pepper spray. Police searched Bar-Jonah's home, uncovering thousands of newspaper pictures of children aged between five and 17, among them some he had been convicted of abducting previously. They also found cannibalistic coded recipe journals featuring dishes called 'barbecued kid', 'little boy stew', and 'lunch on the patio with roasted child'.

More disturbingly, bone fragments identified as belonging to an unknown young male were discovered under his house. Hair from another was found in a meat grinder in his kitchen.

Among the pictures of children found in the house was that of 10-year-old Zachary Ramsey, who had gone missing in 1997 on his return from school. Within days of the child's disappearance, Bar-Jonah had a barbeque for neighbors, where several of the guests complained of 'strange-tasting' meat. He had told them it was venison. Little did the guests know they may have helped Bar-Jonah dispose of the little boy.

There was a mass of evidence that pointed to Bar-Jonah being Zachary's killer—not least his telling the boy's mother, Rachel, that he had 'hunted, killed, butchered and wrapped the meat' of her son. Despite this, she insisted that she did not think Bar-Jonah had anything to do with Zachary's disappearance and believed the child still to be alive. This deep-held belief was confirmed by a psychic she visited. The child's remains have never been found.

The trial for the sexual abuse and attempted murder of the Great Falls boys finally got underway in Montana in 2002. The jury found Bar-Jonah guilty of kidnapping and sexual assault and gave him the maximum sentence of 130 years' imprisonment.

Suffering from severe diabetes, Bar-Jonah was found dead from a heart attack in his cell on April 13, 2008, the true scale of his sick crimes still unknown.

# Sawney Beane

**No one knows the truth about the strange saga of Sawney Beane. The facts about this ancient case of multiple murders are lost in the mists of time, and it is acknowledged that much of the story may be myth more than legend. However, it amply proves that 'serial killers' have been with us through the ages. And it is perhaps illuminating to look back to a time when, although the term had not yet been coined, there were villains whose murderous tally stacked up, not into single figures nor even into the teens, but into the hundreds.**

## Curse Of The Cave-Dwelling Cannibals

**Sawney Beane, reputedly born around 1380,** was the vagabond son of a road-mender and ditch digger who lived near Edinburgh, Scotland. Too feckless to follow his father's trade, he seduced a local girl and was driven out of town. Beane and his mistress fled to Galloway, on the west coast of Scotland, where they lived in a cave and raised a family on the proceeds of sheep stealing and robbing travelers.

However, unlike other historic outlaws of the highway, such as Robin Hood and Dick Turpin, there was nothing romantic about the way of life of the Beanes. For robbery soon turned to murder and murder to cannibalism. Such human monsters are a rare and usually solitary breed but the Beane clan worked as an entire family team. They lived in a deep, tortuous cave system that was accessible only at low tide. The sea flooded some 220 yards (200m) into the cave entrance before the family's hideout was reached.

Over 25 years the evil clan founded by Sawney (sometimes known as 'Sandy') Beane grew, through exclusively incestuous unions, to eight sons, six daughters, 18 grandsons and 14 granddaughters.

Together they made an entire coastal area unsafe for both man and beast. They hunted in packs, like wild animals, attacking groups of up to six travelers on foot or two riders on horseback. Anyone caught would be robbed, slaughtered, and eaten as the most effective means of disposing of their victims and feeding the family. The number of their victims is unknown but, according to folklore, probably exceeded 100; some histories say over 1,000.

The story passed down anecdotally over the years is that when grim tales of the cave dwellers at last reached King James I of Scotland in 1435, he raised a special force to track down and capture the Beanes. It arrived on the Galloway coast just as the Beanes made a fatal blunder. While a group of them were attacking a man and his wife, they were surprised by a party of horsemen and fled, leaving the woman's disemboweled body on the roadside. The royal forces were not far distant and took up the pursuit, using tracker dogs to follow the trail of the fugitives to their subterranean lair.

Although undoubtedly exaggerated over the years, the scene the royal force found within the caves was likened to a human abattoir. Legend has it that hung from the cave roof or laid out on racks were male and female corpses, both whole and dismembered, some fresh, some smoked, some dried, some pickled, and some salted. There were also animal carcasses, stolen saddles, bundles of clothes, provisions, and valuables.

The bestial Beanes, all 48 of them, were shackled and taken to Leith, near Edinburgh, where they were summarily tried and, without exception, condemned to death. Sawney Beane had his hands, feet, and penis severed. The other male members of the clan then suffered the same dismemberment and all were left to bleed to death. As they did so, they were made to watch their womenfolk being tossed alive into three great fires.

**RIGHT:** An artist's impression of the beastly Sawney Beane outside his family's gruesome cave dwelling.

# Bender Family

**The Bender family attracted victims like the flies that buzzed around the dingy Wayside Inn they ran on a dusty Kansas trail. Any passing stranger who appeared to have some money would be invited to their dinner table within the dirty 16ft by 20ft (5x6m) cabin. Many did not live to enjoy their meal, instead ending up being murdered in the most horrific manner.**

# Unwary Wayfarers Slain By Trapdoor Tricksters

**No one knows** when the Benders' murderous reign began, but the end came after Dr William York left his brother's house at Fort Scott, Kansas, on March 9, 1873, to ride home to the town of Independence. He did not arrive, so his brother, a colonel in the US Cavalry, set out to scour the trail. Colonel York's first call was at the Wayside Inn, at the hamlet of Cherryvale, where the Benders offered him food and shelter.

The colonel knew his brother had intended breaking his journey there, and that night he too got to know the unsavory owners. There was old man Bender, a 60-year-old surly East European immigrant, his shrewish wife aged 50, a half-witted son and an ugly, unmarried daughter. They all denied any knowledge of Dr York, blaming bandits or Indians for the brother's disappearance. But because of the colonel's persistent inquiries, they panicked and, hurriedly packing their belongings onto a cart, they fled.

On May 9, another search party on the trail of Dr York found the Wayside Inn abandoned and found several animals, including a small flock of sheep, either dead or dying from hunger and thirst. They also noticed that recent rains had revealed a freshly dug grave. It contained the body of Dr York, his skull smashed and his throat cut from ear to ear.

Further digging revealed the remains of no fewer than seven other victims. All of them had been killed in the same way apart from a small girl. Judging from her position, it was apparent she had been thrown into the shallow grave while still alive. Later, another child's body was unearthed, dreadfully decomposed but probably that of a girl of about eight.

Meanwhile, other members of the search party were investigating the source of a foul smell that permeated

**ABOVE:** The Bender family's humble log cabin, inside which they murdered and robbed at will.

**ABOVE LEFT AND RIGHT:** Sketched portraits of the evil Bender family, who lured unsuspecting travelers to their deaths.

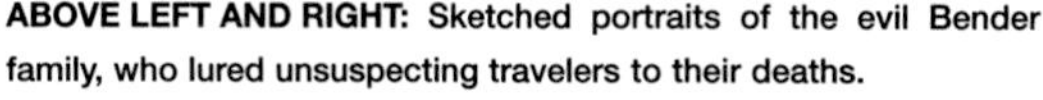

the cabin. Beneath a trapdoor in the floor they found a roughly-dug pit, its floor and walls stained with blood—and the modus operandi of the ghastly Benders gradually became clear.

The family would invite a guest to join them for dinner, always taking great care to ensure he or she was seated with their backs to a curtained-off sleeping area. One of the family would be waiting behind the curtain to smash the victim's skull with a heavy hammer and finish him or her off with a knife to the throat. After searching the body for valuables, it would be dropped through a trapdoor into the revolting cellar below. Then after nightfall, it would be buried in a shallow grave.

Following these grisly discoveries, posses were formed to hunt down the Benders but they were never discovered—at least, officially. Legend has it that one of the several local vigilante patrols caught up with the Benders and local lawmen allowed rough and instant justice to be meted out to them.

# David Berkowitz

**His weapon was a .44 revolver, and at first the New York tabloids tagged him 'the .44-Caliber Killer'. But from the moment when police found a seemingly deranged note at the scene of one particularly senseless double murder, the killer became known for his bizarre nickname: 'Son of Sam'.**

## Sick Taunts Of The Killer Called 'Son of Sam'

**The first of a series of callously teasing letters** was left by the killer after shooting student Valentina Suriani and boyfriend Alexander Esau as they sat in their car in the Bronx in April 1977. Detectives did not know what to make of the rambling missive, in which the gunman complained that he was 'deeply hurt' that the media were referring to him as a woman-hater. He wrote…

'I am not. But I am a monster. I am the Son of Sam. I am a little brat. Sam loves to drink blood. "Go out and kill," commands father Sam…I am on a different wavelength to everybody else—programed to kill. However, to stop me you must kill me. Attention all police: Shoot me first—shoot to kill or else. Keep out of my way or you will die! I am the monster—

BECAUSE CRAIG IS CRAIG
SO MUST THE STREETS
BE FILLED WITH CRAIG (DEATH)

AND HUGE DROPS OF LEAD
POURED DOWN UPON HER HEAD
UNTIL SHE WAS DEAD.
YET, THE CATS STILL COME OUT
AT NIGHT TO MATE
AND THE SPARROWS STILL
IN THE MORNING

**ABOVE:** One of Berkowitz's crazed and chilling handwritten notes in which he appears to describe hammering a victim to death.

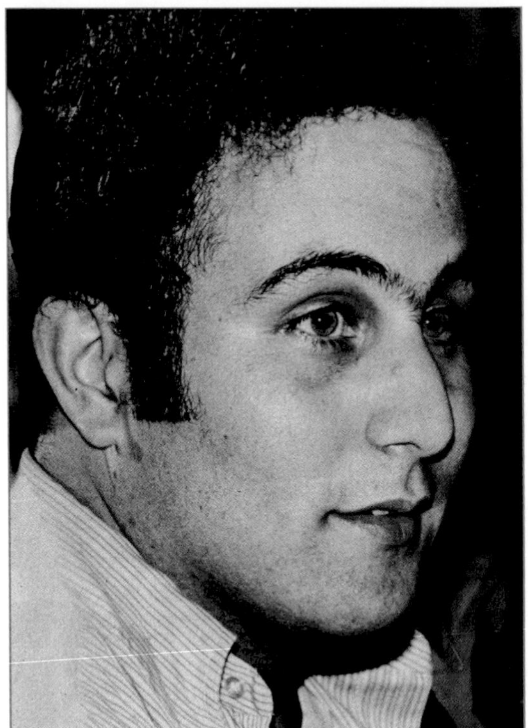

**ABOVE:** A portrait of convicted New York City serial killer David Berkowitz, known as the 'Son of Sam'.

"Beelzebub, the Chubby Behemoth". I love to hunt. Prowling the streets looking for fair game—tasty meat. I live for the hunt—my life. I don't belong on earth. I'll be back! I'll be back! Yours in murder—Mr Monster.'

This 'Son of Sam', this 'Mr Monster' was a plump, chubby-cheeked, 33-year-old bachelor named David Berkowitz. Born illegitimately to a Brooklyn showgirl on June 1, 1953, he was raised by caring, adoptive parents who ran a hardware store in the Bronx. He was deeply affected in his early teens by the death of his doting adoptive mother, Pearl Berkowitz, complaining that her death from cancer was caused by 'evil forces… as part of a master-plan to break me down'. When he was 18, his adoptive father remarried and the disapproving David left home and enlisted in the Army.

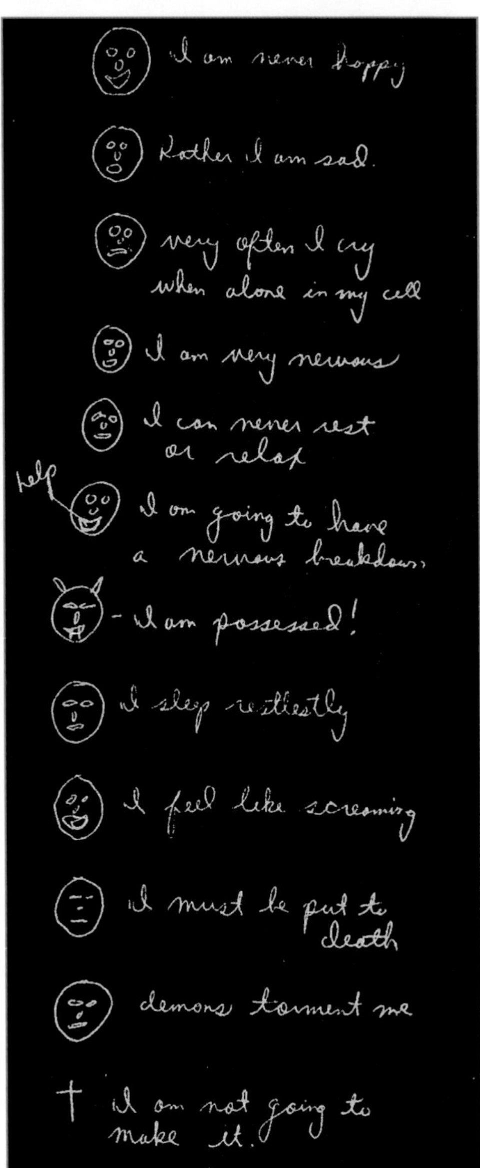

I am never happy

Rather I am sad.

very often I cry
when alone in my cell

I am very nervous

I can never rest
or relax

help

I am going to have
a nervous breakdown

- I am possessed!

I sleep restlessly

I feel like screaming

I must be put to
death

demons torment me

I am not going to
make it.

**ABOVE:** One of Berkowitz's bizarre notes. One line reads: 'I am possessed', another, 'I am going to have a nervous breakdown'.

During three years' service in Korea, he converted from Judaism to fundamentalist Christianity and, once back in the United States, spent his off-duty hours preaching from street corners in Louisville, Kentucky, where he was stationed. In 1974 he returned to the Bronx where, after a spell as a security guard, he joined the US Mail, sorting letters.

It was while working as a mailman that Berkowitz brought fear to the streets of New York for almost exactly one year, from July 29, 1976, to August 1, 1977. He killed six women and viciously wounded another seven. And throughout his mad campaign of carnage, he taunted police with a series of letters bragging about his deeds. Ironically, in his role as a postal worker, Berkowitz may well have handled the mailbags that contained his own letters as 'Son of Sam'.

Berkowitz's first killing seemed wholly random. He laid in wait as a car pulled up in a quiet street in the Bronx and 18-year-old Donna Lauria stepped out, said goodbye to her friend Jody Valente, who remained in the car, and turned to head into her parents' apartment. Berkowitz ran from the shadows, pulled his .44 caliber gun from a paper bag, crouched down and fired three shots. Donna died and Jody was wounded.

The killer struck again on October 23, and once again the targets were two young people in a parked car, this time in the borough of Queens. Detective's daughter Rosemary Keenan, 18, escaped the bullets but her 20-year-old friend, Carl Denaro, was shot in the head and survived.

A month later, two young women sitting on the steps of their Queens home were less lucky. The gunman walked up and wounded both Joanne Lomino and Donna DeMasi, the latter being permanently paralyzed by a bullet to her spine. In January 1977, two bullets shattered the window of a car parked in Queens, one hitting John Diel but the other missing his girlfriend Christine Freund. In the same area in March, student Virginia Voskerichian died with a bullet to the face. Because the bullets all came from the same pistol, a 300-strong '.44 Killer' Task Force was organized, but were hampered by apparent lack of motive.

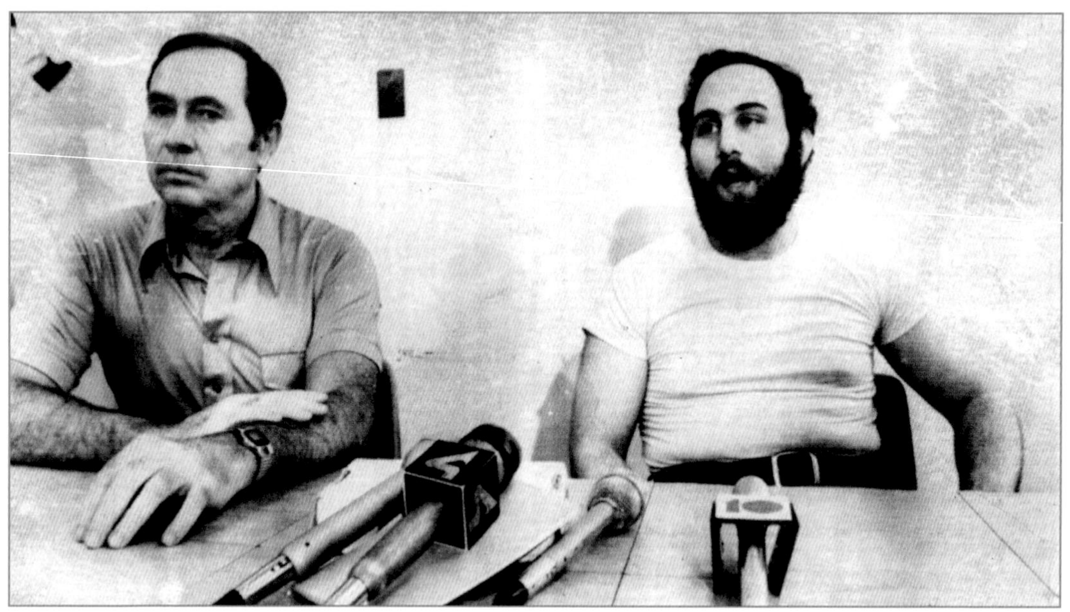

**ABOVE:** Flanked by lawyers and warders, Berkowitz holds a news conference at Attica prison, New York State, in June 1980.

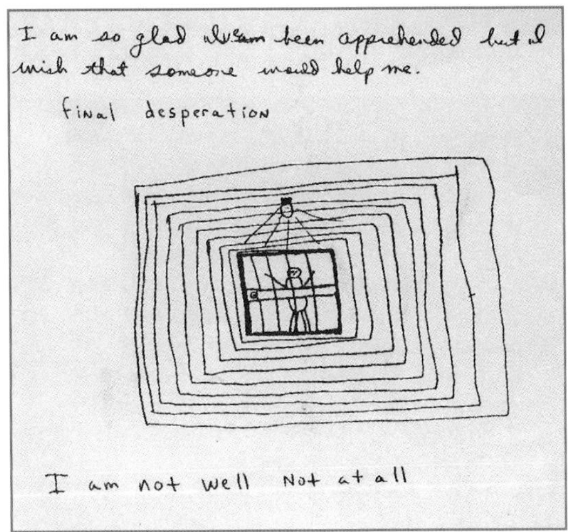


**ABOVE:** Another of Berkowitz's scrawlings, this time after his arrest. He confesses that he is 'not well'.

As his notoriety grew, and the 'Son of Sam' note was found at the scene of the Bronx double murder in April 1977, Berkowitz began sending letters to the rival tabloid *New York Post* and *New York Daily News*. Journalist Jimmy Breslin adopted the very risky tactic of replying in his column on the *News*. One letter from the killer warned him: 'Mr Breslin, sir, don't think that because you haven't heard from (me) for a while that I went to sleep. No, rather, I am still here. Like a spirit roaming the night. Thirsty, hungry, seldom stopping to rest.'

On July 29, 1977, the anniversary of his first attack, Breslin asked 'Son of Sam' in his column: 'Will you kill again?' The very next night, Berkowitz shot dead 20-year-old Stacy Moskowitz and blinded her date, Robert Violante, as they sat in their car in a Brooklyn street.

Berkowitz was finally caught thanks to a $35 parking ticket, issued near the scene of the shooting. A computer trace of the summons showed that it had been slapped on a Ford Galaxie, license plate 561XLB, owned by David Berkowitz. Task Force detectives caught up with it parked outside the killer's apartment—with a rifle protruding from a bag on the back seat and an arsenal of weapons in the trunk. In the glovebox was a letter addressed to police, promising more attacks, including a massacre at a Long Island nightclub where Berkowitz planned to 'go out in a blaze of glory'.

When an unsuspecting Berkowitz emerged from his apartment and stepped into his car, he found 15 guns trained at his head. He had no time to draw the .44 he was carrying in a brown paper bag. 'Okay, you've got me,' he said. 'What took you so long?'

On the evidence of his maniacal letters, Berkowitz could have entered a defense of insanity. Instead, he pleaded guilty to all charges and, on August 23, 1977, he was sentenced to 365 years' imprisonment.

# 'Bible John' and Peter Tobin

**In an interview with a police psychiatrist following his arrest in 2006, murderer Peter Tobin admitted that he had killed as many as 50 women. When questioned about this, he replied: 'Prove it.' Proving it has been tantalizingly difficult. For if police theories are correct, Tobin's crimes stretch back more than 40 years—to a time when a serial killer known only as 'Bible John' stalked the streets of Glasgow.**

## The Baffling Case Of Elusive 'Bible John'

**Are Peter Tobin and 'Bible John'** one and the same? The evidence and the similarities have convinced many, including retired Scottish cops who were on the original case in the 1960s when the unidentified killer strangled three young women.

His first victim was Patricia Docker, 29, found dead in a doorway on February 23, 1968, after spending the previous evening at a Glasgow dance hall. On August 16, 1969, Jemima McDonald, 32, was found dead in derelict apartments. She too had been out to a ballroom where she had met a young man. On October 30, Helen Puttock, 29, was murdered after leaving the same ballroom with a man and her body was found dumped at a bus stop. All the women had been strangled, all had had their handbags stolen, and all were menstruating at the time of their deaths.

Witnesses described the man Helen had danced with on the night she died. He had given his name as 'John', had seemed a 'nice guy' but weirdly quoted Biblical texts and condemned dancehalls as 'dens of iniquity'. The press gave him the nickname 'Bible John'.

Police then lost track of the killer—until 2006 when

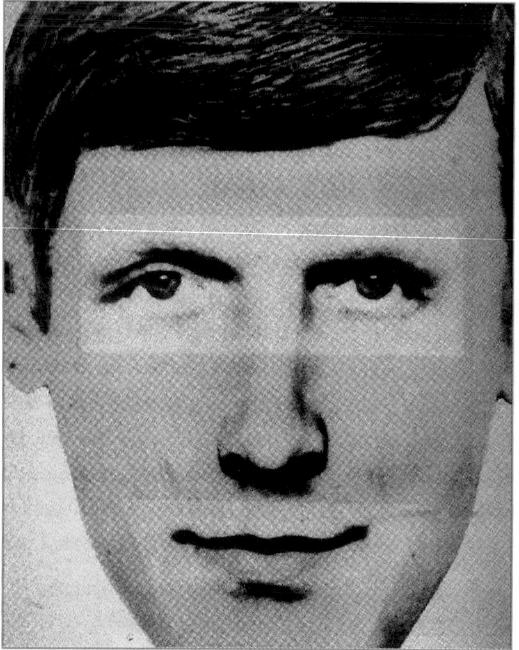

**ABOVE:** A Photofit of 'Bible John', whom Scottish police first sought in the 1960s after he strangled three young women.

**BELOW:** Tobin is taken from Linlithgow Sheriff Court, after a hearing in connection with the Vicky Hamilton murder on November 15, 2007.

retired detective superintendent Joe Jackson, who had been on the 'Bible John' case in the Sixties, was watching TV when he finally glimpsed his suspect.

A 23-year-old Polish student called Angelika Kluk had been murdered, her mutilated body hidden under the floor of a Glasgow church. Now the likely killer had come to light—a drifter, odd-job man and religious crank called Peter Tobin. Jackson's reaction: 'I said to myself, this guy fits the bill. It's as good as we're going to get.'

Tobin, born in Renfrewshire in 1946, had been sent to reform school at the age of seven, had unsuccessfully married three times and had spent a lifetime in and out of prison, including a 10-year term for a double rape in 1993. He would have been 21 at the time of the 'Bible John' slayings.

Tobin's conviction in 2007 for the murder of student Angelika Kluk the previous year allowed the media to point to him as the likely face of 'Bible John'. Indeed, the similarity was striking between a 1969 police drawing of 'Bible John' and Tobin's police mugshot from the same era.

The investigation then moved to southern England, where Tobin was found to have buried the body of 15-year-old Scottish schoolgirl Vicky Hamilton, missing since 1991. Her remains were found at a house in Margate, Kent, where Tobin had previously lived. The skeletal remains of another missing young girl were also found under the patio of the house in Margate.

Already sentenced to life for murdering Angelika Kluk, Tobin, 62, was given a second term in 2008 for Vicky Hamilton's killing and told he could expect to die in jail. Meanwhile, investigations continued over other unsolved cases dating back to the 1960s.

# David and Catherine Birnie

**To label David and Catherine Birnie as the 'Bonnie and Clyde' of serial killers is unfair on Bonnie and Clyde. The American outlaws killed for cash; the sick Australian duo killed for thrills.**

## Predators Who Became Partners In Pure Evil

**The couple, both born in Perth,** Western Australia, in 1951, first met at the age of 12 and were lovers at just 14. Both were from dysfunctional families and both turned to petty crime in their teens.

Quitting school at 15, David became an apprentice jockey but was reported for physically harming the horses. In and out of jail for thefts and assaults, his worst early offense was breaking into an elderly lady's house naked and raping her.

Catherine Harrison, as she was then, also spent some of her teens in prison but, thanks to the encouragement of a parole officer, seemed to be settling down when, at 21, she wed and went on to have seven children.

David Birnie also married in his early 20s and had a baby daughter but in the mid-1980s tracked Catherine down and persuaded her to abandon her husband. She changed her last name to match Birnie's and together the pair began to indulge their sexual fantasies of rape and murder.

On October 6, 1986, student Mary Neilson knocked on the door of their shabby bungalow on Moorhouse Street, in the Perth suburb of Willagee, to buy cheap tires which Birnie had secured through his job at a car wreckers yard. Mary, 22, was forced into a bedroom at knifepoint and raped as Catherine watched. They then drove her to nearby Glen Eagle State Forest where Birnie raped her again before strangling her.

Two weeks later, another body joined Mary's in her shallow grave. The Birnies picked up 15-year-old hitch-hiker Susannah Candy and kept her prisoner for several days, raping her repeatedly before Catherine strangled her.

On November 1, bar manager Noelene Patterson, aged 31, was 'rescued' after running out of gasoline and was taken back to Moorhouse Street, where the Birnies chained her to a bed and repeatedly raped her over three days. They killed her after forcing sleeping pills down her throat and she was buried beside the others.

Three days later, Denise Brown, a 21-year-old computer operator, suffered a similar fate after being picked up at a bus stop. She suffered horribly as attempts to stab her to death failed and she sat up in her shallow grave. David Birnie finished her off with an ax.

The Birnies' murderous rampage ended when a weeping 17-year-old ran naked into a grocery store on November 10 after escaping from the Birnies' house while left briefly unchained. David and Catherine Birnie admitted all charges of rape and murder, and in March 1987 were each sentenced to life imprisonment. While in jail, they exchanged 2,600 letters.

David Birnie hanged himself in his cell in October 2005, the day before he was due in court for raping a fellow prisoner. Catherine Birnie remained incarcerated without hope of freedom after her case was reviewed in March 2009—and her papers marked: 'Never to be released.'

# Lawrence Bittaker and Roy Norris

**There were clear indicators of murderous intent in the early life of Lawrence Sigmund Bittaker. Born in 1940, he dropped out of school at 17 after several brushes with police and juvenile authorities. Thereafter he was in and out of institutions for two decades. In 1961 he found himself being psychiatrically evaluated while in prison in California, where he was found to be 'paranoid' and 'borderline psychotic', with little control over his impulses. Despite this, he was released within two years.**

## Teenage Girls Were Strangled With Wire Coat Hangers

**In jail again in the Seventies,** psychiatrists warned that Bittaker was 'more than likely' to commit new crimes upon his release. Another psychiatrist dubbed him a 'sophisticated psychopath' whose prospects for successful parole were 'guarded at best'. Again the warnings were ignored and Bittaker was released in 1978.

By then, it was too late for the five teenage girls he went on to rape, torture, and murder. His killing spree, committed with his accomplice Roy Norris, lasted between June and October 1979 and briefly brought terror to the Los Angeles suburbs.

Roy Norris, born in 1948, was also a school drop-out. He joined the Navy and served in Vietnam, but was discharged with psychological problems. He was arrested for attempted rape in San Diego in 1969, and while out

**ABOVE:** Lawrence Bittaker (pictured) and his accomplice Roy Norris murdered five young women in a cargo van over five months in 1979.

on bail was rearrested twice for further sex attacks.

Confined to a state hospital as a mentally disordered sex offender, he was freed on probation in 1975, his release papers describing him as someone who would bring 'no further danger to others'. Only three months later he raped a 27-year-old woman and was jailed in California Men's Colony, San Luis Obispo, where he met and befriended Bittaker.

In January 1979, Norris was out of jail again and teamed up with Bittaker in Los Angeles. By October, they snuffed out five young, innocent lives. They abducted the girls in a windowless cargo van with side sliding door which they labeled 'Murder Mack'.

On June 24, while patrolling the coastline of Greater LA, they pounced on 16-year-old Cindy Schaeffer, bundled her into the van, taped her mouth, and bound her arms and legs. Both men raped the girl, then Bittaker strangled her with a wire coat hanger tightened with pliers. They dumped her body in a mountain canyon.

The following month, they picked up hitch-hiker Andrea Hall, 18, and subjected her to multiple rape before Bittaker stabbed her with an ice pick in both ears and, when she wouldn't die fast enough, strangled her. He threw her body over a cliff.

On September 3, the killers spotted two girls on a bus stop bench and offered them a ride. Jackie Gilliam, 15, and Leah Lamp, 13, were kept alive for two days, constantly raped and tortured while the evil pair tape-recorded their victims. Finally, Bittaker stabbed Jackie in both ears with the ice pick and each man took turns finishing her off by strangulation. Norris then battered Leah with a sledgehammer. The bodies were thrown over a cliff.

Their last victim was 16-year-old Lynette Ledford, who suffered a similar fate, eventually being strangled with wire and pliers. Her body was found the following day, November 1, on a lawn in Hermosa Beach.

The couple were apprehended because Norris boasted about the killings to an old prison friend who tipped off the police. Norris testified against his accomplice for a jail sentence that would have him eligible for parole in 2010.

Bittaker was sentenced to death in 1981. He was still on Death Row over a quarter of a century later—answering female fan mail under his favored nickname: 'Pliers' Bittaker.

# Robert Black

**At his trial, Robert Black was described by prosecutors as 'every parent's worst nightmare'. A Scottish child molester and killer, he had a disturbed childhood himself, being fostered and spending his schooldays as a loner prone to outbreaks of mindless violence. His classroom nickname was 'Smelly Robbie'.**

## Every Parent's Worst Nightmare

**His foster mother died in 1958** when Robert was just 11, and he was sent to a children's home near Falkirk, close to his birthplace. He lasted there a year before a fumbled attempt at rape of a local girl caused him to be packed off to a stricter establishment. There he was regularly abused by a male member of staff, and from that time onward, Black associated sex with dominance and submission.

At 15, he left the home and got a job as a delivery boy in Glasgow. He later admitted that, while on his rounds, he molested as many as 40 girls. Seemingly, none of the attacks was reported. Even more astonishing was that, at the age of 17, he got away with what may well have been judged a murder attempt.

He approached a seven-year-old girl in a park, led her to a deserted building, throttled her until she passed out and then sexually assaulted her. He left her unconscious and she was later found wandering the streets confused, crying, and bleeding. Brought to court, he was given no more than a 'good behavior' order after a psychiatric report declared that this was 'an isolated incident'.

Tragically, a chance to stop Robert Black from progressing to full-scale murders had been lost. It would take more than a quarter of a century before the evil pervert was caught and caged. By then, as a burly lorry driver, he had kidnapped, raped, and murdered at least three girls and was a suspect in a string of unsolved child murders across Britain and in Europe.

Black was finally caught in the village of Stow, south of Edinburgh, in July 1990 after being spotted bundling a six-year-old girl into his van. A sharp-eyed postman jotted down the license plate and called police. The girl was found bound and gagged in the back.

Detectives spent four years piecing together the evidence to convict him of murder. They used work records from his job delivering advertising posters to connect him with the scene of each abduction on the relevant day, and later at the sites where the bodies were found.

Eleven-year-old Susan Maxwell was snatched by the scruffy-looking van driver from near her home in the Scottish Borders in 1982. The following year, Caroline Hogg, aged five, was taken from a fairground near her Edinburgh home. Sarah Harper, aged 10, from Morley, near Leeds, was abducted in 1986.

At Newcastle upon Tyne Crown Court on May 20, 1994, Black, then aged 47, was given 10 life sentences, with an order that he serve at least 35 years in prison, for the three proven murders and the abduction of a 15-year-old girl. But police said he could be responsible for 16 further unsolved murders in Britain, France, and Germany.

# Wayne Boden

**Wayne Boden was a serial killer who earned the nickname the 'Vampire Rapist' because of his penchant for biting his victims. It was a trait that led to his conviction on the grounds of dental evidence—one of the first such of its kind in North America and several years ahead of another, more notorious serial killer, Ted Bundy (see page 29). Boden had one other kink: he had a fascination for vampires and, after strangling his victims and raping them, he would bite their breasts to drink their blood.**

## 'Vampire Rapist' Bit His Victims' Breasts

**The gory modus operandi** of the Canadian serial killer caused a two-year reign of terror, first in Montreal and then in Calgary, where Boden carried out his murders between October 1969 and May 1971. His first victim was Shirley Audette whose body was found dumped at the rear of an apartment complex in downtown Montreal. Although she was fully clothed, she had been raped and strangled and had savage bite marks on her breasts. Boden lived next door but was not suspected. It was a missed opportunity to put an early stop to the killer, particularly as a former boyfriend of Shirley told police he believed she had a new man in her life and was 'getting into something dangerous'.

The following month, jewelry store clerk Marielle Archambault happily left work at closing time with a young man whom she introduced to her colleagues as 'Bill'. When she failed to report for work the following morning, Archambault's boss went to her apartment and had it unlocked by the landlady. They found Marielle's fully-clad body on the couch, her pantyhose and bra ripped, her breasts covered with teeth marks.

'Bill' waited two months before striking again. In

January 1970, the boyfriend of Jean Way, 24, arrived at her apartment on a date but got no answer. This was probably because the 'Vampire Rapist' was in her bedroom at the time, hovering over her dead body. When the boyfriend returned later, he found the door unlocked and Jean lying on the bed. She had been strangled and her breasts bitten.

In the cases of two of these murders, there was little sign of a struggle. The girls actually seemed serene in death—one even having a faint smile on her lips. Detectives surmised that the killer had an attraction for girls who wanted and accepted 'rough sex'. These masochistic tendencies may have led the 'Vampire Rapist' to lose control during frenzied and ferocious sex, and asphyxiate the girls before abusing their bodies.

Jean Way's murder was the last in Montreal. 'Bill' had disappeared from that city—only to turn up in another one 2,500 miles (4,000km) away. In May 1971, Calgary schoolteacher Elizabeth Porteous was found murdered in her apartment. On this occasion, the victim had clearly put up a fierce fight for her life before being raped and strangled and her breasts mutilated with bite marks.

From Elizabeth's work colleagues, detectives discovered that she had a new boyfriend named 'Bill' who drove a distinctive blue Mercedes. It was the car in which Jean Way had been seen on the day of her murder. That, plus the clue of a broken cufflink found under Elizabeth's body, led police to Boden.

The clinching evidence came from orthodontists who matched a cast of Boden's teeth to bite marks on his victims. The 'Vampire Rapist' was sentenced in Calgary to life imprisonment for Elizabeth's murder, then returned to Montreal to receive three further life sentences. He died in 2006 of skin cancer, aged 57.

# William Bonin

**It is an indictment of North America's crime-ridden highways that 'Freeway Killer' William Bonin shared his nickname with two other serial killers. By his murder tally, however, Bonin stands out—having raped and murdered as many as 36 young men and boys, 14 for which he was convicted and eventually executed.**

## 'Freeway Killer' Who Raped and Murdered Teenage Boys

**Bonin was born in Connecticut in 1947,** the son of a gambling alcoholic. His mother doted on him and often removed him from his father's frequent rages by having him stay with his grandfather, a convicted child molester. His childhood experiences were to influence him toward a life of sadism and, ultimately, slaughter.

At the age of only eight, he was caught stealing license plates. His first criminal conviction was when he was 10 and was followed by repeated stays in detention centers, where he was sexually abused by older boys. By his teens, back home with his mother, Bonin began molesting younger children. After high school, he joined the US Air Force and served in Vietnam as a gunner, earning a Good Conduct Medal. After a brief marriage ended in divorce, he moved to California.

As a 22-year-old, working as a truck driver and living in Downey, California, he was convicted of his first sex crimes: kidnapping and abusing young boys in four separate attacks. He was diagnosed as mentally disturbed and sent to Atascadero State Hospital, from where he was released in May 1974, with psychiatrists declaring he was no longer a danger.

But in 1979 he began a killing spree that targeted homosexual young men, usually young male prostitutes and sometimes hitch-hikers, whom he would pick up in his van as he cruised around the Los Angeles area.

**ABOVE:** The body count of 'Freeway Killer' William Bonin may have totaled 36 young men and boys.

On many of these sorties, he teamed up with factory worker Vernon Butts, a 22-year-old weirdo who claimed to be a wizard and slept in a coffin.

Their first known murder victim was 14-year-old hitch-hiker Thomas Lundgren. The boy was kidnapped, assaulted, and strangled on May 28, 1979, and his body dumped at Malibu. Before the year was out, seven more teenagers had been killed. More bodies started turning up in early 1980, the youngest victim being 12-year-old James McCabe, who had been abducted, raped, and killed.

Butts later said that, although he had been sickened by his first killing, he went on to actively enjoy raping, torturing, and murdering. He told police: 'After the first one, I couldn't do anything about it. Bonin had a hypnotic way about him.'

Extraordinarily, Butts was not Bonin's only accomplice. He also recruited two mentally subnormal 19-year-olds, James Munro and Gregory Miley, and a fourth accomplice, who was aged only 15. It was Bonin's attempt to involve a fourth teenager into his killing games that led to his arrest. The horrified 18-year-old tipped off police who set up a surveillance of Bonin. On the night of June 11, 1980, they caught him in the act of assaulting a 15-year-old boy in the back of his van. Rounded up by police, all four of Bonin's accomplices gave evidence against him to avoid the death sentence. Butts hanged himself in his cell and the others served jail terms.

Bonin confessed to abducting, raping, and killing 21 boys and young men, although he was a police suspect in at least another 15 other murders. He was eventually charged with 14 of the murders. He showed no remorse and said simply: 'I couldn't stop killing. It got easier with each one we did.' In a later prison confession, he added: 'If I had not been arrested I would still be killing. I couldn't stop killing.'

Convicted on all counts, Bonin was sentenced to death by Judge William Keene in January 1982 but it was to be another 14 years before the execution was carried out. On February 23, 1996, he was taken from Death Row to the old gas chamber at San Quentin Prison and became the first person to be executed by lethal injection in California.

# Werner Boost

**Werner Boost, born in 1928, the illegitimate son of an East German peasant, was a child thief who originally made a living transporting refugees across the Iron Curtain. Because of subsequent events, it may well be that some of the escapees, having entrusted Boost to get them across the border, were not helped out of a miserable life in the East but out of life altogether.**

## Death At The Double

**LEFT:** Werner Boost (pictured) and his accomplice, Franz Lorbach, carried out a string of murders in 1950s Germany.

**His murderous character became clearer,** however, after Boost relocated to Düsseldorf in 1950 and became a killer who preyed on courting couples. His first known attack in the city was made with an accomplice, Franz Lorbach. In January 1953, the pair crept up to a car parked in a quiet suburban street and disturbed lawyer Bernd Serve and his 19-year-old male lover. Dr Serve was shot through the head but the lover was only beaten and robbed.

The murderous duo's next crime, in October 1955, was to earn Boost the nickname the 'Düsseldorf Double Killer'. Again accompanied by Lorbach, Boost robbed and battered to death Thear Kurmann and her boyfriend, 26-year-old baker Friedhelm Behre, after they left a restaurant. Their bodies were discovered a month later trapped in their car in a water-filled gravel pit.

Boost carried out his final double killing in February 1956. The charred bodies of Peter Falkenberg and 20-year-old secretary Hildegard Wassing were discovered in a smoldering haystack. Both had been bludgeoned and robbed, and Falkenberg had been shot through the head. The bloodstained car in which they had been attacked was also discovered.

A further attempt at double murder took place in May of that year in woodland outside the city but failed because the woman's screams alerted passers-by. In the same area on June 10 a forest ranger spotted an armed man apparently tracking a young couple. Boost surrendered to the ranger, protesting his innocence of any crime.

Evidence linking him to the 'Düsseldorf Double Killer' was slim and Boost might have got away with murder if Lorbach had not buckled under police interrogation, admitting his role in the killings and naming his accomplice. Lorbach told police that Boost's favored method was to sedate the couples then rape the women before killing them. Excusing his own part in the crimes, he claimed he had been 'hypnotized' into committing them.

Boost was sentenced to life imprisonment on December 14, 1959, for the murder of Dr Serve. Lorbach was jailed for six years. Despite police suspicion, evidence linking the two men to the other murders could not be proved.

# Ian Brady and Myra Hindley

**Tough cops wept when they first listened to the tape. Now, when played in a hushed courtroom, hardened reporters were also reduced to tears. No one there that day in 1966 would ever forget the harrowing recording. It was of a little girl's voice, pleading for her mother and begging for mercy.**

## Tiny 'Moors Murders' Victim Taped Pleading For Mercy

**The recording was of Lesley Ann Downey,** at 10 the youngest victim of 'Moors Murderers' Ian Brady and Myra Hindley. It was made by the evil couple as the little girl was put to death, her plaintive cries accompanied by the sounds of torture and sexual assault. The only other voice was Hindley's, coldly

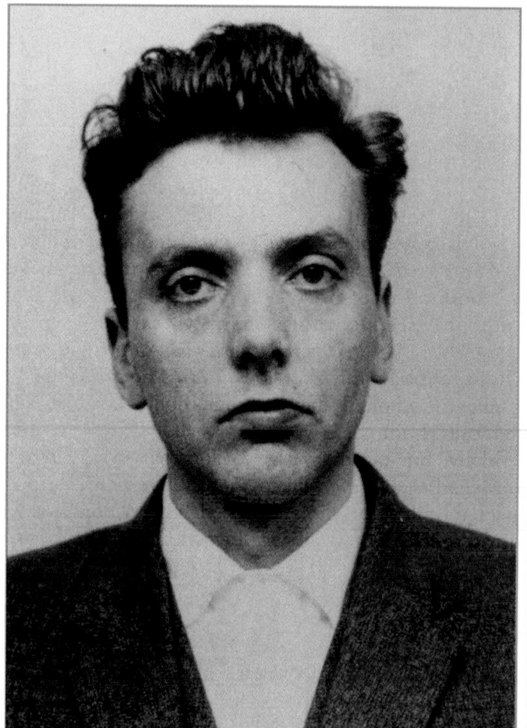

**ABOVE:** Ian Brady was sentenced to life imprisonment on May 7, 1966. The judge told him and his accomplice that they were 'evil beyond belief.'

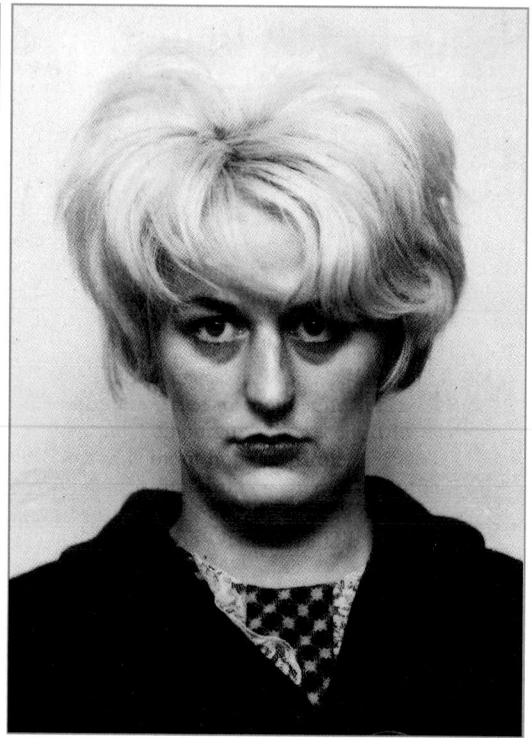

**ABOVE:** A portrait of 'Moors Murderer' Myra Hindley taken during her trial. While in prison, Hindley claimed to be a reformed character, but she was never released and died in 2002.

ordering the child to 'shut up' and 'be quiet'. The 16-minute tape ended with a scream.

The 'Moors Murderers' are, to an entire British generation, the epitome of evil. Between 1962 and 1965, Brady and his lover Hindley abducted, tortured, and murdered at least five, possibly eight, children or teenagers. Most of the bodies were buried on bleak Saddleworth Moor, on the hills outside Manchester.

Brady, born in 1938, the illegitimate son of a Glasgow waitress, was a teenage burglar before moving to Manchester in 1954, settling into a job as a clerk. There he encountered 19-year-old typist Myra Hindley in 1961. It was a meeting of evil minds. Brady was a sadistic fetishist who drew a willing Hindley into his perverted games. They took pictures of themselves having sex while dressed in leather, brandishing whips and acting out Nazi crimes. Soon the games turned to reality.

In July 1963, Hindley lured 16-year-old Pauline Reade onto Saddleworth Moor, where Brady raped her then hit her over the head with a shovel before cutting her throat. Four months later, 12-year-old John Kilbride was taken to the moor, held down and molested by Brady before being strangled and buried.

In June 1964, Hindley asked another 12-year-old, Keith Bennett, to carry some shopping for her, then invited him for a trip across the moor. There the boy was abused and strangled, Brady taking photographs of the body before burying it.

Ten-year-old Lesley Ann Downey disappeared while attending a Christmas fair on December 26. She was taken to Brady's home and forced to pose nude for pornographic photographs before being killed.

In October 1965, the couple invited Hindley's brother-in-law, David Smith, to their suburban home. Brady talked openly to him about previous murders but, fearful that he might go to the police, tried to implicate him in a fresh killing. Brady lured 17-year-old Edward Evans to the house and attacked the teenager with a hatchet—having first ensured that Smith's fingerprints were on the murder weapon.

Smith pretended to play along with Brady and even helped him and Hindley clear up. Then he ran to the police. He told detectives that, after the killing, the bloodstained couple had sat around laughing and drinking wine. Brady had boasted to him: 'It's the messiest yet. It normally only takes one blow.'

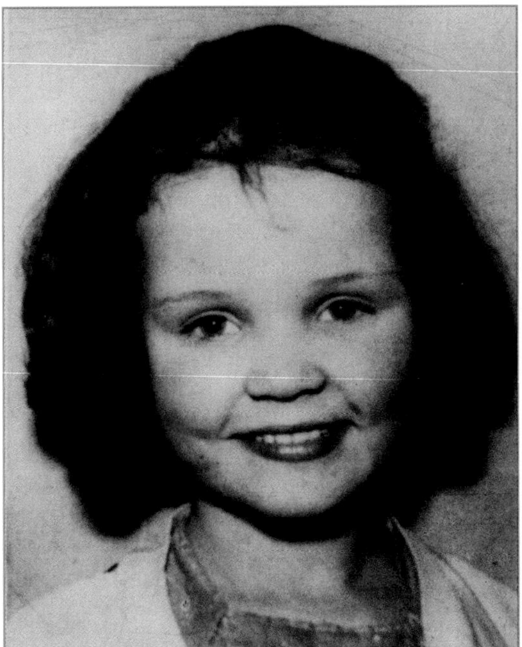

**ABOVE:** A family photograph of Lesley Ann Downey shortly before her death at the hands of the 'Moors Murderers'.

**ABOVE:** Hindley (left) was complicit in all the crimes. She is still Britain's most notorious female serial killer.

With Brady and Hindley under arrest—the latter coolly denying any part in the killings—police searched their house. They found a photograph of Hindley posing next to John Kilbride's shallow grave on Saddleworth Moor. Other photographs showed poor Lesley Ann Downey in pornographic poses. But the most horrifying discovery was the recording made of her dying cries: 'Please take your hands off me a minute, please. Please, Mum, please. I can't tell you. I cannot breathe. Please God. Why? What are you doing with me?'

That damning tape was finally played at the trial of Brady and Hindley at Chester Assizes, which ended in May 1966 with the couple being found guilty of the murder of the little girl and of Evans. Handing down life sentences, the judge told the killers: 'You are evil beyond belief.'

While incarcerated, Brady 'confessed' to five other murders but, being diagnosed as suffering from paranoid psychosis, no further charges were brought. The killer went on hunger strikes in a vain bid to end his life.

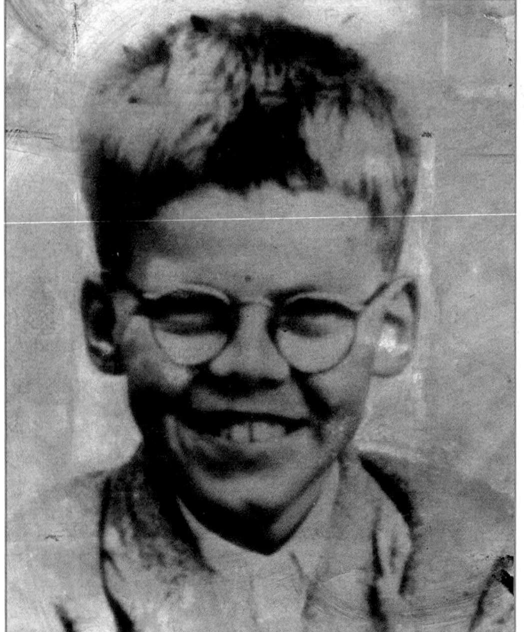

**ABOVE:** John Bennett was the third victim of the evil duo. Hindley lured him onto Sadddleworth Moor where Brady strangled him.

**ABOVE:** Manchester police excavated large areas of Saddleworth Moor in the hunt for bodies.

By contrast, Myra Hindley fought for her release, claiming to be a wholly reformed character. Despite controversial campaigns to free her, she ultimately became Britain's longest-serving female prisoner and, after 36 years in jail, died of heart problems in 2002.

Still reviled because of her crimes against children four decades earlier, her passing at the age of 60 still made front-page news. One typical headline read: 'At last Myra is where she belongs—HELL.'

**ABOVE:** Police officers dig near the site where Lesley Ann Downey's body was discovered, in 1965.

**ABOVE:** Ian Brady in police custody prior to his court appearance for the Moors Murders for which he was later convicted.

# Gary Ridgway

Gary Ridgway pleaded guilty to 48 murders in November 2003, making him the worst, confirmed serial killer in America's history at that time. In a statement read in court, he said he killed so many women that he had a hard time keeping count. By way of explanation, he said he hated prostitutes and did not want to pay them for sex.

## 48 Fell Victim To 'The Green River Killer'

**ABOVE:** Gary Ridgway was a frequent user of prostitutes, but rather than pay them for sex he murdered them instead.

**The so-called 'Green River Killer',** named for the river south of Seattle where the first victims were found, had confounded detectives for two decades. The remains of scores of women, mainly runaways and prostitutes, turned up near ravines, rivers, airports, and freeways from the early 1980s. Ridgway had been a suspect ever since 1984, but it was 16 years before advances in DNA technology linked him to the bodies of four of his earliest victims.

Gary Leon Ridgway was born in Utah in February 1949 but grew up south of Seattle, where the household was dominated by his violent mother who discouraged him and his two brothers from mixing with friends. At the age of 13, Ridgway was still a bed-wetter. He was of low intelligence and did badly at school. At 16, he lured a six-year-old boy into woods and stabbed him. The victim survived and recalled Ridgway walking away laughing and saying: 'I always wondered what it would be like to kill someone.'

**ABOVE:** Investigators search for the remains of one of 'Green River Killer' Gary Ridgway's victims at an unknown location.

Ridgway got a job as a painter at a trucking company. He was married three times and fathered one child. At the time of his arrest, his third wife was still with him. His first two told police he liked sex outdoors—and detectives were intrigued to discover that these couplings took place at or near where victims' remains were found.

The hunt for the murderer began in July 1982 when the body of a 23-year-old woman was found on the bank of Green River in King County, Washington. Only one month later and half a mile away, the body of a 16-year-old was discovered.

Throughout the rest of the 1980s and 1990s, the 'Green River Killer' murdered 48 or more women in and around Seattle and Tacoma. Most of the victims were either prostitutes or teenage runaways picked up along Pacific Highway South and strangled. Their bodies, usually naked, were often dumped in clusters, sometimes posed. Ridgway would often scatter items he had collected from others, such as cigarettes, receipts, and gum, around the sites to confuse police.

It had long been a mystery to detectives as to why so many women should so trust the killer that they would accompany him to wild areas. It transpired that Ridgway carried in his pickup truck toys belonging to his son, and would show the boy's photograph to victims to put them at ease. He even took some victims to his house and showed them his son's room to demonstrate they had nothing to fear.

An FBI profile of the killer indicated that he had a

**ABOVE:** With strong evidence of his guilt in 48 murders, there was little chance of Ridgway escaping justice.

**ABOVE:** The Washington police forensic investigation centered on land adjacent to the state's Green River.

deep hatred of women, was possibly a married man who came from a broken home and probably hated his mother. It also suggested that the killer would be aged between 20 and 40, white, a heavy smoker who liked to drink and someone with a background of sexual crime. It was an accurate portrait of Gary Ridgway.

The killer's arrest in 2001 was due to improved DNA testing. Ridgway had provided a DNA sample during a 1984 investigation into the murders. That sample now linked him directly with four of the Green River victims from that period. These were the four murders Ridgway was initially charged with. When the case finally came to court in November 2003, however, it took eight minutes to read out the names of all 48 victims with whose murders he was charged.

Ridgway successfully plea-bargained to escape the death penalty and instead, in December 2003, heard King County Superior Court Judge Richard Jones hand out 48 life sentences with no possibility of parole. He was also sentenced to an additional 10 years for tampering with evidence for each of the 48 victims, adding 480 years to his 48 life sentences.

**ABOVE:** When Ridgway's court case opened the first eight minutes were spent reading out the names of his many victims.

In 2004, prosecutors released videotape of Ridgway's confessions to them. In one, he admitted responsibility for the deaths of 65 women, and in another claimed to have murdered 71. He also confessed to having sex with victims' bodies—but said he began burying the later victims so that he would resist the urge to revisit them.

# Joel Rifkin

**Joel Rifkin was a landscape gardener who murdered and dismembered at least 17 prostitutes between 1989 and 1993 sometimes storing their bodies in the suburban home he shared with his adoptive parents.**

# Man Who Kept Clippings On Killers

**Born in 1959, the son of unwed teenage parents,** Joel was adopted by Ben and Jeanne Rifkin at three weeks of age. They settled in the New York suburb of East Meadow, Long Island, where Joel, despite a high IQ, did badly at school, attributed to the constant bullying of the loner by his classmates who called him 'The Turtle' because of his shy, awkward manner and habitual slouch.

As a teenager, he visualized himself as a knight in shining armor, as this adolescent poem suggests: 'A siren temptress calls me near / a stranger beyond darkness haze / pleading from within the shadows / and though I be helpless to help her / help her I must.'

But his dreams of heroism dissipated in a failed college course and a string of short-term jobs. His only girlfriend over the next decade described him as 'depressive'. Instead, Rifkin turned to prostitutes for comfort, picking them up in Brooklyn and Manhattan.

In 1987, his adoptive father committed suicide to end the pain of cancer, thereby increasing Rifkin's depression. He became increasingly obsessed with violence, collecting books and press clippings on serial killers of prostitutes, including Gary Ridgway (see page 178) and New York's Arthur Shawcross (see page 185).

He began emulating their brutal crimes in 1989. Rifkin's first two victims have never been found or identified. He killed one prostitute in 1989 and another in 1990, dismembering their bodies and dropping the pieces into rivers or canals. Over the next four years, he is believed to have killed 15 more, sometimes taking them back to East Meadow, on other occasions killing them in his car.

Bodies were turning up in a variety of locations. One girl he strangled was found in a plastic bag, another inside a trunk in the East River. Four victims were

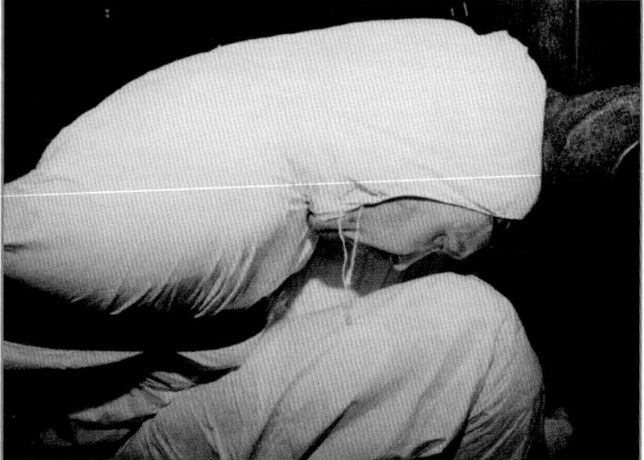

**ABOVE:** A bound Joel Rifkin is transferred to District Court on June 29, 1993 in Farmingdale, New York after confessing to murder.

**ABOVE:** Rifkin at the Nassau County Courthouse in Mineola, NY, in December 1993 for a pre-trial hearing.

found wedged into oil drums which were then rolled into creeks. Some bodies were found in the countryside, but one dead prostitute was dumped in a vacant lot at JFK airport.

Rifkin was finally caught in June 1993 when police spotted his pickup truck with no license plates. After a high-speed chase, he crashed into a utility pole directly in front of the courthouse in which he would eventually stand trial. In the back of the truck was the dead body of his latest victim, aged 22. A search of his home recovered dozens of items of personal effects of the dead girls—plus a chainsaw stained with blood. Rifkin was found guilty of nine murders in 1994 and sentenced to life.

# Danny Rolling

**Danny Harold Rolling was born in Shreveport, Louisiana, in 1954 to a police officer father who was abusive to both him and his mother. After leaving school, he failed to hold down a steady job and slid into a life of crime, being jailed for robberies. During yet another argument with his father, Rolling attempted to murder him before fleeing to the university town of Gainesville, Florida, where he was to commit some of the most gruesome murders America has known.**

## Campus Carnage Of The 'Gainesville Ripper'

**He was tagged the 'Gainesville Ripper'** in August 1990 after attacking students Christina Powell, 17, and Sonja Larson, 18, whom he savagely killed as they slept in their shared house. He placed tape over their mouths to stop them from screaming. He stabbed Sonja repeatedly and then went downstairs to rape and knife Christina before pouring washing-up liquid over her body in an attempt to destroy any DNA evidence that could identify him.

His next victim, Christa Hoyt, 18, met the same grisly end. She too was raped and her body sliced from throat to stomach and then washed in caustic cleanser, leaving a complete absence of blood.

The cleansing of the bodies became the killer's 'signature', along with the rearranging of the bloodied corpses in such a way as to highlight the carnage in the rooms. In the case of Christa Hoyt, he decapitated her and set her head on a shelf, surrounding it with carefully arranged mirrors—one positioned to reflect

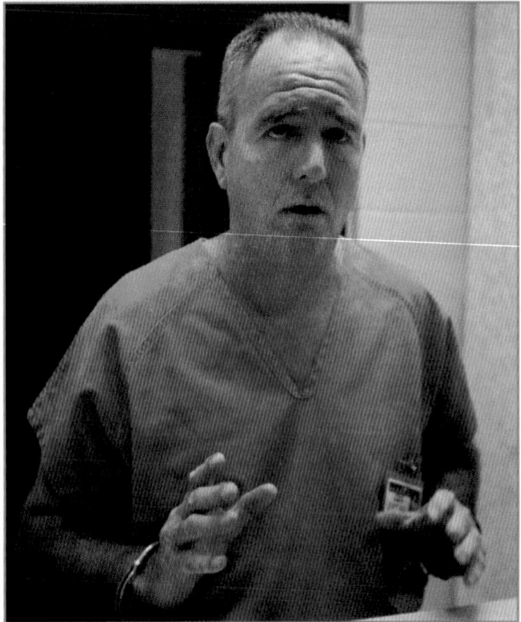

**ABOVE:** After 15 years in maximum security prison, Danny Rolling was executed by lethal injection in October 2006.

ABOVE: Rolling, the 'Gainesville Ripper', is led into court to answer for his crimes on May 31, 1991.

the grisly scene out to anyone passing by her window.

Next victim was Tracey Paules, 23, and her roommate, 23-year-old Manuel Taboada, a strapping 6ft (1.83m), 210lb (95kg) football star. They were both taken off-guard and stabbed to death 30 times. Later the same day, Rolling robbed a bank using a 9mm pistol, which police found soon afterward at a campsite where he had been hiding out. Rolling stole a car and carried out a series of thefts until he was caught after holding up a supermarket.

When police ran a check on the small-time thief, a violent past was revealed. Not only did the attempted murder of his father come to light but there were similarities between the Gainesville murders and a triple murder in the previous year, 1989, in Rolling's home town. In that case, 24-year-old Julie Grissom had

ABOVE: A spokesman for the Florida Department of Corrections briefs the media about Rolling's imminent execution in October 2006.

been stripped, murdered, and her body posed. Her father William, 55, and eight-year-old nephew Sean, who had also been in the house, had been killed, too. Tape had been used to bind them and their bodies had been cleaned.

Rolling was charged in September 1991 with several counts of murder. He pleaded guilty in court and was subsequently convicted and sentenced to death. The 52-year-old serial killer lodged a last-ditch appeal which was rejected by the US Supreme Court.

Rolling was executed by lethal injection on October 25, 2006, and pronounced dead at 6:13pm. He had showed no remorse and had refused to make any comments or offer any apology to the relatives of his victims, several of whom were present at his execution as witnesses.

# Efren Saldivar

**By their own nature, it is notoriously difficult to apportion blame in the case of hospital killings. Leading forensic scientist Henry Lee, speaking in Los Angeles after one particularly horrifying case, said murders by nursing staff were the most difficult serial killings to detect and on which to obtain a conviction. 'You have to figure out who the victims were long after they were buried,' he said. 'Then you have to link them to the suspect. Prepare to fail.'**

## Rookie Nurse Killed From The Age Of 19

The case the scientist was referring to was that of Efren Saldivar, by then known as the 'Angel of Death', who confessed to murdering 50 patients while working as a respiratory therapist in a Los Angeles hospital. Texas-born Saldivar had got the job at the Glendale Adventist Medical Center after graduating from a brief course at North Hollywood medical college in 1988. He worked the night shift, when there were fewer staff on duty, killing his patients by injecting a paralytic drug which led to respiratory or cardiac arrest.

His 10 years of quiet killing came to an end in 1998 when, acting on a tip-off from another member of staff, phials of muscle relaxant were found in Saldivar's locker. The 32-year-old nurse was taken to the local police station, where he made a confession. He said he

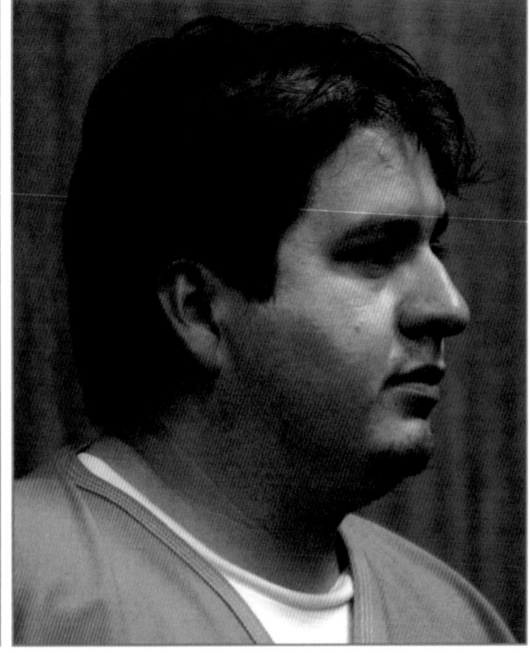

**RIGHT:** Sick respiratory therapist, Efren Saldivar confessed to killing 50 patients at a Los Angeles hospital between 1988 and 1998.

had killed his first patient a decade earlier when he was 19 and fresh out of training. The victim, an elderly woman terminally ill with cancer, had been suffering, so Saldivar suffocated her.

He claimed his next victim by introducing a lethal drug into her intravenous drip tube. His first lethal injection was in 1997. After that, he injected more and more elderly patients—according to him, picking only those who were under a 'Do not resuscitate' order. The drugs he used were Succinylcholine and Pavulon.

The case against Saldivar seemed in doubt when he suddenly recanted his confession. To gain a conviction, 20 of the most recently buried patients had to be exhumed—and six of those bodies contained large amounts of Pavulon. Presented with this evidence, the fickle nurse confessed all. He said he had killed the patients because there were too many of them and his department was understaffed.

Apart from the pathology evidence, there were two key witnesses who clinched the case against Saldivar. A fellow respiratory therapist was granted immunity in exchange for testifying that she had given him the Pavulon and knew the use to which he was putting it. A second witness, who had been a patient at Glendale in 1997, told how she had inexplicably blacked out for some hours after Salvidar had attended her.

Although his confession to 50 killings was considered to be an underestimate—some authorities putting his tally at over 100—Salvidar was charged with only six counts of murder. In court in March 2002, he pleaded guilty, having been told that he would escape the death penalty if he confessed. He also apologized to the families of those he had killed. He was given six consecutive life sentences.

# Arthur Shawcross

**Known also as the 'Genesee River Killer' after the place many of his victims were found, Arthur John Shawcross was convicted of some of the most savage slayings and cannibalistic perversions that America had known in recent years. And the fact that he was able to kill and kill again was largely down to a tragic blunder—for he claimed most of his victims after being paroled early following the murder of two children.**

## Cannibal Returned To Eat Rotting Corpses

**Born in 1945 in Kittery, Maine,** Shawcross's parents moved to Watertown, New York State, where he was a surly, aggressive child with a particularly low IQ. As a teenager, Shawcross had a tendency toward bullying and violence, and received several probationary sentences for minor crimes. In 1967, he was drafted to Vietnam, where his sadistic tendencies seem to have flourished. According to his own accounts, he raped, slaughtered, and cannibalized two Vietnamese peasant girls during a combat mission on his tour of duty.

Back on United States soil, Shawcross was well into his third violent marriage when, in May 1972, a neighbor's son, 10-year-old Jack Blake, disappeared from his home in Watertown, New York. It would be five months before the boy's body was finally located. He had been sexually assaulted and suffocated. Four months later, the body of eight-year-old Karen Hill was found under a bridge. She had been raped and murdered, and mud, leaves, and other debris had been forced down her throat and inside her clothing.

Witnesses linked Shawcross to the two murders and, in October 1972, he pleaded guilty to manslaughter. Due to lack of evidence tying him to Jack Blake's death, Shawcross was charged only with Karen Hill's killing. He received a 25-year jail sentence, of which he served 15 years.

**ABOVE:** A police mugshot of Arthur Shawcross taken in January 1990. Later that year he was convicted of killing 10 women.

Released on parole in March 1987, he settled in Binghamton, NY, but angry citizens learned of his bloody history and ran him out of town. After two other communities turned him away, desperate parole authorities finally smuggled the homicidal pedophile into Rochester, NY. Neglecting to alert the police and sealing Shawcross's criminal record to avoid further public outcry seemed the only way to keep him from being uprooted again, but this gross incompetence would later cost more victims their lives.

It wasn't long before Shawcross began killing again, but now he preyed primarily upon prostitutes. In the spring of 1988, mutilated corpses started turning up in woods and marshland, under ice and floating in streams near the Genesee River. The women had been either strangled or battered to death and most, as in the case of his first victim, 27-year-old prostitute Dorothy Blackburn, had undergone a vicious attack revealed by bite marks in the groin area.

As more bodies turned up in similar condition, detectives knew that this was the work of a serial killer, and one that indicated previous criminal or possibly military experience. Yet as Shawcross' criminal records had been sealed, he was not a suspect. Eleven victims were found dead or went missing in the space of less than two years before police finally caught up with the killer.

**ABOVE:** Shawcross after pleading guilty on first degree manslaughter in the deaths of two children, in October 1972.

**ABOVE:** A painting by Shawcross from 2001 entitled 'What Dreams Are Made Of'. It was part of a display of inmate art at the New York Legislative Office Building in Albany.

In January 1990, the body of a 34-year-old prostitute June Cicero was discovered by aerial surveillance in the Rochester area. Quite by chance, as the helicopter flew above, Shawcross was reliving the pleasure of the attack by masturbating at the bridge above where the body lay on the frozen river. His vehicle license plate was noted and he was later arrested.

Shawcross confessed to all the murders after a piece of jewelry given to his fourth wife was traced back to one of his victims. In his confession, he stated that he killed one woman because she bit him, another for trying to steal his wallet, a further was murdered because she called him 'a wimp' and one simply because she made too much noise during sex.

He admitted that he would sometimes return to his victims' decomposing remains weeks after the murder to cut out and eat pieces of the corpses, and he bragged of doing similarly disgusting things to young Jack Blake's body after killing the boy.

In December 1990, Shawcross was convicted of killing 10 of the women. His lawyers' attempts to obtain a lighter sentence—citing mental illness and blaming a supposedly abusive upbringing and a traumatic spell in Vietnam—were rejected and he was given 10 life sentences. Three months later, Shawcross pleaded guilty to strangling a further woman whose body had been found in November 1989, in woods in neighboring Wayne County and he received a further life sentence.

While serving time at the Sullivan Correctional Facility in New York for the murder of the 11 women, Shawcross complained of pains in his leg and later died from a massive coronary on November 10, 2008.

# Lydia Sherman

**In her sick and twisted mind, Lydia Sherman was taking care of her family and doing her very best for them. By the time her atrocities had been discovered, she had aided three husbands, six of her own children, and two step-children through agonizing deaths to their merciful ends.**

## How 'Black Widow' Diposed Of Family

**Born in Burlington, New Jersey,** in 1824, Lydia was married at the age of 17 to a 40-year-old New York policeman, Edward Struck, and the couple had six children in quick succession. All was well until the cop was dismissed from the force, accused of cowardice. He fell into a deep depression. Lydia could not bear to see him in such a state, and so purchased a few cents' worth of arsenic to 'put him out of the way'. He died in 1864, the doctors thought of consumption.

Finding herself a widow with six children to support—and, according to her twisted logic, having considered the best course of action for all the family—she poisoned her three youngest children. Baby William, four-year-old Edward, and six-year-old Martha Ann all died on the same day. Next of her offspring to meet an agonizing end was 14-year-old George. Having lost his job bringing in $2.50 a week, she didn't want him to become a burden on the rest of the family.

When little Ann Eliza, aged 12, took ill with fever and chills, she laced her medicine with arsenic. It took her four days to die, the cause of death being declared as 'typhoid'. Two months later, her elder daughter, also named Lydia, was struck down with fever and died in convulsive agony, again diagnosed as 'typhoid'.

With nothing to keep her in New York, Lydia moved to Connecticut and was quickly married to an elderly widower, Dennis Hurlburt. Within a year, Lydia was a widow again, a very wealthy one this time, having poisoned him, too.

In September 1870, she married Horatio Sherman, himself a widower with four children. Just two months after the wedding, Lydia dispatched baby Frankie, and the following month pretty 16-year-old Ada. The sudden death of two of his children devastated Sherman and he took to the bottle. Lydia tolerated his drunkenness for a few months but her patience ran out in May 1871, and Sherman took to his bed with stomach pains and diarrhea. He was dead within a week.

Given the frequency of tragic deaths in Lydia's past, foul play was suspected and a post-mortem was carried out, revealing a liver saturated with arsenic. Lydia's relentless murder spree was over. The 'Black Widow', as she was called, stood trial in 1872 and, convicted of second-degree murder, was sentenced to life imprisonment. She died in jail in 1878.

# Harold Shipman

**A jubilant cry of 'Yes!' rang out from one of the deceased's relatives after the guilty verdict was announced in the case against Dr Harold Shipman. Britain's 'Doctor Death' was going to prison for life. That day, January 31, 2000, ended a chilling chapter in criminal history. For Shipman's 24-year-long trail of corpses made him the country's most prolific serial killer ever.**

## 'Doctor Death': Britain's Most Prolific Serial Killer

**The doctor was convicted** of murdering 15 patients. A year later, a government report put the number of his victims at 236, of whom 218 could positively be identified. That immediately placed him just behind recent history's most prolific serial killer, Colombian Pedro López, dubbed the 'Monster of the Andes' (see page 134).

Shipman hid his murders behind the mask of a respected suburban doctor. His victims tended to be elderly females, although the 20 percent who were males included his youngest, aged 41. The doctor hoarded lethal drugs like candy and often caringly patted his victims' hands as he injected them with heroin along with an assurance that it would cure their illness or at least ease their suffering.

Dr Harold Frederick Shipman graduated from Leeds

**RIGHT:** Harold Shipman hid behind a mask of caring GP to murder at least 236 of his patients over a 24-year period.

**ABOVE:** 'Doctor Death' ended his own life while in Wakefield Prison, hanging himself in his cell in January 2004.

School of Medicine in 1970 when he was aged 24. In 1976, while practicing in West Yorkshire, he pleaded guilty to forging prescriptions and stealing drugs, and asked for 74 other offenses to be taken into consideration. He next got a post conducting baby clinics in County Durham but was supervised throughout because of his past criminal record. By the end of 1977, he was considered to have sufficiently rehabilitated himself to be allowed back into general practice and moved to Hyde, Greater Manchester, where he worked as a GP through the 1980s and 1990s. But Shipman was far from rehabilitated.

Shipman's first murder victim in Hyde was believed to have been a 76-year-old who visited him in September 1984 complaining of a cold. On a follow-up home visit, he said he found her 'lying dead on her bed'. There was then an average of one suspicious death a year until Shipman left the Hyde group practice where he was working until 1992 and founded his own surgery in 1993. Then the number of deaths escalated—eight that year, starting with a 92-year-old who was found dead within hours of a visit by Shipman.

It was neither suspicious police nor worried patients who brought Shipman's deadly bedside manner to a close. It was the intervention, in March 1998, of a 28-year-old local undertaker, Deborah Bamroffe, who decided 'there were just too many deaths for a one-

**ABOVE:** Elaine Oswald, believed to have been the first intended victim of the serial killer in 1974, arrives to give evidence against him.

doctor surgery'. She voiced her suspicions to one of the doctors who had been countersigning Shipman's deaths for cremation purposes. Within days, coroner John Pollard was briefed and he called in Greater Manchester Police. However, Shipman still managed to kill three more patients before his arrest.

One of them was a fit and active 81-year-old, Mrs Grundy, who was found dead at her home in June 1998. Shipman gave the cause of death as old age—but when it was discovered that her will left her entire £386,000 estate to the doctor, her daughter contacted police. The will had been typed on Shipman's typewriter and had his fingerprints on it. Mrs Grundy's body was exhumed and lethal levels of morphine were found.

Shipman, by then a 52-year-old married father of four, was arrested in September and brought to court in Preston the following October, when he denied one charge of forging the will and 15 charges of murdering old ladies. 'All of them died most unexpectedly,' said the prosecuting counsel, 'and all of them had seen Dr Shipman on the day of their death.' He added that Shipman's drive to kill was fed by a God-like belief that he had power over life and death.

After the jury returned guilty verdicts, the judge, Mr Justice Forbes, told Shipman: 'These were wicked, wicked, crimes. Each of your victims was your patient. You murdered each and every one of your victims by a calculating and cold-blooded perversion of your medical skills. For your own evil and wicked purpose, you took advantage and grossly abused the trust each of your victims put in you. I have little doubt each of your victims smiled and thanked you as she submitted to your deadly administrations. None of your victims realized that yours was not a healing touch.'

Shipman was jailed in top-security prisons and told he would never be released. He carried out his own death sentence, hanging himself in his cell at Wakefield Prison, West Yorkshire, on January 13, 2004.

# Joseph Smith

**George Joseph Smith, born 1872, became known as the 'Brides In The Bath Murderer' because of the manner in which he disposed of three of his five wives. The first of these spouses, Caroline Thornhill, whom he married in 1898, was a petty thief, just like her husband. They fell out, however, and she tipped off police about his crimes, resulting in a jail sentence. Once free, he sought revenge but Caroline survived by emigrating to Canada.**

## Wooing Ways Of 'Brides In Bath' Murderer

**Smith, of Bethnal Green, London,** then used a series of pseudonyms for his subsequent, bigamous marriages. Beatrice Mundy died by drowning in July 1912 still clutching a piece of soap in her hand. Alice Burnham left a large clump of hair in her death bath. Smith had taken out insurance policies on the lives of his wives and he lived well on the proceeds.

The murder of Smith's final victim, Margaret Lofty, followed an identical pattern. A clergyman's daughter, he established that she already had a nest egg and wooed her under the alias 'John Lloyd'. With a £700 policy on her life and a freshly written will safely in his hands, Smith married her on December 17, 1914. On the evening of the very next day, their landlady heard splashing noises from the bathroom and, true to form, the latest bride was found 'accidentally' drowned.

But Margaret's murder proved literally a fatal mistake for Smith. Margaret had been a bride for only one day, and her death therefore made front-page news, revealing suspicious similarities with the previous

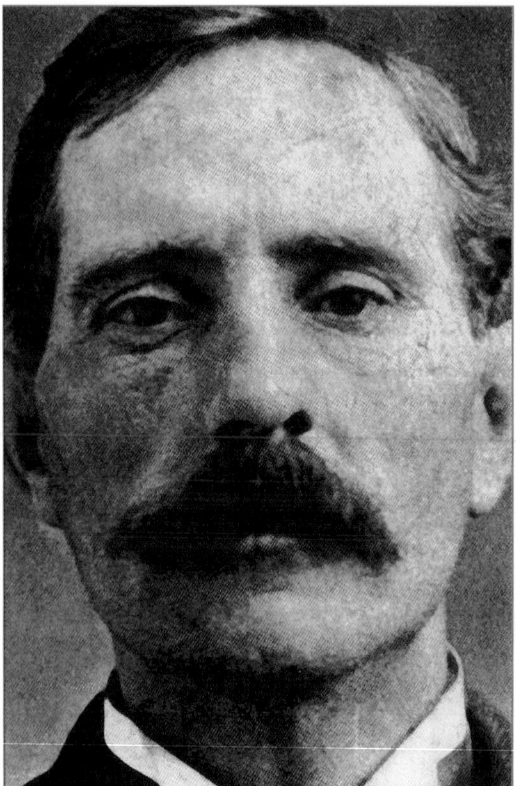

**ABOVE:** Joseph Smith was hanged in August 1913. He drowned three of his five wives in a bath tub.

deaths. 'Bride's tragic fate on day after wedding' ran one headline; another read 'Bride found dead in bath'. The reports were seen by relatives of his previous victims and police were waiting for 'John Lloyd' when he turned up at a solicitor's office to collect the money from his murdered wife's insurance policy.

The bodies of Beatrice Mundy, Alice Burnham, and Margaret Lofty were exhumed but Smith was charged with only one murder, that of his first victim. The courtroom drama was played out at the Old Bailey against the backdrop of news pouring in from the battlefields of the Western Front. One odd aspect of the case was the appearance of a bathtub which was filled with water so that a female volunteer could demonstrate how easy it would have been for a killer to drown a victim in it. She performed the task so convincingly that she passed out and had to be revived. Smith's behavior in court was outrageous, attacking the judge, jury, and his own lawyers. 'It's a disgrace to a Christian country,' he screeched at the judge. 'I might be a bit peculiar but I'm not a murderer.' The jury disbelieved him. Smith was found guilty and, quaking with fear, he was hanged at Maidstone Prison on August 13, 1915.

**ABOVE:** Smith with Beatrice Mundy, his first victim in July 1912. She was found dead, still clutching a piece of soap.

# Wayne Ford

**He was arrested after he walked into the Humboldt County Sheriff's office in Eureka, northern California, in 1998 with a woman's severed breast in his pocket and confessed to horrified cops that he was the serial killer they had been hunting. His name was Wayne Adam Ford.**

## Tearful Confessor Bore A Grisly Memento

**The previous night,** November 2, 1998, Ford, a 37-year-old truck driver, had been slumped over a motel bar, unsure whether to drink himself into a stupor or unburden his conscience. When the barman asked him if he was all right, Ford told him all he wanted to do was get drunk and blow his brains out.

His brother Rod joined him at midnight and the pair sat up most of the night talking. At daybreak, they drove to Eureka and Wayne Ford made his startling confession. Shedding tears and clutching a Bible, he said he had killed and mutilated four women and strewn their body parts in rivers and ditches across California.

To support his claim, he produced a plastic bag containing the severed breast of a 29-year-old prostitute he had picked up two weeks earlier. She had been found the next day dumped in an aqueduct after being bound, raped, battered around the head, strangled, and mutilated.

A search of Ford's trailer-park home revealed body parts of other girls in his freezer and buried nearby. He told detectives that he was in the habit of picking up prostitutes or hitch-hikers and taking them back to his trailer for bondage games. When that went too far, he would strangle them and mutilate the bodies.

Despite his detailed description, police failed to identify his first victim, killed in 1997. He said he had chopped up her body, storing her legs in his freezer and burying other parts by the banks of northern California's chillingly named Mad River. A second victim had also had a breast hacked off, which psychiatrists said was a clear signal of the killer's hatred of women.

Police had sufficient evidence for the four slayings but were still puzzled as to what had driven the quiet family man to become a serial killer.

The all-Californian boy, born in 1961 to a military family, had served in the US Marines but was discharged in 1984 following a mental breakdown. He took a job driving a bus for disabled children before

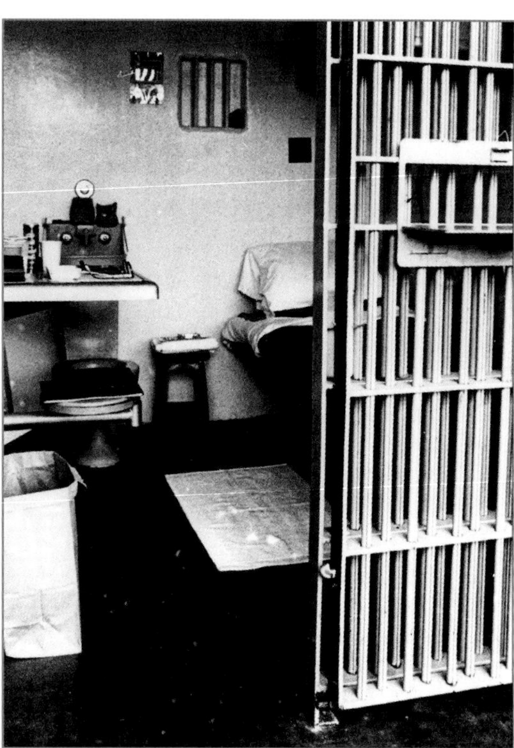

**ABOVE:** A Death Row cell at San Quentin prison, similar to that inhabited by serial killer Wayne Ford.

becoming a long-haul trucker. He attended a Bible study group and frequented a Christian bookstore. The only clue as to what may have tipped him over the edge was a feud with his estranged second wife who would not allow him to see his toddler son.

It was not until June 2006 that Ford was tried and found guilty of four counts of first-degree murder. He was sentenced to be executed—joining California's 600-plus inmates on Death Row. The case did not close then, however.

Despite his supposedly frank confession back in 1998, Ford was suspected of as many as eight other murders. Which put into question the notion that he was that rare breed, a truly remorseful serial killer.

'It's a rarity, almost without precedent,' said Mike Rustigan, a criminologist at San Francisco State University. 'Serial killers usually delight in trying to outwit the police—and they have absolutely no sympathy for their victims. To see genuine remorse in a guy capable of such savagery is extremely surprising.'

# Michel Fourniret

**In what was to be one of France's worst serial killer cases of all time, 66-year-old Michel Fourniret was convicted in 2008 of the murder, rape, and attempted rape of nine people between 1987 and 2001. The victims, mostly French girls between the ages of 12 and 21, were either strangled, shot or stabbed with a screwdriver and were, according to prosecutors, targeted in an effort to feed Fourniret's obsession with virgins.**

## Evil Abductor Who Had Obsession With Virgins

**Fourniret, a former carpenter,** forestry worker, and school supervisor, was sentenced to life imprisonment and his wife, Monique Olivier, a 59-year-old nurse, was sentenced to 28 years with no possibility of parole for helping him lure his victims to their deaths.

Fourniret confessed to his crimes after his wife gave information to the police, apparently fearing a conviction similar to the 30-year sentence handed down to Michelle Martin, wife of Belgium's notorious pedophile and murderer Marc Dutroux (see page 64). Even though Olivier claimed to have not been involved in the abductions and murders, prosecutors believed she played a vital role. Olivier, latterly accompanied by her baby son, Selim, was used as a lure to put potential victims at ease. And once Fourniret had abducted his victims, he would order Olivier to watch him rape and kill them.

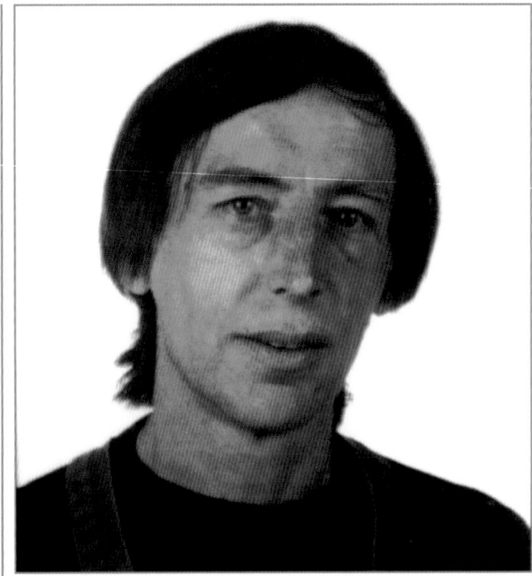

**ABOVE:** Michel Fourniret's evil lust for virgins knew no bounds and saw him rape and murder at least nine victims over a 14-year period.

Fourniret, dubbed the 'Ogre of the Ardennes' after the forested border region between France and Belgium where many of his crimes occurred, was a known pedophile and had already served three years of a seven-year sentence for trying to abduct a 13-year-old Congolese girl. Some of Fourniret's victims were buried within the grounds of his château on the Franco-Belgian border, a property he and his wife had purchased after stealing the spoils of a bank robber with whom he had shared a prison cell.

Fourniret's youngest victim was a 12-year old Belgian girl, Elisabeth Brichet, who disappeared after playing with a friend in Namur in 1989. Olivier helped to trap Elisabeth so that Fourniret could strangle her. Elisabeth's disappearance was long thought to be at the hands of Marc Dutroux—until Fourniret led police to her burial site on his estate.

Olivier was also the accomplice in the killing of Natacha Danais. At just 13, Natacha was kidnapped, sexually assaulted, and stabbed to death near Nantes, western France, in November 1990. Her body was found three days later on a beach on the French Atlantic coast. The couple had lured Natacha into their van in the car park of a supermarket and Fourniret stabbed her during an attempted rape. The coroner suggested Fourniret sexually assaulted the girl after killing her.

**ABOVE:** Police teams excavate the grounds of Fourniret's house in July 2004 looking for the remains of one of his victims.

**ABOVE:** A Belgian investigator outside Fourniret's house in Sart-Custinne, shortly after his arrest in July 2003.

During the trial, at Charleville-Mézières, northeast France, in March 2008, state prosecutor Francis Nachbar described the couple as 'inhuman and cruel criminals, the likes of which our country could have never imagined'. He called the serial killer a 'necrophiliac monster' and said that, together with Olivier, they formed a 'devil with two faces'.

The jury heard Fourniret admit that he had a sexual obsession with virgins. He told the court: 'I remain an extremely dangerous individual.' Although he was convicted of the murder, rape, and attempted rape of nine people between 1987 and 2001, it is believed the tally of his victims is higher. Fourniret faced charges in three other cases, including the 1990 killing of British student Joanna Parish, 20, who was working as a teaching assistant when she was raped and murdered.

In court, Fourniret's wife Monique proved herself a more enigmatic character. She had no prior criminal record before meeting the killer, to whom she wrote in reply to his advert for a pen pal while he was serving a prison sentence in the 1980s. Her lawyers sought to portray the short, gray-haired woman as the weak and fearful wife of an overpowering and violent husband, who would have killed her and their son if she had lifted a finger to intervene.

However, state prosecutor Xavier Lenoir described her as a willing accomplice, a 'bloody muse' and a 'deceitful witch' who displayed 'a deafening silence' to the screams of girls being raped by her husband. Found guilty of complicity to murder, Monique Olivier expressed some remorse at the end of the trial, saying: 'I regret everything that I have done. That is all.'

**ABOVE:** Fourniret leaves Dinant court house in handcuffs after an appearance in July 2003.

# Wayne Gacy

**It was a late hour to attend a job interview but 15-year-old Robert Piest was eager. As he prepared to leave the family home in Des Plaines, Illinois, on the evening of December 11, 1978, his only thought was the prospect of earning some extra cash for the school vacation. His appointment was for 9pm at the local pharmacy where his prospective employer, a building contractor, was carrying out renovation work.**

## Foul Smelling Morgue Of The 'Killer Clown'

**As he stepped out of the front door,** his mother urged him to return speedily. It was her birthday and a family party was getting into full swing. When there was still no sign of Robert by midnight, his worried mother phoned the police to report that he had not returned. He never did.

As soon as police established the identity of the builder Robert had been due to meet, they realized that this was not simply a 'missing persons' case. John Wayne Gacy, aged 36, had a long criminal record as a sexual deviant.

After Piest's disappearance, the local force decided to keep a watch on Gacy. He boldly invited the officers sitting outside his home to pop in for a cup of coffee. The cops immediately smelled a strong odor, which Gacy put down to a drainage problem. A warrant was obtained and Gacy was arrested as police began a search of the house.

What they discovered was one of the most gruesome scenes in the history of American crime. No fewer than

**ABOVE:** Several thousand protestors stage a Gacy Day Parade in May 1994, to celebrate the murderer's imminent execution.

29 bodies were found covered with lime and dirt in the 'crawl space' beneath his home and in the plot surrounding it. The victims ranged in age between nine and their mid-20s. Some were homosexuals and some were men who had worked for, or sought work from Gacy. All had endured savage sexual torture.

Gacy, born in Chicago in 1942, was the son of a Danish mother and Polish father who was abusive toward him. The young Gacy suffered from dizzy spells in his youth, the result of being hit in the head by a swing at the age of 11. Nevertheless, he completed a good education at business school, moving to Iowa and becoming a successful shoe salesman.

When he married Marlynn Myers in 1964, he took a management position in his father-in-law's fast-food business. At this point, Gacy seemed the most normal of family men. He was a pillar of the community in the city of Waterloo, Iowa, being a leading light in the Junior Chamber of Commerce. But disturbing forces were coming to the surface.

In 1968 he sexually assaulted a young male employee at the Waterloo fried chicken restaurant business which he managed. The terrified boy was handcuffed while 280lb (127kg) Gacy subjected him to a vicious attack. The boy fought back against attempts to sodomize him and force him to perform oral sex and afterward went to the police.

Gacy was convicted of sexual molestation and given a sentence of 10 years' imprisonment. He served only 18 months, his reputation as a model prisoner convincing his parole board that he was no longer a risk to the public, but it was long enough to send his life into a tailspin. His wife divorced him, taking their two children, so he moved back to his hometown of Chicago.

In 1971, he was questioned by police for trying to force a teenage boy into having sex, but the case was dropped after the boy failed to turn up for the preliminary hearings.

A second marriage, to Carole Hoff in 1972, also ended in failure. Police were later to learn how Hoff was puzzled by his lackluster sexual performance and terrified of his violent temper. Also, she complained to him constantly about the fetid smell that hung around the house.

Gacy worked to regain his social standing and began his own construction business. He became involved in the local political scene. He was also much in demand as a children's entertainer, his character being 'Pogo the Clown'. But there was nothing funny about the pornography-addicted Gacy; all the while, he was a predatory serial killer on the loose.

Shamefully for the police, one incident that could have stopped him in his tracks went largely unpunished.

**ABOVE:** Chicago Police use a ground penetrating radar device to seach for the bodies of those murdered by Gacy.

In March 1978, 27-year-old Jeffrey Rignall told police how he had been approached by a fat man driving a distinctively colored Oldsmobile car. Invited to sit in the passenger seat for a smoke of cannabis, he had been rendered unconscious when a chloroformed handkerchief was held to his face.

Rignall remembered regaining consciousness in his abductor's house where he was beaten with whips and repeatedly raped. He promised that he would leave Chicago forever if Gacy would free him, and the following morning he was dropped off in Chicago's Lincoln Park.

When police failed to launch a full investigation, Rignall launched his own search for Gacy's car and turned him in. Gacy denied all knowledge of any homosexual rape and, as there were no witnesses to challenge his statements and alibi, the incident resulted in only a misdemeanor charge.

When police raided the builder's home at 8213 West Summerdale Avenue nine months later, the stench of rotting flesh was unmistakable.

Stored in the cramped 'crawl space' were seven corpses in different stages of decomposition. Eight more were dug out of crude lime pits in the backyard. In total, the remains of 29 teenage boys and young men were accounted for in the house and grounds. Having run out of space, another five victims, including Robert Piest, had been thrown into the Des Plaines River.

Gacy's explanation for his crimes was a hatred of homosexuals. He denied that he was one himself, and pleaded not guilty by reason of insanity at his trial in Chicago in February 1980. The plea was rejected and he was sentenced to death. After a failed string of appeals, he was executed by lethal injection at Stateville prison, near Chicago, on May 10, 1994. His last reported words to a warder were: 'Kiss my ass.'

# Gerald Gallego

**Sociologists and forensic psychiatrists might argue that Gerald Armand Gallego never really stood a chance, given his difficult background. Born in 1946, he never met his father, who was locked up in San Quentin at the time. Gallego Sr. was a triple-killer who was executed in a Mississippi gas chamber at the age of 28.**

## Sick Coupling Of The Genius And The Sadist

**Gallego Jr. seemed destined** to go much the same way. A burglar at the age of six and a sexual offender at 12, he wed at 17 and by the age of 32 had married seven times. At 22, he was jailed for armed robbery. He went on the run in 1978 after his daughter complained to police that he had been abusing her from the age of six.

Thereafter, Gallego embarked on a killing spree with a strange accomplice: 22-year-old Charlene Williams, a bisexual, drug-taking violinist with a genius-level IQ. The pair would tour central California, southern Oregon, and Nevada by van, procuring victims to fulfill Gallego's sex-slave fantasies. The girls would be lured into the van with the promise of drugs, whence Gallego would pounce on them, rape them, and murder them while Charlene sat coolly in the front seat.

Their first known murders were in September 1978 when two girls, aged 16 and 17, were enticed into the van in Sacramento. Gallego repeatedly raped them throughout the night before bludgeoning them, shooting them, and leaving their bodies in a ditch.

Possibly their most horrific crime was the June 1979 murder of 21-year-old Linda Aguilar who was four months pregnant when Charlene offered her a ride at Gold Beach, Oregon. Her body was found in a shallow grave with her legs and hands tied and her skull shattered. A post-mortem revealed that the injuries had not killed her—but that she had been buried alive.

Later that month, girls aged 13 and 14 were lured into the van at the Washoe County Fair, Nevada. Driving through the desert, Charlene watched through the rear-view mirror as Gallego repeatedly raped the girls. Parked up, he then watched Charlene force them to perform sexual acts on each other before beating them to death with a shovel.

Gallego and Charlene, now bigamously married, killed 10 people before finally being identified. In November 1980, Craig Miller and Beth Sowers were leaving a dance in Sacramento when a woman brandishing a gun forced them into the back of a van. A friend tried to follow them and took down the license plate.

The kidnapped couple were later found dead in separate locations but police at last caught up with the killers. Charlene Gallego turned state's evidence when she realized she faced a death sentence. She was sentenced to 16 years in jail and was freed in 1997.

Gallego was tried in both California, where he was sentenced to death in June 1983, and in Nevada, where a year later he was again condemned to death. He remained on Death Row through a series of appeals until his death through rectal cancer in July 2002.

**ABOVE:** Gerald Gallego calmly lights a cigarette as he hears the jury's verdict in his murder trial on April 11, 1983 in Martinez, California.

# Luis Garavito

**Colombians are accustomed to violence, but not on this scale. Described in South America as 'the world's worst serial killer', Luis Alfredo Garavito confessed to the murder and rape of 140 boys over a period of five years. The number of his victims, based on the locations of skeletons listed on maps that Garavito has drawn in prison, could eventually exceed 300—possibly even beating the 'score' of his compatriot Pedro López (see page 134).**

## Is This The World's Worst Serial Killer?

**The mutilated corpses** of the mostly male victims, aged between eight and 16, have been discovered near more than 60 towns in at least 11 of Colombia's 32 provinces. The hunt for more corpses has now moved to neighboring Ecuador, where Garavito once lived.

Most of the bodies so far unearthed since his capture in 1999 had been beheaded and bore signs of having been tied up and mutilated. The killer's 'signature' method of execution meant that police forces across the country, who once thought they were seeking a number of serial killers, now know the murders are the work of only one man: Luis Alfredo Garavito, aka

'Goofy' (because of his prominent front teeth), 'The Madman', 'The Priest' or simply 'La Bestia' (The Beast).

Born in December 1956 or January 1957 in Colombia's western coffee-making region, Garavito was the oldest of seven children. He was regularly beaten by his father and claimed to have been raped by two male neighbors. Ill educated, he was considered a simpleton and managed only menial jobs. He was also an alcoholic.

He probably committed his first murder in 1992 but his killing spree started in earnest in 1994. His prey were poor or homeless children lured by the promise of money, food, drink or drugs. Many of them were the children of street vendors who had been left unattended in parks and at city traffic lights to beg money from motorists.

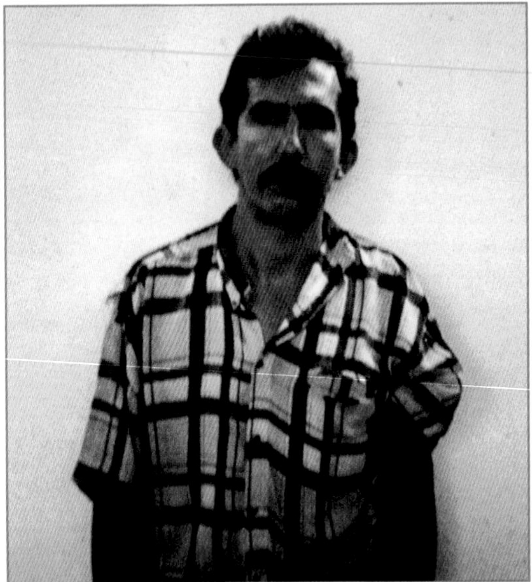

To win their confidence, Garavito would pretend to be a street vendor or beggar himself. He also posed as a cripple and even a monk, hence his nickname 'The Priest'. Led to a quiet location, he would tie the children, torture, rape, and kill them by cutting their throats. Finally, wherever possible, he would decapitate them.

Since Columbia has one of the highest murder rates in the world, little was done about the discovery of a single child's body. And since Garavito frequently moved around the country, the killings appeared to be spasmodic and unrelated.

Authorities were unaware that such a monster was on the loose until a mass grave was discovered in 1997. The bodies of 25 boys were in a ravine beside an overgrown car park in the western city of Pereira. The victims had their throats slit. Some showed signs of torture and rape.

Police initially believed the children were massacred in some sort of black magic ritual. Authorities also considered social cleansing, organ trafficking and a pedophile gang. But when another 16 bodies were found a few miles away and a further 27 in a bordering county, they finally realized they were looking for one of history's worst serial killers.

After an 18-month investigation, Garavito was arrested in the eastern city of Villavicencio in April 1999 on suspicion of attempting to rape a child. That's when the 42-year-old monster confessed to killing 140 children. He was eventually charged with murdering 189. Because the death penalty had been abolished in Colombia, Garavito was sentenced to 835 years in prison.

**LEFT:** Luis Garavito was charged with murdering 189 young boys during the 1990s, but the final death toll may prove to be far higher.

# Donald Gaskins

**Born Donald Henry Parrott Jr. in March 1933, he became 'Pee Wee' Gaskins following the marriage of his mother, the nickname being acquired because of his diminutive 5ft 4ins (1.62m) stature. With a violent stepfather, Gaskins's home life was, he later said, 'unbearable'. He grew up unruly and, as a youth, was sentenced to reform school for planting a hatchet in the head of a woman who upset him. She surprisingly survived.**

# Pervert 'Pee Wee' Claimed Over 100 Murder Victims

**'Pee Wee' might have been small** but he had a ferocious temper and was feared in the town of Prospect, South Carolina, where he drove around in a hearse and boasted about his 'personal graveyard'. Many believed him—and were right to do so.

Gaskin carried out a string of arson attacks, burglaries and an attempted murder, for which he received a prison sentence. While incarcerated, he killed a fellow prisoner whom he claimed had sexually abused him, and this earned him a further nine-year sentence for manslaughter.

Following parole in 1962, Gaskins committed more offenses, including the rape of a 12-year-old girl, and served further prison terms. Surprisingly, he was granted parole once more in November 1968, but it was not until 1975 that the real extent of his evil came to light. Police were investigating several disappearances around Florence County, including that of a 13-year-old local girl, when, because of his record and due to a tip-off by a former burglary accomplice, Walter Neeley, suspicion fell on the obvious suspect.

**ABOVE:** The 13 murders committed by Gaskins included those of a pregnant woman and her baby daughter.

**ABOVE:** Donald Gaskins directs officers to an area in Florence County, South Carolina, where human bones were found.

Gaskins was captured trying to escape over the state line and was initially charged with eight murders, most of the victims being neighbors who, in some small way, had offended him. Eventually, he confessed to 13 slayings over the previous five years. They included the murders of his own 15-year-old niece, her 17-year-old friend and, most horrifically, a pregnant woman and her baby daughter.

Gaskins led police to remote woodland east of Prospect where they uncovered the bodies of three men and three women, killed by having their throats cut or by gunshot, execution style. One mile away, the gruesome discovery was made of the bodies of the pregnant woman and her baby girl—who, at just 20 months old, had been raped.

Questioned about the abhorrent act, Gaskins described it as 'the best sexual experience of my life'. He later told police: 'I am one of the few that truly understands what death and pain are all about. I have a special kind of mind that allows me to give myself permission to kill.'

In May 1976, Gaskins was found guilty of the murders, along with his burglary accomplice Neeley, who had been charged with complicity in three of the killings. Both were sentenced to death, later commuted to life imprisonment.

But Gaskins had not yet finished killing. While serving his nine life sentences, he accepted a contract to murder a Death Row inmate, Randolph Tyner, a task he carried out with explosives, removing half his head and laughing during the process. For this, Gaskins finally received the death penalty, being convicted in 1982 and eventually going to the chair in September 1991.

Before his death, Gaskins wrote his autobiography outlining what he termed his 31 'serious murders' and introducing a further 80 or 90 recreational 'coastal kills'. Describing the first of these, carried out in September 1969, he recalled picking up a girl hitch-hiker, torturing, then disemboweling her before burying her body on the Carolina coastline. This was his first of many 'pleasure kills'.

Although the authorities have been unable to substantiate the full numbers of his claimed victims, 'Pee Wee' Gaskins still goes down in history as one of America's most prolific killers.

# Edward Gein

**Edward Gein has a unique claim to infamy. His heinous deeds were so macabre that they were used as the basis of not one but three Hollywood movies. He was the inspiration for the character of schizophrenic transvestite Norman Bates in Hitchcock's *Psycho*, as Leatherface in *The Texas Chainsaw Massacre* and, through his liking for wearing human skin, as Jame 'Buffalo Bill' Gumb in *The Silence of the Lambs*. No morbid fiction, however, could hope to match the horrors perpetrated by Gein, who exhumed corpses from graveyards and fashioned trophies and keepsakes from their bones and skin.**

## Psycho Who Inspired Three Movies

**Edward Theodore Gein** was born in 1906 to an alcoholic carpenter and a strict Lutheran mother. He and his elder brother Henry were not allowed to mix with other boys but made to work long hours on the family's poor farmstead near Plainfield, Wisconsin.

After Edward's father died of drink in 1940, his widow Augusta became even more possessive of her sons. Four years later, Henry went missing while fighting a brush fire—Edward being suspected of fabricating an 'accident'—and shortly afterward Augusta suffered a stroke. Edward nursed her for 12 months until she died in December 1945.

The large, ramshackle farmhouse now became a time capsule, the boarded-up rooms unchanged from the moment of his mother's death—with her corpse remaining behind the locked door of her bedroom.

Gein, then aged 39, grew fascinated with corpses and began making night-time visits to three local graveyards to exhume recently buried bodies and investigate their sexual organs. They were all female and, generally, they were of the age of his mother.

His sickness progressed from adorning himself with bits of their flesh to draping himself in the skin and parading around the house wearing a woman's scalp on his head, a woman's chest over his own, and women's genitalia strapped to his groin. He would arrange a dead woman's skin over a tailor's dummy as though he were somehow trying to resurrect his mother.

Finally, Gein graduated to murder. And although the tally of his two known victims would not normally qualify him as a 'serial killer', the nature of his crimes and the suspicion that more corpses may have been 'created'

**ABOVE:** Edward Gein (right) in custody. Gein was the inspiration for the character of Norman Bates in Hitchcock's *Psycho*.

rather than exhumed have made him notorious.

In December 1954, he shot bar owner Mary Hogan, dragged her body home on a sled, skinned it and dissected it. Over the next three years, he put an end to an unknown number of victims, probably including two abducted teenage girls, before striking for the last time. In November 1957, he shot dead store owner Bernice Worden, decapitated and disemboweled her corpse, then hung it like a deer's carcass.

When police visited the farmhouse, they found a stomach-churning array of artifacts, including lampshades, belts, and socks made of human skin, skulls mounted as ornaments and skullcaps used as bowls. In this weird, stinking charnel house were the remains of the two known victims, as well as body parts including those of two teenagers.

After being judged 'incompetent to stand trial', Gein was locked in a mental institution for 10 years before doctors finally gave the go-ahead for a trial in November 1968. Found guilty of murder but legally insane, he was returned to a mental institution in Madison, Wisconsin, where he died of cancer in July 1984.

# Harvey Glatman

**Harvey Glatman was an ugly, jug-eared career criminal who pretended to be a professional photographer to lure the beautiful women he would not otherwise have a chance of attracting. He murdered three times during the 1950s and earned himself brief notoriety as the 'Lonely-hearts Killer'.**

## Death At The Hands Of A Jug-Eared Monster

**Born in 1927 and raised in Colorado** and New York, Glatman exhibited sadomasochistic tendencies from his teens, when he would break into women's apartments, tie them up, molest them, and take pictures as souvenirs. He was caught in 1945 after pulling a toy gun and ordering a woman to strip. Charged with attempted burglary but set free on bail, he kidnapped another woman and molested her before letting her go. Glatman went to prison for eight months.

On his release, he moved to New York where he was rewarded for a spate of street muggings and burglaries with a five-year stretch in Sing Sing. Upon his further release in 1951, he made his home in Los Angeles, where he set himself up as a TV repairman. But the sight of California's sun-kissed beauties turned him back to crime and, using false names and credentials, he began posing as a professional photographer to entrap them.

In August 1957, he arranged to meet blonde model

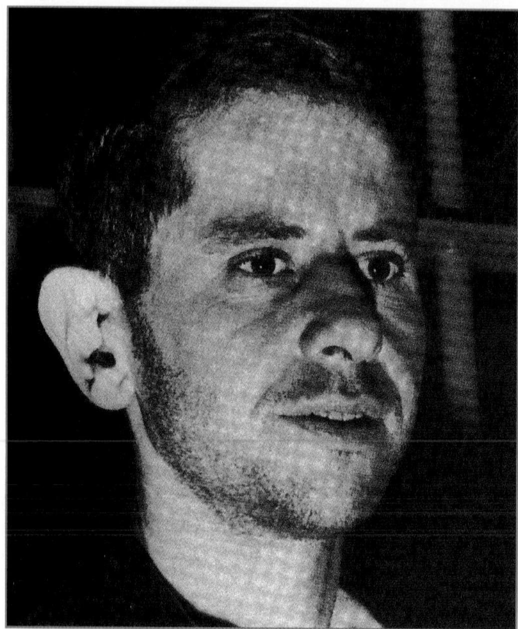

**LEFT:** Posing as a photographer, Harvey Glatman murdered three young women in the Californian desert in 1957 and 1958.

Judy Ann Van Horn Dull for a picture shoot 'for a detective magazine'. He picked her up at her apartment and drove her to his makeshift Hollywood studio where he tied her up for some bondage shots. But instead of freeing her, he assaulted her before driving her into the desert where, at gunpoint, he made her pose for obscene photographs. Finally he tied a noose around her neck and slowly throttled her.

Shirley Bridgeford, a 24-year-old divorcee, was the next to die, in March 1958. After meeting her through a dating agency, he drove her into the desert where he bound and gagged her before strangling her. He photographed her suffering right up to the moment of her death.

Four months later, Glatman talked his way into the apartment of model Ruth Mercado, 23, bound her, bundled her into his car and again drove her into the desert to meet the same fate.

The killer's last target, 27-year-old model Lorraine Vigil, managed to turn the tables on her attacker as he tried to tie her up in his car in a dark Los Angeles side-street. She bravely wrested his gun away from him despite suffering a flesh wound to the leg in the struggle. As they rolled out of the car and onto the sidewalk, they were spotted by a passing motorcycle cop who pounced on Glatman.

A search of his home revealed photographs of the three dead girls that finally sealed his fate. He confessed to the three known murders and led detectives to the bodies in the desert. Glatman was also suspected of the 1954 killing of an unidentified girl in Boulder, Colorado. Found guilty of first-degree murder, he was executed in the gas chamber at San Quentin on September 18, 1959.

# John Glover

**John Glover's series of murders earned him unchallenged notoriety as Australia's worst serial killer. He was the 'Granny Killer'. His known crimes, the battering to death of six elderly women for which he was jailed for life, were horrific enough. But police who investigated those killings believe there were many more.**

## 'Granny Killer' Was Australia's Worst

In 2005 Glover committed suicide at the age of 72 in Lithgow Prison, New South Wales. He was found hanging from a crude noose attached to a shower fitting in his cell.

John Wayne Glover, born in 1932, came from a broken family, left school at 14 and emigrated to Australia from Britain in 1957 with 30 shillings in his pocket and no qualifications other than his driver's license. In 1962, he was convicted of assaulting two women in Melbourne and put on probation for five years. Three years later, he was convicted of 'being unlawfully on premises' and was jailed, a police officer marking his file with the notation that he would probably become a 'serious sex offender'.

Glover married in 1968 and the couple moved to Sydney to live with the bride's parents in the North Shore suburb of Mosman. There is no evidence of Glover killing over the ensuing 20 years, by which time he was 57 and had two children.

Early in 1989, and soon after his mother's death, he attacked an 84-year-old, but she survived and provided police with an accurate description of her assailant. On March 1 of that year, he claimed his first murder victim, Gwendolin Mitchelhill, 82. On May 9, he murdered Winifred Ashton, 82. He struck three times in June of that year, assaulting women residents of retirement homes. In August he battered an old lady in the street, and in October, pretending to be a doctor, he molested a blind nursing home inmate. Later that month, he violently attacked another retirement home resident, smashing her face into a brick wall. The victim gave a clear description, which provided police with an Identikit picture—of a young man, possibly a teenager.

In November, he murdered Margaret Pahud, 85, in Lane Cove and the very next day attacked and killed Olive Cleveland, 81, at a retirement community in Belrose. Later that month, he followed Muriel Falconer, 93, to her home in Mosman and battered her to death, but left a clear footprint at the scene.

In January 1990, he entered Sydney's Greenwich Hospital and molested an elderly woman, who pressed an alarm button. Glover fled, downed a bottle of Scotch, wrote a suicide note saying there would be 'no more grannies', then got into a hot bath. He survived but by now was a prime suspect and under police surveillance.

Nevertheless, he managed to strike one last time, on March 19, 1990. The victim was Joan Sinclair, with whom he had a longstanding but apparently platonic relationship. He went to her Beauty Point home, smashed her head with a hammer, removed her pantyhose and strangled her with it. He then ran a bath, swallowed sleeping pills and a bottle of Scotch, slashed a wrist and waited to die. At that point, police burst in and found him in a coma.

At his trial, Glover pleaded not guilty on the grounds of diminished responsibility. A psychiatrist said pent-up hostility toward his mother and then his mother-in-law was the trigger for the crimes. Judge James Wood had no sympathy for the plea and gave Glover consecutive life sentences, ordering: 'He is never to be released.'

His wife agreed. She never went to see her husband in jail, instead leaving Sydney for New Zealand with their daughters. Her husband, she said, would be 'better off dead'. That was not the view of New South Wales Police, however. They wanted him to confess to further crimes, so easing the pain for families of at least five other murder victims.

The unsolved killings included that of a woman he knew, Sydney socialite Florence Broadhurst, found bludgeoned to death in her apartment in 1977. Seven other elderly women were murdered in similar style in the Sydney area, and two close to where Glover once lived in Melbourne.

But prison visits by murder squad detectives could elicit no more than vague hints from Glover right up until his suicide in September 2005.

# Belle Gunness

**It is quite likely that Belle Gunness got away with murder—at least 18 and possibly more than 40 of them. For, although police closed their files after finding what they thought was the lady's corpse, it is highly likely that she faked her own death and continued her murderous career 'from beyond the grave'.**

# Wily Widow Wooed Victims With Words Of Love

**ABOVE:** Belle Gunness invited many rich male suitors to stay at her home...then murdered them with a meat cleaver.

**Belle was not her real name.** She was born Brynhilde Paulstadder, a stonemason's daughter, in Trondheim, Norway in November 1859. At the age of 24, she arrived as an immigrant to the United States and married a Swede, Mads Sorenson, who died in suspicious circumstances. Although his body was later exhumed, no evidence of foul play was detected.

Sorenson was insured—and so was the couple's house, which burned down shortly afterward. Belle invested in a bakery, which also burned down, although this time the insurance company refused to pay up.

Belle moved to Indiana, where she married widower Peter Gunness, and they settled on a lonely farm near the town of La Porte. He was persuaded to take out heavy life insurance and was dead shortly afterward, his head crushed by a blunt object. According to his widow, a sausage grinder had fallen from a shelf under which he had been sitting and split his skull.

That was not the version of events that was reported by their 14-year-old adopted daughter, Jennie, who went to the police to report Mr Gunness's slaying. They did not believe her and she returned home, only to be murdered too.

Now a widow in her 50s, Gunness found difficulty making the mortgage payments on her farm, so she advertised for suitors through the matrimonial columns of newspapers. One of her adverts read: 'Rich, good-looking woman, owner of a big farm, desires to correspond with a gentleman of wealth and refinement, object matrimony. No replies by letter will be considered unless the sender is willing to follow an answer with a personal visit. Triflers need not apply.'

Gunness would invite prospective suitors to stay at the farm but insisted they bring along a sum of money to prove their willingness to invest in the property. Belle would feed them, sleep with them, then drug them. Once comatose, she would hack them to death with a meat cleaver, dispose of the body and make off with their savings.

To one deluded suitor, Andrew Helgelein, she wrote: 'My Andrew, I love you. PS, Be sure and bring the $3,000 you are going to invest in the farm and for safety's sake sew them up in your clothes, dearest.' Andrew traveled from his home in South Dakota and was never heard of again.

Belle's one-woman crime wave ended in 1908, although the circumstances surrounding her demise are still shrouded in mystery. It appears that Belle had an accomplice in many of her crimes, a hired handyman and lover, Ray Lamphere. They had recently fallen out, however, and Lamphere had gone to police with a seemingly far-fetched tale of 42 murders having been committed at the farm over the past four years. They had disbelieved him and Lamphere had been fired by his employer.

On the night of April 28, the farmhouse was burned to the ground. Lamphere was seen running from the scene and police assumed he had torched the farm in revenge for his firing. He was subsequently jailed for a year for arson. Yet it is far more likely that the arsonist had been Gunness herself. Inquiries were being made by relatives of the missing Andrew Helgelein and it is probable that she wanted to cover her tracks and simply vanish.

This she seemed to have successfully achieved. When police searched through the burned-out farm buildings, they found several bodies. Fourteen male corpses were discovered in a pigsty, and among the ashes in the basement of the house were the burned bodies of Gunness's four children. Alongside them lay the headless body of a woman—presumed to be that of Belle herself because her false teeth were recovered nearby. However, the corpse was considerably shorter and lighter than the strapping widow and there were traces of poison in it. Had Belle Gunness lured yet another victim to the farm, this time a woman, and callously murdered her alongside her own children in order to conceal her escape?

**RIGHT:** Gunness with three of her four children. Their bodies were later found, almost certainly murdered, in the basement of her farm.

# Fritz Haarmann

**Werewolf scares were common in the Middle Ages, as evidenced by the case of Peter Stump (see page 195). But this was the 20th century—and the notion of a half-man half-beast prowling the streets of a German city, even in the dark days following World War One, was an obvious nonsense.**

# The 'Werewolf' Who Bit Boys To Death

**Yet this was the period** when the defeated country found itself sucked into the kind of monster-hunting hysteria that belonged to an earlier age, as people by the dozen mysteriously vanished from the streets. At the same time, housewives became suspicious about cuts of meat they had bought—and it was suggested to police that the odd-tasting joints might be human flesh.

Soon it would be proved that a monster was indeed on the loose. His name was Friedrich 'Fritz' Haarmann, and he would soon become known by the epithets 'Werewolf of Hanover', 'Vampire of Hanover' and 'Butcher of Hanover'. His prey was young boys, over the years, his victims numbered at least 27 and possibly as many as 50.

Haarmann found his prey by prowling around Hanover's central railroad station, luring young male prostitutes and vagrants back to his apartment and killing them by biting through their throats while sodomizing them. He would then chop up his victims and sell the flesh as black market pork.

Born in 1879, young Friedrich adored his invalid mother but hated his father, a railroadman who rejected him as feeble minded. He turned to petty crime, his center of operations being the railroad station. There, even the charity workers manning the soup kitchens for the poor and homeless came to regard Haarmann as one of their team. And the police saw him as a useful source of criminal information.

They were forced to question their informer in September 1918, however, when it was reported to them that a missing 17-year-old youth had last been seen in his company, but the killer was cleared. At his trial six years later, he was to boast: 'When the police examined my room, the head of the boy was lying wrapped in newspaper behind the oven.' Haarmann now believed he was invincible. The following year he teamed up with a homosexual lover, 20-year-old Hans Grans, who picked out victims for Haarmann to abduct. Grans made a living by selling the clothes of the murdered young men—even instructing his elder partner to murder a boy 'because I like what he's wearing'.

As newspapers wrote hysterically about the 'Werewolf of Hanover', one claiming that 600 people had disappeared in the city within a year, the finger of suspicion increasingly pointed to Haarmann. In June 1924, police raided his apartment and discovered blood-splattered walls and heaps of clothes of varying sizes. Haarmann broke down and confessed everything.

At their trial in December 1924, Haarmann and Grans were jointly charged with the murders of 27 boys aged 12 to 18. Grans was sentenced to life imprisonment, served 12 years and died in Hanover in the early 1980s. Haarmann was sentenced to be executed and was beheaded by guillotine.

**ABOVE:** The 'Werewolf of Hanover', Fritz Haarmann, who murdered at least 27, and possibly as many as 50, young boys.

# Archibald Hall

Archibald Thompson Hall, the son of a Glasgow postman, experienced a taste of the good life at 16 when he was seduced by an older woman. They attended the best hotels and enjoyed the finest restaurants, and this made Hall determined that the elegant lifestyle would be his from then on.

## The Butler Did It—In Savage Style

His youthful misdeeds began modestly: collecting for the Red Cross, but keeping much of the charitable proceeds in his own pocket. From this, it was a small step to more serious theft, and in 1943, at the aged of 19, he embarked on a crime spree that earned him several brief terms in prison and two spells in mental institutions.

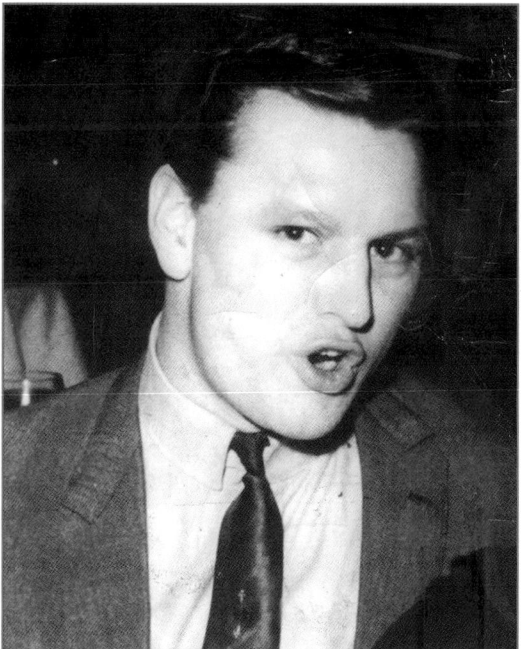

**ABOVE:** Archibald Hall, aka Roy Fontaine, a fake butler whose yearning for the high life led him to murder.

**ABOVE:** Hall committed his first murder after being released from prison in 1977.

Then, in 1951, Hall reinvented himself as 'Roy Fontaine' and became a 'gentleman's gentleman'. Using forged references, he gained positions as a butler, which allowed him to live the high life he so yearned for. Among his stunts over the next five years were intercepting an invitation to a royal garden party where he met the Queen, posing as a rich Arab to fool jewelers, and playing the part of a wealthy American to gain access to exclusive functions.

A string of thefts from his employers caught up with him in 1956 when he was given a 30-year jail term. Paroled in 1963, he was back inside the following year, only to escape and go on the run for two years before his recapture.

Free again in 1977, Hall played his usual trick of creating fake references to obtain a post as butler to Scottish heiress Lady Peggy Hudson. On his recommendation, David Wright, a homosexual lover from prison, was taken on as gardener on her Dumfriesshire estate. It was a short-term position for Wright—because when the pair fell out, Hall shot him and buried him in a shallow grave.

Hall's next post was in London with wealthy ex-MP Walter Scott-Elliott and his wife Dorothy. In ailing health, Scott-Elliott was an easy mark for Hall, who called in two accomplices, Mary Coggle and Michael Kitto, to help relieve him of his valuables. When Mrs Scott-Elliott caught the two men in her bedroom, Hall suffocated her. Then, with her body stuffed into a car boot and her drugged husband in the back seat, the three conspirators drove to Scotland, where the old man was also killed and both bodies buried in the countryside.

Hall's next victim was his accomplice Coggle who, when she refused to return Mrs Scott-Elliot's stolen jewelry, was also killed and her body dumped in a stream. The remaining two villains then returned to England, breaking their journey at the Cumbria home of Hall's hated half-brother Donald, a pedophile just out of prison. Hall placed a chloroform-soaked cloth over the man's face and drowned him in his bath.

With yet another body in the car boot, Hall and Kitto returned to Scotland where, during a meal stop, a suspicious hotel manager phoned police and the pair were arrested. Tried for different murders in both London and Edinburgh, both received life sentences, Hall's being without hope of parole.

From his cell, Archibald Hall wrote his autobiography, published in 1999 under the title *A Perfect Gentleman*. He died in prison in October 2002 at the age of 78.

# Donald Harvey

**How Donald Harvey ever got a job working in hospitals is a mystery to many of the families of those he murdered. In 1987, he confessed to killing between 85 and 100 patients. His mental state made it difficult to sift fact from fiction, however, and, in three separate trials, he was convicted of 40 murders.**

## Scourge Of The 'Angel Of Death'

**Born in 1952** and raised in Booneville, in the Appalachian Mountains, Harvey was a homosexual obsessed with the occult. He also had a fascination for all things medical. At the age of 18, he took a part-time post as a junior orderly at Marymount Hospital in London, Kentucky. There, he was later to confess, he killed 12 patients in 10 months by suffocation or removing their oxygen supply 'to ease their suffering'.

In 1972 he joined the US Air Force but was discharged less than a year later and was subsequently committed to the Veterans' Administration Medical Center in Lexington, where attempts were made to cure his mental disorders by the application of electroshock therapy. Undeterred by this dramatic treatment, Harvey disguised his recent medical history and secured part-time jobs as a nursing assistant at two Lexington hospitals and as a clerk at a hospital in Fort Thomas. There are no records of any deaths at his hands in those hospitals but the killings started anew when he moved to Ohio in 1975 to work at the Cincinnati Veterans' Association Medical Center in jobs ranging from nursing aide to laboratory technician to mortuary assistant.

**ABOVE:** Donald Harvey during a court appearance. The Cincinnati prosecutor called him 'a compulsive killer'.

Harvey literally got away with murder for 10 years. In 1985, he was searched by security guards and was found to be carrying hypodermic needles, cocaine-snorting equipment, and a .38 caliber pistol. He was fined $50 and fired but that was no impediment to his getting another hospital job. Within a few months he picked up a new post as a nurse's aide at the city's Drake Memorial Hospital.

Patients were now regularly dying at Harvey's hands, his methods including injecting air into their veins, sprinkling rat poison on their food, disconnecting life support machines, and suffocation with plastic bags and wet towels. He sometimes inserted a coat hanger into a catheter, causing an abdominal puncture and subsequent peritonitis. His favorite methods, however, were poisoning by arsenic, cyanide, insulin, morphine or fluid tainted with hepatitis B or HIV.

Harvey's colleagues were now calling him 'Angel of Death' because so many patients died on his shifts. Yet it took an autopsy on one of his victims to reveal that a poisoner was on the loose. Harvey was arrested in April 1987 and was found to have kept a diary of his crimes. It revealed that during his 10 years at the Cincinnati Veterans' Association Medical Center, he had murdered 15 patients. In his 13 months at Drake Memorial, he murdered another 23. He had also attempted to murder his gay lover, Carl Hoeweler, after they had fallen out. Hoeweler ended up in hospital but survived. So did Hoeweler's mother, to whom he had also administered poison. His father was similarly admitted to hospital but died in May 1983 after Harvey had visited him and sprinkled more poison on his food.

As Harvey's trial date loomed, the killer began a spate of plea bargaining to avoid Ohio's death penalty. In an apparent bid to demonstrate insanity, he first confessed to 33 murders, then 50, then 80-plus. The view of the Cincinnati prosecutor's office was clear, however: 'This man is sane and competent but is a compulsive killer.'

In court in Cincinnati on August 18, 1987, Harvey was given four consecutive 20-years-to-life sentences after pleading guilty to 25 counts of murder. A further trial opened in Kentucky in November, when he pleaded guilty to 12 murders at the Marymount Hospital and was sentenced to eight life terms. Back in Cincinnati in February 1988, he pleaded guilty to three further murders and three attempted murders, drawing three further life sentences. That made a total of 40 murders—far short of his last confessed total of 87. Since Harvey is notable for keeping his crimes undetected over 17 years, their true extent may never be known.

# Javed Iqbal

**Javed Iqbal never completed his 700-year jail sentence, of course. The serial killer with the most victims in the history of Pakistan was found dead in his cell in Kot Lakhpat prison on the morning of October 8, 2001. Iqbal and one of his accomplices Shahzad Sajid had apparently committed suicide by hanging themselves with bedsheets, though their deaths looked suspiciously like murder. Autopsies revealed that they had recently been beaten.**

## Letter To Newspaper: 'I Killed 100 Kids'

**Iqbal (full name Javed Iqbal Mughal),** born in Lahore in 1956, had a relatively privileged upbringing, his father being a well-off businessman in the city. His son followed in his footsteps. Yet in December 1999, at the age of 42, he wrote the most astonishing letter to a Lahore newspaper. He confessed to killing 100 children and mocked police for failing to catch him. Then he went on the run.

The fugitive became the target of Pakistan's biggest ever manhunt. It was a month before he turned himself in at the offices of a newspaper, telling journalists that he feared that the police would kill him. He allegedly confessed: 'I have no regrets. I killed 100 children. I could have killed

**RIGHT:** Javed Iqbal was Pakistan's most prolific serial killer. 'I killed 100 children', he boasted. 'I could have killed 500.'

500. This was not a problem, nor was the money. But I pledged to kill 100 and I never wanted to violate this.'

Although he later reneged on his confession, the evidence against him was overwhelming. In a sickening rampage, he had plucked children from the streets of Lahore, sexually abused them, throttled them, then hacked their bodies to bits. The 100 he had killed had all been aged between six and 16. In his letter, he had claimed to have strangled and dismembered the victims, mostly runaways and orphans, and disposed of their bodies using vats of hydrochloric acid. He had then dumped the remains in a river.

Police who swooped on his three-bedroom apartment found bloodstains on walls and floors and on the chain with which he had strangled many of his victims. There was a huge vat of acid but the remains of only two children. However, there were photographs of some of the missing youngsters. Tearful parents were able to identify only 25 out of the 100 ill-fated children, mainly by their belongings which the murderer had kept in five sacks.

Four accomplices, teenaged boys who had shared Iqbal's home, were arrested. One of them died in police custody, apparently by jumping from a window. When the remaining three appeared in court with Iqbal in March 2000, they pleaded not guilty to charges of murder, abduction, and sodomy. Astonishingly, so did Iqbal himself.

At their trial, the court heard evidence that one of Iqbal's young helpers, 19-year-old Shahzad Sajid, had purchased sulphuric and hydrochloric acid to fill his master's vats. On March 16, 2000, Iqbal was found guilty of 100 murders and Sajid of 98. The third accused, aged 15 at the time of his arrest, was found guilty of complicity in 13 killings and the youngest boy, then just 13, of aiding in three killings. The two minors were given extended jail sentences of 162 and 42 years respectively.

The judge then sentenced Iqbal and Sajid to life sentences, in the ringleader's case specifically 700 years, being seven years for each of the bodies he had dissolved in acid. He added that he wished he could have made the punishment fit the crime under Islamic 'Qisas' law—by having the pair strangled in a public park in front of their victims' families, cut into 100 and 98 pieces respectively, and thrown into an acid bath.

# Colin Ireland

**Colin Ireland made the leap from morbid daydreamer to serial killer as a conscious lifestyle choice. Labeled London's 'Gay Slayer' in the tabloid press, he reveled in his notoriety. As his crimes were reported in the newspapers, he would telephone detectives to taunt them. 'I've got the book,' he once said. 'I know how many you have to do.' The 'book' was the FBI handbook which stated that only someone who had murdered 'one over four' could count as a serial killer. Colin Ireland was desperate to achieve that level of infamy—which is why, after his fifth victim, he jubilantly boasted: 'I've done another one.'**

## Sick Revenge Of The Gay Slayer

**Ireland was a burglar and robber** who decided to become a serial killer as a New Year resolution at the beginning of 1993. With two failed marriages behind him, he claimed to be 'a normal guy'—but his obsessive hatred of homosexuals proved him otherwise. The survival enthusiast launched his vendetta against them after being fired at Christmas 1992 from the night hostel for the homeless where he worked in Southend, Essex, following a row with a gay man.

Intent on revenge, he began frequenting the

Coleherne pub, in London's Earl's Court where, on March 9, 1993 he met 45-year-old theater director Peter Walker and was invited back to his apartment for a sadomasochistic sex session. There, Ireland bound him, whipped him, placed a plastic bag over his head and suffocated him. Two days later, he rang the Samaritans charity to request someone go round to the address to feed Walker's two pet dogs.

**ABOVE:** Police mugshot of 'gay slayer' Colin Ireland, who decided to become a serial killer as a New Year's resolution in 1993.

Ireland struck again on May 29 after being invited to the apartment of 37-year-old librarian Chris Dunn. Ireland handcuffed him to his bed, beat him with a belt and held a cigarette lighter to his testicles before strangling him.

Ireland's next fatal Coleherne assignation was with Perry Bradley III, 35-year-old son of a US Congressman, who invited the killer back to his stylish apartment in Kensington on June 4. Bradley agreed to be tied up and handcuffed to the bed but was then strangled. Ireland's pick-up four days later followed a similar pattern. Andrew Collier, a 33-year-old warden at an old people's home, ended up being spread-eagled on his own bed, beaten, and strangled.

Encouraged by the way his crimes were being reported but frustrated that police had not taken his 'crusade' sufficiently seriously, Ireland phoned Scotland Yard and again taunted them: 'Doesn't the death of a homosexual man mean anything? I will do another. I have always dreamed of doing the perfect murder.'

Ireland's final murder was far from perfect, however. On June 13, he tortured and strangled Emmanuel Spiteri, a 42-year-old chef. But within days, police knew the face of his killer, because the pair had been caught on a security camera. When they apprehended Ireland, they recognized his voice from the anonymous phone calls. A single fingerprint he had left at Collier's apartment was further evidence.

At the Old Bailey in December 1993, Ireland was handed five life sentences after Lord Justice Sachs told him: 'The fear, brutality, and indignity to which you subjected your victims are almost unspeakable. You expressed a desire to be regarded as a serial killer. That must be matched by your detention for life.'

# Jack The Ripper

**One of the most infamous serial killers, yet with only five murders to his credit over a relatively brief period of less than three months, Jack the Ripper or the 'Whitechapel Murderer' still fascinates and mystifies experts and amateur sleuths alike. More than a century later, researchers pour over the gory evidence and clues he left behind, trying to put a name to this savage slayer of the East End of London.**

# The Unanswered Question: Who Was 'Jack The Ripper'?

**What is certain, from the surgical precision** the Ripper used to mutilate and disembowel his victims, is that he (or even she) was no stranger to anatomy or handling a scalpel. Each victim had her throat slashed, was disemboweled, and her entrails removed.

Jack first struck on August 31, 1888, the victim being a 42-year-old prostitute, Mary Ann Nichols, known as 'Pretty Polly'. The police surgeon reported that 'only a madman could have done this' and commented on the skill with which he had used his knife. Local residents were so upset by the murder that they petitioned to have their street renamed. It was duly retitled Durward Street but no longer exists.

ABOVE: Bucks Row, renamed Durward Street, where the body of the Ripper's first victim, Mary Ann Nichols, was discovered.

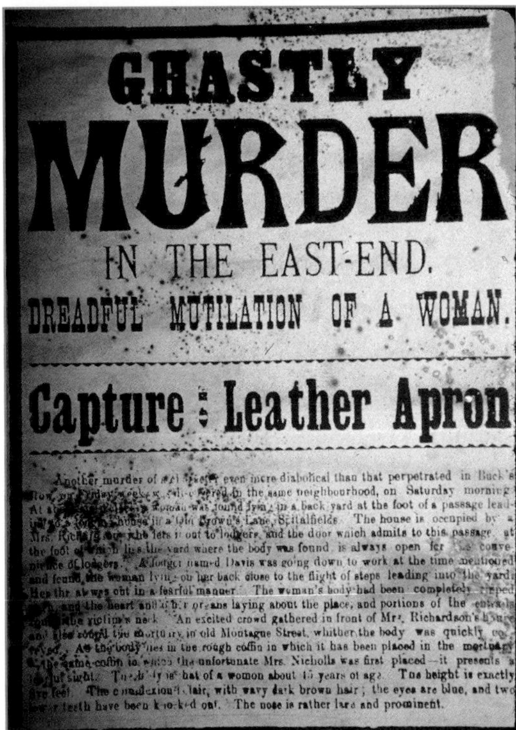

GHASTLY MURDER

IN THE EAST-END.

DREADFUL MUTILATION OF A WOMAN.

Capture : Leather Apron

Another murder of [illegible] even more diabolical than that perpetrated in Buck's Row [illegible] in the same neighbourhood, on Saturday morning. At [illegible] woman was found lying in a back yard at the foot of a passage leading [illegible] house in [illegible] Brown's Lane, Spitalfields. The house is occupied by a Mrs. Richardson, who lets it out to lodgers, and the door which admits to this passage, at the foot of which lies the yard where the body was found, is always open for the convenience of lodgers. A lodger named Davis was going down to work at the time mentioned and found the woman lying on her back close to the flight of steps leading into the yard. Her throat was cut in a fearful manner. The woman's body had been completely ripped [illegible] and the heart and other organs laying about the place, and portions of the entrails [illegible] the victim's neck. An excited crowd gathered in front of Mrs. Richardson's house and also round the mortuary in old Montague Street, whither the body was quickly conveyed. As the body lies in the rough coffin in which it has been placed in the mortuary [illegible] the same coffin in which the unfortunate Mrs. Nicholls was first placed — it presents a fearful sight. The body is that of a woman about [illegible] years of age. The height is exactly five feet. The complexion is fair, with wavy dark brown hair; the eyes are blue, and two lower teeth have been knocked out. The nose is rather large and prominent.

ABOVE: A newspaper report on the death of Annie Chapman, on September 8, 1888.

Just a week later, Jack struck again, butchering 47-year-old 'Dark Annie' Chapman. Her disemboweled corpse lay alongside her few paltry possessions and her still-steaming entrails. Following this murder, a Fleet Street newspaper received a letter purporting to be from Jack. He told how he was targeting prostitutes and wouldn't stop until he was caught. He also described how he would cut the ears off his next victim, 'just for jolly'.

Victim Number Three was 44-year-old Elizabeth 'Long Liz' Stride, found in Whitechapel on September 30. Although her throat was cut, her body remained intact, leading the police to believe Jack had been disturbed. However, the very same day, he struck again. Catherine Eddowes, 46, a drunkard recently released from police cells after causing an affray, was discovered

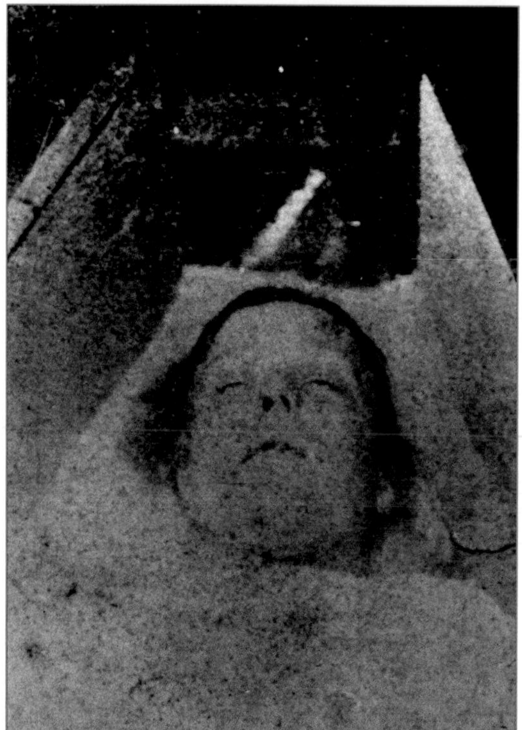

**ABOVE:** A mortuary photograph of 42-year-old prostitute Mary Ann Nichols, known as 'Pretty Polly'.

disemboweled, with her intestines draped over her shoulder. As promised, her ears were missing and her face had been hacked off. A chalk message was scrawled on a nearby wall: 'The Jewes (sic) are not men to be blamed for nothing.'

This fueled a theory that the murders were being committed by a Jewish ritual slaughterman. Others believed the killer must be an insane surgeon, or possibly a butcher. Indeed, Inspector Robert Sagar, a leading officer in the investigation, later revealed that a chief suspect lived in Butcher's Row, Aldgate. He was kept under close surveillance, but his friends committed him to a private asylum. After his incarceration, the killings stopped.

Mary Kelly, at age 25 the Ripper's final and youngest victim, met her grisly end on the night of November 9 in her own apartment, giving Jack plenty of time to mutilate her body in private. Her horrifying remains were discovered the next day by her landlord when he called to demand his rent. After this final murder, London waited with baited breath, but the killings had ended.

Fascination with the case for modern-day criminologists has never faded. There have been endless publications and television investigations on the grisly subject, all speculating on Jack's identity.

Several authors favor Montagu John Druitt, an impoverished barrister with some medical training. His body was found floating in the Thames a few weeks after Mary's murder. Another theory is that Jack was

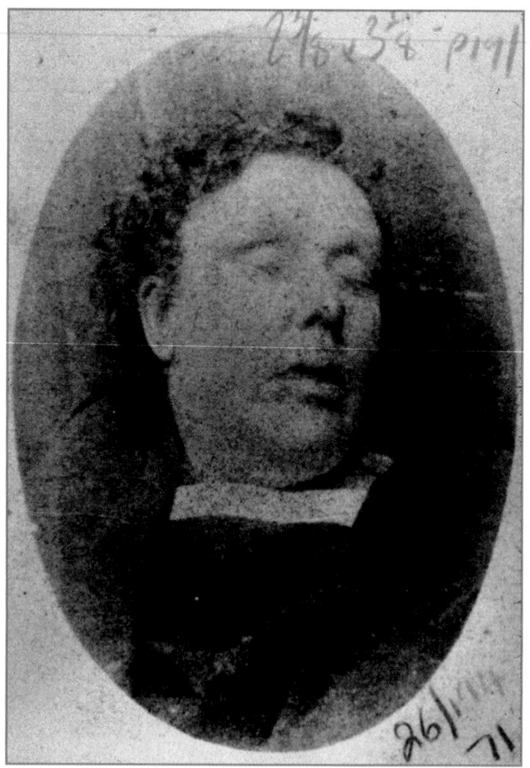

**ABOVE:** The body of Annie Chapman was discovered alongside her steaming entrails, meaning she was very newly killed.

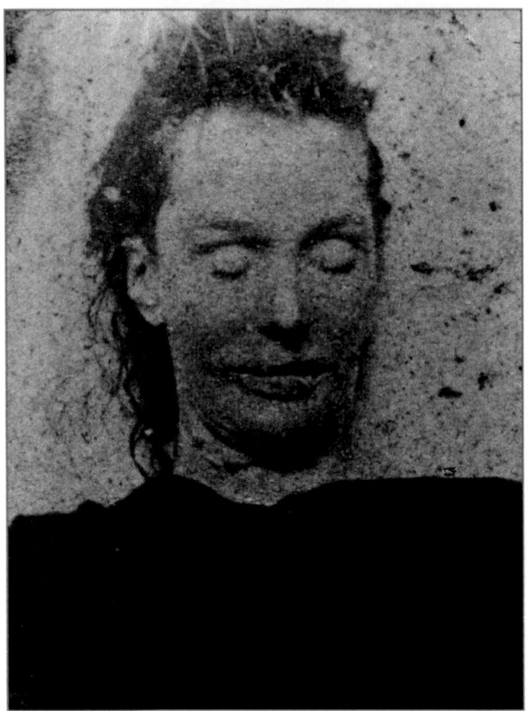

**ABOVE:** The corpse of Elizabeth Stride. She had her throat slit but was not mutilated, leading police to believe the killer was disturbed.

really Jill, a twisted midwife and abortionist. Other names include William Bury, who was hanged for murdering his prostitute wife five months after the last Ripper murder, and Aaron Kosminski, a Polish Jewish hairdresser known to be a prostitute hater. Even Prince Albert, a grandson of Queen Victoria, fell under suspicion. It was believed that he had contracted venereal disease which sent him insane.

Author Melvin Harris named Robert D'Onston Stephenson as his prime suspect in his respected book *The True Face of Jack the Ripper*. Stephenson was obsessed with black magic, had some medical experience, and had boasted of killing a black woman in West Africa. Harris believes Stephenson killed his wife, who disappeared in 1887, perhaps giving him the taste for murder. Stephenson became a self-professed expert on the Ripper murders, even having detailed articles published on the subject.

A diary discovered in 1993 in Liverpool was said to prove that James Maybrick, a wealthy cotton broker, had committed the atrocities. Crime writer Patricia Cornwell suspected Walter Sickert, an artist whose works reflected the murder scenes. In 1996 an American doctor named Tumblety was implicated by a television documentary, which suggested he killed after discovering his wife was a prostitute. His effects upon his death contained a collection of preserved female reproductive organs.

The mystery intrigues thousands each year who come to visit the capital and join one of the guided tours of the area where Jack dispatched his victims. But after so long a gap and so much speculation, the question remains unanswered: Who was Jack the Ripper?

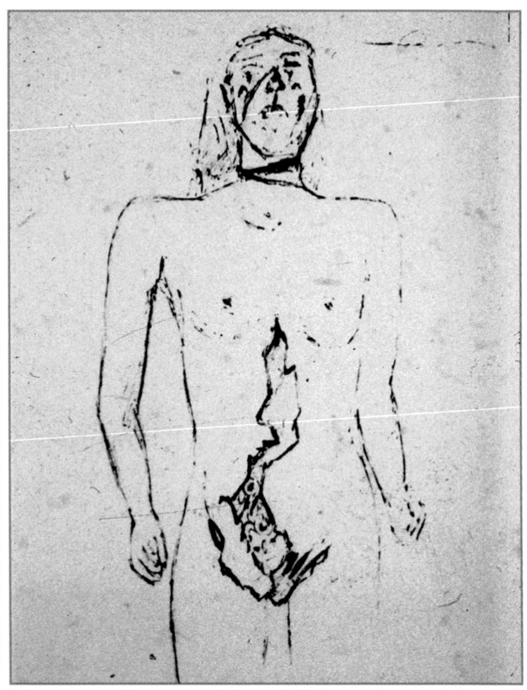

**ABOVE:** A mortuary sketch of the violated body of the Ripper's penultimate victim, Catherine Eddowes.

# Jack The Stripper

**Beneath the glitz and glamor of the swinging Sixties, London was a city in fear. Seventy years after Jack the Ripper conducted his reign of terror, killing prostitutes in the East End, the body count had begun again. And, like his mysterious predecessor, this new butcher, nicknamed 'Jack the Stripper', was never caught.**

## Did 'Jack The Stripper' Die Of Shame?

**The first possible 'Stripper' victim** was prostitute Elizabeth Figg, dragged out of the River Thames in June 1959. She had been strangled. Another probable victim was 22-year-old Gwyneth Rees, found in a shallow grave on the banks of the Thames in November 1963. She had been sexually assaulted and was naked apart from one stocking.

In February 1964, the body of Hannah Tailford, aged 30, was recovered from the river. She was naked apart from her stockings, her panties having been stuffed down her throat. In April, when the nude body of yet another street girl, 26-year-old Irene Lockwood, was found floating in the river, alarm bells began to sound at Scotland Yard. At this stage, although the incidents were

**ABOVE:** Detective Superintendent William Marchant of Scotland Yard holds up an Identikit picture of his prime suspects.

**ABOVE:** A policeman and young volunteers near the spot on the Thames towpath where the body of Gwyneth Rees was discovered.

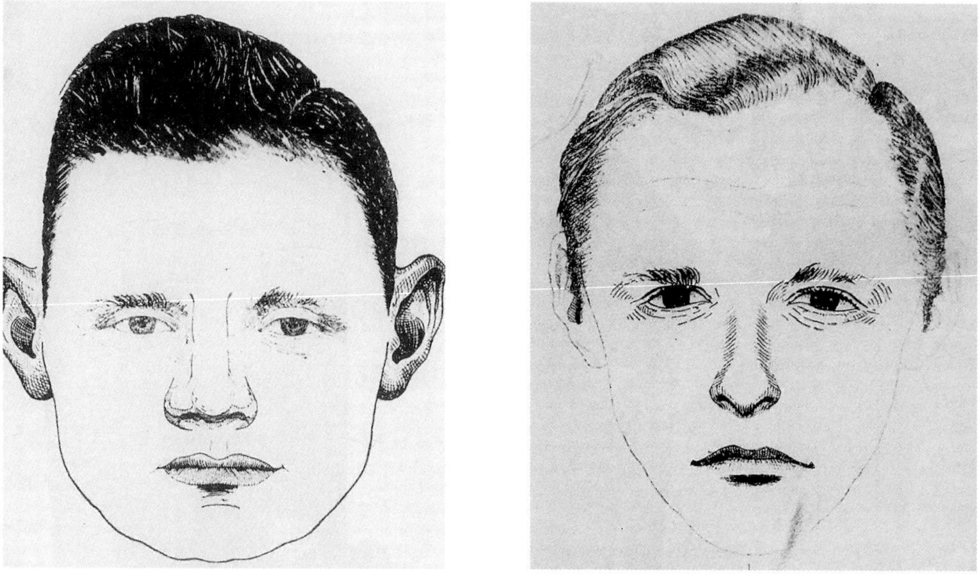

**ABOVE:** As the Stripper was never caught, it is not known if these Identikit images were a good likeness.

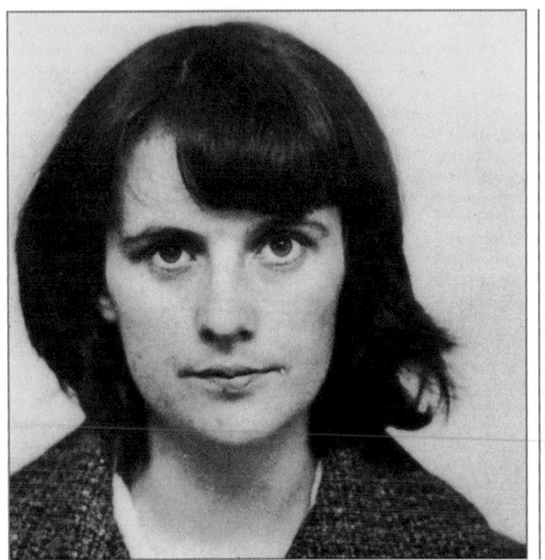

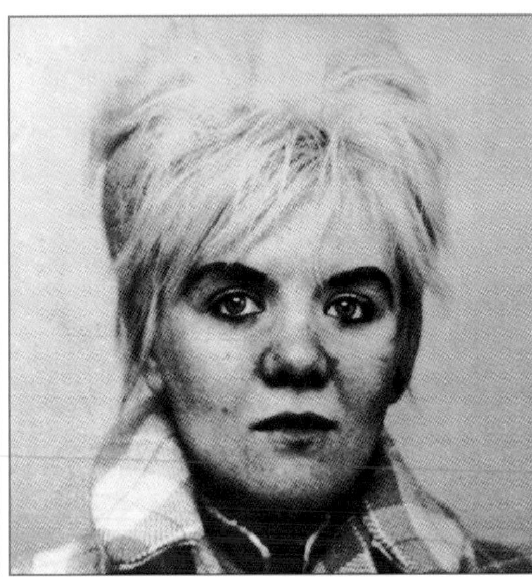

**CLOCKWISE FROM TOP LEFT:** Gwyneth Rees, discovered on a towpath in November 1963; Irene Lockwood, whose naked body was found floating in the Thames in April 1964; 21-year-old prostitute Margaret McGowan; and Bridget O'Hara, the Stripper's final victim.

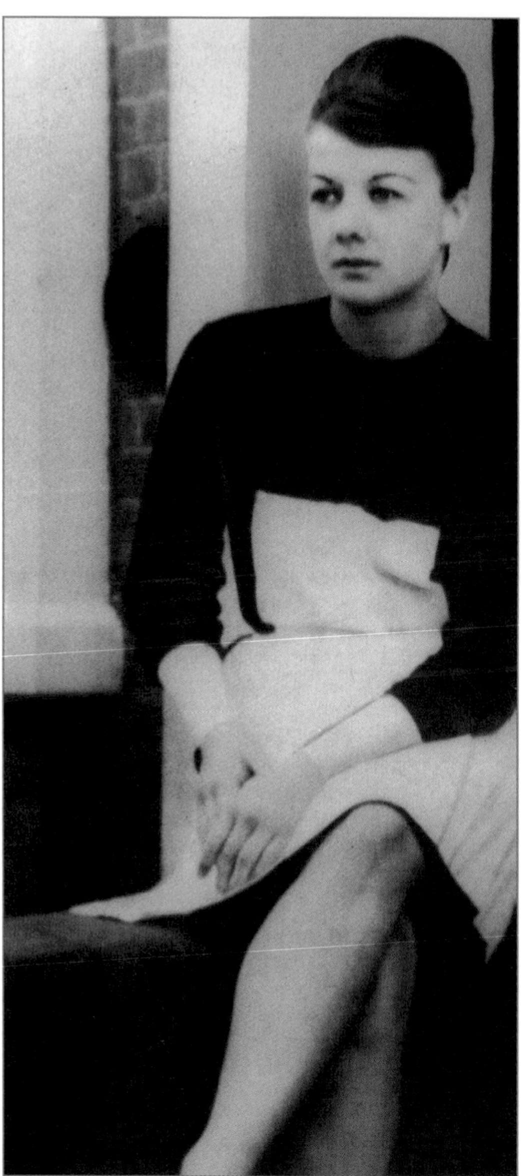

**ABOVE:** Prostitute Helen Barthelemy, whose naked body was found in a London sports field on April 24, 1964.

**ABOVE:** Policemen guard a spot on the edge of a North Acton playing field where the corpse of Bridget O'Hara was found.

concentrated within a few miles of each other in West London, there was no firm link between the victims.

That same month, Helene Barthelemy, age 20, became the first victim found away from the river. Her naked body had traces of multi-colored spray paint, suggesting it had been kept in a paint store before being dumped beside a sports field. In July, 21-year-old Mary Fleming was discarded, nude and lifeless, on a garage forecourt, her body bizarrely arranged with legs crossed and chest slumped forward. The body of Margaret McGowan, 21, was found in November with the familiar traces of paint on her skin. Last to die was 27-year-old Bridget O'Hara, found in February 1965 in shrubbery on an industrial estate. Her corpse was partially mummified, as if it had been stored in a warm, dry place.

Police now had their first lead. The Heron Trading Estate, where Bridget's body had been dumped, contained a car body-shop from which flecks of paint were emitted through an air extractor. They questioned all 7,000 workers on the estate without success.

Like the 'Jack the Ripper' killings, the 'Stripper' reign of terror seemed to cease on its own, and there were few solid clues for police to follow. But the policeman in charge, Chief Superintendent John Du Rose, subsequently professed his certainty that the killer was a security guard on the Heron Trading Estate, his rounds including the paint store where at least some of the bodies may have been stored after death. In March 1965, a month after Bridget's murder, just such a guard gassed himself, leaving a note saying: 'I cannot stand the strain any longer.'

Pointing to the man's guilt, Du Rose wrote in his memoirs, *Murder Was My Business*: 'The man I wanted to arrest took his own life… (but) because he was never arrested or stood trial, he must be considered innocent—and will therefore never be named.'

However, the cessation of the crimes is not proof, and it is still unclear whether the murders listed above are the work of one man or more. Police put the killer's tally at a certain five, a probable six, and a possible eight. But there remains doubt over the numbers because the first possible victims did not entirely fit the killer's modus operandi: asphyxiation during sex. For this reason, the Scotland Yard file on 'Jack the Stripper' remains open to this day—just as it does on his more famous namesake 'Jack the Ripper'.

# Hélène Jégado

**An illiterate French peasant girl, Hélène Jégado once complained: 'Wherever I go, people died.' They certainly did—because she poisoned them, her victims including her masters, mistresses, their relatives, her fellow servants, and her own sister. As many as 36 people are known to have succumbed to her habit of lacing their food and drink with arsenic.**

## 'Wherever I Go, People Die'

**Born in Lorient, Brittany,** in 1803 and orphaned in childhood, Hélène entered a convent as a novice when she was in her early 20s. She was expelled from her first convent for stealing and from a second convent when the nuns suspected they were being poisoned. They did not inform the authorities, thus failing to save many innocent lives.

Apart from her spells in holy orders, Jégado worked throughout the region as a domestic servant, usually for members of the clergy. The seemingly pious servant could not resist stealing from her venerable masters, however, and she covered up her petty thieving by poisoning potential witnesses. Jégado would mix arsenic with their food and, upon their agonizing deaths, would go into convincing mourning.

Her first suspected poisoning was in 1833 when she was working for a family in Guern, Brittany. In the space of three months, seven members of the household and their house guests died suddenly, including the parish priest and her own visiting sister. Her apparent sorrow and pious behavior was so convincing she was not suspected. Coming shortly after a cholera epidemic the previous year, the deaths were attributed to natural causes.

After an initial spate of killings between 1833 and 1841, Jégado seems to have stopped for eight years before a final spree starting in 1849. That year, while working as cook for a family in Rennes, Jégado was fired for theft but, before leaving, poisoned the entire

household. All recovered, but in her next job in the city, working for a university professor, two of his servants died mysteriously. An autopsy revealed arsenic in the second victim's body and Jégado was suspected.

Her mistake was protesting her innocence too volubly, revealing details of the murders that had yet to be put to her. Initially accused of 17 killings, the poisoner was eventually brought to court in December 1851 on three charges of murder and three of attempted murder. Her behavior in court was bizarre, from pronouncements of innocence to loud and violent outbursts against her accusers.

She was led to the guillotine on February 26, 1852, and executed in front of a large crowd in the town center of Rennes.

**LEFT:** An engraving of the execution, by guillotine, of serial poisoner Hélène Jégado.

# Genene Jones

**Genene Jones was a pediatric nurse who is feared to have lethally injected up to 47 infants and children in her care over a four-year span in clinics around San Antonio, Texas, in the early 1980s. Jones, it appeared, thrilled in putting children in mortal peril and thrusting herself into the role of heroine when they pulled through. Sadly, many did not.**

## Tiny Innocents Fell Victim On The 'Death Shift'

**Jones had always been viewed** by many of her colleagues as a strange character. Born in 1950, her nursing career started shakily, with her having to leave a number of nursing positions because of her difficult and sometimes aggressive behavior. Despite this, she landed a job in the intensive care section of the pediatric unit of Bexar County Medical Center Hospital. There, it was apparent to colleagues from the onset that she was odd. She was described variously as an unlikeable character, one who wouldn't take orders and a 'bragging attention seeker'.

It was noted by hospital staff that when a baby died, Jones would be grief-stricken as if it were her own child. She would sit by the body for hours and insist on taking it to the morgue herself. Despite her peculiar behavior, she had the support of her Head Nurse, who liked and protected her. This, it appears, gave Jones a feeling of invincibility.

In 1981, Jones was granted authority to oversee the hospital's sickest children, giving her access to an unlocked cabinet of freely available medications on the ward. It was not long before babies started dying on her shifts—at one point as many as seven in two weeks. The babies had been admitted because of common childhood symptoms such as fevers, vomiting or diarrhea but, while in Jones's care, they developed unexplained seizures and went into cardiac arrest.

One of those babies was month-old Rolando Santos, who was being treated for pneumonia. His unexplained cardiac arrest, extensive bleeding, hemorrhaging, and finally coma all occurred or intensified on Jones's shifts. The baby recovered only when he was placed under 24-hour surveillance.

**ABOVE:** Many of the babies in the care of Genene Jones suffered cardiac arrest. During one two-week spell in 1981 she killed seven.

Jones's on-duty hours became known as the 'Death Shift', because of the many occurring resuscitations and deaths. Her boss, Dr. James Robotham, head of the pediatric unit, made a formal complaint about her after an autopsy on one of the babies in her care revealed traces of Herapin, a drug that causes the heart to stop. Tragically, hospital administrators decided not to follow up on an investigation that could draw negative attention to their hospital, but they asked for the drug to be carefully monitored within the ward.

Further infant deaths continued but, with Herapin restricted, toxic amounts of another drug, Dilantin, began to come up in laboratory tests. When investigators failed to pin the deaths on just one nurse, a staff restructure was ordered and Jones was moved away from pediatrics.

She immediately resigned and, in 1982, she joined a newly opened pediatric clinic in Kerrville, Texas. After she started work there, seven children succumbed to seizures in a two-month period, culminating in the death of 15-month-old Chelsea Ann McClellan, who was treated by Jones in a routine check-up.

As with all the other six babies who had unexpected seizures, Chelsea had immediately been transferred to Kerr County's Sid Peterson Hospital. From the sheer volume of children admitted, staff there became suspicious, especially since the babies normally recovered quickly once in their care.

A doctor at Sid Peterson Hospital investigated the deaths and discovered a similar spate of emergencies at Bexar County Medical Center Hospital where Genene Jones had previously worked. At last the finger of suspicion was pointed at the 'Death Shift' nurse.

Chelsea's body was exhumed in October 1982 and it was found that a powerful muscle relaxant, Succinylcholine, had been injected. In February 1983, a grand jury was convened in San Antonio to look into a shocking total of 47 suspicious deaths of children at Bexar County Medical Center Hospital. All had occurred over a four-year period coinciding with Jones's tenure at that facility.

Jones was finally indicted on charges of poisoning Chelsea McClellan and went on trial for that single murder in January 1984. She was sentenced to 99 years in prison and earned another 60 years in a second trial the same year when she was found guilty of injuring Rolando Santos by injection.

Jones's final death count may never be known because hospital officials at Bexar County Medical Center Hospital shredded records of her employment and activities, thus destroying crucial evidence that was under the grand jury's subpoena. But it has been speculated that Jones may have murdered almost 50 helpless infants dating back to the beginning of her nursing career in 1977.

Jones will serve only one-third of her sentence because of a law in place at the time to deal with prison overcrowding, meaning she will receive automatic parole in 2017. She is currently eligible for early parole every two to three years, but has been constantly denied it.

# Patrick Kearney

**Patrick Kearney became known as the 'Trash Bag Killer' and the 'Freeway Killer' because his victims were found scattered along Californian roadsides. The first epithet is the one that has stuck—mainly because, in the sick 1970s, there were so many murderers roaming the United States West Coast highways. 'Freeway Killer' is a nickname Kearney had to share with two other separate serial killers, William Bonin (see page 23) and Randy Kraft (see page 122).**

## Dismembered Bodies Were Mark Of The 'Trash Bag Killer'

**Born in Texas in 1940,** Patrick Wayne Kearney was a sickly child who was bullied at school. He was to admit years later that he fantasized about killing people from his teen years. After a brief marriage ended in divorce, he moved to California and took a job in Los Angeles as an electronics engineer for Hughes Aircraft Co. He was withdrawn and avoided small talk with colleagues.

He killed his first victim, a hitch-hiker, around 1965 and claimed several more victims over the next two years before he teamed up with a younger, homosexual lover, David Hill, and the pair moved to a rundown house at Redondo Beach.

The California 'trash bag' case officially opened on April 13, 1975, when the mutilated remains of 21-year-old Albert Rivera were discovered near San Juan Capistrano. Over the next seven months, five more bodies were found dumped between Los Angeles and San Diego. All the victims were drifters or young men who frequented gay bars. All came to a similar end, stripped naked, shot in the head with a small-caliber gun, dismembered, and their body parts packaged in plastic garbage bags which were left by the roadside.

As the number of corpses continued to mount, detectives realized that the abduction of gay men seemed to be linked to the company of two particular, mysterious prowlers, but they had no idea of their identities. The last known victim of Kearney and Hill was 17-year-old John LaMay, who left his home in March 1977 to meet an acquaintance he had named to his parents only as 'Dave'. Five days later, the teenager's dismembered body was found beside a highway near Corona. Police questioned LaMay's gay friends, one of whom was able to identify 'Dave' as David Hill. The net was closing in on the evil duo, who fled to Mexico and laid low.

The pair were eventually caught, not by fleet-footed

detective work, but by their dramatic appearance at Riverside County Sheriff's office on July 13, 1977. Kearney, then aged 37, and Hill, 34, walked up to the desk, pointed to a wanted poster and announced: 'We're them!' They had decided to turn themselves in under pressure from family members.

The evidence against Kearney and Hill included fibers, binding tape, and a bloodstained hacksaw found at their Redondo Beach home. But when the older man assumed full responsibility for the murders, the Riverside County Grand Jury refused to indict Hill, and the charges against him had to be dropped through lack of evidence—to the great frustration of investigating officers. Hill fled California and returned to his home town of Lubbock, Texas.

Kearney, who explained that killing 'excited me and gave me a feeling of dominance', signed confessions to 28 murders but was initially charged with the deaths of only three of them, including John LaMay, whose blood it was on the hacksaw. At his trial in December, he was sentenced to life imprisonment, having been spared the death penalty because of his cooperation in clearing up other cases. The judge said: 'This defendant has perpetrated a series of ghastly and grisly crimes. I can only hope he will never be released. He appears to be an insult to humanity.'

Kearney was back in court in 1978 to plead guilty to the murders of 18 boys and young men and to provide information relating to a further 11 gay victims, bringing the probable total of his victims to 32, including two children, aged five and eight. Given a fresh string of life sentences, he spent his years in Californian state prisons as an avid writer of essays and of letters to his many, sick-minded pen-pals.

# Edmund Kemper

**Edmund Emil Kemper, otherwise known as 'The Co-ed Killer' because of the female college students he targeted, could hardly be described as a normal child. Born in December 1949, his parents separated when he was nine and young Edmund lived mostly with his grandparents on a ranch in North Fork, California. He had a terrible relationship with his mother, who would constantly belittle and humiliate him. Finding it difficult to make friends, Kemper lived in a fantasy world involving the torture and slaughter of helpless animals. The decapitation of his pet cat was an indication of his future trademark.**

## He Practiced Killing By Decapitating The Family Cat

**At the age of 15,** Kemper shot his grandmother three times with her own gun, then dispatched his grandfather with a shot to the back of his head. He was diagnosed as paranoid and psychotic and committed to Atascadero State Hospital, where he used his time expanding his fantasies. On release in 1969, he was ready to start his trail of sickening killings and mutilations.

Disappointed at being turned down for the police force—he was too tall at 6ft 8ins (2.03m)—Kemper frequented bars used by off-duty cops, gradually becoming a regular participant in their conversations about guns. He even customized his car to resemble an unmarked police vehicle. During this time, he often picked up young female hitch-hikers, indulging in bizarre sexual fantasises involving murder and necrophilia.

It was in May 1972 that he started to put his preparations into practice. Kemper embarked on a spree of murders, picking up hitch-hikers, killing them, having sex with them, and then dissecting them. Two hitch-hiking students, Mary Ann Pesce and Anita

Luchese, never reached their destination. His next young victim was a 15-year-old Korean girl, Aiko Koo, on her way to a dance class. He suffocated her, raped her and, after a few beers in a local bar, cut off her hands and head.

In 1973, now living back home with his mother in Santa Cruz, Kemper struck again. The first of his next three victims, Cindy Schall, was shot before he had sex with the body. Her head was buried in his backyard and other body parts thrown off a cliff. Cindy was followed by Rosalind Thorpe and Alice Lui. He abused Alice's headless body in the apartment of his mother, who throughout had no idea of her son's depravity.

Just one month later, on Easter Sunday, Kemper battered his mother to death with a hammer while she slept. He decapitated her—some reports detailing that he performed oral sex on her head before using it as a dartboard. He stuffed her voice box into the waste disposal unit 'to put an end to her constant nagging'. He ended his killing spree by strangling Sally Hallet, his mother's friend, having invited her for dinner while his mother's mutilated body lay in a cupboard.

**ABOVE:** Kemper's evil fantasies prompted him to cut off the hands and head of one helpless 15-year-old female hitch-hiker.

**ABOVE:** Aged 15 Edmund Kemper was imprisoned for murdering his own grandparents, but he was released...to kill again and again.

Kemper fled the murder scene and, with the two women's heads in a bag in his car, he drove aimlessly for 18 hours until, reaching Pueblo, Colorado, he used a payphone to call Santa Cruz police and make a full confession. He had to make several calls before they would believe him.

At his trial in October 1973, he pleaded insanity but was found guilty of eight counts of murder. He asked for the death penalty but received life imprisonment at Folsom maximum-security jail.

# Bela Kiss

**Perhaps it was the infidelity of his wife that made Bela Kiss resort to murder. Certainly, he gained sympathy from neighbors in the Hungarian town of Czinkota when, in 1912, he told them that Marie Kiss, some years his junior, had found herself a lover and the couple had run off together.**

## Kiss Of Death For Lonely Widows

**Kiss, however, took immediate advantage** of his new bachelor status. He replaced his wife with an elderly housekeeper, and invited a regular flow of women to his home, 10 miles (16km) from the capital Budapest.

This seemingly romantic period in his life ended in November 1914 when, at the age of 34, he was drafted into the Hungarian army and sent to fight in Serbia. In the spring of 1916, word got back to his home town of Czinkota that Kiss had been killed in action and had been buried at the battlefront.

That, it seemed, would be the last anyone would hear of Bela Kiss. But in June of that year, a squad of soldiers visited Czinkota looking for illegally stockpiled gasoline, in severely short supply during the First World War. In the course of their search, they visited Kiss's home and discovered a number of suspicious oil drums in a workshop where he had carried out his trade as a plumber and tinsmith.

Prizing open the lid of one, they found the perfectly preserved naked body of a woman. The contents of a further six drums was the same. Each woman had been garrotted and then pickled in alcohol.

A search of the surrounding countryside revealed another 17 drums, each with a pickled corpse inside. One contained Marie Kiss, another her lover Paul Bikari, who was the only man among the 24 victims.

Kiss's motives had been both sex and robbery. From papers and letters found in his house, it became clear that Kiss had been advertising himself under the name Hoffman as a 'lonely widower seeking female companionship'. He had, it appeared from the bodies, been successful at attracting lovelorn females.

He had also been successful at avoiding the consequences of his murderous ways. For Kiss had not died on the battlefield, as reported. He had simply switched name tags with a dead comrade and was now on the loose.

Bela Kiss was later spotted back in Hungary in the spring of 1919. Someone who had known him as 'Hoffman' spotted him on Budapest's Margaret Bridge across the Danube—the place where at least two lonely widows had last been seen with him. There were three further reports of Kiss. In 1924, a fleeing French Foreign Legionnaire told police about a fellow deserter who had boasted at his proficiency with the garrotte. His name was Hoffman.

In 1932, New York homicide detective Henry Oswald, who earned the nickname 'Camera Eye' because of his memory for mugshots, chased a man he was convinced was Kiss through Times Square before losing him in a subway. He again proved elusive in 1936, fleeing before police could check out a 'Mr Hoffman', the aged janitor in a Sixth Avenue apartment block. Bela Kiss was never caught.

# Randy Kraft

**The epithets applied to Randy Steven Kraft when arrested in 1983 included the 'Scorecard Killer' and the 'Freeway Killer'. Another was 'California's worst-ever serial killer', because Kraft's case stands out among the spate of slayings at that time—in that he probably accounted for as many as 67 murders.**

## Sick 'Scorecard' Of A Sadistic Mutilator

**Kraft, born in 1945,** was a star pupil at high school in Westminster, California, and at his college, at Claremont, where he joined the Reserve Officer Training Corps and, unlike many of his peers,

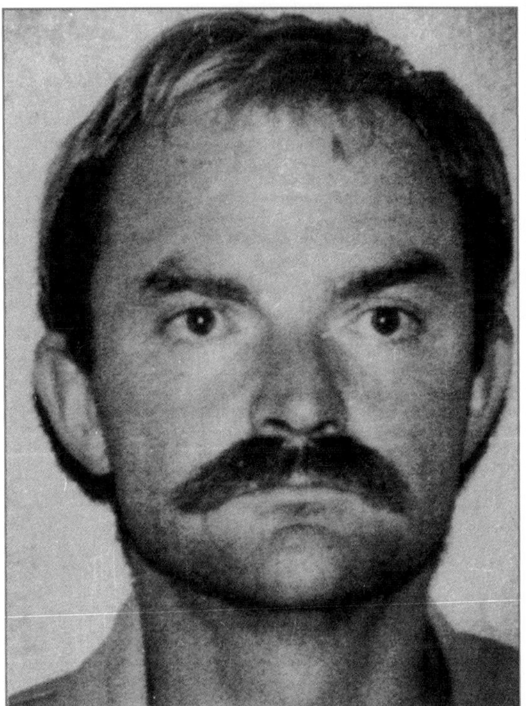

**ABOVE:** A face of pure evil. Randy Kraft was dubbed 'California's worst-ever serial killer.' His murder count probably totaled 67.

demonstrated in support of the Vietnam War. In 1964, he campaigned for right-wing presidential candidate Barry Goldwater. The following year, he began working as a bartender at a local gay club.

Kraft joined the US Air Force in 1968 but was discharged only a year later on undisclosed 'medical grounds'. He went back to bartending for a while, but his especially high IQ of 129 was finally put to use and he went on to forge for himself a successful business career. A computer expert, he became a sought-after trouble-shooter for companies' technology problems, earning himself a large salary. But it was while on these business journeys up and down the Pacific Coast that Kraft picked up homosexual partners and murdered them.

His first suspected victim was Wayne Dukette, a 30-year-old gay barman missing since September 1971 and whose decomposing body was found beside a highway near San Juan Capistrano. Kraft's first confirmed victim was Edward Moore, a 20-year-old Marine whose body was found near Seal Beach in December 1972. He had been strangled and sexually assaulted.

For the next two decades, dozens of what were believed to be Kraft's victims turned up along the freeways of California and Oregon. The victims were young men and teenage boys. Many were in the military, hitch-hiking their way between homes and bases. Some were teenage runaways. Others were picked up by the killer in gay bars.

Kraft's method of dispatching his victims varied; they had been strangled, shot in the head or had died as a result of torture. Most of the bodies showed signs of sexual mutilation by a sadistic killer. It was established that some of his victims had been alive and conscious while Kraft hacked at their genitals.

In May 1983, highway police stopped Kraft near San Diego for drink-driving and were surprised to discover that his passenger was dead. Terry Gambrel, a 25-year-old Marine, had died either of strangulation or an overdose of drugs. Also in the car was a briefcase containing a notebook with the killer's own detailed account of his murders—his 'scorecard'. It gave names, places, how the victims were murdered, and the mutilations carried out.

The briefcase also held 47 photographs of young men, some naked, some dead. Among those pictured were victims whose deaths were on the police 'unsolved' list. One of them was shown lying dead on the couch at Kraft's house in Huntington Beach, where police found property and fibers that helped identify further victims: three from Oregon and one from Michigan, both in locations where Kraft visited in his work. It was suspected that he had also killed on business trips to New York, Washington, and Ohio.

Kraft confessed to none of the murders and, by manipulating the legal system, managed to delay his trial for five years. He stretched the hearings out over 13 months, running up a bill for his Orange County trial of $10 million. But time ran out for him in May 1989 when he was finally convicted of 16 counts of murder and sentenced to death.

He remained on San Quentin's Death Row, raising a

**ABOVE:** Kraft (right) during his much delayed trial costing $10 million. He was eventually convicted of 16 murders in May 1989.

string of appeals to delay justice. Meanwhile, of Kraft's suspected 67 victims, 22 bodies remain unrecovered and unidentified.

There was one more mystery that remained unsolved: had Randy Kraft always acted alone? Forensic evidence in two cases point to an accomplice: an extra set of footprints and semen that did not match Kraft's DNA. His trial prosecutors believed that Kraft's roommate, Jeff Graves, occasionally helped him carry out or cover up the killings. Graves died of AIDS before police could question him, so the matter was never raised in court.

# Joachim Kroll

**When police finally caught up with German 'Cannibal Killer' Joachim Kroll, they found themselves interrogating a pathetic, mentally retarded 43-year-old lavatory attendant, small and balding with tinted glasses, who embarrassedly told them he had killed so many people that he could not remember the details.**

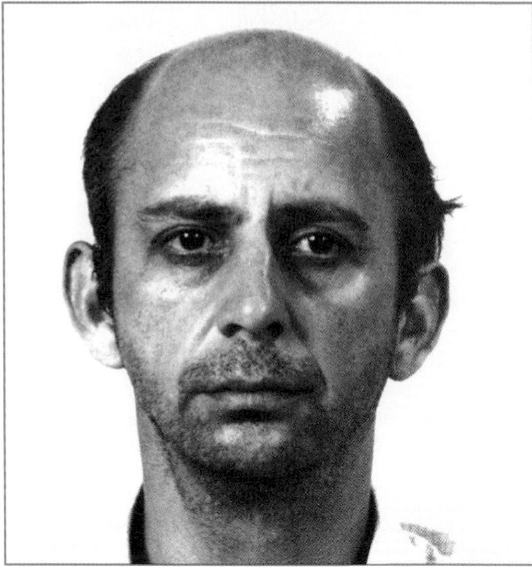

LEFT: When police raided the home of Joachim Kroll they found him cooking a meat stew...containing a child's hand.

# Cannibal Who Killed For The Cookpot

**As they searched his rooms** in Duisberg, an industrial city of the Ruhr, they found plastic bags filled with the flesh of his victims. Cuts of meat were laid out on plates in the refrigerator. And on the stove was a stew of carrots, potatoes…and a tiny human hand.

Kroll admitted killing at least 14 women and children between 1955 and 1976, their ages ranging from four to 19. Most had been raped and slices of flesh taken from their bodies. He said he had begun raping women in 1955, when he was aged 22, but had discovered that he was unable to have sex with a conscious woman.

He committed his first murder shortly afterward, his victim being a 19-year-old girl whom he lured into a barn and strangled. Four years and four victims later, he began cannibalizing the bodies. After raping and strangling a 16-year-old girl, he carved slices from her buttocks 'because meat in the shops is so expensive'.

Kroll was later to tell detectives that he only ate those he considered to be young and tender. When they checked through the files, they found that the skinnier of the victims had been left with their bodies unbutchered.

Kroll would surprise his victims and strangle them quickly. Afterward he would strip the body and have intercourse with it. Among Kroll's younger victims were two 13-year-old girls whose buttocks, thighs, and forearms he carved steaks for his dinner table. But it was two murders of mere youngsters that caused the German press to howl for the apprehension of the 'Ruhr Hunter', as he was then known—while freshly labeling him the 'Cannibal Killer'.

In 1966 he strangled five-year-old Ilona Harke in a park, raping her and carving chunks of flesh from her buttocks and shoulders, and in 1976, he snatched four-year-old Marion Ketter from a street, took her to his apartment and cut up her body.

Kroll was caught only because, while performing his duties as a lavatory attendant in the apartment complex where he lived, he had warned a neighbor not to use a

ABOVE: The bespectacled rapist, murderer, and cannibal admitted he could only have sex with his victims after they were dead.

particular toilet because it was 'stuffed up with guts'. It was in fact blocked with the remains of Marion Ketter.

Now relabeled in the press as the 'Duisburg Man-Eater', Kroll tried to explain his vile habits by complaining to police about the price of meat in the stores. In custody, the simpleton believed that he would be freed again after undergoing an operation to cure him of his homicidal urges. Instead he was charged with eight murders and one attempted murder.

In April 1982, Kroll was convicted on all counts, given nine life sentences and sent to a secure hospital for the criminally insane. He died of a heart attack in 1991.

# Peter Kurten

**One of 13 children, home life for Peter Kurten was brutal and harsh. His father was an alcoholic and beatings were commonplace, as was the sight of his father raping his mother and sisters. At the age of nine, the local dog catcher initiated him into the act of bestiality. It was then that Kurten developed an insatiable fascination for spurting blood—and for murder. In 1893, when he was just 10 years old, he drowned two young friends while out on the Rhine on a raft together.**

## Evil Bloodlust Of The Vampire Of Dusseldorf

**As a teenager on the streets** of Dusseldorf, Kurten embarked on a career of petty crime, including arson and housebreaking, receiving a two-year prison sentence. On his release, he progressed from torturing animals to attacking women. He savagely beat and raped a girl in woods at Grafenburg and left her for dead. The traumatized victim never reported his vicious attack. This was followed in May 1913 by the murder of eight-year-old Christine Klein. Kurten discovered her during a burglary. He cut her throat and raped her, relishing the sound of her blood gushing to the floor.

His killings were curtailed by the arrival of World War One, which Kurten spent entirely in prison for desertion and petty crimes. On his release in 1921, he took a job in a local factory and got married. His wife was an ex-prostitute but she did not satisfy Kurten for, over the next few years, he had several mistresses, all of whom seem to have enjoyed his penchant for sadistic torture. He achieved his orgasms by wounding them and watching their blood drip. It was not long before he transferred his sick practices to strangers, now drinking blood from horrific wounds he inflicted, thus earning the nickname 'The Dusseldorf Vampire'.

The citizens of the city were now living in terror, believing there was a vampire prowling their streets. Kurten struck next in 1929, when he stabbed to death two sisters, aged five and 14, followed by an attack on a 26-year-old housemaid who, despite her appalling injuries, survived. On another day, he killed again, cutting down three victims within 30 minutes.

For his next attacks, Kurten chose to hammer his victims to death before stabbing them. The more wounds, the longer he had taken to reach orgasm. Poor little Gertrude Albermann, aged just five, had 36 separate stab wounds. She was the last of Kurten's murder victims, although his vicious attacks continued.

In May 1930, he befriended Maria Budlick, a 21-year-old maid. He took her first to his apartment and then, on a walk through Grafenburg woods, he raped and half-strangled her. But she survived and, although inexplicably she did not immediately go to the police, she was later able to provide as evidence the address to which Kurten had taken her: 71 Mettmannerstrasse.

Meanwhile, realizing that the police were closing in on him, Kurten told his wife his grisly secret, and it was she who tipped off the police. Kurten remained calm throughout his arrest and subsequent trial. His counsel failed to convince the jury of his client's insanity and Kurten was sent to the guillotine on July 1, 1932. He asked if he would hear the sound of his own blood gushing from his neck—forecasting that it would be 'the pleasure to end all pleasures'.

**ABOVE:** Two photographs of Peter Kurten after he was taken into police custody in May 1929.

# Ilshat Kuzikov

For some reason, the Soviet Union has bred a high proportion of serial killers with a penchant for cannibalism. One of the most enthusiastic of recent times was Ilshat Kuzikov, a St Petersburg street sweeper. Neighbors in Ordzhonikidze Street recalled him as a cheery, likeable man who was always ready to help his elderly neighbors with jobs around the house. He was devoted to his cat, Dasha, but appeared to have few human friends. He was also on the register at his local psychiatric hospital.

## Special Ingredients Of A Killer's Kebabs

**In November 1992,** a piece of human torso turned up in the basement of a house close to Kuzikov's home. Police failed to link him to the crime, just as they failed to make the connection two years later when the severed head of a vagrant was found in a communal trash dump on Ordzhonikidze Street. But in August 1995, another severed head was found, this time belonging to one of Kuzikov's fellow psychiatric patients, Edik Vassilevski. Police realized the two men were friends and made 35-year-old Kuzikov their main suspect.

When they raided the dingy apartment block in which he lived, detectives found a plastic bag hanging outside a window in the cold, which contained human flesh marinating with onions, probably destined to be for Kuzikov's evening meal. In the hallway leading to his front door were two arms and two legs. And when they broke into his single-room Apartment 22, they found a human abattoir. Near the oven was a casserole dish containing human bones. Nearby was a small sack of human ears and other parts. Pickle jars sat around the room filled with vinegar and what turned out to be pickled human meat. On a shelf was a fizzy drink bottle full of blood. Next to it was an old gherkin jar used to store dried skin and ears. And, last but not least, there was an aluminum cooking pot containing the last remains of Edik Vassilevski. He had been cut up for Russian-style kebabs.

As he was sent to an institution for life, psychologists said Kuzikov was a sexual sadist for whom cannibalism was the ultimate way of controlling his victims. As he put it himself in interviews with police: 'You know, I always wanted to be a surgeon, but it's better to be a cannibal. If you're a surgeon you have to put the body back together and you stop having any control over it. But a cannibal kills and then he can do what he wants with the body. After he kills, he owns it forever.'

# Leonard Lake and Charles Ng

**To outsiders and even close members of his family, Leonard Lake was a model citizen. He was a volunteer firefighter and a charity worker with the elderly. But behind this façade, he was a sadistic murderer who kidnapped his victims before subjecting them to terrifying torture and mutilation, capturing the images on film which he then sold from his perverted mail-order business.**

## Deadly Partnership Of The Sickest Of Killers

**His interest in photography** and film started in his childhood in San Francisco when his mother encouraged Leonard to take pictures of young naked girls and to take pride in the human body. She could never have guessed that these early movies and photographs were just practice for his later 'snuff movies'.

Lake had a variety of jobs, from teacher to circus performer, but in 1966 joined the Marine Corps. During his service, he spent two years undergoing psychiatric treatment for unspecified mental problems before his discharge in 1971. He then moved to San Jose, California, and had a short-lived first marriage. Lake was known to be making porn movies featuring his wife and several other women at that time.

In 1981 he moved again, to rural Ukiah, California, joining a commune whose residents dressed in 'Renaissance' style clothing and led bizarre lives. While living at the commune, he married Cricket Balazs, who became another star of his sadomasochistic movies.

At this time, he met Charles Chitat Ng, the son of a wealthy Hong-Kong based businessman, who had been sent to boarding school in England after being arrested at the age of 15 for shoplifting. He was expelled from that school for theft and continued his education in San Francisco, joining the Marines in 1981. However, unable to stop his thieving ways, he was caught stealing weapons worth $11,000 and sentenced to 27 months in a military jail. He managed to escape and made his way back to San Francisco, where he applied to an advertisement in a survivalist magazine for a 'mercenary'.

The advert had been placed by Lake, who was himself a 'survivalist' and believed the 'holocaust' was coming. He had constructed a sick fantasy in his mind that he labeled 'Operation Miranda', where he saw himself in total world domination surrounded by his 'sex-slaves'. When he and Ng met up, a barbarous partnership was forged. The year was 1982; Lake was aged 37, Ng aged 21, and a three-year killing spree was about to begin.

It was Ng's clumsy shoplifting habit that was to bring to light the horrific murders he and Lake were committing in the wooded hills in Wisleyville, Calaveras County, about 150 miles (240km) east of San Francisco. In June 1985, police officer David Wright responded to a call about an oriental man attempting to shoplift a $75 vice from a South San Francisco store. By the time Wright arrived, the young thief had fled but his older friend was vainly trying to pay for the item.

The officer became suspicious and ran a vehicle check, which revealed that the car belonged to a local businessman, Paul Cosner, who had been reported

**ABOVE:** A grinning Leonard Lake on one of his wedding days. It's not known if his two brides were aware of his grisly activities.

missing. Lake gave his name as Robin Scott Stapley, a further police check revealed Stapley to be 26 years old and also missing.

Lake was arrested and taken to the police station where he was momentarily left with a pencil and paper to write out his statement. He calmly wrote a note begging forgiveness from his wife and family—and took a cyanide capsule he always carried on his person. He collapsed and died four days later, never having regained consciousness.

Finding an electricity bill on Lake, the police contacted the local Calaveras County sheriff, who confirmed that a young oriental man and a 'Charles Gunnar' lived at a ranch in Wisleyville. He had been keeping an eye on the pair as they were always advertising second-hand furniture and effects for sale and he thought these were possibly stolen goods.

When officers arrived at the small woodland cabin, they were horrified and sickened. Charred human bones were found in shallow graves, along with decomposing human remains. Inside the house they found bloodied women's clothing, a box containing shackles, and a collection of chains, hooks, and manacles hanging from the bedroom walls and ceiling. In an outhouse they found a blood-stained chainsaw.

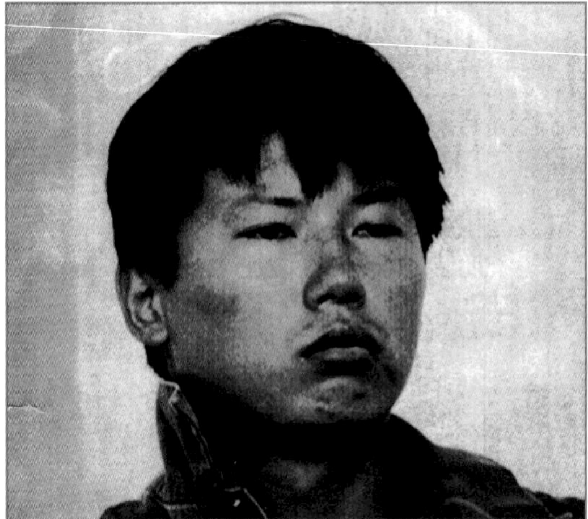

**ABOVE:** Charles Ng's compulsive shoplifting habit led to the arrest of the deadly duo, and signaled the end of their murderous spree.

But worse was to come. The discovery of a subterranean bunker a few days later provided more gruesome evidence of the activities of Lake and Ng. Lake had filmed and photographed their terrified victims, chained and shackled to beds or a chair, as they were tortured, raped, and sexually abused. Some movies showed the final terrifying moments of the victim's life. Ng and Lake found this 'snuff movie' trade a most lucrative addition to their already established drug-trafficking business.

In the course of fingerprint checks, it was discovered that Lake was wanted under another name for burglary in Humboldt County, where police discovered he had started another bunker. It was here they found the remains of Lake's own brother, Donald, murdered when he had come asking for a loan. The grave of Charles Gunnar was also discovered, a colleague of Lake's from the Marines, whose identity he had later taken.

Among the known victims of Lake and Ng were two babies, taken from their mothers and used to get the women to perform sickening sex acts with empty promises of their return. And all recorded by Lake for his own video library. For variety, Lake and Ng had set some victims free in the woods, only to be hunted down like animals with rifles or doused with gasoline and burned alive.

With one murderer dead, the investigation focused on tracing Ng. Again it was his bungled attempts at shoplifting that were to give him away. In July 1985, he was caught stealing in Calgary, Canada, and wounded an officer during capture. Initially, he denied any involvement in the murders, although he admitted knowledge of them. He was sentenced to four-and-a-half years for armed robbery in Canada, during which time he fought extradition to California to face the murder charges.

After a long extradition battle, Ng was finally handed over to the United States authorities and convicted of 11 murders, the victims being six men, three women, and two babies. The trial was one of the longest and most expensive in Californian history. He was sentenced to death on June 30, 1999, and is languishing on Death Row in San Quentin State Prison, where he has submitted a string of appeals in his attempt to beat the might of the American legal system.

# Henry Lee Lucas

**Was Henry Lee Lucas the worst serial killer in American history? Given the glaring inconsistencies in his various confessions, it is impossible to know. He admitted to being, among other things, a cannibal, Satanist, contract killer, and born-again Christian. He claimed more than 500 murders. He might be responsible for over 100. He was convicted of just 11. Perhaps not even Lucas himself could filter fact from fiction in his warped and addled brain.**

## America's Worst Serial Killer?

**Lucas was born in 1936,** the youngest of nine children whose home was a one-room log cabin in Blacksburg, Virginia, where his alcoholic father ran an illegal whiskey still. Lucas Sr., who had lost both legs when a freight train ran over his drunken body, was later frozen to death when his wife locked him out of the cabin in mid-winter. She also starved, abused, and brutally beat her youngest son, probably causing him brain damage. He was once in a coma for three days after she hit him with a plank. She earned her living as a prostitute and allowed young Henry to watch her satisfying her clients.

Henry later said of his mother: 'I was brought up like a dog. No human being should have been put through what I was.' In 1960, at the age of 23, he took revenge on her by stabbing her to death. It was also suggested that he may have raped her.

Lucas was committed to a mental institution but, against his own better judgment, was chosen for release on parole in 1970. 'I told them not to let me loose', he said. 'I told them I would do it again. They wouldn't listen.' He was soon back inside with a four-year sentence for kidnapping and attempted rape, his victim being a woman who had rejected his advances.

Released again in 1975, by which time he was aged 39, Lucas became a drifter, roaming the American South and taking short-term jobs. In Florida in 1976, he teamed up with Ottis Toole, a transvestite. They became friends and, according to Toole, lovers. The pair

**ABOVE:** Henry Lee Lucas was a self confessed cannibal, Satanist, and contract killer—but how many did he murder?

**ABOVE:** A local sheriff at Stoneburg, Texas, points to the site where an 80-year-old victim of Lucas had been buried.

continued on the road together taking with them Toole's 12-year-old niece, Becky Powell, who was on the run from a juvenile detention center.

The unprepossessing Lucas—tattily dressed, unshaven, with straggly hair, and a glass eye—and Becky, who was slightly retarded, seem to have had a genuinely deep affection for each other. It was possibly the only such relationship he had ever enjoyed, and it ended in 1982 when Becky disappeared while the couple were drifting through Texas. By then, Toole and Lucas had split up, the former returning home to Florida and later being jailed for arson.

In October 1982, Texas Rangers were investigating the disappearance of an 80-year-old widow at Stoneburg when inquiries led to a squalid hut, dubbed by locals 'the Chicken Shack'. There, they found the dagger that had killed the old lady.

Under interrogation, Lucas confessed not only to her murder and posthumous rape but a catalog of sex-murders across the Deep South and Southwest states. He told of rapes and torture, kidnapping and mutilation, death by gunshot, knife, rope, and even crucifixion. Some were carried out by him alone, some with Ottis Toole. Among his solo victims, he said, was the feeble-minded Becky.

Detectives at first believed the confessions were a fantasy, possibly dreamed up to justify a plea of insanity. But Lucas was often able to produce irrefutable

**ABOVE:** Lucas is led by Texas Rangers to the site of one of the many unsolved murders they hoped he would confess to.

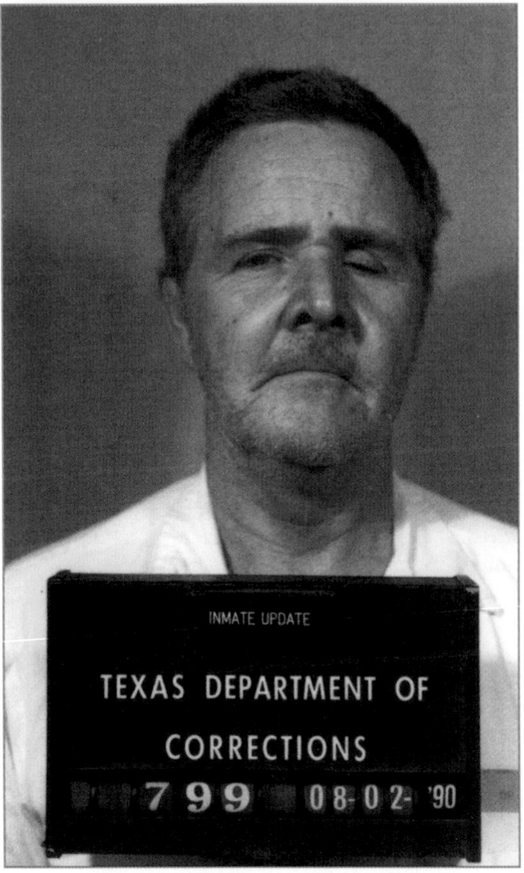


**ABOVE:** A prison mugshot of Lucas in a Texas jail. While incarcerated his own estimate of his murder tally rose to 600.

evidence. He recalled how he had scattered pillow feathers over the body of a 76-year-old lady he had bludgeoned to death—information that had never been released to the media. Police also obtained verification of many of the crimes from Toole, who consequently had a death sentence added to the 20 years he was serving for arson.

Toole, who died in prison of cirrhosis of the liver in 1996, told Florida investigators: 'We picked up lots of hitch-hikers. Lucas killed most of the women himself. Some of them would be shot in the head and the chest, and some of them would be choked to death, and some of them would be beaten in the head.'

Meanwhile, in Texas, Lucas's official murder confessions rose to 360, although he hinted that he had committed 500 or more—which would have made him the worst serial killer in American history. Some of these confessions he later retracted. But in many cases, his claims enabled the bodies of missing persons to be recovered, most having been raped, sometimes after death.

Lucas needed to be locked up for life. His 1983 trial for the murder of the Texas widow—during which he shocked the judge by telling him he should take into account 'another 100' murders—resulted in a 75-year sentence. Then came his trial for murdering Becky, during which he sobbed in court and told the jury that he loved her and didn't want her dead.

His case wasn't helped by a videotaped confession in which he said: 'I had sex with her. It's one of those things that I guess got to be part of my life, having sexual intercourse with the dead.' A sentence of life imprisonment resulted, after which a smiling Lucas shook hands with the prosecutor and said: 'You did a good job.'

In prison, Lucas continued recalling murders he had supposedly committed all over the country. A list of female victims from 19 different states produced a spate of requests from other forces for samples of hair and saliva. But over the months, the information he gave became increasingly bizarre. Lucas's own estimate of his victims eventually grew to about 600. In 1983, frustrated representatives of law enforcement agencies from 19 states gathered in Louisiana to exchange information on Lucas and Toole. They concluded that there were links between the pair and 81 murders, and many of those cases were thereby closed.

Convicted of only 11 of his indeterminate number of murders, with a further 20 murder charges pending, Lucas languished on Death Row in Texas. In June 1999, as a fresh execution date neared, doubts arose about his guilt in the case of one his unidentified victims, and Texas governor George Bush Jr. stepped in to commute his death sentence to one of life imprisonment. Lucas died of natural causes in March 2001.

# Robert Pickton

**Pig farmer and serial killer Robert 'Willie' Pickton is currently serving the longest sentence available under Canadian law for murdering six women; feeding their remains to his pigs and hanging and skinning one victim on a meat hook. The women, who disappeared between 1997 and 2001, are only a fraction of the total number Pickton is thought to have slaughtered, as the six cases were the only ones where adequate body parts survived.**

## Women Were Butchered And Fed To The Pigs

**Pickton, born in British Columbia** on October 24, 1949, was well-known for the parties he threw for prostitutes and bikers. He lured the women to his farm in Port Coquitlam, just outside Vancouver, with the promise of money and drugs.

Most of his victims were prostitutes and drug addicts from Vancouver's Downtown Eastside, and police were accused of paying insufficient heed to these 'missing persons' cases over the course of the past 20 years. But in February 2002, they raided Pickton's scruffy pig farm in an unrelated investigation into illegal firearms and discovered property and identity cards of some of the women listed as missing.

In the farm's slaughterhouse, they dug up human remains—from body parts to minute traces of DNA—until the count came to 30. Four could not be identified

**ABOVE:** Robert Pickton was convicted of six murders, but the remains of many other nameless victims were fed to his pigs.

**ABOVE:** The common-law husband of Mona Wilson holds a photograph of his partner. She died at the hands of Robert Pickton.

**ABOVE:** A police forensic officer searches for evidence. Various human remains were found in the farm's slaughterhouse.

but the other 26 were among the names of 67 women who had disappeared from the Downtown Eastside.

In the freezers, they found skulls of two women among the most recently reported missing. Some carcasses were cut in half, like slaughtered pigs, with hands and feet stuffed inside.The remains of one victim was in a garbage bag and her blood-stained clothing was found in the trailer in which Pickton lived. Part of another victim's jawbone and teeth were found in the ground beside the slaughterhouse. Much of the evidence, however, had been devoured by pigs long before the police search.

**ABOVE:** Police trailers set up in April 2002, during the extensive on-site murder investigation at Pickton's farm.

**ABOVE:** A spokesman for the Crown Counsel speaks outside court following a preliminary hearing during Pickton's murder trial.

**ABOVE:** An artist's impression of Pickton's trial in January 2007. He was sentenced to life imprisonment.

At Pickton's trial in January 2007, a former farm employee, Scott Chubb, testified that Pickton told him the way to get rid of 'junkies' was to inject them with a syringe filled with windshield washer fluid. A syringe with the fluid was found in Pickton's trailer. Another witness, Andrew Bellwood, testified that Pickton demonstrated how he killed the women. He produced a pair of handcuffs, a leather belt, and a thin wire with loops on the end and showed him how he strangled the women while having sex with them.

The most disturbing story the jury heard from a witness was told by Lynn Ellingsen. After waking up from a crack binge at the farm one night, she had gone

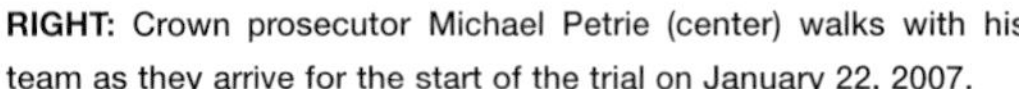

**RIGHT:** Crown prosecutor Michael Petrie (center) walks with his team as they arrive for the start of the trial on January 22, 2007.

outside to the barn because she saw a light on. When she opened the door, she saw a body hanging from a chain. Beside the body was a bloodied Pickton, who warned her that 'she'd be next' if she said anything.

Further damning evidence at the trial came from a conversation Pickton had with an undercover police officer posing as a cellmate, in which he confessed to 49 murders. He told the officer that he wanted to kill another woman to make it an even 50, and that he was caught because he was 'sloppy'.

In the largest serial murder case in Canadian history, the jury of seven men and five women took 10 days to reach a verdict. In December 2007, Pickton received a mandatory life sentence, with no possibility of parole.

# Jesse Pomeroy

**When a number of children were abducted and sadistically tortured in the backstreets of 19th-century Boston, Massachusetts, few could believe that the foul sexual assaults could have been committed by anyone but a sick adult. Yet the culprit was found to be a 12-year-old boy: Jesse Pomeroy, a gangling child with a hare lip, one completely white eye, and extremely low intelligence.**

## The Ugly Kid Who Killed 27 Times

**Jesse, born in 1860** and raised in a South Boston slum tenement, was shunned by other children because of his obvious disabilities and unprepossessing appearance. His revenge for being ostracized was a terrible one. Between December 1871 and September 1872, a number of children were snatched from the streets, sadistically tortured with whips, knives, and pins and left unconscious.

Jessie was sent to West Borough Reform School but was handed back into the care of his mother two years later. The 14-year-old sadist immediately sought fresh victims, both male and female.

In March 1874, he murdered nine-year-old Katie Curran, whose body he buried in the basement of his mother's dressmaking store. Five weeks later, the body of four-year-old Horace Mullen was found on a Boston beach. He had been beaten, stabbed 15 times and his throat cut.

The ensuing manhunt turned into a boy-hunt when the evidence pointed toward Pomeroy. When police

**ABOVE:** Child killer Jesse Pomeroy as a much older adult. He spent more than 40 years of his life sentence in solitary confinement.

asked him if he had killed the little boy, whose body was the first to be found, Jesse replied: 'I suppose I did.' Shamed by the arrest of her son, Jesse's mother moved house—and the new owners found 12 corpses buried in her trash-strewn yard. He eventually confessed to torturing to death 27 youngsters.

At his trial in December 1874, Jesse Pomeroy was accused only of the single murder of Horace Mullen. He pleaded insanity but was found guilty and sentenced to death. There were appeals for mercy to be shown to such a young offender and the sentence was commuted to life imprisonment—but to be spent entirely in solitary confinement.

Pomeroy began his solo existence on September 7, 1876, when he was transferred from the Suffolk County Jail to a single cell at the State Prison at Charlestown, and began his life in solitary. He was 16 years and 10 months and would spend more than 40 years entirely alone in his cell before finally being allowed to mingle with other convicts. He had used his lonely decades in solitary to study and he ended up writing his autobiography which chronicled his early life and terrible crimes. In 1929, in frail health, he was transferred to Bridgewater Hospital for the Criminally Insane, where he died on September 29, 1932, at the age of 73.

# Dennis Rader

**To his neighbors, he was a pillar of the community, a churchgoer, a scout leader, a respectable family man. What they failed to see in him was the sickening serial killer who managed to evade justice for 30 years. His name was Dennis Rader, but he was better known by his nickname 'BTK' because of his method of murder: Bind, Torture, Kill.**

## 'BTK' Was His Nickname. It Stood For 'Bind, Torture, Kill'

**His sick crime spree left 10 dead.** He strangled four members of one family, hanged an 11-year-old girl from a sewer pipe to watch her die, photographed the bodies of his victims and taunted police by sending them trophies taken from the corpses.

Yet, to most who knew him, father-of-two Rader seemed 'an ordinary guy'. A US Air Force veteran, he was an attentive parent who took his children on camping and fishing expeditions. He ran his son Brian's scout troop. He was an usher at his local church in Wichita, Kansas, where he worked as a 'code compliance officer', enforcing petty rules for the city authority.

**ABOVE:** Dennis Rader was an apparent pillar of the community, but behind the facade he was a serial killer who claimed 10 lives.

ABOVE: A news conference outside the Sedgwick County Courthouse in Wichita, Kansas on March 1, 2005.

He was, however, a secret sadist, with the classic serial-killer background of torturing small animals. His depths of evil finally found full expression in 1974 when, at the age of 28, he burst into the home of the Otero family, held them at gunpoint, bound, and gagged them. Joe Otero, 38, his wife Julie, 34, and nine-year-old son Joey were strangled one by one. But it was the fate of 11-year-old Josephine 'Josie' Otero that was to send a wave of revulsion through the Kansas town.

Josie's body was found hanging from the basement sewer pipe. Her hands were bound behind her back and she wore nothing but socks and a sweater. The rest of her clothes were in a pile by the foot of the stairs, left by her killer before he carried out a sex act on her corpse.

His next victim was 21-year-old student Kathryn Bright, who returned home with her younger brother

ABOVE: Police work in front of Dennis Rader's house in Park City, Kansas, following his arrest in February 2005.

Kevin to be confronted by a gun-toting intruder wearing a black stocking cap, camouflage jacket, and black gloves. Rader tied them up and stabbed Kathryn to death. Kevin was shot in the head but survived.

Police at first failed to link the attack to the Oteros massacre—but Rader seemed to want recognition for his crimes and wrote to the *Wichita Eagle* newspaper, claiming to be 'BTK', bragging about the slaughter and promising to kill again. He did not do so for three years. Then, in March 1977, mother-of-three Shirley Vian, 24, was found bound and strangled in her Wichita home. A plastic bag had been placed over her head and her panties had been removed as a trophy.

**ABOVE:** A manacled Rader, flanked by police officers. The evil killer was sentenced to 175 years in prison.

Nancy Fox, a 25-year-old secretary, was next. Rader broke into her home, handcuffed her and stripped her, before assaulting her and finally throttling her with a belt. To ensure recognition for the crime, Rader rang police from a payphone to report the murder. As 'BTK', he later sent letters to local media asking: 'How many do I have to kill before I get some national attention?'

'BTK' then went to ground for almost eight years and police assumed he had died. But in April 1985, his urge to kill returned and he murdered his 53-year-old neighbor, Marine Hedge. Rader took her body to the Christ Lutheran Church where he was congregation president, placed the corpse on the altar and took bondage photos before dumping it in a ditch.

The following September he entered the home of Vicki Wegerle, 28, after posing as a telephone repairman and strangled her. His final victim was Dolores Davis, 62, abducted and strangled in 1991. He dumped her body under a bridge—then returned to place a mask over the corpse's head and take photographs. As always, he performed a sex act at the scene.

Police failed to link the latest deaths to the earlier 'BTK' murders until, in 2004, Rader again wrote to the local media, sending them and the police trophies from his crimes. They included pictures of Vicki Wegerle's body, Nancy Fox's driving license, and a doll symbolizing Josie Otero's murder.

'BTK' was finally captured in February 2005 when a floppy disk he sent to a TV station was traced to Rader's church. Confronted with a DNA test that matched him with a sample found in Josie Otero's body 31 years earlier, Rader admitted all 10 murders.

In a written confession, he said: 'Josephine, when I hung her really turn(ed) me on. Her pleading for mercy…then the rope took (hold); she helpless; staring at me with wide terror fill(ed) eyes, the rope getting tighter-tighter.'

At his trial in August 2005, the bespectacled 60-year-old looked relaxed as he admitted planning further murders, adding: 'I was thinking about it but I was beginning to slow down.' Since the crimes were committed before Kansas reintroduced capital punishment, the judge handed down the maximum prison sentence he could deliver: 175 years with no chance of parole.

# Michael Lupo

**Michael Lupo was an outrageous homosexual who claimed to have had 4,000 lovers. He indulged in sadomasochistic activities of the weirdest kind, including slitting the scrotum of his partners so that he could massage their testicles. And when he began killing some of those gay partners, he gained the nickname 'Wolf Man of London'.**

## Crazed 'Wolf Man Of London'

**Before arriving in Britain in 1975** at the age of 22, the ex-choirboy had served in an elite Italian commando unit. He got a job as a hairdresser in London, and worked his way up to owning a fashion and make-up store, which he grandly called a 'styling boutique'. His clients were said to include some of London's High Society names, with gay lifestyles they were eager to keep secret.

Lupo bought himself a house, one room of which he kitted out as a torture chamber. But his kinky promiscuity was to cost him his life, and that of four others. For after he was diagnosed with AIDS, he began a bloody rampage, slaughtering four men whom he picked up in bars—his weird 'calling card' being to slash their naked bodies and smear them with excrement.

Police inquiries began in March 1986 when the body of a 37-year-old man was found in a derelict apartment in Kensington, London. The investigation made no progress because there was no connection between victim and perpetrator. But Lupo was already a killer. He was responsible for the murder of a young hospital worker, found strangled in West London, and an unidentified man who was killed beside the River Thames, near Hungerford Bridge. And Scotland Yard subsequently passed their case file to forces in Germany and the United States because of similar mutilation murders in Berlin, Hamburg, Los Angeles, and New York at times coinciding with Lupo's travels.

In April 1986, a 24-year-old man was found strangled to death with his own scarf on a railroad embankment in Brixton. It was the discovery of this final victim that convinced police a serial killer was at large. His existence sent terror through the capital's gay glitterati.

Lupo was arrested on May 20 after two terrified men who had managed to escape his orgiastic clutches went to police with their stories. In July, under his full name Michele de Marco Lupo, he was found guilty at the Old Bailey of four murders and two attempted murders and was sentenced to life in prison, where he died from an AIDS related illness in February 1995.

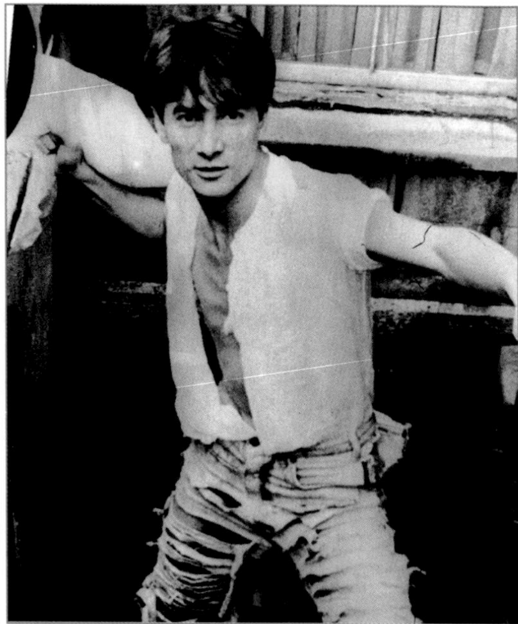

**ABOVE:** Ex-choirboy and full-time hairdresser, Michael Lupo, killed four gay lovers in London in the 1980s.

# Picture Credits

**Getty Images**
7, 10 Hulton Archive
11 New York Times/Archive Photos
14 Jeff J. Mitchell
22 (left) Evening Standard, (right) Keystone
23 (left) Evening Standard, (right) Keystone/Hulton Archive
24 (left) Keystone/Hulton Archive, (right) Keystone
25 (top) Evening Standard, (bottom) William H Alden
26 (both) King County Prosecutor's Office
27 Elaine Thompson-Pool
28 (left) King County Prosecutor's Office, (right) Keystone/Hulton Archive
29 (left) Bob Strong/AFP
32 Scott Nelson/AFP
37 AFP
38 (left) Greater Manchester Police
41 Popperfoto
42 David Martin/AFP
43 (bottom left) Bruno Arnold/AFP, (top right) Jean-Christophe Verhaegen/AFP
44 Bruno Arnold/AFP
45 (top) Eugene Garcia/AFP, (bottom) Jay Crihfield/AFP
63 (left) Hulton Archive
63 (right), 64 (both), 65 (both) Express
66 Jim Gray/Keystone/Hulton Archive
67 (top) Evening Standard/Hulton Archive
68 (all), 69 (left) Keystone/Hulton Archive, (right) J. Wilds/Keystone/Hulton Archive
71 The Bridgeman Art Library
88 Getty Images
89 (top left) Jeff Vinnick/AFP, (bottom left, top right, bottom right) Don MacKinnon
90 (top) Felicity Don/AFP, (bottom) Jeff Vinnick
92 Sedgwick County Sheriff's Office
93 (both), 94 Larry W. Smith

**Press Association**
30, 31, 34, 35, 38, 47, 48, 49, 50, 51, 59, 60, 72, 75 (both), 77, 78, 79 (both), 81.



To Katie, Leonie and Mike
Who, in the interests of research, braved more gore and guts than any homicide detective would experience in a lifetime. My sincere thanks to them.

TRUE CRIMES

# CRIMES OF PASSION

igloo

igloo

This edition published in 2010
by Igloo Books Ltd
Cottage Farm
Sywell
NN6 0BJ

www.igloo-books.com



A copy of the British Library Cataloguing-in-Publication
Data is available from the British Library.

10 9 8 7 6 5 4 3 2 1

ISBN 978-0-85734-396-3

Printed and Manufactured in China

# Contents

# Anibal Almodovar

**A serial womanizer who was quick to anger, Anibal Almodovar became so furious at his new wife's insistence that he give up his wayward sexual lifestyle that he killed her just weeks after the wedding. Unfortunately for him, he did not stop to consider that it might not just be witnesses that could place him at the scene of the murder. The evidence that convicted him came from somewhere no one would have suspected.**

**An extremely handsome man and former sailor,** 25-year-old Puerto Rican Anibal Almodovar was working as a porter in New York City when he met a waitress in a Manhattan bar and married her. Two years younger than her new husband and strikingly pretty herself, Louise Almodovar assumed that as a married man her husband would give up the one-night stands

**BELOW:** An aerial view of Central Park, where Anibal Almodovar dumped the body of his wife Louise.

and frequent flings he had been so used to enjoying. But she was wrong. The couple hadn't been married more than a few weeks when it became apparent to her that Almodovar was still pursuing the same lifestyle; he made few efforts to hide the fact from his wife. She protested and a violent argument broke out, after which Almodovar stormed out of the apartment.

Unwilling to give up on her marriage so quickly, Louise later called him at a local bar and asked to meet so they might try and resolve their problems more calmly. He agreed and told her that he would see her in Central Park. Louise's body was found among tall grass in the famous park on November 2, 1942. The ripped sleeve of her jacket suggested that she had struggled furiously, and the chief medical examiner concluded that she had been throttled by a killer who had placed two fingers from each hand on her windpipe.

Unable to identify the corpse and assuming that it was a random killing committed by one of the many dubious characters that could be found in Central park at night, the police department was initially at a loss. But when reports of a missing woman whose husband was a known cheat and violent bully came in, they scented a murderer.

Almodovar was brought in for questioning and his clothes taken away for examination. The seeds found in the turn-ups of his trousers would later prove crucial in convicting him of his wife's murder.

At first, Almodovar made a full confession, telling police he had lost control when Louise nagged him about seeing other women. He said he had strangled her and left the scene. However, when the case came to trial, on February 24, 1943, he retracted the confession. The police, he said, had forced it out of him under duress. Now he maintained that he had nothing to do with Louise's death.

Unfortunately for him, the seeds that had been found in his trousers were from rare plants growing at the murder scene. They had been planted there as a nursery experiment and could not be found anywhere else in New York. What's more, as a professor of biology and botany explained to the court, as the seeds found on Almodovar's trousers only matured within a week of the murder, the evidence placed Almodovar at site on the night Louise was killed. Anibal Almodovar's was the first case in US legal history to rely on botanical evidence to get a conviction. He was found guilty and sentenced to death in the electric chair.

# Tracie Andrews

**A former boyfriend would later recall, "When Tracie gets angry her eyes go wild," and the parents of her victim have spoken of their fear that she will kill again if ever released. For Tracie, it seems that rage is never far from the surface and if roused to passion she can be deadly, as Lee Harvey found out.**

**The relationship of barmaid and former model** Tracie Andrews and her fiancé Lee Harvey was a stormy one. Both had tempers and—as neighbors would later tell the police—often had violent arguments. The row they had while driving to their home in Alvechurch near Worcester, England, on December 1, 1996, was no different from the rest, except in the way it ended. Tracie's uncontrollable temper finally snapped completely and, in a frenzy of rage, she pulled a knife and stabbed Harvey 15 times.

Two days later, she appeared at a press conference appealing for information about Harvey's killer. She told the cameras and waiting reporters that Harvey had been the victim of a road rage attack by a man with "staring eyes." Her story was that a "tatty" Ford Sierra had followed them flashing its lights, before drawing level when they stopped. The driver then got out and knifed Harvey. The police described the attack as "particularly vicious" and the killing was highly publicized in the national press.

**ABOVE:** Tracie Andrews arriving at Birmingham Crown Court on July 29, 1997, to hear the verdict in her murder trial.

Either wracked with guilt or in fear of being found out, Tracie took a drug overdose the next day, but survived. She was arrested in hospital on December 7, while recovering. The police had been unable to find any witnesses to the road rage attack and not a single member of the public had come forward. All the evidence pointed to the killer being closer at hand.

Even after she had been charged and released on bail, Tracie maintained her story, but she could not stop the truth seeping out. At her trial the jury heard that Harvey had been obsessively jealous over her and accused her of seeing other men. The neighbors told their own stories of screaming rows.

Tracie Andrews was found guilty of murder at Birmingham Crown Court on July 29, 1997. Sentenced to life in prison with the recommendation that she serve a minimum of 14 years, she immediately lodged an appeal claiming she was the victim of a miscarriage of justice because of the publicity about her case. It was thrown out in October 1998.

Two years later, Tracie finally admitted she had killed Lee Harvey, and in 2005 a television documentary was made about the case. A prison source said, "Andrews has… admitted to the murder, which has surprised a lot of people. Although she has accepted her guilt, nobody really believes that she feels much remorse. She sees this as her first step on the way to parole. Andrews is manipulative and devious. Officers believe she will say or do anything to get out of jail."

**BELOW:** The sleepy village of Alvechurch was shocked by the murder of Lee Harvey in 1996.

# Arnold Axilrod

**A man whose sexual appetites were matched only by his depravity, dentist Arnold Axilrod drugged his patients so that he could rape them while they were unconscious. He also kept a lover, and when she fell pregnant the evil man decided to terminate the fetus, and his mistress with it.**

**On the morning of April 23, 1955,** John J. Cowles, Jnr., of the Cowles publishing empire was backing his Pontiac out of his garage, in Minneapolis, when he noticed what appeared to be a bundle of clothes in the alley. The "bundle" was the body of a young woman. Her face had been scratched and bruised, and her throat had a bluish mark. Police were called and when they searched the woman's coat pockets found a wallet containing a five-dollar bill, a doctor's prescription slip, and a driver's license. The woman was identified as Elizabeth Mary Moonen aged 21.

An autopsy revealed that she had been strangled, and that Elizabeth had been three months pregnant. It also found traces of semen in her vagina, which suggested that she had had intercourse just prior to her death. It seemed likely that her sexual partner would also be her killer. Here the mystery deepened, for police enquiries found that Elizabeth's husband was a serviceman stationed in Korea.

The starting point in the hunt for Elizabeth's lover was Dr. Glen Peterson who had issued the prescription found in Elizabeth's wallet, and he immediately pointed police in the right direction. He told them that she had named the baby's father as local dentist Arnold Axilrod, 49, who had a reputation as something of a ladies' man.

In fact, Axilrod was much more sleazy than a simple womanizer. His surgery was above a seedy nightclub called the Hoop De Do, and his patients were mainly nightclub performers and hat-check girls. Despite the fact that he had a spotless reputation, there were doubts about his activities. In late 1954, a phone call had been received by the police during which an anonymous woman told an officer that Axilrod had sedated her to operate on her teeth and then raped her while she was unconscious. But as she refused to give her name or file a complaint, the allegation was never investigated.

Axilrod buckled quickly under police questioning. He admitted that he'd given Elizabeth a ride on the evening of her death, and said that the two had quarreled after she accused him of being the father of her child. He claimed she had also threatened to expose him. The next thing he knew, Axilrod continued, was that he'd blacked out and when he came to, Elizabeth was no longer in the car. What he said next surprised the police. When they told him that she had been strangled, Axilrod replied, "If she was strangled, I must have done it. I was the only one there." He later withdrew that statement.

When the case hit the newspapers, 20 women came forward to say they had also been drugged by the dentist. One was Elizabeth's sister who said that Axilrod had talked suggestively to her. Axilrod went on trial for murder in Hennepin County District Court in late 1955. Despite public outrage, the evil dentist was not convicted of murder though. At the end of his trial, the jury found Axilrod guilty of manslaughter and given a prison sentence.

# Arthur Bagg

**When jealousy enters an already unbalanced mind, the results can be tragic. And few minds have been as fevered as Arthur Bagg's. His was a life lived in fantasy, worshipping the mythical Count Dracula, and the murder he committed was every bit as ghastly as any from a horror story.**

**When 17-year-old Marjorie Patricia Rosebrook's stabbed and mutilated body was found** beneath a viaduct outside Johannesburg, South Africa, suspicion immediately settled on her boyfriend, artist Arthur Bagg. The detectives' certainty that they had found the killer hardened when he told them that he hadn't been with Marjorie on the day of the murder—November 23, 1937. In fact, they already had several witnesses who reported that they had seen the couple together.

Determined to get a confession, the police continued to interrogate the 23-year-old. Eventually he broke down and willingly took officers to the scene of the crime, even going so far as to re-enact the killing for them. In a jealous rage over her conduct with another man, he had had stabbed her twice. Nevertheless, that didn't explain the mutilation and there was also the question of Marjorie's missing clothes and the murder weapon. At this point Bagg's co-operation dried up, for the full extent of his lunacy was yet to be uncovered. He tried everything he could to stop a police search of his home, and once there it soon became apparent why.

Beneath the floor of his bedroom was a secret earthen chamber hidden by a trapdoor; a "ritual site" where Bagg worshipped Count Dracula. It was also where he had hidden the murder knife and Marjorie's blood-stained clothing. Along with the incriminating evidence detectives found a piece of leather on which Bagg had carved the words, "I hereby defile the living God and serve only the Dark One, Dracula; to serve him faithfully so I may become one of his faithful servants."

Ironically, it was the evidence that he had tried to conceal that would save Bagg from execution. At his trial, on February 28, 1938, he withdrew his confession to Marjorie Rosebrook's murder and claimed she had committed suicide. He said he had only told police he had killed her to save her from shame. But after two hours deliberation, the jury found Bagg guilty of murder and he was sentenced to death. However, after assessments of his mental state were made—which took into account his strange shrine to the vampire—the sentence was commuted to life imprisonment. Bagg was released in 1947 after serving nine years.

**BELOW:** Arthur Bagg's obsession with Count Dracula led him to commit the horrendous murder of Marjorie Rosebrook.

# Lorena Bobbitt

**Although Lorena Bobbitt did not actually kill her husband, she inflicted on him a terrible—and now infamous—wound. In an odd twist of fate, she was not punished for her crime and instead became something of a heroine to feminists.**

It was an incident that grabbed headlines around the world. John Wayne and Lorena Bobbitt returned to their home in Manassas, Virginia, on June 23, 1993, after an evening of partying and drinking, and Lorena would later allege that Bobbitt raped her. She told a court that it was just the latest abuse in a long list of others. Her husband was often violent toward her and made no secret of the fact that he was having sex elsewhere. On one occasion, she said that he had forced her to terminate a pregnancy against her wishes. This time, however, John Wayne would pay a terrible price for his behavior.

**ABOVE:** Lorena Bobbitt waving to cheering demonstrators as she leaves the Prince William County Courthouse in Manassas, Virginia.

After the attack, as John lay sleeping, Lorena got out of bed to fetch a glass of water from the kitchen. As the tap was running, she spotted a carving knife and, as she stared at it, the years of abuse that she had suffered at the hands of her husband all came flooding back. Overwhelmed with anger and

**BELOW:** The knife used by Lorena Bobbitt to cut off the penis of her husband.

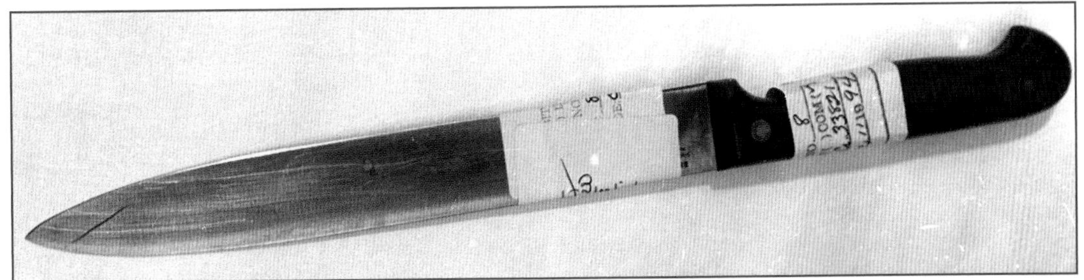

At this point Lorena came back to her senses, and realizing that she had committed a terrible crime she called the emergency services. Bobbitt was rushed to hospital while police combed the field for his penis. It was eventually found and the police packed it in ice and rushed it to the hospital. It took nine-and-a-half hours in surgery to successfully re-attach the severed body part.

Lorena defended her actions in court by maintaining that she had been the victim of constant abuse. Her lawyers told the jury that suffering from depression and post-traumatic stress disorder she had simply snapped. While John Wayne denied all of his wife's allegations, Lorena was able to supply witnesses to support her claims and she was eventually found not guilty of sexually wounding her husband.

In 1994, it was John's turn to face the judgement of the court. He stood trial for raping Lorena, but he, too, was acquitted.

By 1995 the couple were divorced. Although she had tried to avoid media attention, Lorena Bobbitt had by now become a feminist icon, and in the years that followed she founded Lorena's Red Wagon, an organization devoted to bringing an end to domestic violence. She later obtained a degree and gave birth to a daughter by a new partner, though when she and John were both guests on the Oprah Winfrey Show in 2009 she insisted that she would never marry again. John Wayne Bobbitt, however, used his new notoriety

**ABOVE:** Lorena Bobbitt (left), being escorted from the courtroom in the Prince William County Courthouse, Virginia, following the not guilty verdict.

hardly knowing what she was doing, Lorena Bobbitt picked up the knife, walked back to the bedroom, and sliced off more than half of Bobbitt's penis. Then she picked up the severed organ and drove a short distance before throwing it into a field.

in a different way. He formed a band called The Severed Parts and appeared in adult movies. He also continued to abuse women and after two more court cases for domestic assault was convicted in 2004.

**LEFT:** John Wayne Bobbitt (center) arriving at the Prince William County Court House for the first day of his wife's trial on charges of malicious wounding.

**BELOW:** Supporters of Lorena Bobbitt hold signs and shout their support as she leaves the courthouse.

# Mary Bolton

From almost the day that she was married, in 1922, Mary Bolton was a dreadful thorn in her husband's side. And as time went on she became more and more unbalanced, to the point where she was willing to kill rather than lose him.

**A good-natured, hard working,** and patient man Charles Bolton most certainly didn't deserve the woman he married. Almost immediately after the wedding, he realized that he had made a terrible mistake: Mary nagged him constantly and made wild accusations. Each day he went to his office and each night he returned home to face her jealousy. She was convinced that he was having affairs and became so frenzied in her rage that she would even beat him and, on one occasion, slashed his face with a razor. The hapless Bolton was forced to tell police who came to investigate when neighbors reported the violent row that he had cut himself shaving.

None of Mary's accusations was true. Bolton was a decent man and despite his wife's temper tried hard to make their marriage work. His protestations and attempts to calm Mary were futile though, and the strain was affecting his work. His employers even suggested that due to his personal problems he might be better off working for himself.

After enduring her emotional and physical torments for 14 years, Bolton finally came to the end of his tether, and filed for divorce on January 25, 1936. Mary, however, was not going to let him get away so easily and spent months harassing him to change his mind. And when she realized that Bolton was determined to be rid of her, she decided that she would get rid of him first.

Mary bought a revolver on June 11, and drove to her husband's office. All the way her rage grew and by the time she was riding the elevator to the 10th floor her fury was uncontrollable. Finding her husband in his office, Mary fired six shots. As Charles Bolton lay bleeding to death on the floor, she asked, "Why don't you get up and stop faking?"

Mary Bolton was originally sentenced to death in the electric chair but this was later commuted to a sentence of life imprisonment. However, Mary did not fancy spending the rest of her life—perhaps another 40 years—behind bars. She died on August 29, 1943, after slashing her wrists with a pair of scissors.

# Lizzie Borden

**Not all crimes of passion are triggered by lust or passion turned sour. For Lizzie Borden it was hatred of her stepmother and a domineering father, as well as good old-fashioned greed, which turned her into a brutal killer. Perhaps one of the most famous murderers in history, Borden was never convicted of her crime, but looking back it seems almost impossible that she got away with it. Never able to give a clear account of her whereabouts at the time of the double murder, she was lucky enough to have a judge who owed her defense counsel a favor and she also threw herself on the sympathy of the jury, and their misplaced belief that a mere woman could not have committed such a frenzied slaying.**

**Born in Fall River, Massachusetts,** in 1860, Lizzie's mother died when she was just two years old. Her father married again, a woman called Abby Gray who was 10 years his junior, and as Lizzie and her sister, Emma, grew up they came to despise their stepmother. To them she was a simple gold-digger who was frittering away their inheritance. Matters came to a head when their father, who was notoriously mean with money gave his wife's sister a large sum to save her from financial ruin. Lizzie wanted revenge.

The opportunity presented itself in the summer of 1892. Emma had gone to stay with friends at the nearby country town of Fairhaven while Lizzie remained at home with just a maid in the house along with Lizzie and her stepmother and father.

On August 4, Lizzie's father was away from the house for a short while. Around 9.30am, Mrs Borden was cleaning the steps to a spare bedroom when she was struck from behind with an axe. The blow to her head was enough to kill her instantly, but eight more rained

**ABOVE:** A colorized photograph of Lizzie Borden from the late 19th century.

down in quick succession. The same fate awaited her husband when he returned home an hour or so later; a killing blow was landed and again followed by a ferocious attack on his already dead body. Both heads were later removed for specialist forensic examination, which revealed "injuries consistent with a frenzied, almost psychopathic, attack, although both victims died with the first blow such was the force with which it was delivered."

The alarm was raised when the maid, Bridget Sullivan, heard Lizzie screaming, "Come down, come down. Father's dead. Someone came in and killed him!" The police were soon on the scene and under questioning, Lizzie's own story changed constantly from the outset. First she said she had been out in the yard when her father was killed, then she "remembered" that she had actually been in the barn. At the inquest that would change again, with Lizzie recalling that she had been in the kitchen when her father returned home. Although at one time she also said she had been on the stairs, she maintained that she had not noticed her stepmother's body there.

Nevertheless, the early investigation focused on John Morse, the brother of Mr Borden's first wife, who had recently stayed with the family for a few days. That avenue of investigation proved short-lived when Morse provided a solid alibi. The police were left with just two suspects—Lizzie and Bridget Sullivan. Quickly they narrowed it down to one as it was established that the maid had no motive for the crime while Lizzie had made no secret of the fact that she hated her stepmother. Her contradictory statements were also arousing suspicion.

By the time Lizzie Borden came to trial in June 1893, public opinion was already behind her. The folk of Massachusetts could not bring themselves to believe that one of their own, a God-fearing woman, could have committed such a crime. Lizzie had also cannily appointed one of the best criminal lawyers in the state to defend her. George Robinson was a former governor of Massachusetts and, crucially, had been responsible for appointing one of the three judges who now sat on the bench before him. The judge repaid the favor by agreeing with Robinson that damning transcripts of Lizzie's questioning at the inquest, during which her story had changed several times, were inadmissible. The prosecution case looked weaker and weaker, having finally to rest on the fact that Lizzie Borden was at the house at the time of the murders and that her evidence was conflicting.

Lizzie and her lawyer did their utmost to secure the jury's sympathy. Midway through the 10-day hearing she appeared to collapse in a faint, while Robinson later pointed to the soberly dressed, neat figure, saying: "To find her guilty, you must believe she is a fiend. Gentlemen, does she look it?" The tactic worked. The jury found Lizzie not guilty and she was set free. On

**ABOVE:** The Borden house in Fall River, Massachusetts where the grisly murders were committed.

being acquitted of murder, she inherited much of her father's money and used it to buy a house in a wealthy suburb. Suspiciously, Bridget Sullivan returned to Ireland soon after with, it was often said, a large quantity of cash from the late Mr Borden's bank account given to her by Lizzie.

The jury may have been convinced of her innocence, but the public was not so satisfied. and as the years passed it became the widespread belief that Lizzie had gotten away with murder. She may have escaped the law, but for the remainder of her days would be taunted by a popular rhyme: "Lizzie Borden took an axe. And gave her mother forty whacks. When she saw what she had done. She gave her father forty-one!"

Lizzie Borden initially lived with her sister and then by herself until she died aged 67 in 1927. She was buried in the same family plot as those who died on that sweltering August day 35 years before.

# Cordelia Botkin

**Cordelia was most definitely a "woman scorned." Having won her younger lover, he deserted her and returned to his wife. Love turned to seething fury and when Botkin's attempts to ruin his marriage failed, there was only one course of action left: revenge. Not on the man who had broken her heart, but on the woman who had taken him from her.**

**At 41 years old, Cordelia Botkin** was a sophisticated woman of the world. Separated from her wealthy grain broker husband, he nonetheless supported her financially, leaving her free to indulge a busy social life and numerous flirtations. But when she met John Preston Jack Dunning in 1896, she felt a powerful attraction that appeared to be mutual. He was 32, nine years her junior, and a highly regarded reporter for the Associated Press in California. Soon the couple were involved in a passionate affair. It was not Dunning's first, and when his wife found out that once again he was cheating on her, she decided that she had had enough. She left, taking their small daughter away to her father's home. Cordelia was overjoyed. With Mary Dunning out of the picture she could at last take a more public position in her lover's life.

The affair lasted three years. During that time, Dunning began to drink more and more heavily, and became addicted to gambling. Eventually, he was sacked by the Associated Press after embezzling $4,000 dollars to pay gambling debts, and though he found work on local San Francisco newspapers was quickly fired by them too; this time for habitual drunkeness. Homeless and penniless, Dunning was forced to move into the hotel where Cordelia lived. There, he surveyed the wreckage of his life and decided to clean up his act.

Well aware of Dunning's talent, in 1898 the Associated Press agreed to give him another chance and hired him as their lead reporter. It meant leaving San Francisco, but he seemed all too keen to return to the life he'd had before it had all gone so disastrously wrong. Although Cordelia pleaded with him desperately, her agonized pleas fell on deaf ears. Dunning left her, was reconciled with his wife, and left for news assignments in Cuba, where he became a hero at the battle of Santiago Bay when he helped save survivors of the Spanish battleships that were sunk.

**BELOW:** The California State Prison at San Quentin where Cordelia Botkin lived out her final days.

Already heartbroken, when Cordelia heard of her faithless lover's new success and the mended relationship with his wife, she became incensed with jealousy. Having supported and loved Dunning through all his troubles, it was the final humiliation. At first she tried to vent her rage by sending Mary Dunning anonymous letters that gave intimate details of all her husband's affairs, but it didn't have the effect she had hoped. More radical measures were called for.

One morning, Mary Dunning was delighted to receive a box of candies at her father's home in Delaware. An unsigned note attached said, "With love to yourself and baby," but the fact that the handwriting was the same as the poison-pen letters she had received obviously didn't register. Mary ate three and shared the rest. The candy contained a real poison this time: arsenic. Two days later, Mary was dead, alongside her sister Harriet. Miraculously, four others who had eaten the sweets survived.

It didn't take the police long to follow the trail back to Cordelia. Mary's father noticed that the note accompanying the candy was in the same hand as the poison pen letters his daughter had been receiving, and the box of candy was traced back to San Francisco. Cordelia Botkin denied the murder charges, but the case against her was open and shut. She was convicted in December 1898 and again at a retrial in 1904.

Sentenced to life, she eventually died in 1910 at San Quentin State Prison, her life destroyed by jealousy. And hers was not the only one. If vengeance on the man she loved was what she was after then Cordelia succeeded. The loss of his wife and the ensuing scandal tipped Dunning into a downward spiral. He died, virtually destitute, before she did.

# Leone Bouvier

**Leone Bouvier's life was one of abuse, and when the man whom she believed would save her from it betrayed her too, it proved too much for her to bear.**

**The daughter of a drunk father and unsympathetic mother**, at 16 years old, Leone Bouvier had already lost her virginity during a fumbled encounter in a field and been taken advantage of by various local lads. Illiterate and unloved, she had little in life to look forward to when she met a 22-year-old garage mechanic named Emile Clenet. For the first time Leone believed that someone cared about her. Clenet would visit her on a Sunday, take a hotel room, and the couple would spend the day making love, taking rests to laugh together and talk about marriage.

But like many a naive young girl, she was deceived. While Clenet certainly enjoyed the promise of certain sex on a Sunday, he had little love for her. Leone had already suspected that he had a cruel streak, but in a haze of love she had made excuses for him. And when she fell pregnant in 1951 she continued to trust him. On hearing the news, Clenet refused to live up to his responsibilities and instead, callously told his teenage lover to get rid of the baby. Leone obediently had a termination. It left her ill; the headaches and depression she had previously suffered from grew so bad that she eventually lost her job at a shoe factory. Her drunk father beat her when he was told that she would no longer be bringing a wage home. In desperation Leone cycled 30 miles to Nantes in the hope of finding comfort in the arms of her lover, but Clenet briskly told her she had broken the "Sundays only" rule and refused to speak to her.

Jobless and abandoned by her lover and family, Leone lived on the streets and earned money for food the only way she could; by prostituting herself. Despite all that had happened she still loved Clenet and hoped against hope that they might marry, but as time passed their meetings became few and far between and, when he did show up, he showed no compassion for her plight. Much of her life was now spent at the docks where she sold her body. Sick, heartbroken, betrayed, and with her thoughts dwelling on revenge, Leone spent what little money she had on a pistol.

Still, disaster might have been averted if Clenet had returned just a little of the love that Leone had given him. But it was not to be. At a final meeting, during which the couple visited a carnival, Clenet announced he was to leave France to work in North Africa. Leone begged him to stay, but he simply shrugged and told her that he would never marry her. In response Leone pulled his reluctant face to hers for a parting kiss. Then she shot him at point-blank range in the neck.

Leone was arrested in a convent at Angers where she had sought shelter with her sister who had become a nun several years before. She was charged with murder and brought to trial in December 1953. Fate still had one final misfortune for her. Although she had killed a man, if anyone deserved to be treated leniently under the French traditions of the *crime passionnel* it was Leone Bouvier. Nevertheless, she was unlucky enough to be assigned an unsympathetic judge. When he heard that her sister was a nun, he chastised Leone for not making anything of her own life, and even the appearance of a drunk father and long-suffering mother in the dock did nothing to sway him. He told her that killing her lover as he bent to kiss her was an act of gross atrocity and took no notice of Leone's weeping or her whispered words, "But I loved him."

After deliberating for just 15 minutes, the jury saved Leone from a death sentence by finding her guilty of murder without premeditation. However, she received the full penalty of the law: a life sentence with a minimum of 20 years to be served.

# Elliot Bower

**It is rare indeed that someone who confesses to killing a love rival is set free, yet in Paris in the mid-1800s that is exactly what happened. The British defendant used the French plea of crime passionel rather than premeditated murder, and he was set at liberty, with many even agreeing that he had done the honorable thing by slaying his wife's lover.**

**Like many men of his time,** Elliott Bower was a hypocrite whose double standards are easy to see in these more enlightened days. An English foreign correspondent working in Paris, he thought nothing of betraying his wife, Fanny, with a series of women. Such was his arrogance that he hardly bothered keeping his numerous mistresses a secret from her. For the unfortunate Fanny Bower, life became a series of heartbreaks as she discovered time and again that her husband had been cheating on her with yet another. Needless to say, while Bower pleasured himself with the ladies of Paris, his wife was expected to be completely faithful and uncomplaining.

Emotionally crushed after her husband's latest fling was revealed to her, Fanny finally turned in desperation to a close friend of her husband's who had always been kind to her. Saville Morton was also a foreign correspondent, working for a rival newspaper, and during happier times he had become almost part of the family, dining often with the Bowers and accompanying them for Parisian nights out. Now, Morton's relationship with the distressed Fanny deepened into something more and, as time passed, they became lovers. Soon, Fanny fell pregnant.

When the child was born (Fanny's fifth), she instantly declared it to be, "just like Morton!" At first, fearing scandal, Morton stayed away, but his lover's fragile emotional state had been further weakened by the birth of another man's child. She summoned Morton to her bedside and banned her husband from the room. He must have been suspicious, and his fears were confirmed on the night of October 1, 1852. At last called to his wife's side, he heard her confess in a fevered outburst that he was not the father of her child.

In a frenzy of rage that he—the serial adulterer—should be deceived in his turn, he confronted his former friend. Morton admitted everything. Bower, in a fury, took up a long carving knife and ran him through with it.

To escape punishment Bower deserted his family and fled to England. But soon came the news that French police considered his act a *crime passionnel*, and not premeditated murder. Knowing that this would be treated much more leniently, Bower returned to France and gave himself up. At his trial, which started on December 28, 1852, Bower listened to the heated defense put up by his counsel; that he had been driven to kill because of Morton's seduction of his wife, his close friend's dishonorable and treacherous behavior, and the ultimate humiliation of the birth of a child which was not his. In fact, he was presented to the jury as the real victim of the affair, and the murder of his wife's lover not only understandable, but a deserved punishment and an act of honor.

He was lucky to be tried in a country that prides itself on having the legal defence of a *crime passionnel*. Perhaps he would not have been given such a sympathetic hearing anywhere else. Acquitted of the crime, and virtually hailed as a hero by the French press, Bower left the court a free man.

# Martha Bowers

**Taking another human life is a terrible crime and one that affects killers in different ways. Some suffer the torture of their own conscience as they realize what they have done, others remain defiant. A few seem to feel no remorse whatsoever. When Martha Bowers husband died she threw herself on his body, weeping hysterically. But less than two hours later she was spotted laughing and joking with her lover.**

**Martha Bowers married her third**—and final—husband in San Francisco in 1902, but such happiness she may have had with Martin Bowers, a bridge builder, did not last long. Martha was not the type to be satisfied with just one man and before her marriage was a year old she was enjoying the attentions of a lover, Patrick Leary. It wasn't long before Bowers became aware of his wife's infidelity, and he insisted that the affair must come to an end.

Soon after, on June 5, 1903, a doctor was called to their home. Martha asked Dr. Carl Von Tiedmann if he could prescribe medicine for her husband saying that he had become ill as a result of ptomaine poisoning caused by eating too much ham. Over the following days, Martin's condition deteriorated until a second doctor was called in. This time, Bowers was taken to a convalescent home and finally he began to recover. After a month he was judged fit to return home. Not long after, he was critically sick again and was rushed to hospital where he died on August 25, with his wife pouring out her grief over his lifeless body.

Harry Bowers—Martin's brother—was perplexed. Something about the death didn't seem quite right. He requested a full postmortem be carried out, which found four grains of undissolved arsenic in Martin Bowers' stomach. By now the possible murder was making news reports and caught the eye of a pharmacist who recalled a woman coming to him on August 20, with a prescription for arsenic. He told police the prescription was memorable because though signed by a Dr. McLaughlin, it was written on a plain sheet of paper and not a normal prescription form. However, the description of the woman the pharmacist gave turned out not to match that of Martha, but it did lead police to her sister, Zylpha Sutton.

In Bowers' home, police found a school composition book with a page torn out. It matched that upon which the phoney prescription had been written and so, too, did the handwriting in the book. The police also heard from witnesses of how Martha had been seen playfully cavorting in public with Patrick Leary less than two hours after the death of her husband.

With further revelations about how Martin Bowers had attempted to put an end to the affair, it was more than enough to condemn her. Martha Bowers was found guilty on January 20, 1904, and sentenced to life imprisonment. Her sister Zylpha was released through lack of evidence.

# Maria Boyne

**Maria Boyne's murder of her husband was committed simply because she could not bear to lose anything she thought of as hers. While she wasn't prepared to part with her lover she had no intention of losing her London home in a divorce either. In her attempt to have it all though, as so many killers had found out before her, she made sure that she lost everything.**

Maria's eight-year marriage was over in all but name when she took a knife to her husband. She was already pregnant by her 24-year-old lover, Gary McGinley, and divorce was imminent. The only thing Maria was afraid of was that she might lose her house in the legal battle with her husband. In the weeks before the killing, she told her friends that she just wanted Boyne dead so that she could bring McGinley into her home.

Finally, her murderous intentions were fired up by a particularly vicious argument with her husband. Maria grabbed a knife and brutally stabbed him 31 times, then calmly took a gold chain from around his neck. She would use the money raised from pawning it to celebrate her husband's death with a passionate night in a hotel with McGinley. Boyne's body was found by his elderly father, Michael, who would die soon after giving evidence in the trial. The shock he received on finding his son's bloody corpse meant he too became a victim of Maria's crime.

Maria couldn't evade justice for long, though she was prepared to go to any lengths to do so. In fact, when it became clear that she would face trial for her crime she threw her lover to the wolves, telling the police that it was he who had killed Boyne. No one was fooled. The jury cleared the apparently naive McGinley, but Maria faced the full penalty of the law, damned almost as much by her own lack of remorse and her attempts to shift the blame as by the crime itself. As Judge Paul Worsley, told Maria, "You were motivated by sex and selfishness. You were scheming and devious."

In February 2009, the 30-year-old Maria was found guilty at the Old Bailey, London's central court, murdering Boyne in his bed in April 2008. She was sentenced to life on March 4 and told she would serve a minimum of 24 years in prison. In seeking to serve only her own needs she had killed an innocent man and left two young children, as well as her baby daughter, motherless. In an emotional and touching statement shortly before he died, Boyne's father told the press, "My son thought the world of her despite her numerous affairs. He loved her."

# Betty Broderick

**After putting so much time, emotional energy, and effort into helping her husband achieve his dreams, to be betrayed at a time when she should have been enjoying the fruits of her labors was a brutal injury for Betty Broderick to suffer. Her life, which had once promised so much, was torn to shreds. The only thing that could satisfy her was the deaths of those who had caused her so much grief.**

**Betty and Dan Broderick married in April 1969** after meeting at a football game and both shared the same dream: They wanted to be wealthy, secure, and happy—a family that had it all. During the first years of hardship, the couple put everything into their hopes for the future. Dan enrolled in law school, while Betty took jobs to support him. When their four children came along she took sole charge of them, allowing her husband to concentrate on finishing his studies and starting a career. He was offered a job at an established law firm in San Diego, California, and Betty—still determined to do her bit—took a job as a cashier at a restaurant in the evenings.

As the years passed, the Brodericks' dreams of financial security came true. They bought a beautiful house in the affluent Coral Reef suburb of La Jolla in San Diego, became members of exclusive clubs, and took foreign vacations. But along the road to success the shared goals and the loving closeness that had bound them together was lost. Dan became ever more distant from the family. He rarely saw the children and when he and his wife did spend time together it was usually at one of the legal functions or parties that Betty came to detest.

It was at one of these events that Betty overheard a stray comment from her husband that would mark the beginning of her breakdown into emotional chaos. Dan, who was talking to a friend, asked, "Isn't she beautiful?" After a brief moment of delight, Betty soon realized that Dan hadn't been talking about her but Linda Kolkena, a receptionist at the law firm.

Dan now became even more detached from his family than he had been before, and made no secret of his distaste for the woman who had worked so hard to help him climb the ladder of success. On one occasion he told Betty that he was tired of his life and that she was "old, fat, ugly, and boring." Meanwhile, he had taken Linda Kolkena on as his personal assistant.

Betty found out just how calculating her husband could be at the beginning of 1985. Having announced that he was moving the family to a new, bigger, rented house; soon after their belongings were unpacked Dan deserted them and returned to their old home. In a fit of anger and hoping that Dan might realize just how much she had done for him, Betty took all their children and dumped them on him. Her plan, however, backfired badly. Dan hired a housekeeper and finally began to spend more time with his children. Not only did he cope admirably, but his relationship with the children flourished. Betty, meanwhile, was sidelined. His relationship with Linda now openly acknowledged, Dan filed for divorce, and as a top lawyer he was not an easy opponent in a legal battle.

Having lost everything and faced with a long and painful fight, Betty's state of mind began disintegrating. She ignored legal advice, failed to turn up at court hearings, and left a series of telephone messages littered with obscenities and abuse. They would soon come back to haunt her during the divorce proceedings in court. But when she lost custody of the children and Dan took out an injunction preventing her from visiting her old home, something in Betty snapped.

She bought a gun and on November 5, 1988, drove to Dan's home, let herself in with a key she had stolen from her eldest daughter, and made her way to the bedroom. Seeing two shapes beneath the covers of the bed she used to share she shot them both. Dan and Linda were killed instantly.

In court, Betty's defense lawyers claimed that she had been driven to the edge of sanity by the latest developments in the long and bitter divorce battle and had gone to the house to reason with her husband one last time and to commit suicide if she failed to win his sympathy. But while the jury accepted that Betty suffered from psychological disorders they could not help but see the crime as being calculated and premeditated. The prosecution made full use of the hysterical messages Betty had left on her husband's answer phone and, again, they helped paint a picture of a bitter, vindictive woman.

Betty's first trial ended in a hung jury with two jurors preferring a manslaughter verdict rather than murder. At her second hearing, the jury returned a verdict of two counts of second-degree murder, and Betty Broderick was sentenced to two consecutive terms of 15 years to life and two years for the illegal use of a firearm. She was ordered to serve a minimum of 21 years before becoming eligible for parole.

# Elizabeth Brown

**The tale of the last woman ever to be hanged in Dorset, England, is a sorry one, for Elizabeth Brown's was a true crime of passion, committed in a moment of heartbroken anger. It is also a tale that has left a lasting mark. Her death was watched by a 16-year-old reporter named Thomas Hardy, who would go on to be one of Britain's greatest novelists. Elizabeth's tragic story made such an impression on him that it formed the basis of his greatest novel, *Tess of the D'Urbervilles*.**

**An attractive redhead**, Elizabeth Brown married her husband John later in life than was usual in the mid-19th century. He was 20 years her junior, and it was rumored that he wed only for his wife's money, though the gossip doesn't have the ring of truth to it. Elizabeth was certainly not wealthy; both she and her husband were employed as servants. The couple settled down to married life in the village of Birdsmoorgate, near Beaminster in Dorset, and it soon became obvious that the relationship was not a happy one. Elizabeth became convinced that her youthful husband was unfaithful, and one fateful day in 1856 she was proved right. Returning home unexpectedly one night, Elizabeth caught her husband beneath the blankets of their marriage bed with another woman. Broken-hearted and humiliated she flew into a rage and a violent quarrel followed. Elizabeth hit out at John who in turn lashed her with a whip. She seized an axe and in the heat of the moment caught him a fatal blow.

Elizabeth then made a mistake that would eventually lead to her own death. Had she told the truth then it is very likely that the circumstances of her husband's death would have been taken into account, and she would have been treated leniently. Instead, the frightened woman told police that her husband's fractured skull had been caused by the kick of a horse. Her story was not believed, she was charged with murder, and went on trial at Dorchester Assizes where she continued to protest her innocence. It did not take a jury long to return a guilty verdict and she was sentenced to death by hanging. Only then did she tell what had really happened.

Although there was a swell of public support for Elizabeth, the Home Secretary refused to grant a reprieve because Elizabeth had lied for so long. She was taken to the scaffold at Dorchester prison on August 9, 1856, and—in a further cruel injustice—delivered into the hands of the infamous hangman William Calcraft, Britain's principal executioner from 1829 to 1874. He was noted for his "short drops," which meant a slow and agonizing death by strangulation rather than a cleanly broken neck.

A crowd of nearly 4,000 people gathered to watch Elizabeth accept her fate with calm and dignity. She had chosen a tight-fitting black silk dress for her execution. The noose was ill-fitting and Elizabeth's death was far from instant. A later report noted what a "fine figure she showed against the sky as she hung in the misty rain," and how "the tight black silk gown set off her shape as she wheeled half round and back" in her death throes. This grisly and salacious report was written by the young Thomas Hardy.

**OVERLEAF:** The acclaimed English novelist, poet and dramatist, Thomas Hardy who attended the execution of Elizabeth Brown at Dorchester Prison as a young reporter.

**BELOW:** An illustration from Thomas Hardy's *Tess of the D'Urbervilles*: Elizabeth Brown's tragic story made such an impression on Hardy that it formed the basis of his classic novel.

# Ernest Brown

**Dorothy Morton's first mistake was to cheat on her husband with Ernest Brown. Her second was to try and end the affair. For her lover had killed before and was determined to keep her by doing so again.**

**Having begun an affair with one of her husband's employees**, a worker on his successful Yorkshire cattle farm, Dorothy Morton soon realized that she had made a terrible misjudgment. Her lover, Ernest Brown, was bad tempered and aggressive. Try as she might, he wouldn't let Dorothy finish the relationship. Instead, he continued to badger her for sex and treat her as if he owned her. On September 5, 1933, Brown found out that Dorothy had been swimming with another man and flew into a terrible rage during which he punched her to the ground. In fear for her life, Dorothy ran from her lover to the main house and stayed there, waiting for her husband, Frederick, to return. Instead, she heard the sound of a shot outside. Soon after, Brown appeared saying he had killed a rat in the barn. Dorothy waited in vain for her husband. In the early hours of the next morning, she heard an explosion and looked out to see the farm garage on fire. She grabbed her baby and with companion Ann Houseman, ran from the house to report the fire to the police.

When the flames were finally put out, the badly burned body of Frederick Morton was discovered among the cinders. He had been shot in the stomach then he and his two cars were doused with petrol and torched in an attempt to destroy evidence.

Ernest Brown was arrested and charged with murder. He was tried at Leeds Assizes and was soon found guilty. However, as the case had proceeded, it came to light that Brown had also murdered a woman called Evelyn Foster nearly two years earlier. She had offered a lift to a "smartly dressed man" with a bowler hat on January 6, 1931, and he had leaned over to touch her intimately as she drove. When she stopped the car to throw him out, he knocked her unconscious before setting fire to the car with her in it. Burned almost beyond recognition, Evelyn Foster had managed to whisper the man's description to police from her hospital bed before she died, and after Brown's arrest, police realized he was a match. Already sentenced to death it made no sense to try Brown for an earlier crime, but on the day of his execution—February 6, 1934—a chaplain told him, "You should use these last few moments to confess your sins and make your peace with God." As the hangman placed the noose around his neck, Brown murmured "Otterburn," the name of the village where Evelyn had lived.

# Albert Burrows

**A violent thief who had previously been arrested for horse stealing, cruelty to animals, and assault, when Albert Burrows met Hannah Calladine he added bigamy to the long list of crimes on his charge sheet. It was not, however, the last one he would commit.**

**Born in Cheadle Hulme**, Derbyshire, England, in 1871, by the time World War I broke out, Albert Burrows had amassed an extensive police record. Although he sometimes worked as a laborer on building sites, he was not above raising extra income to take home to his wife and daughter through stealing and his temper had also landed him in trouble on more than one occasion. He was a man who felt that laws and morals just didn't apply to him. So when he began working in an ammunition factory and met a younger woman to whom he was attracted the fact that he already had a wife and child did not stop him starting an affair with her. As far as Hannah was concerned Burrows was a widower whose daughter was being looked after by a housekeeper friend in Glossop and when she fell pregnant in May and Burrows proposed, she accepted. The couple were married in October.

For a short while Burrows was able to secretly support both families, but when the war ended he found himself unemployed and unable to keep up payments. Added to which, Hannah had begun to have suspicions about her husband and wrote a letter to his daughter in Glossop. Burrows first wife was shocked to discover that there was another Mrs Burrows, and her husband was prosecuted, serving six months for bigamy.

Burrows returned to his original wife when he was released, but found that Hannah had obtained a legal order that he financially support her and her infant son, as well. When he couldn't pay up, she had him arrested and he was imprisoned for another three weeks. The situation was no better when he came out the second time. With no job and two families to maintain, Burrows was soon behind on payments again.

The situation grew even worse when Hannah arrived on his doorstep in a cold night just before Christmas in 1919 with his son and Elsie (her daughter from a previous relationship) and demanded to be taken in. With his outraged wife protesting, Burrows allowed Hannah to stay, saying that she couldn't be turned away on such a night—his wife walked out the following day. Hannah ended up staying the final three weeks of her life with her former husband.

On January 12, 1920, Burrows again appeared in court, but this time he had solved his problems. He told the justices that Hannah had found a good job and left taking the children with her. Mrs Burrows returned to the family home soon after. Finally, it seemed that Albert Burrows had put the stresses and strains of supporting two families behind him. The true extent of his crimes, however, would later come to light in the most appalling way.

On March 4, 1923, a four-year-old boy named Thomas Wood went missing after having been seen with Burrows. He was quickly taken into custody and under police questioning broke down. The truth that was to be unravelled made his previous crimes look like minor misdemeanors. Burrows admitted that he had sexually assaulted the small boy, then dropped him down a mine shaft. When it was searched, little Thomas's body was indeed found, and alongside were the remains of Hannah Calladine and her two children, Albert, and Elsie.

The trial of Albert Edward Burrows for the murder of Hannah Calladine, 32, and her fifteen-month-old son was held at the Derbyshire Assizes and began on July 8, 1923. The horrified jury took less than a quarter of an hour to bring in a verdict of guilty. With the death sentence already passed, the authorities didn't waste any time bringing the cases for Elsie or Thomas Wood to court and Burrows paid for his crimes at Bagthorpe Gaol in Nottingham on the August 8, 1923 with a noose around his neck.

# William Burton

**A cheat and a liar, William Burton, made sweeping promises in order to seduce the young woman who had caught his eye. He had no intention of keeping them though, and when he found out that she was pregnant the cold-hearted Burton decided she had become a problem.**

**As a 29-year-old rabbit catcher at Manor Farm** in the Dorset village of Gussage Saint Michael, William Burton was no great catch himself, though he possessed a certain amount of charm. It had won him a respectable wife, who worked as a schoolteacher, and the couple had recently welcomed a baby to their flat above the village post office. Burton was dissatisfied though. His wife was somewhat older than him and now a mother. His passion for her was waning, just as it was growing for another woman.

At Manor Farm there was a beautiful young cook named Winifred Mary Mitchell. Burton became determined to have her. He gave her the full benefit of his rough charm, but she was not the type of woman to give her love easily. For two months he tried to seduce her, and still she resisted, knowing that he was married man with a young child.

Winifred was finally won over when Burton promised to take her to Canada where they could begin a new life together. Convinced that Burton loved her enough to leave his family behind, Winifred's reluctance was cast aside. Burton's promises were empty. What had started for him as a challenge and then an enjoyable sexual liaison abruptly became a liability when Winifred fell pregnant. He could see only one solution that didn't involve the inconvenience of either making good on his promises or having his cheating brought to light with the birth of an illegitimate child.

On March 29, 1913, Burton again promised Winifred that they would soon run away together and arranged to meet her in a secluded spot. He then borrowed a gun, saying he needed it to kill a cat. When his lover arrived for their illicit tryst, he shot her and buried her body in a shallow grave.

Unfortunately for him, on May 2, the corpse was discovered, and when police discovered scraps of passionate letters Burton had written to Winifred, he was arrested. William Burton was found guilty of murder and became the last man ever to be hanged at Dorchester Prison on June 21, 1913.

**ABOVE:** An aerial view of Dorchester prison, William Burton was the last man to be hanged there.

# Kitty Byron

**The law is supposed to stand apart from public opinion, but in Kitty Byron's case her conviction for murder was followed by such an outcry that the Home Secretary himself stepped in, saving her first from the gallows and later allowing Kitty's release from prison after she served just six years of a life sentence.**

**Kitty Byron's was a woeful tale**. She had the misfortune to fall in love with Arthur Reginald Baker. In public, Baker seemed to be respectable married man and was a member of the London Stock Exchange. However, in private Baker was a heavy drinker and prone to outbursts of violent temper, during which he often attacked his mistress. On one occasion he almost strangled her.

Baker lived a double life, with his wife in one home while Kitty was set up in lodgings on Duke Street in the West End of London. As far as the landlady was concerned the couple were Mr and Mrs Baker and unremarkable except for their furious arguments, which often ended in violence. On the evening of November 7, 1902, there was a particularly vicious quarrel that ended with Kitty appearing on the landing in her nightdress to avoid her lover's fists. The next morning, tired of the fighting, the landlady gave them two months' notice to leave.

The relationship calm down for a while after the incident, but it seems that Baker was growing bored of his mistress. After taking Kitty a cup of tea before leaving for work one morning, he took the landlady to one side and confessed she was not his wife, but a girl of "no class." He assured her that he would make sure Kitty left the premises the very next day.

Unfortunately for Baker, a housemaid overheard the conversation. The news, which she quickly passed on to Kitty, would cost him his life. On hearing how her abusive lover now planned to coldly abandon her and have her thrown out of her home, Kitty uttered the words that would come back to haunt her at her trial. Baker would die, she said, "before the day is out."

The landlady was mystified. Why, she asked, did Kitty stay with a violent, drunken bully if they were not married? Kitty's reply was short and simple: "Because I love him," she said, before going out to buy a sharp knife. She then sent a note via a post office messenger boy to Baker at his office. It read, "Want you importantly. Kitty."

Baker came at once, following the boy back to the post office where Kitty was waiting. As he approached the woman he had beaten so often she pulled the knife from where it was hidden in her muff and stabbed Baker twice.

Her trial began in December 1902 and Kitty's was a pathetic figure as she stood weeping in the dock. While admitting that she had killed Baker, she said that she did not know what she was doing and pleaded not guilty to murder. Public sympathy was with her, but the judge's less so. While the defense pleaded manslaughter, he did not agree and summed up in favor of a murder verdict though with a strong recommendation that the court should be merciful. But clemency was not forthcoming: Kitty was found guilty of murder and sentenced to death.

However, her fortunes were about to take a dramatic turn for the better. The trial had been widely reported in the press, and the public mood was that the sentence was far too harsh considering how Kitty had suffered at Baker's hands. While she awaited the gallows, a petition was circulated and 15,000 signatures collected before it was handed to the Home Secretary. It included the names of clerks who had worked with Baker in the City and knew exactly the type of man he was. A reprieve was duly granted, and Kitty's sentence reduced to life imprisonment. In 1907 it was reduced again and she was released from prison in 1908.

# Frederick Bywaters

**Percy Thompson was the victim of a classic crime of passion. In refusing to divorce his wife, Edith, so that she and the man she adored could be together, he brought the anger of both down upon his head. But while the lovers both eventually hanged for his murder, it is likely that only one of them was guilty.**

**In 1916, Percy Thompson married Edith Graydon.** He was 21 and she was just 18, and the couple settled down to their life together in Ilford, Essex, England. Percy was a clerk at the Pacific and Orient shipping line, and Edith was a bookkeeper at a millinery firm. For almost six years, they enjoyed a life of quiet domesticity, but that was before Edith was swept away by a passion that she had never imagined possible.

In the summer of 1921, the Thompsons joined a group for a holiday visit to the Isle of Wight. Among the party was 19-year-old Frederick Bywaters, a shipping line employee and a confident young man

**ABOVE:** Frederick Bywaters, seated, at the inquest into the death of Percy Thompson.

with a strong personality. The mutual attraction between him and Edith Thompson was explosive. Before the short vacation was over, Edith confided to her sister that she no longer loved her husband.

Overwhelmed by her feelings for Bywaters, Edith set out to persuade her husband to allow him to become a lodger at their home, telling him that the extra money would be useful. Reluctantly, Thompson agreed, and Bywaters moved in. But such was his love for Edith that Bywaters could not be satisfied with the role of lover. Although the affair was made easy by the fact that he lived under the same roof as his mistress, he could not bear to watch her pretending to still be a dutiful wife. Before long, he confessed to Thompson that he and Edith were deeply in love and asked him to divorce her so that she would be free to marry again. Thompson was understandably furious. A huge argument erupted and Bywaters was thrown out of the house. Edith was told that her affair was at and end.

Nevertheless, the lovers continued to see each other whenever it could be contrived and, when they couldn't meet, sent each other long, passionate letters. In September 1922, Bywaters' ship docked in England. On the afternoon of October 3, he and Edith had a secret rendezvous in a London teashop. Later that night she and her husband went to the theater and returned late to Ilford. As they walked home an assailant leaped from the darkness. It was Bywaters.

As the young man repeatedly plunged a knife into Percy, Edith screamed and cried for help, pleading with her lover, "Oh don't, oh don't!" Her reaction was, said witnesses at her trial, one of genuine horror. She also pleaded with a doctor who rushed to the scene to save her husband's life. However, she did not tell the police that she knew the attacker though the thin protection this brought Bywaters soon failed. After talking to neighbors and discovering the stack of letters Edith had received from her lover, a motive for murder was established. Edith and Bywaters were arrested.

At their trial, the prosecution alleged that the murder had been planned that afternoon at the teashop rendezvous. Bywaters denied it and told the jury that he had tried to reason with Thompson again and ask him to divorce Edith, and in the ensuing an argument Thompson had threatened to shoot him. He insisted that he had acted in self-defense and even so had only meant to injure, not kill.

**ABOVE:** Frederick Bywaters being led from Ilford police station in Essex following his arrest for the murder of Percy Thompson.

However, the couple were betrayed by their own letters. When the prosecution produced 62 of them, sent from Edith to Bywaters, they painted a damning picture of adulterous lovers plotting to kill the man who stood between them. In each, Edith referred to her lover by his pet name "Darlint" and many told how she was trying to kill her husband by putting glass into his food, "Big pieces too, not powdered." She also wrote of trying to poison Thompson: "He puts great stress on the tea tasting bitter." And more: "I am going to try the glass again when it is safe." In one particularly passionate letter Edith wrote, "This thing that I am going to do for both of us—will it ever, at all, make any difference darlint? Do you understand what I mean? Will you ever think any the less of me?"

In response, Bywaters told the court there never had been a real plot to murder Thompson. The letters were just the fantasies of two people who adored each other but were forced apart. The letters also contained references to an abortion that Edith had had when she found she was carrying Bywaters' baby and it is interesting to note that such was the morality of the time that the ignorant jurors interpreted many of the phrases in the letter referring to the terminated pregnancy as being further death threats. Edith's defense counsel, however, made no attempt to clear up the jurors' misunderstandings. He feared that the knowledge that she had not only cheated on her husband but aborted her lover's child would lose the jury's sympathy completely.

The case against the lovers was strong, yet there was one thing in Edith's favor. A single hard fact that the defense case finally rested upon. The pathologist's report stated that no glass or traces of poison had been found in the body of Percy Thompson.

There was to be no mercy, however. The judge—Mr Justice Shearman—took pleasure in detailing Edith's "wicked affection" for her lover in his summing up, saying, "This is a squalid and rather indecent case of lust and adultery." The jury took two hours to consider their verdicts. Edith Thompson and Frederick Bywaters were pronounced guilty and the judge sentenced them to hang. They died on the gallows on the morning of January 9, 1923.

To the end, Bywaters remained both dignified and determined to protect the reputation of his beloved Edith. From his condemned cell, he wrote in her defence, saying "For her to be hanged as a criminal is too awful. She didn't commit the murder. I did. She never planned it, she never knew about it. She is innocent, absolutely innocent."

**BELOW:** Crowds lining up outside the Old Bailey, London, during the trial of Edith Thompson and her lover, Frederick Bywaters, for the murder of her husband.

# Cheryl Crane

**Over the years Hollywood has been the scene of many murders, some every bit as dramatic as those on-screen. But there have been few stranger cases than the slaying of gangster Johnny Stompanato by the 14-year-old daughter of movie star Lana Turner.**

As has often been the case with Hollywood folk, while Lana Turner enjoyed a thriving career in the movies her private life was much less successful. It was while she was coming to terms with the collapse of her most recent marriage that she received a telephone call that would end in death, and a murder trial for Lana's young daughter, Cheryl Crane. At the end of the line

**RIGHT:** Cheryl Crane, daughter of actor Lana Turner, sits in a chair at the time of her trial for the murder of gangster Johnny Stompanato.

**BELOW:** American actor Lana Turner (center), wearing dark sunglasses, sitting next to her ex-husband, Stephen Crane, in a courtroom during the murder trial of their daughter, Cheryl Crane.

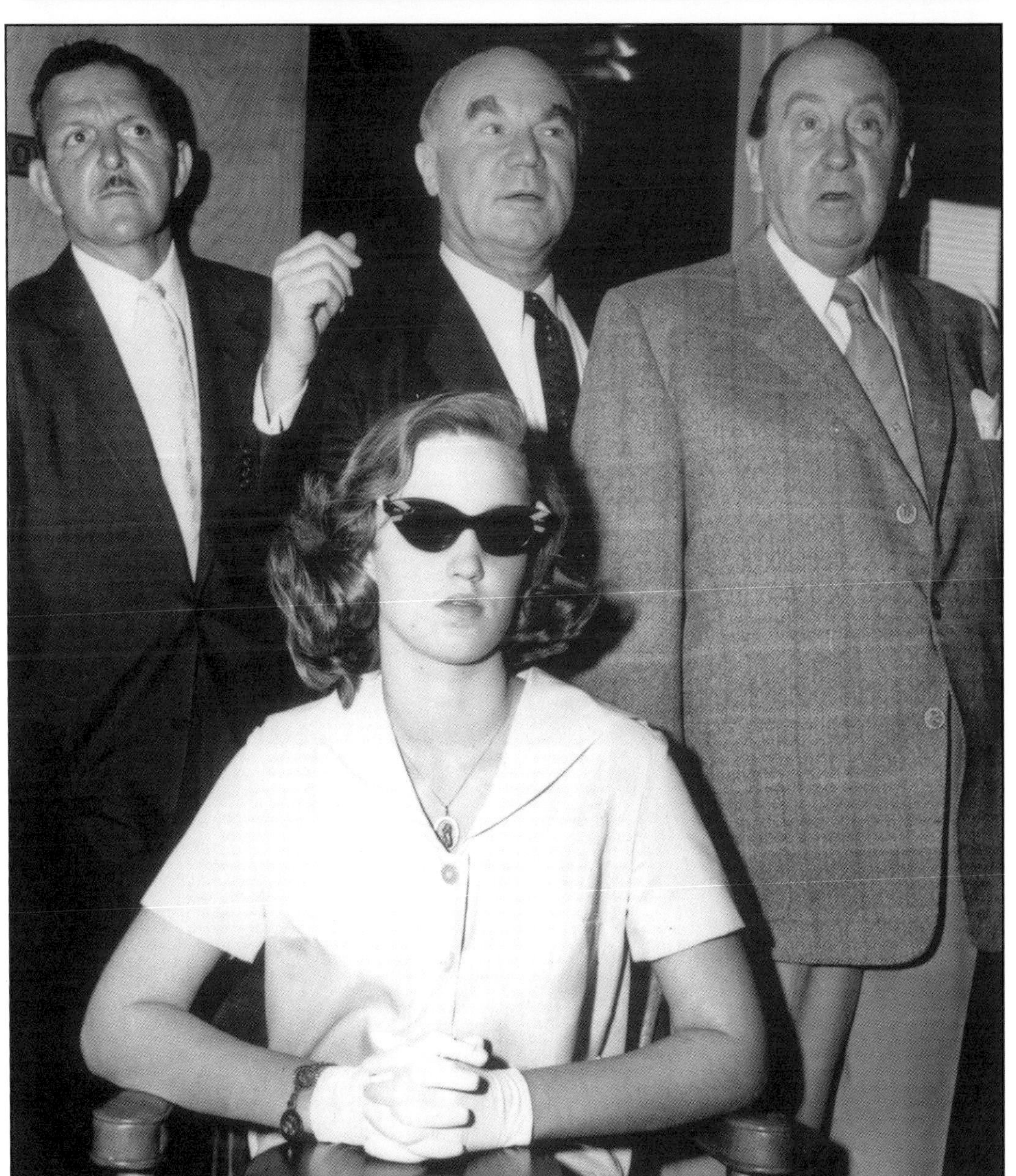

was a man, a complete stranger, who told the star that they had mutual friends and asked her out on a blind date. Showing an incredible lack of judgement, Lana agreed and so began a torrid relationship with local criminal Johnny Stompanato.

An ex-U.S. Marine, con-man, and associate of known gangsters, Stompanato was a smooth talker who soon insinuated himself into Lana's bed, her Los Angeles mansion, and her bank account. And once he was firmly installed in her life things quickly turned sour. Stompanato bullied and abused his famous lover and gambled her money away. Lana's daughter Cheryl regularly begged her mother to end the relationship, but Lana replied, "I'm too afraid." As a court would later hear, Stompanato was an associate of big-time gangsters Bugsy Siegel and Mickey Cohen, and had

**ABOVE:** High-angle view of American actor Lana Turner (right) seated in a courtroom, surrounded by reporters during the trial of her daughter, Cheryl Crane.

already told Lana what would happen if she tried to leave him, threatening, "I'll mutilate you. I will hurt you so you'll be so repulsive that you'll have to hide forever." On another occasion he told her, "When I say hop, you hop. When I say jump, you jump."

Such threats became ever more frequent and on the night of April 4, 1958, Stompanato and Lana had a violet argument during which he again threatened to scar her, shouting, "I'll get you if it takes a day, a week, a month or a year. If I can't do it myself, I'll get someone who will. That's my business."

Outside the door Cheryl was listening. In fear for her mother's life and driven to a frenzy of hatred by the gangster's threats, she fetched a long-bladed kitchen knife, ran into the room, thrust it into Stompanato's stomach, and killed him.

As might be expected for a case involving such a high-profile celebrity, the ensuing inquest was a sensational. On live television, audiences greater than any she had received before watched Lana Turner give an account of the events leading up to Stompanato's death and a passionate defense of her daughter. As a minor, Cheryl did not appear in court, but gave evidence in writing. Her statement read: "They had an argument and he was threatening Mother. He said he would kill her and hurt Daddy, Grandma, and me. He said he had ways of doing it. My mother was very frightened. I went down to the kitchen and got the knife. I took the knife up to the room in case he hurt mother. I rushed into the room and stuck him with the knife. He screamed."

The jury returned a verdict of justifiable homicide, effectively clearing Cheryl of blame for the killing. On hearing it, a friend of Stompanato leaped up in the public gallery and shouted, "It's lies, all lies. The girl was in love with him as well. He was killed because of jealousy between mother and daughter." Cheryl was released from a juvenile prison to resume normal life with her movie star mother. The scandal had no ill-effects on Lana's career. In fact, she earned an $2 million from her next film, *Imitation of Life*—an incredible fee at the time. She needed the money: Stompanato's family sued her and received an undisclosed settlement.

# Dr. Hawley Harvey Crippen

**The case of Dr Crippen is one of the most famous in the history of crime. Involving a nagging, unfaithful wife, a sexually charged affair, a desperate escape, and grisly remains found in a basement, Crippen's tale contains all the ingredients of a thriller novel.**

**Crippen was an American doctor**, who worked as a consultant ear specialist in England despite not being qualified to practice medicine outside of the United States. Flamboyant and dressy, he was charming in public but hid his private turmoil. All was not happy in the Crippen household.

Following the death of his first wife, Crippen had married again in 1892 at the age of 31, to a young woman of 19 named Cora. They had a complicated courtship. At the time, Cora was already the mistress of a stove manufacturer who paid for the singing lessons that would eventually propel her onto the London music hall stage under the name Belle Elmore. While she eventually agreed to be Crippen's wife, marriage did nothing to settle Cora. She liked to be center stage; to be adored and admired. Like many others of the same temperament, she tried to satisfy her need for attention in the arms of numerous men. Her string of lovers included an ex-boxer and several of the lodgers who took rooms with the Crippens. Meanwhile, she grew contemptuous of her husband and her bad temper often spilled over into nagging and arguments.

So, when Crippen met a 17-year-old Polish typist named Ethel Le Neve and was attracted to her, he felt no guilt. After all, he knew that Cora had affairs and made his life a misery. He hired Ethel as his bookkeeper and—surprisingly—the pair remained on professional, terms for seven years before becoming lovers.

It was Cora's vicious tongue that sealed her fate. When Ethel fell pregnant and had a miscarriage, Cora was quick to humiliate her husband, claiming to her music hall friends that the baby could have been fathered by any one of a number of men that Ethel had been sleeping with. Such accusations were rich, coming from a woman who delighted in her many affairs, and drove Crippen into a rage. Cora, he decided, had to die.

Crippen's chose poison as the cleanest murder method and accordingly gave his wife a strong dose in a nightcap on January 31, 1910. But when that didn't have the required effect he simply shot Cora in the back of the head, then dismembered her body and buried it in the cellar, covering the parts in quicklime to help them decompose more quickly. To cover his tracks he then told her friends that she had rushed to the bedside of a sick relative in the United States. As time passed and she didn't return, he said that she had become seriously ill, and then that she had died. Nevertheless, Cora's friends were suspicious. They alerted the police who questioned Crippen and searched the house. Although on that occasion they found nothing, Crippen was spooked, and decided to flee.

**BELOW:** A photograph of Dr. Crippen from 1910, the year he is alleged to have poisoned his wife and dismembered he body before fleeing across the Atlantic Ocean.

Together with Ethel, who was disguised as a boy, Crippen boarded the SS *Montrose*, which was bound for his homeland. But back in London the police returned and, finding the house deserted, this time searched more thoroughly. Before the ship left harbor, the tale of the grisly remains found in the coal cellar were splashed all over the newspapers along with Crippen's photo. And as the boat steamed out toward America, a copy caught the eye of the captain of the SS Montrose. Recognizing one of his passengers, he famously sent a message to shore, which read: "Have strong suspicion that

Crippen London cellar murder and accomplice are among saloon passengers." Crippen became the first murderer to be caught by wireless telegraph.

At the trial, Crippen gallantly played down Ethel's involvement in his wife's death, and she was acquitted of murder. Crippen also pleaded innocent, saying the remains found at the house on Hilldrop Crescent were not those of his wife, but the jury did not believe him. he was found guilty of murder and hanged on November 23, 1910.

However, it appears Crippen did not kill his wife after all. In 2007, DNA analysis of the body in Crippen's cellar suggested that the body was not Cora's. Instead the murder victim was an unknown man!

**OVERLEAF:** 39 Hilltop Crescent, London: The house where Dr Crippen was alleged to have murdered his second wife Belle Elmore.

**BELOW:** A detective leads Doctor Hawley Harvey Crippen from the SS *Megantic*, upon arrival in England, in August 1910.

# Dr. Philip Cross

**For some men entering the twilight of their lives, a new passion with a much younger woman is a chance to turn the clock back to a time when they were young and vigorous. Such infatuations can be so all-consuming that they become deadly.**

**Dr. Philip Cross had long preferred women** who had a fresh glow of youth about them. When he married at the age of 44, his wife Laura was just 22. For 18 years, the couple lived comfortably and happily at Shandy Hall in the village of Dripsey, County Cork, Ireland. Dr Cross's practice was successful, and over the years the couple were blessed with six children. However, the contentment of the Cross family home came to an abrupt end when Laura took on a new governess for the children.

Effie Skinner was just 20, by then more than 40 years younger than Cross, and not strikingly pretty. Nevertheless, she had a youthful charm that immediately attracted Cross. Soon he had become totally besotted. Although the strength of his lust threatened to overwhelm him, Cross tried to suppress the emotion, but one day as Effie stood before him reporting on the children's' progress he could contain himself no longer. He leaned over and kissed her.

Cross regretted it immediately, fearing that the

shocked and unresponsive Effie might tell his wife or—even worse—that she might leave. Effie had no wish to give up a comfortable job though, and stayed quiet. But the longer she was in the house, the more intense became Cross's lust until it became so obvious that Mrs Cross could not help but notice. She immediately sacked Effie even though she protested that any sexual inclination was all on the doctor's side.

The governess left for Dublin and was pursued there by Cross. Now, at last, away from his wife's watchful eyes he allowed his passion free reign. Effie succumbed to his advances. It seems that finally having the object of his lust robbed Dr Cross of what remained of his senses, for he was now determined that she must become his wife, and mistress of Shandy Hall, whatever the cost. And the price that must be paid to satisfy his passion was Laura Cross's life.

It was easy for the doctor to arrange his wife's death. Having procured a good supply of arsenic, which he said was to be used for sheep dip, he began to poison her. As she grew unwell, the doctor reassured her that it was not a serious illness and gave her a remedy that contained yet more arsenic. Within a month she was dead. And within two weeks of that, Philip Cross was married to Effie Skinner.

Had he not been so quick to wed his mistress, Cross may never have been discovered, but Laura's friends and family were already suspicious about her death. She had always been a healthy, robust woman and never displayed any of the symptoms of the heart problems that Cross had said killed her. Although he tried to keep his new marriage secret, when he brought Effie back to Shandy Hall it couldn't be hidden for long. Suspicions became accusations, and the police exhumed Laura's body. A postmortem found no sign of heart disease, but plenty of arsenic and strychnine. Dr Philip Cross went on trial for murder at the Munster Assizes in Cork and was found guilty on December 18, 1887.

# George Crossman

**George Crossman's were not really crimes of passion in the true sense, yet the murders he committed are worth mentioning here because they were all in the name of love. A serial womanizer and bigamist, he married seven women—that we know of—and one by one he killed them.**

**At the age of 32**, George Crossman was married to his fifth wife. His first three marriages had all been legitimate, but this was his second wedding conducted under a false name. Wife number five was a widowed nurse called Ellen Sampson. After her joyous wedding day in January 1903, she returned with her husband to her new home in Ladysmith Road, Kensal Rise, north London, without the slightest suspicion that it was already the home of wife number four, Edith. As soon as their wedding night was over Ellen became surplus to requirements. Crossman smashed her over the head and hid her body in a trunk in the attic. By the time Edith returned home from visiting friends everything in the house was normal. She would never know that her husband had found time for a bigamous marriage and a murder while she was away.

Incredibly Crossman and Edith lived a fairly happy married life for the next two years, though that certainly would not have been the case if she had known the truth: she was not legally married (there was yet another wife in the background), there was a body rotting in a trunk at the top of the house; and during that time Crossman married wives six and seven during trips away from home.

It was only when the couple's lodger William Dell started to complain about the awful smell coming from one of the upstairs room that Crossman's murdering secret was revealed. In March 1904, Crossman hastily tried to get the trunk out of the house, but it was too late. By then William Dell had already alerted police about what he strongly suspected was the smell of a rotting body, and Crossman was caught in the act or trying to remove the trunk on March 23. He managed to dash past the police, who gave chase. The certain knowledge that he was going to die a painful death on the gallows was too much for Crossman. After running almost a mile, he stopped to cut his own throat from ear to ear with a razor.

# Sir John Henry Delves Broughton

**The murder of a known womanizer in Kenya will probably never now be solved, but the prime suspect remains Sir Henry Delves Broughton. However, though he stood trial for the killing, with the help of his young wife—whose lover was the victim—Sir Henry was found not guilty of killing his rival.**

**Kenya's White Highlands** were once nicknamed "Happy Valley" due to the excessive drink, drugs, and sex parties enjoyed by its wealthy inhabitants in the days when Kenya was still a colony of the British Empire. Foremost among the hedonists was Josslyn Victor Hay, 22nd Earl of Erroll and Baron Kilmarnock. Locally, he was known as "The Passionate Peer," for the 39-year-old aristocrat was a sophisticated, handsome, sexual predator; an accomplished seducer, whose favorite line was, "To hell with husbands."

On November 30, 1940, Hay was drinking at the Muthaiga Club, a watering hole favored by the wealthy British, when two recently arrived strangers entered. Sir John Henry "Jock" Delves Broughton was a property magnate and racing fanatic in his late 50s and on his arm was an ash-blonde beauty—26-year-old Diana Caldwell whom Sir Henry had married only weeks before the pair had emigrated to Kenya. Hay later told friends, "Never can I remember a woman having such an immediate impact on me. I saw her eyes boring into me and I knew then that I must have her. I walked over to her while Jock was at the bar and said to her, Well, who is going to tell Jock—you or I?'"

It did not take long for Hay to seduce the beautiful young bride. On January 18, 1941, Diana confessed to her husband that she had fallen madly in love, and reminded him of an extraordinary pact that Sir Henry had made with her before they were married. Aware of the great differences in their ages, Sir Henry had promised that if Diana ever fell in love with a younger man he would provide her with a quick divorce and several thousand pounds a year afterward. He had never expected the marriage to come to an end so quickly though. Instead of immediately honoring his promise, he asked his wife to take a three-month trip with him to Ceylon and told her that if she would just promise to reconsider then she could even bring Hay along.

Diana considered the generous offer for a couple of days and then rejected it. She walked out on Sir Henry, telling him that she was going to live with Hay.

Three days later, Sir Henry called the police to report a break-in. Two revolvers, some money, and a cigarette case had been stolen. The same day he saw his lawyers about a divorce and later wrote the following words to a friend: "They say they are in love with each other and mean to get married. It is a hopeless position and I'm going to cut my losses. I think I'll go to Ceylon. There's nothing for me to live in Kenya for."

At 3am on January 24, 1941, a truck driver discovered Hay's body slumped under the dashboard of his car, which had left the road and plunged into a ditch only three miles from Sir Henry's home. He had been shot through the head at point-blank range with a .32 caliber revolver.

Strangely, the police didn't announce that they were treating it as a murder case until January 25, by which time the body had already been buried. But once they

**RIGHT:** Sir John Henry "Jock" Delves Broughton, pictured at the first day of York races in England in 1937.

did, Diana quickly came forward and accused her husband of cold-bloodedly killing her lover out of jealousy. Sir Henry was taken into custody. In another odd turn of events, however, Diana relented almost immediately. By the time police formally charged Sir Henry with the murder, she had flown to Johannesburg to hire top criminal lawyer Harry Morris to defend her husband. It was to be a worthwhile investment.

Morris called experts to prove that the three bullets fired at Hay could not have come from any gun owned by Sir Henry. The accused also performed masterfully in the dock, at one point saying, "She could ask who she liked. I should not have tried to stop her in any event. I see no point in it. We met every day at the club and I cannot see it makes any difference if a man comes to stay the night. In my experience of life, if you try to stop a woman doing anything, she wants to do it all the more. With a young wife the only thing to do is keep her amused." What motive, it was asked, could a man so coolly accepting of his wife's infidelity have in murdering her lover?

On July 1, 1941, Sir Henry Delves Broughton was found not guilty of murdering Josslyn Hay. The file on the crime has never been closed, and the murderer has never been caught. Sir Henry committed suicide in Liverpool on December 5, 1942, leaving a note that said he had found the strain of the trial and publicity too much to bear. Diana returned to Kenya where she remained until her death in 1987, a rich, enigmatic, extravagant lady to the last.

# Geza de Kaplany

**Most men who marry a beautiful and glamorous young wife celebrate their good luck in winning a woman that so many other men desire. But for Geza de Kaplany, his wife's good looks were a reason for jealousy and suspicion. When he was struck by impotence and could no longer make love to her, he found a solution to his problems: if he couldn't have her, then he would make sure that no one else wanted her.**

**Born in Hungary in 1926**, Geza de Kaplany was working in a hospital in San Jose, California, when he met 25-year-old Hanja. She was 10 years his junior, a glamor model and ex-showgirl who had her choice of men, but the doctor's own good looks attracted her and she fell in love. He, in turn, was smitten by the lovely young creature and soon the couple were joined in marriage. Less than a month later, Hanja was brutally and fatally mutilated by her husband.

It began with an obsession that other men in their apartment building were pursuing the eager Hanja, but de Kaplany's unravelling mental state also meant that he could no longer sustain an erection. Sunk in black thoughts and comparing his own inadequacy to his gorgeous young wife's obvious sexual allure, he came to an insane conclusion: Hanja must be made ugly.

On the evening of August 28, 1962, loud classical music flooded the Ranchero Palms Apartments in San Jose, accompanied by equally loud blood-chilling screams. Neighbors quickly called the police, but by the time they arrived it was already too late. Hanja was found tied to her bed. De Kaplany had poured sulfuric and nitric acids over his wife, and mutilated her with a knife. She suffered third degree corrosive burns over 60 per cent of her body with most of the brutality focussed on her genitals. So bad was the damage that one of the ambulance crew had to be treated for burns sustained simply by touching her skin. Maimed beyond comprehension, still Hajna de Kaplany fought for her life. It proved to be a losing battle. After 33 days in hospital, she succumbed to her injuries.

De Kaplany told police that Hajna had been unfaithful to him, and that he had just wanted to destroy her beauty rather than kill her. Somewhere in his twisted mind he was aware of the horror of his crime: When he saw police photographs of his wife

**ABOVE:** Dr. Geza de Kaplany, who tortured his wife with acid on her face and knife wounds to much of her body.

wounds he broke down. At his trial in 1963, de Kaplany pleaded not guilty to his wife's murder on the grounds of insanity. He claimed to suffer from multiple-personality disorder and said that the sadistic crime was not committed by him but by his alter ego, Pierre de la Roche. Nevertheless, de Kaplany was convicted of first degree murder, though due to his irrational behavior before and during the trial he was sentenced to life imprisonment rather than death.

De Kaplany actually served less than 12 years for his insane and deadly attack. He was released in 1975 amid protest and accusations that gruesome postmortem photographs of Hajna de Kaplany had been removed from his file prior to review by the California State Parole Board. After working in Taiwan as a medical missionary he broke parole conditions and got a job at a hospital in Munich in 1980. However, when his past became known he was swiftly fired. Incredibly, he found another woman willing to be his wife and became a naturalized German citizen in order to avoid extradition back to America.

**BELOW:** Hajna de Kaplany, pictured in her showgirl days. Her beauty, combined with her husbands insane jealousy, led to her horrific death.

# Nannie Hazle Doss

What drove Nannie to kill was not love and passion, but the lack of it. As hard as she tried to find a husband who would match up to the dashing men in the bodice-ripping books and true romance magazines she had become addicted to, none of them ever did. And to make way for the next unlucky husband, one by one they had to die.

**Nannie Hazle Doss**—who also became known as "Arsenic Annie," the "Jolly Black Widow," and the "Giggling Grandma"—was a cuddly creature with twinkling eyes and a wide smile by the time she finally stood trial for her crimes. Beneath the sweet exterior was a woman who killed without a second thought. She had been born Nancy Hazle, in 1905 in Blue

**RIGHT:** Nannie Doss pictured with her grandchildren, in a courthouse corridor during a hearing to decide her fate for the death of her husband, Samuel Doss.

**BELOW:** Nannie Doss looks happy and relaxed as she talks with homicide detective Captain Harry Stege before her arraignment on a charge of murder.

Mountain, Alabama, and, in a similar tale to many women who turned murderer, led a miserable childhood. Beaten cruelly and forced to work on the family farm by a father who may also have sexually abused her, Nancy—now known to all as Nannie—escaped her hellish home at the age of 15 by marrying a man named Charlie Braggs who she had met only four months previously.

The marriage was doomed from the start. Braggs insisted that his mother come live with the newlyweds in Tulsa, Oklahoma, and before long started staying away from home for nights at a time while he played around with other women. Meanwhile Nannie was swamped with children—the couple had four daughters in four years—and having failed to find the love for which she had always yearned, turned to drink and lost herself in romance magazines.

Nevertheless, as it turned out Braggs was the most fortunate of her five husbands, though the same can't be said for two of the children. He returned home one day in the spring of 1927 to find them dying on the floor (they were later alleged to have been Nannie's first victims) and he walked out, taking the surviving oldest child and leaving his wife with the youngest. He later said that he had left, "because I was frightened of what she would do." His instinct probably saved his life. Braggs filed for divorce and it was finalized the next year, by which time Nannie had already lined up husband number two.

This one didn't last long. He failed to satisfy and within a year of the marriage Frank Harelson died of stomach trouble. Husband number three must have come closer to fulfiling Nannie's fantasies because he survived until 1952 before the same death took him, too. Number four, Richard Morton, left a healthy insurance policy, and by now Nannie had hit her stride and felt that she no longer needed to confine herself to husbands. In short order, Nannie's mother, her two sisters, and the nephew of one of her deceased husbands were added to the list of mysterious deaths.

It was only upon the death in 1954 of Nannie's fifth husband, Samuel Doss, that an autopsy was ordered. It was discovered that there was enough arsenic in him to kill 20 men. Arrested, she chuckled and giggled through police interrogation, not appearing to understand the gravity of her crimes. She was still smiling when, at her trial, the court was told that her estimated tally of victims was 11. Nannie Doss showed neither regret nor remorse and calmly explained that she had poisoned the last four of her five husbands because they were, "dullards." None of them had lived up to the glamorous fictional men in her paperbacks and magazines. She was sentenced to life imprisonment and died in prison of leukaemia in 1965.

**BELOW:** Nannie Doss, pictured in a mug-shot taken in Tulsa, Oklahoma in October 1954.

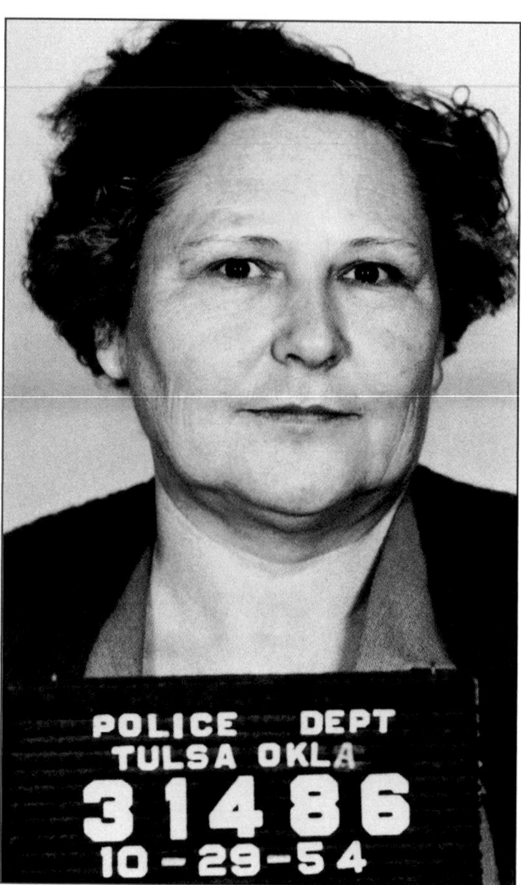

# Ruth Ellis

**Since immortalized in literature and film, the tale of the last woman in Britain to be hanged is one of tangled relationships and immorality set in the murky world of sleazy London nightclubs. It is also a warning. When someone allows their life to slide into depravity, the results can be disastrous.**

Ruth Ellis began life as Ruth Hornby in the Welsh seaside town of Rhyl. Born on October 9, 1926, as she grew up her one ambition was to get out of the stifling town and away from her unhappy childhood home. By the age of 17, she was working in a factory in London during the war years and had met a Canadian serviceman. He took the opportunity of being on the opposite side of the Atlantic from his wife

**OVERLEAF (LEFT):** Ruth Ellis, in a photograph probably taken in the flat above her club on the Brompton Road in Knightsbridge, London.

**OVERLEAF (RIGHT):** The Magdela public house in London where Ruth Ellis shot her husband David Blakey.

**BELOW:** Ruth Ellis posing in stockings and suspenders, in a picture taken by a Captain Ritchie in 1954.

ALES
CHARRINGTON'S
STOUT
CHARRINGTON'S
FINE ALES
CHARRINGTON'S
WINES & SPIRITS
BOOKSELLER
NEWSAGENT

and children to have an affair with the pretty young teenager and showered Ruth with gifts while escorting her around London's nightspots. Sadly, his passion waned when he found out that his young lover was pregnant. Like many girls of her day, Ruth was literally left holding the baby when the war ended and her boyfriend returned to his family.

Devastated, Ruth declared that she would never trust or love a man again and persuaded her mother to take care of her infant son. Then she returned to London to seek work. One particular advert caught her eye, it read, "Wanted. Model for Camera Club. Nude but artistic poses. No experience necessary." Ruth attended an interview, stripped off her clothes, and was awarded a job posing for photographers who rarely bothered to fill their cameras with film. She also happily escorted the men who paid to look at her naked out to dine and dance in London's West End.

It wasn't long before Ruth forgot her pledge not to become involved with men and she took up with another who saw her as an easy target. Morris Conley owned the sleazy Court Club, had served time for fraud and illegal gambling, and employed women who would satisfy all needs of his customers. Ruth soon became an employee and quickly mastered the art of flirting with the men who came to the club and tricking them into buying fake Champagne and overpriced food. For her troubles, Ruth received a ten percent commission on top of her five pounds a week wage. However, there was even more money to be made by allowing customers to purchase her body as well, and Ruth proved herself a willing and able prostitute. As one client later reported, "She was an artist. She gave you the full treatment and by the time she had finished you felt on top of the world." At the same time she was also sleeping with Conley who felt he had the right to sex with his hostess employees. They were rewarded for complying with gifts of beautiful gowns, and should they refuse the dresses were slashed, and the girls fired.

At the age of 23, Ruth fell pregnant again, but this time opted for a dangerous backstreet abortion. Within a year, she was married to 41-year-old divorced dentist George Ellis and pregnant again, though there was no guarantee that the child was her new husband's. Nevertheless, Ruth decided to keep the baby and her daughter was duly placed in the care of her mother while Ruth and George continued to live a decadent lifestyle in London's seedier hangouts. The marriage wasn't destined to last though. Ruth's husband was an alcoholic with a violent temper, and the couple were constantly separating and reuniting as passion and possessiveness alternated between contempt and hatred between them. Eventually, George used doubts over their daughter's paternity as an excuse to desert his wife. By 1951 they were divorced.

With George's financial support withdrawn, Ruth returned to her job at the Court Club, which by now had become the Carroll Club, though the activities within its walls hadn't changed in the slightest. Ruth's enthusiasm for her work was rewarded with a rent-free, two-bedroom Mayfair apartment supplied by Conley while her expertise as a prostitute brought numerous gifts from clients. One admirer bought her a race horse, Ruth's wardrobe was filled with expensive designer clothes, and her purse with bundles of banknotes given to her by rich, international businessmen. She now counted celebrities among her friends including the World Champion racing driver Mike Hawthorn, who introduced Ruth to the man that would end her life.

David Blakely was engaged to another girl when he took up with Ruth. Three years younger than her, he followed a by now well-established pattern in Ruth's lovers, turning violent and abusive when drunk. But unlike previous boyfriends he had had a decent education at a public school, and when sober had excellent manners and treated her with more respect than most other Carroll Club customers. For once Ruth was sleeping with a man because she wanted to, rather than because he was just part of the job. When she became pregnant again in 1953, Blakely seemed ready to take responsibility. As Ruth would later recall, "David was very concerned about my welfare. Although he was engaged to another girl, he offered to marry me and he said it seemed unnecessary for me to get rid of the child, but I did not want to take advantage of him. I was not really in love with him at the time and it was quite unnecessary to marry me. I thought I could get out of the mess quite easily. In fact, I did so with the abortion."

After the latest pregnancy was terminated, Ruth's

affections for Blakely waned and she began seeing other men without his knowledge. Among them was company director Desmond Cussen whose help she began to rely on. Due to Blakely's jealousy and suspicions about her activities, Ruth had not been able to entertain clients at the Carroll Club and had subsequently lost her job. Cussen set her up in a flat and became a frequent visitor. Nevertheless, she was still sleeping with Blakely and their relationship had become increasingly stormy, swinging from warm embraces to violent arguments. And despite her own infidelities and the fact that he was still engaged to Mary Dawson, when she found out that he was having another affair—with an au pair—Ruth was furious. On one occasion she drove to the house where the girl worked and, seeing her Blakely's car outside, proceeded to smash every window at the front of the house.

Then, surprisingly, for a short while, Ruth's life looked as though it might finally settle down. Blakely broke off his engagement to Mary Dawson and proposed to Ruth. She was delighted and told friends that it was a turning point in her life. The relative peace and happiness was just the eye of the storm though. Blakely was still visiting his au pair lover and quickly became tired of Ruth's possessiveness. One night in January 1955, while drunk, he punched Ruth so hard in the stomach that she miscarried his child. The years of brutal, drunken rows, dalliances with other partners, and terrible behavior finally came to a head on Easter Sunday that year.

The lover she had so much hope for had turned out no better than any of the other men in her life, so Ruth

**BELOW:** The gun that Ruth Ellis used to shoot David Blakely.

**ABOVE:** Crowds gathering outside Holloway Prison before the execution of Ruth Ellis.

made her way to the Magdala public house in Hampstead, north London. In her bag was a .38 Smith and Weston revolver given to her by Desmond Cussen who not only showed her how to use it, but also drove her to the pub that night. On seeing Blakely in the Magdala, Ruth was overwhelmed with an icy, calm fury. As she later explained to a court, "I had a peculiar idea to kill David."

When Blakely left the pub with his friend Clive Gunnell, headed towards a night of pleasure with his au pair girlfriend, he heard Ruth scream "Get out of the way Clive!" Then a bullet ripped into him and he fell. Ruth fired three more shots as Blakely lay in the gutter. His life of womanizing and drinking was over.

Ruth went on trial at the Old Bailey on June 20, 1955. The jury took just 14 minutes to find her guilty of murder, and the sentence was death by hanging. Many suggested that she had brought it upon herself, having shown no remorse in court and making it perfectly clear her one intention on the night in question was to kill her lover. Nevertheless, there was an immediate public outcry. While no-one disputed that Ruth was a murderer, the campaign against capital punishment in Britain had lately been gathering pace, and to hang a woman who had been so taken advantage of and abused by so many men was deemed too harsh. On July 13, 1955, more than 1,000 people gathered outside Holloway Prison crying for Ruth to be reprieved. They added their voices to the many petitions sent to the Home Secretary. One petition alone bore 50,000 signatures.

The protests fell on deaf ears. Ruth's head was put through a noose and moments later the trapdoor beneath fell away. Writing in the Daily Mirror newspaper that day, the popular columnist Cassandra moved the nation with the words, "If you read this after nine o'clock in the morning, the murderess Ruth Ellis will have gone. The one thing that brings stature and dignity to mankind and raises us above the beasts of the field will have been denied her—pity and the hope of ultimate redemption."

Ruth Ellis was buried in an unmarked grave within the walls of Holloway Prison. In the early 1970s the prison underwent a program of rebuilding, during which the bodies of all executed women were exhumed for reburial elsewhere. Ellis's was reburied at St. Mary's Church in Amersham, Buckinghamshire. The headstone in the churchyard was originally inscribed "Ruth Hornby 1926–1955," but in 1982 it was destroyed by her son Andy shortly before he committed suicide.

# Sergeant Frederick Emmett-Dunne

**Often, the victims of crimes of passion are the innocent people who happen to be close to those caught up in powerful emotions. The murder of Sergeant Reginald Watters, for example, shows how love can set an otherwise decent man to kill his best friend.**

**Tall, handsome Sergeant Frederick Emmett-Dunne** and his five-foot, one-inch friend Sergeant Reginald Watters were stationed in Duisburg, Germany, as part of the British post-war occupation force. While in Germany, Watters met and married a beautiful ex-nightclub singer called Mia. At first, Emmett-Dunne tried to repress his feelings for his mate's wife, but the more time he spent in their company the more his passion for her grew and the more he came to resent the fact that his unremarkable, short friend had married her when she should have been his. Slowly the bonds of friendship were overwhelmed by jealousy, to the point where Emmett-Dunne was prepared to kill the man he had once shared so much with.

On November 30, 1953, the body of Reginald Watters was found hanging from the banister at his barracks on the British Army base. It was Emmett-Dunne who broke the news to Mia, telling the widow that he would be constantly at her side to help her through her ordeal. He also gave a statement to the police saying that he had driven Watters back to his quarters at 7pm the night before, bid him good night, and left. The doctor who conducted the postmortem concluded that death was caused by shock, brought on by strangulation. Watters, he wrote on his report, had committed suicide by hanging.

There was something amiss though. Despite the verdict, gossip began to circulate. It was whispered that

Watters had committed suicide because his wife was having a secret fling with his best friend. The marriage of Mia and Emmett-Dunne in England just seven months later did nothing to still the wagging tongues.

But it wasn't just gossips who were suspicious of the events. The marriage was also viewed with suspicion by one of the official army criminal investigators named Sergeant Frank Walters. He had previously been bothered by the suicide verdict, too, and did not believe that Watters was type to take his own life, no matter how serious his personal problems were. When he heard about the wedding, Walters contacted Scotland Yard to report his concerns.

In February 1955 an order arrived at British headquarters in Duisburg to exhume Watters' body. Examination by a more experienced pathologist revealed that he had died not by hanging, but by a "severe blow across the front of the throat"—just the kind of blow that might have been inflicted by someone trained in unarmed combat. At the same time Emmett-Dunne's half-brother Ronald, who had been a private at Duisburg, confessed to his own involvement in Watters' death. He told investigators that he had helped Emmett-Dunne hang Watters up on the bannister after his panicked half-brother told him he had killed him by accident.

Emmett-Dunne was arrested at the home in Taunton, Somerset, he shared with Mia. Despite his claim that he had acted in self-defense when Watters threatened to shoot him and had only meant to stun, he was charged with murder. The case, held before a seven-man army court, was covered extensively in the British and German press. On July 1955, Emmett-Dunne was found guilty of murder and sentenced to death. However, he escaped a fate that many thought he richly deserved. West Germany had abolished capital punishment, and foreign army bases had to conform with the law of the country. Instead Emmett-Dunne was given a life sentence. He served 10 years in Britain before being released.

# Dr. Yves Evenou & Simone Deschamps

**Twice divorced Yves Evenou had the good fortune to find his third wife in the strikingly beautiful and young Marie-Claire. But though she was undoubtedly stunning, she could not satisfy his cravings for perverted sex games: for that he turned to an older, plain woman. And when his desire for both waned he formed a plan to get rid of them in one disgusting act.**

**What Simone Deschamps lacked in looks** she more than made up for with her zealous participation in sexual masochism. Almost as soon as she came into his surgery one day in the mid-1950s Dr Yves Evenou realized that she was a woman with whom he could explore his secret dark lusts. Before long he had moved his sex partner into the flat below the one he shared with his wife, Marie-Claire. It was a perfect arrangement for Evenou; a loving, respectable and beautiful wife in one flat, and a subservient mistress willing to satisfy all his perverted desires, in the flat below. Evenou even told a friend, "She may not be beautiful, but she knows how to love."

A willing conspirator in the duping of Marie-Claire, Simone even made herself useful to her lover's wife, helping her with chores around the house that were too heavy for the sickly doctor's wife. But as Simone and Evenou pushed their sexual boundaries to the limit, so the doctor grew ever more tired of his wife and his lover, too, and began plotting to get rid of them both in one foul swoop. To a twisted and sadist mind such as his, the plan he hatched must have had an elegant simplicity: he would incite Simone to kill

**RIGHT:** Dr. Yves Evenou (center) following his lawyer, Charles Marcelpoll, in a lobby of the Palace of Justice of Paris.

Marie-Claire and then inform on her to the police. The plan also had the merit of providing one last, horribly depraved, sexual thrill.

Evenou warmed his lover up to the idea slowly. One night he told her, "My first two wives left me of their own accord but this one sticks like mustard plaster." After a day or two, he announced, "I feel that I should kill her, or maybe that you should do it for me." By the following day, after six glasses of port, the doctor appeared to make his mind up. "We must kill her," he told Simone. Without a word, she rose from her chair, went to the local hardware store, and bought a knife.

That evening Marie-Claire complained of a toothache, and her husband suggested a sleeping pill to ease the pain. As soon as she was asleep, Evenou rang the apartment below and Simone arrived within moments, naked except for a coat and shoes, which she slipped off. Then Evenou gently uncovered his wife's breast and said, "Strike here!" Simone obeyed. Marie-Claire woke in a shock as the knife plunged into her body and cried out, "Simone!" and then, "No! No!" But Evenou held her in his arms and whispered, 'There, there, everything's all right'. Befuddled with drugs and not yet feeling any pain, Marie-Claire relaxed, and Simone struck her again and again: 11 times in all. Then the lovers kissed. When it was over, Simone went to the bathroom to wash her hands, and Yves Evenou slipped out of the door. A few minutes later he arrived at the police station and told them that Simone Deschamps had murdered his wife.

What may have been an elegant plot in Evenou's mind didn't stand up to police investigations and questions. He was arrested alongside his sado-masochistic lover, but escaped trial by dying before the case could be heard. For her part in the murder, however, Simone Deschamps received a life sentence.

# Dr. Renzo Ferrari

**When Tranquillo Allevi drank from a bottle of liqueur that contained enough strychnine to kill 500 men, the Italian police were baffled at first, but one by one they exonerated his wife's lovers until they found the man who poisoned him.**

**At 38, Renata Allevi was a sophisticated woman** of the world. She loved her wealthy dairy farmer husband who kept her in all the luxuries she could want, but also delighted in the intrigue and passions of her illicit liaisons and kept a stable of men to admire her. Nevertheless, the charmed life she had been leading shuddered to a halt on August 26, 1973.

Two days earlier a bottle of liqueur had arrived from Milan with a note explaining that the established Italian drinks manufacturer who made it was planning a sales campaign in the local area and asking Tranquillo Allevi if he would consider becoming the company's local representative. Allevi was an influential and highly popular man, and often received this kind of offer, so when the bottle arrived Renata thought nothing of it. She signed for it and left it on her husband's desk. When he returned he put it in the refrigerator to cool and then forgot about it.

On the 26th, after taking his wife out to dinner at a local restaurant, Tranquillo Allevi went to his office to entertain two friends. He remembered the bottle and took it from the fridge, poured three glasses, and—while his friends politely sipped their drinks—knocked his back in one. Death came quickly. Allevi was screaming by the time the liquid hit his stomach and his body quickly went into uncontrollable spasms. He was rushed to hospital but died soon after he was admitted. The diagnosis was obvious, for his friends too showed signs of poisoning, though mercifully their small sips saved them from death.

The police immediately suspected Renata, but it was apparent that her grief was genuine, and she made no

**ABOVE:** Renzo Ferrari gesturing in front of microphones as he answers questions by the president of a Court of Assizes in Imperia on the Italian Riviera, during his 1964 trial.

secret of the fact that she had signed for the bottle and even suggested to her husband that he put it in the fridge. Perplexed they looked elsewhere, but Allevi was a popular man and had no enemies that anyone knew of. Then, reluctantly, Renata admitted that she had three lovers with whom she regularly met: her husband's book-keeper, an army officer, and the veterinary surgeon who looked after Allevi's herds.

Another clue was the bottle itself, which had been sent from Milan on August 23. Checks with the drinks company confirmed that though over 100 complimentary bottles had been sent out, Allevi's name was not on the mailing list and the accompanying letter was not on the company's headed paper. Tests showed that a massive dose of strychnine had been injected into the bottle through the cork.

The police began to question Renata's lovers. The first two had alibis to prove that they had been nowhere near Milan the day the parcel was posted. The book-keeper had been with a client in San Remo, while the army officer had been in Tuscany on maneuvers. Detectives were left with the veterinary surgeon, Dr. Renzo Ferrari, who had been in Milan on that very day to renew his professional license. He had also purchased strychnine. And a check on the town hall offices Ferrari used in his post as a local government officer, revealed the typewriter upon which the accompanying letter had been written.

On September 1, 1973, Ferrari was charged with the murder of Tranquillo Allevi. At his trial the truth finally emerged. He pleaded not guilty, and his defense counsel told the court that he had no motive. Ferrari, they argued, had recently become engaged to the daughter of a wealthy family and had broken off his purely sexual relationship with Renata. He was looking forward to a good future and there was no reason to jeopardize it. Renata, however, painted a very different picture for the jury and one that fit the facts. On the witness stand she said that her husband had found out about the affair and that while she saw other men for pleasure it was him she loved, so she had agreed to finish with Ferrari. On being notified that their affair was over, Ferrari refused to accept it and when she told him, "I will never return to you", he had replied, "We will see about that."

A representative of the drinks company supplied the final, damning, piece of evidence. He stated under oath that no sample had been sent to Mr Allevi. However, one bottle had been dispatched, with an invitation on company notepaper, to one Dr. Renzo Ferrari.

The jury did not need any further evidence. Ferrari was found guilty of murder with premeditation on May 15, 1974. His combined sentence amounted to 30 years, including consecutive terms for the attempted murder of Allevi's two drinking companions. Although he has never admitted to it, it is very possible that the murderer had hoped that Allevi and his wife would open the bottle together and that he would thus have killed both of them. Once the bottle was delivered, Ferrari had no way of controlling who drank the poisoned liqueur, which suggests that he did not care which of the Allevis he murdered.

# Sheila Garvie and Brian Tevendale

**In retrospect it is hardly surprising that Max Garvie was eventually murdered, for the sex games he delighted in grew so astonishingly depraved that it was almost inevitable that sooner or later there would be an emotional backlash.**

**In 1955, Sheila Watson** considered herself lucky to have landed Max Garvie for a husband. He was handsome, rich, and the owner of a large farm in Fordoun, Kincardineshire, Scotland. Over the following years the couple had two daughters and a son and had Max not been so bored of his tranquil existence the family might have enjoyed a happy family life. At first Garvie tried to liven up his life with the expensive toys of the rich. He filled his driveway with fast cars and bought a private plane, but nothing seemed to bring the satisfaction he craved and he eventually began looking for excitement elsewhere.

It started innocently. Garvie created his own so-called "nudist colony," and groups of his wealthy, thrill-seeking friends were invited to weekend parties where they would frolic naked within a triangle of trees and thick bushes Garvie had planted for just that reason. It was not long, however, before the guests' inhibitions were set aside completely and Garvie's nude parties turned into sex orgies.

Sheila Garvie wasn't interested, and tried to ignore the naked flesh and debauched scenes in her garden. Instead, she tried to shield the children from what was happening outside the house and shrugged off her husband's continual demands that she join in the fun. Eventually, however, she was worn down by his pestering. Sheila gave in and went on to become a willing, and even enthusiastic, member of the group.

By this time West Cairnbeg Farm had become known locally as "Kinky Cottage," and guests at the house were playing a dangerous game of jealousy and broken rules. Garvie took his sexual adventures further with homosexual couplings and then brought 20-year-old Brian Tevendale into his home—not for his own

**ABOVE:** Sheila Garvie on her way to the High Court at Stonehaven, Scotland, in 1968.

pleasure but for Sheila's. His wife was appalled at the idea. She saw sex sessions in the company of her husband as acceptable, but not the intimacy of one-to-one lovemaking.

Nevertheless, she gave in again. One night in 1967, when Tevendale was staying over, his bedroom door was suddenly opened and a naked, shivering Sheila shoved into the room by her husband. Garvie had at last broken his wife's will. Now the games took a new turn with Garvie and Tevendale tossing a coin to see who would sleep with Sheila. When Garvie lost he insisted the three go to bed together. Then Garvie started an affair with Tevendale's sister, Trudi Birse, wife of a policeman. Trudi joined in four-in-a-bed romps with the Garvies and her own brother. Trudi's husband even joined in, though Max thoughtfully arranged another female partner for him.

Still Garvie craved new sensual pleasures and further erotic adventures. Growing bored with Trudi, he suggested to Sheila that they both move on to new bedmates. Sheila refused. The one thing her husband had not considered was that amid all the debauched coupling real affection might blossom, but now his wife was passionately in love with Brian Tevendale. Used to getting his own way, Garvie tried to come between them. The man who had forced them together now tried to prize them apart.

On the morning of May 15, 1968, Sheila Garvie reported her husband missing to the police. She said when she had woken up that morning, Garvie was not in bed or anywhere to be found. Whether to cover her tracks or because she was genuinely innocent, Sheila confided in her mother, Edith Watson, that she thought Tevendale had killed her husband, and an appalled Mrs Watson went straight to the police.

Max Garvie's putrefying remains were eventually found in the drains of Laurieston Castle, St. Cyrus—Tevendale's home village—on August 17, 1968. The police's investigations led them straight to the depraved goings-on at the farm and Sheila Garvie, Brian Tevendale, and one of his friends, Alan Peters, were arrested and charged with Garvie's murder.

The sensational trial began at Aberdeen High Court on November 19, 1968. While details of the sordid events became public, Sheila and Tevendale accused each other of the murder. Sheila claimed she woke in the middle of the night to discover Tevendale and Peters had murdered her husband; Tevendale said the killing was Sheila's idea and he had gone along with it because of his infatuation with her. The prosecution, however, maintained that Sheila and Tevendale had plotted the murder together in order to stop Garvie from splitting them up. They suggested that on the night Garvie died, Sheila had slipped out of the marital bed to let Tevendale and Peters into the house and given them a gun. She then watched as Tevendale used it to smash Max's skull before putting a pillow over his face and shooting him in the head. The men then wrapped the body in a blanket, put it in the boot of Peters's car, and dumped it in the drains of Laurieston Castle. Throughout the proceedings, both the jury and the nation were horrified by the perverse events and the crime itself. One juror fainted when the yellowed skull of Max Garvie was produced as part of the prosecution evidence.

In the end, the prosecution prevailed—barely. The jury unanimously found Tevendale guilty of murder and Sheila was also found guilty by a majority verdict—enough under Scottish law to sentence her. The case against Peters was not proven.

Tevendale and Sheila were both released from prison in 1978, but never saw each other again choosing to lead anonymous lives. Tevendale married and became the landlord of a public house in Perthshire. He died in 2003. Sheila married twice—she was divorced once and then widowed—and led a quiet life running a bed and breakfast.

# William Gardiner

**The so-called Peasenhall Mystery of 1902, is one of the most notable of murder cases in British criminal history with a cast of characters reads like an Agatha Christie novel. William Gardiner was a Sunday school teacher, devout church minister, and married father of six; the victim—Gardiner's pregnant lover—a choir girl at the village church. Officially "unsolved" it is likely that Gardiner would have been convicted had it not been for the alibi provided by the very wife he had been cheating on.**

**The affair between 23-year-old Rose Harsent and Gardiner** was much gossiped about in the small Suffolk village of Peasenhall. She was a domestic servant who sang in the choir and he taught Sunday school and delivered sermons from the pulpit. While it was rumored that Gardiner was only one of several men that Rose was involved with, the pair appear to have been irresistibly attracted to one another. Some said that the vicar had been called upon to intervene after they were caught in a compromising situation, but even his warnings had failed to cool their passion and the secret trysts continued.

On June 1, 1902, Rose was found dead by her father at Providence House where she worked. Her half-naked body was at the foot of the stairs with the throat cut from ear to ear. There were wounds on her shoulders and her nightdress was burned. It seemed that whoever had killed Rose had tried to set fire to her to destroy the evidence. Further examinations of her body revealed that she had been pregnant.

It did not take long for Gardiner to become the prime suspect. A police search of Rose's room soon turned up a note in his handwriting addressed to her and arranging a secret midnight meeting. He was arrested two days later.

Gardiner's trial began on November 7, and the case against him was strong: A bloodied knife had been found at his home (though Gardiner said he had used it to kill rabbits) and neighbors spoke of a late-night bonfire in the Gardiner's garden on May 31. The police suggested that Gardiner and his wife had been burning his blood-stained clothes. Nevertheless, Mrs Gardiner insisted that they had passed an unremarkable evening together before retiring to bed where they had both stayed until morning.

Of the 12 jurors, 11 thought Gardiner guilty, but without a unanimous verdict a retrial was ordered to begin on January 21, 1903. Again, the jury failed to reach a unanimous decision, this time with 10 of their number finding him innocent. Arrangements were quickly made for yet another trial, but before it began the Home Office decided that there was no prospect of securing a conviction and lodged a verdict of *nolle prosequi*—not proven. The case against Gardiner was dismissed and he was released from custody, having neither been convicted or acquitted.

# Lilian Getkate

**Every so often, someone slips through loopholes in the law, and so it proved in the case of Lilian Getkate. A former Brownie leader and church-goer, Lilian fully expected to serve a prison sentence for the crime of shooting her husband with his own rifle, but despite failing to convince many that she had good cause to kill, the jury found her guilty of the lesser charge of manslaughter and sentenced her to just 200 hours of community service. In a second stroke of luck, Lilian's conviction preceded a change in the law by just three weeks. Under the new ruling anyone convicted of manslaughter using a firearm was to be sentenced to at least four years jail time.**

**Lilian's was a problematic case.** Her defense lawyer told the jury that she had been subjected to years of constant abuse by her husband, Maury. During their 16 years of marriage she had been dragged by her hair, made a virtual prisoner in her own home, raped, and threatened with death. Lilian also claimed that what finally provoked her to kill was her husband threatening to sexually abuse their daughter. According to a report in the Canadian newspaper, the Ottawa Citizen, Maury Getkate had been a tall, well-built man; a "paramilitary buff and aspiring ninja" who had a collection of "exotic weaponry." Two psychiatrists who examined and interviewed Lilian testified that she fitted the criteria for "battered woman syndrome."

The evidence was not so clear-cut though. Relatives and friends of the couple gave a different story, saying that to all outward appearances the Gatkates had been a happy, ordinary couple, devoted to their children and Lilian more than satisfied to be a stay-at-home mother. Maury Getkate, they said, was a hard-working, successful professional admired by his colleagues.

In fact, as crown prosecutor Julianne Parfett pointed out to the court, the only evidence they had for Lilian's plight came from Lilian herself. "No one could corroborate it," Parfett stated. "Not a bruise, not a hospital record, not a police report. Nothing... that's what is most troubling about this one. We simply say, 'Yes, you were abused. Fine. You walk.' That's what this sentence was all about. I think it's an appalling message to send to the public." With no third-person testimony or physical evidence to corroborate Lilian's tales, Parfett suggested that, at most, she may have suffered "moderate abuse."

Nevertheless, a jury made up of 10 women and two men found Lilian guilty only of the lesser charge of manslaughter, and she was ordered to do community service and attend meetings of Co-Dependents Anonymous, a support group for emotionally dependent people. It was not a verdict that pleased Ms Parfett. After hearing the sentence, she said, "The decision to spare her jail sends a message that women can kill, claim they have been abused, fail to prove it, and remain free." Lilian's defense lawyer, Patrick McCann, was quick to respond, saying, "There's a long tradition in Canada that women who have been abused by their husbands or partners and have reacted to that and killed the man, have been convicted of manslaughter and not received custodial sentences. This is nothing new."

In the middle of the legal fuss was Lilian Getkate. She was as surprised as anyone to be walking free. And her surprise must have turned to relief when it was announced that from January 1996 there would be mandatory prison sentences of at least four years for manslaughter offences in which firearms are used. Lilian shot her husband in December 1995.

# Chester Gillette

**Born to a deeply religious family, Chester Gillette traveled around the United States during his formative years. By the time he reached age 22 in 1905, Gillette had settled in New York City where he worked as a foreman at his wealthy uncle's shirt factory. It was here that he met the pretty young secretary Grace Brown, who was just 18 years old.**

**Grace fell for the dashing nephew of the boss**, and in a whirl of passion she was soon sleeping with him. The result was a pregnancy. Expecting Gillette to make an honest woman of her, Grace returned to her family home to come to terms with approaching motherhood and to await a marriage proposal. It never came. Instead, Grace discovered that Gillette had never been faithful and was now openly seeing other women. The final blow came when she discovered that the man she loved had met an attractive and wealthy socialite at a dance, and that he had become engaged to her. Her heartbroken letters to her lover became increasingly desperate, but still Gillette would not acknowledge her or the coming baby. Eventually, with nowhere left to turn, Grace threatened to tell Gillette's uncle the whole story and expose his dreadful conduct.

The threat seemed to work. In July 1906, Gillette told Grace to pack for a weekend trip away. Excited, and possibly believing that the trip would involve a wedding ceremony, she packed her entire wardrobe. Gillette, meanwhile, packed almost nothing.

At first the couple checked into a rented cottage on Tupper Lake in Herkimer County, but the resort was too busy for what Gillette had in mind. At his insistence, they moved onto Big Moose Lake, taking separate rooms in a hotel there. Gillette then hired a rowing boat under the name of Carl Graham (careful to matching the initials on his suitcase) and rowed his pregnant teenage lover out onto the water. When they were some distance way from the shore, Gillette battered Grace with a tennis racket, then tipped her over the side, and rowed back alone. The unconscious Grace was left to drown. Gillette's social climbing ambitions were safe.

Back on shore, Gillette tried to cover his tracks by moving on to the Arrowhead Hotel on Eagle Bay. However, he made a fatal error in asking the check-in clerk if there had been any reported drownings. When

**ABOVE:** Chester Gillette's heartless murder of his one-time lover led to his eventual execution.

**ABOVE:** Grace Brown's only crime was to fall in love with the wrong man—who turned out to be a killer.

Grace Brown's body surfaced the next day, the clerk remembered Gillette's strange question, and the killer came under immediate suspicion. The tennis racket used to bludgeon Grace was found on the shore of Big Moose Lake, and under police questioning Gillette was nervous and shifty.

In court, the jury heard the extent of Gillette's callousness as Grace's heart-rending letters to her lover were read out, one by one, by the lawyers acting for the prosecution. He was found guilty of murder on December 4, 1906, and sentenced to death in the electric chair.

# Gary Grinhaff

**While some killers' fury vents itself in an uncontrollable outburst of deadly rage, others channel it into a cold, calm plan for revenge. Convinced that the affair that his wife had confessed to was still continuing, Gary Grinhaff approached murder—and his own suicide—in a highly methodical manner.**

**Grinhaff discovered the affair his wife, Tracey,** had been having in February 2008. A few weeks later he confronted her, and in order to try and resolve the situation peacefully her lover and his wife were called over to discuss it. It was an unusual step, but seemed to work; the unfaithful pair agreed that they would end their illicit relationship.

Over the following weeks though, Grinhaff became convinced that Tracey had not kept her promise so, ignoring his wife's protests of innocence, he set about to prove that she was still arranging secret love trysts. First he bugged her car so that he could listen to conversations and fitted it with a tracking device. Then he secretly bought another car in which he could follow her undetected. By May 1, he had the proof he needed. Tracey was a cheat, and with the same efficient calm Grinhaff made plans for retribution.

At 6am on the morning of May 3, 2008, the Grinhaff's three-year-old daughter Niamh woke her older sister Chloe. She was standing on the landing outside her parents' bedroom crying because she couldn't find her mother. Thirteen-year-old Chloe went to investigate and found her mother and father's bed empty and the duvet laying on the floor. Downstairs she found the note in the kitchen pinned to the cooker hood. It was in her father's handwriting and gave her certain instructions. The teenager phoned a neighbor who told the girls not to go to school and contacted the police.

When the police arrived they found signs of an attack in the Grinhaff's bedroom, though an effort had obviously been made to make it tidy and to hide bloodstains from the two girls. Later, the bodies were discovered. Tracey Grinhaff's was found in the shed at the back of her garden. She had been strangled and bludgeoned to death with a heavy object. Shortly after, police found Gary Grinhaff's corpse in woodland nearby. He had killed himself by cutting into his own leg and arm with the saw attachment to his cordless electric drill. They later also found the car that Grinhaff had used to follow his wife, with notes inside so that his daughters wouldn't discover them. One was addressed to the wife of Tracey's lover and read, "This cannot go on; this is my only way out."

At the inquest assistant deputy coroner Donald Coutts-Wood said that Grinhaff had gone to considerable lengths to confirm his wife had resumed her affair and once satisfied had set out to kill her. He recorded verdicts that Mrs Grinhaff was unlawfully killed and that her husband committed suicide.

# Albert Guay

**There are no words to describe the sheer depravity of Albert Guay's crime. Even if we cannot understand the minds of many of the murderers who have been pressed to kill by their passion we can, at least, begin to imagine how a person may have come to feel so violently angry that they wished to punish the person who caused their pain or stood in the way of their future happiness. But Guay's crime goes far beyond that, for in planning to murder the wife who stood between him and his teenage mistress he saw no obstacle in causing the deaths of 22 other people, four of them children.**

**Joseph-Albert Guay was born on January 12, 1919.** The youngest of five children he was spoiled as a youngster and the temper tantrums that followed his not getting exactly what he wanted were something that he would take into adulthood with him. As a young man Guay sold watches and jewelry on commission and when World War II broke out, he got a job at Canadian Arsenals Limited at St. Malo. There he met the woman who was to become his wife, Rita Morel. When the arsenal closed in 1945, Guay left with a little money, which he spent on buying a jewelry and watch repair shop. Life should have been sweet for the shop owner and his new wife, but from the start the couple argued frequently, and the fights grew worse after the birth of their child. The shop was not doing well and the financial strain was added to by a new tension in the house. Like many immature men, Guay felt slighted that he was no longer the center of attention in his own household. His natural inclination toward jealousy and possessiveness grew more pronounced as he realized his needs now came second to that of his son. Eventually, after eight years of marriage, he decided that the only way he would feel important again was to find someone who doted on him as his wife once did.

The girl he chose was 17-year-old nightclub waitress Marie-Ange Robitaille, who liked to be called Mary Angel. To help prevent his wife finding out about his pursuit of a teenager, Guay gave a false name when he first met her and it became the name he used throughout their relationship, which—despite his own family's financial worries—was conducted at an apartment Guay paid for. He also promised to marry her. Duped by his lies, Marie-Ange had no reason to doubt that she was not being seriously courted by a gentleman called Roger Angers who dearly wished to walk down the aisle with her.

But despite his careful tactics to avoid discovery Rita found out everything, and chose the place to confront her husband to cause the maximum damage to his affair. When Guay visited Mary-Ange at her parents' home one day, he found his wife waiting for him and the

**RIGHT:** Albert Guay, pictured with his wife Rita, who was one of the victims of the plane crash that he callously engineered.

secret life he had built completely destroyed. Mary-Ange was ordered out of the house by her appalled mother and father and the Guays soon followed, arguing viciously. When they returned home Rita packed some clothes and took the couple's five-year-old daughter to live at her mother's house.

If Rita had meant to finish his relationship, she failed. None of this seemed to bother Guay. He continued to see his young lover, and in most respects his life was little changed. The confrontation had, however, altered the relationship with Mary-Ange forver. Now she insisted that Guay make an honest woman of her and told him that if he didn't then she would end the affair. With divorce in the largely Catholic province of Quebec rare in the 1940s, Guay realized that the only way could marry his pretty young lover was to bring about 28-year-old Rita's death.

Initially, Guay considered killing his wife with poison, but he was afraid of discovery. After all, there were numerous people who knew he had a good motive for killing his wife. Instead, he concocted a twisted plan that he thought no-one would ever suspect. He traveled frequently by plane in his business as a jeweler to deliver or pick up items for his shop and came to the conclusion that if he could get his wife to take his place while he planted a bomb that would bring the plane down then there was every chance of the crime remaining undiscovered. And if he could time the bomb so the wreckage landed in the St. Lawrence River, any evidence would be washed away.

The more he examined his idea, the more he liked it, but there was a drawback. For a murder on this scale he would need the help of others. Unfortunately, he knew just where to find them.

The rewards that Guay must have promised those willing to join his evil scheme must have been huge, but he soon had his co-conspirators. The first was one of his employees, wheelchair-bound watchmaker Genereux Ruest, who would help him build and package a time bomb. Although Ruest had worked in the munitions factory alongside Guay, he did not have the detailed knowledge required for bomb-making or, indeed, how to go about blowing up a plane so he and Guay decided that a trial run would be needed. In preparation, the pair consulted local explosives experts, using the bizarre cover story that they needed to dynamite a pond. With all the information he needed and with help from Guay, Ruest worked on the bomb-making project from his wheelchair. He eventually created a simple, but effective, timed device from 20 sticks of dynamite, an alarm clock, and a battery. The second person that Guay enlisted was 41-year-old Margeuritte Pitre. She was Ruest's married sister and another former mistress. It would be her job to deliver the bomb to its destination.

All Guay had to do now was persuade Rita to make the plane journey. Guay insisted to his estranged wife that though their marriage was all but over, there was no reason why she shouldn't continue to help him with the business. It was imperative, he told her, that she should go to Baie Corneau to collect some jewels he had ordered from the mining community. Rita refused, but her estranged husband insisted that he was too busy to go himself and pointed out that her income depended on him doing well. When she protested again he told her that he had already bought the ticket. He failed to mention that he had also taken out a $10,000 insurance policy on her life, on top of another for $5,000 that he had purchased back in 1942. Finally, Rita agreed, though the couple argued fiercely as Guay drove her to Quebec City airport on the morning of September 9, 1949. They continued their row inside.

Meanwhile, Pitre was also on her way to the airport in a taxi. She had with her a very heavy parcel, which she told airport authorities was a religious statuette that had to be delivered to a Mr Larouche at an address in Baie Comeau. The 26 pound parcel was duly checked in as freight.

Shortly afterward, Rita boarded the Canadian Pacific Airlines DC-3 together with 22 other passengers. The plane was five minutes late leaving Quebec City and took off at 10.25am, a delay that upset Quay's carefully laid plan. It climbed into the sky and headed northeast toward the St. Lawrence River. And exploded 20 minutes later, scattering debris over the shore of the river rather than into the water. A fisherman near Sault-au-Cochon, 50 miles north of Quebec City, later told how he saw the smoking plane crash toward Cap Tormente on the wooded north shore of the river. Other witnesses said the plane's engines were still running as it hit the ground, which meant that investigators could immediately rule out engine failure as the cause of the crash.

Five workers at a nearby railway line witnessed the terrifying sight, too, and rushed to the scene. But there was nothing they could do. As flames flashed through the aircraft it was clear there would be no survivors. One of the rail workers gave a report to Montreal's La Patrie newspaper, saying: "Arms, legs, and severed heads were lying on the ground. The forward part of the plane looked intact. The bodies were piled up in there as if they had been thrown forward when the plane crashed... There was nothing we could do so we rushed to alert the railway authorities."

News of the disaster was soon being broadcast on radio stations throughout the province and police and Mounties descended on the crash site. The dead included the four crew, four children, and three American executives from the Kennecott Copper Corporation. Guay and his co-conspirators had succeeded in the murder of Rita Guay, but, in total, the lives of 22 other people were also lost. And all so that Albert Guay could marry his teenage sweetheart.

However, Guay would never make his trip down the aisle. Forensic analysis of the plane's debris soon revealed traces of dynamite and investigators concluded the plane had crashed following the explosion of a time bomb in the forward baggage compartment. Within days, Pitre, Guay, and Ruest were arrested. The investigation into the explosion had thrown up many clues, but the one that led straight to Guay was found in a simple tally of the freight list. All but one of the items on board were from regular shippers, and were easily checked. There was, however, no record of the sender of the "religious statuette." Nevertheless, a conversation with the taxi driver who took Pitre to the airport revealed her address and he also remembered that the lady dressed in black had specifically warned him not to drive over any bumps in the road. The driver recalled the woman had added, "These aren't eggs I'm carrying."

When police called at the home of Margueritte Pitre she wasn't there. In fact, she was in hospital recovering from a failed suicide she had attempted after realizing the enormity of the crime she had helped commit. Believing that the police were already watching her, Margueritte had taken an overdose of sleeping tablets. She lived, but only to face death by less gentle means. Under interrogation she maintained that she had not known what the package she had delivered contained, but no-one believed her. Neither did anyone believe her story that Guay had threatened to bankrupt her if she didn't help him, though the tale that he had encouraged her to commit suicide after the crash seemed slightly more plausible.

Before his arrest Guay had presented himself to the world as a man deeply in mourning for his beloved wife. He urged investigators to "get to the bottom of this" and carried a large cross of flowers to Rita's funeral and placed it on her coffin, telling a priest,""If God wanted it, I accept." He was, however, swiftly forced to drop the pretence after he was arrested on September 23, 1949. and charged with murder.

Reust's arrest followed soon after. The three killers appeared at separate trials at the Supreme Court of Canada throughout 1950 and early 1951. Guay was charged with the killing of 22 people along with the assassination of his wife and found guilty. Imposing the death sentence, the judge told him, "Your crime is infamous. It has no name."

Albert Guay was hanged on January 19, 1951, in the Bordeaux Jail near Montreal. As was the ritual there, a chime sounded seven times to announce the execution of a man. (It sounded ten times to announce a woman's death.) Newspapers reported that his last words were, "Well, at least I die famous."

Reust fruitlessly claimed that he had not known his homemade bomb would be used to kill people. There were witnesses, however, who had seen him on the terrace of a hotel on the day of the crash; a vantage point he had chosen because it offered a fine view of the aircraft's course and, therefore, of the crash itself. Ruest was taken to the gallows in his wheelchair and hanged on July 25, 1952.

Pitre's trial began in March 1951, too late for Guay to testify against her as he had done against Reust in an effort to avoid the death penalty. Although she protested her innocence throughout, she was also found guilty and became the last women to be executed in Canada on January 9, 1953.

# Catherine Hayes

**The death of the last woman ever to be executed at Tyburn, London's infamous killing ground, was as gory as the one she inflicted on her husband. Catherine Hayes had an appetite for the wild side of life. She enjoyed nothing more than heavy drinking and romping with her two teenage lovers. However, her fun was spoiled by the presence of a husband. For Catherine the answer was simple: John Hayes must die.**

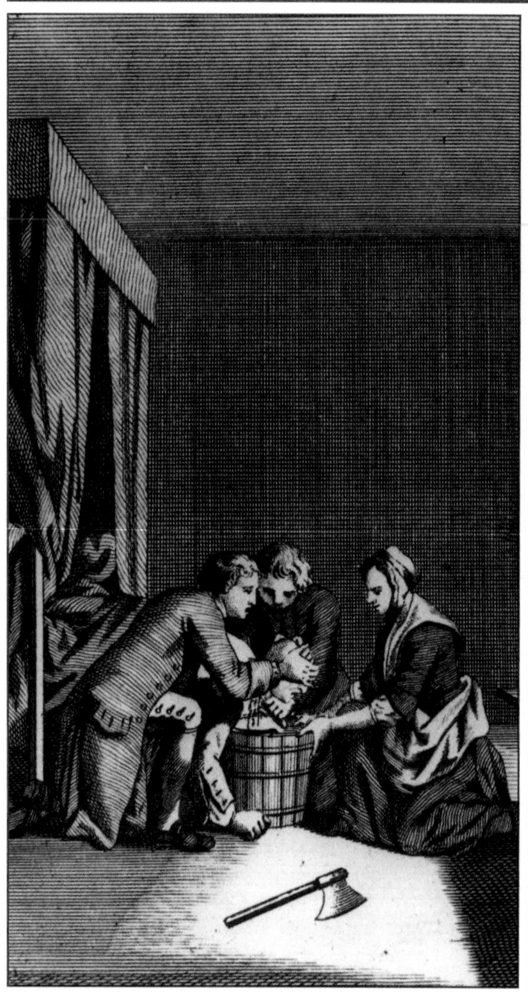

**The method Hayes chose for murder was direct and extreme**, as might be expected of a woman who delighted in her own wildness. And it didn't take much to convince her two strong and virile young lovers to help. Catherine Hayes, Thomas Billings, and Thomas Wood prepared for their evening's work by drinking at the Brawn's Head tavern in London's New Bond Street. They then returned to the Hayes' home and, pretending to be friendly, plied John Hayes with enormous amounts of drink.

After drinking six pints of wine, Hayes staggered to his bed and collapsed. Even had he been conscious Hayes would have been in no state to defend himself from what happened next. Billings smashed him on the back of the head with a coal hatchet, fracturing his skull, and as Hayes gurgled in his death throes, Wood entered the room and hit him twice more. Then Catherine joined her young bedmates, and all three of them decapitated the body.

Hayes' head was taken in a blood filled bucket to be thrown in the River Thames, while the rest of his body was dismembered and stuffed in a trunk that was hidden in the local woods. However, in their haste and drunkenness, Wood and Billings made a mistake. Hayes' head was not washed away on the tide, but came to rest on the river's shore. Night watchmen soon discovered it, and the next day it was paraded on a pole around the streets of London in a ghastly identity parade.

**LEFT:** Catherine Hayes hacking off the head of her husband John Hayes with the aid of her young lovers, Thomas Billings and Thomas Wood.

**RIGHT:** Catherine Hayes being strangled and burned at the stake for the murder of her husband. The flames were so high that the executioner dropped the rope, and she was in fact burned to death.

It did not take the law long to catch up the murderous trio, and all three were found guilty at the Old Bailey, London's central criminal court, on April 30, 1726. Catherine Hayes and her lovers each received a death sentence. While in Newgate Prison awaiting her execution, Catherine sent letters to Wood and Billings showing remorse for involving them in the horrendous act. In a perverse twist, it was later whispered that she had also confessed that Billings was actually her son from a previous affair. Wood caught a fever in prison and died before he could be executed.

On May 14, Catherine Hayes was driven on a cart to be burned at the stake. Reports of the time tell us that, "She was fasten'd to the stake by an iron collar round her neck, and an iron chain round her body, having an halter also about her neck, which the Executioner pulled when she began to shriek. In about an hour's time she was reduced to ashes."

# Frances Howard & Robert Carr

**For the young Frances Howard, daughter of the Earl of Suffolk, the temptations of sexual adventures at the court of King James I proved too great to resist. Caught up in a web of passion that may have involved the king himself, she conspired to poison her lover's other sexual partner.**

**Young, beautiful, and from an old noble family,** Frances Howard was an excellent marriage prospect. She was duly married off to the teenage Earl of Essex in 1610. However, either his sexual interests lay elsewhere or he was simply too young to appreciate the pleasures of the bed chamber. The marriage was not consummated, and soon after Frances' new husband left court bound for a long stay in France.

The passionate young woman, left alone in a court simmering with sexual intrigue, soon found herself tempted to join in and before long was sharing her bed with a young, handsome page called Robert Carr. While Carr was also involved in a homosexual relationship with Thomas Overbury, who was 11 years Carr's senior, he seems to have been more than happy to satisfy Frances' appetites. In addition to this pair of sexual partners, it was also whispered that Carr was the king's bedmate too! He was certainly much favored by the monarch, and while Carr and Frances pleasured each other on nights that Carr didn't spend in someone else's bed, he rose quickly in the king's service. Having been given a position in the Royal court, Carr, in turn, employed Overbury as his secretary.

Trouble began to brew with the return the Earl of Essex, Frances' husband. The earl was now eager to prove himself a man and whisked his wife off to the country in order to finally consummate their marriage. Sadly for him, his clumsy approaches were rejected by a woman who was, by now, more used to the expert touch of her youbg bisexual lover. Frances refused to have sex with him, and the frustrated earl instead sought a divorce. The marriage was dissolved by the Archbishop of Canterbury.

The divorce came as a shock to Thomas Overbury. Convinced that a now single Frances would steal Carr away from him , he became hysterical and made such a public scene that King James had him thrown into the cells at the Tower of London. In fact, both Frances and Carr were eager to be rid of Overbury, whose revelations were an embarrassment to both of them. With the help of Sir Gervase Elwes, Governor of the Tower, and a chemist's assistant, they conspired to have the poison mercuric sublimate administered to Overbury in his cell. It was a foolhardy plot, for while Overbury might be imprisoned for the moment in order to stop his tongue, he was known to be one of the king's homosexual lovers. The king would be furious if the poisoning were discovered. Nevertheless, the plot went ahead. Overbury died on September 15, 1613, after enduring five months of agony.

It looked as though the murder would go undetected, but—in another unexpected twist—the chemist's assistant was struck down with a fatal illness and made a deathbed confession. Elwes and three other men involved in the plot were put on trial and executed in late 1615, while Carr and Howard were tried the following year and also sentenced to death. However, possibly due to the king's lingering affection for Carr, the penalty was waived, and the pair were instead confined in the Tower. After six years of imprisonment, they were allowed to return to their homes in the country. After all that had happened, their passion had turned to mutual hatred. Howard died of a disease of the womb when she was 39; Carr lived on. It is said that a while later, King James held his former lover and sobbed uncontrollably on his shoulder.

# Gus Huberman

**What must be one of the strangest cases in the history of crime began as a simple extramarital affair and ended with a husband shot dead. In between, Gus Huberman's older mistress literally treated him like a pet. Imprisoned in the attic, he was fed, watered, and played with as the mood took her.**

**Gus Huberman attracted Dotty Walburger's attention when he was just 16 years old.** While her husband Bert was wealthy and successful, he was much given to the pleasures of the table and had grown so obese that he could no longer climb the stairs. For a woman who had her own appetites, which had nothing to do with food, the young and energetic boy who worked for a local paint company was a stark contrast to the man she had married. It was not long before the teenager and Dotty were conducting a passionate affair,

Noticing the difference in his wife and suspicious of the relationship with her new young friend, Bert Walburger hired a private detective to trail them and it didn't take long for the truth to be revealed. Faced with proof, Dotty confessed her infidelity and asked for a divorce, but Walburger refused, fearing that the court would award Dotty—and thus her lover—with a large portion of his fortune.

Unable to get rid of her husband and forced to promise that she would give her young lover up, Dotty took desperate measures. She knew that Bert was in no condition to reach the top parts of the house and her solution, while bizarre, was elegantly simple: she smuggled Huberman into the attic. Now she could indulge herself whenever she pleased while never appearing to leave the house. Whenever the Walburgers' moved home—which they did often as Bert's business flourished—Huberman secretly came with them. Dotty was careful to always insist on a tall house with a large attic space.

The situation might have continued indefinitely, but for a violent argument that broke out between Bert Walburger and his wife on August 29, 1922. Hearing it from the attic and fearing for his mistress's safety, Huberman crept down the stairs carrying a revolver that he would later tell a court he always kept handy in case of burglars. He arrived just in time to see Dotty punched to the floor. As his wife fell, Walburger looked up to find himself being watched by his wife's lover, who he had believed to have been long gone. In a fresh rage, Walburger attacked Huberman and during the fight the gun went off. Walburger lay dead. Dotty later claimed the whole incident had happened while she hid in a wardrobe.

Gus Huberman's trial lasted five weeks, during which the press began calling him "The Phantom in the Attic." While the details of the case were undeniably shocking, Huberman's plight roused enormous sympathy. He was just a young boy who had been seduced and then kept like an animal by a woman more than old enough to know better. Finally though, it was a moving speech by Huberman's lawyer that saved him from the charge of murder. Earl Wakeman, defending the lad, told the court that his client was an orphan who had known misery all his life.

Huberman was found guilty, but not of murder but the lesser charge of manslaughter and sentenced to three years in prison. However, he had served longer than this while awaiting trial and was allowed to go free at once. By the time Dotty Walburger was put on trial separately, Huberman had found himself a wife. Dotty was also acquitted when the legal system felt Huberman had been through enough and did not deserve to appear at a court again.

# Lila Jimerson and Nancy Bowen

**When artist Henri Marchand had a casual fling with Native-American Lila Jimerson, he said it was of no great consequence to him; just another brief sexual encounter in a long line. It was a fling that would end in murder, however. But though the woman who actually committed the deed was easy to find, the case proved so difficult to untangle that we will probably never know who really plotted to kill Clothilde Marchand. Nevertheless, it is interesting to note that before the jury reached their final verdict, Marchand had taken a new, young wife.**

**On March 6, 1930, Nancy Bowen,** a 66-year-old Cayuga Indian from the nearby Cattaraugus Reservation walked into the home of Henri Marchand, artist for Buffalo's Natural History Museum. Inside the house, Bowen confronted Marchand's wife Clothilde and asked her, "Are you a witch?" Taken aback by the question, Mrs Marchand jokingly replied yes. On hearing the answer, Bowen beat Clothilde with a hammer, stuffed chloroform-soaked paper down her throat, and left her for dead.

When the Marchands' youngest son Henri came home from school he found his mother sprawled across the first floor landing and ran to the nearby museum, bringing home his father and two brothers. At first it was thought that Clothilde had died from falling down the stairs, but the medical examiner soon found bloody gashes, the odor of chloroform, and signs of a furious struggle on the body of the tiny Frenchwoman. The police were brought in and after questioning Henri Marchand and an associate who boarded with him, began looking for 39-year-old Lila "Red Lilac" Jimerson.

She was arrested alongside Bowen, who had retained broken pieces from Clothilde's glasses and scraps of her bloodstained clothing. But what appeared a straightforward murder for revenge would prove anything but. The court would have to sift through strange accusations, denials, and counter accusations to try and make some sense of the case. Throughout the trial there was also a strong smell of racism, with District Attorney Guy Moore at one point referring to Jimerson as a "filthy Indian."

The prosecution alleged that Lila Jimerson—determined to exact revenge for her callous treatment at Marchand's hands—had fixed upon Clothilde's reputation as a white witch as a means of getting back at him. The French woman, like many of her nation, enjoyed picking and eating wild mushrooms and her love of these "strange hellish vegetables" was considered evidence among some of the Native-American community that she practiced magic. So Jimerson convinced Nancy Bowen, whose husband Charley had recently died, that Clothilde had used her dark powers to cause his death. Bowen was thus primed to exact Jimerson's revenge for her by killing her faithless lover's wife.

During the first trial, Marchand admitted the affair, but told the court it had come about as a matter of professional necessity between artist and model. He added that he had had more affairs than he could remember, dismissing Jimerson as a minor fling. The rest of the trail did not proceed well. Jimerson, who suffered from tuberculosis, collapsed. The federal government also attempted to meddle with the proceedings by enlisting the help of a top-flight lawyer, Richard Harkness Templeton, to defend Jimerson, leaving District Attorney Moore incensed and shouting in court for Templeton to be removed. At the end of the turbulent hearing no verdict was reached.

By the time a second trial came to court, 53-year-old Marchand was remarried to an 18-year old girl and, with the financial support of the Seneca and Cayuga tribes, Jimerson had hired an excellent attorney. Jimerson continued to deny the charge and accused Marchand of the killing, saying that he had told her he wanted to hire assassins to kill his wife. Then in a dramatic reversal—and from a hospital bed—she changed her plea to guilty for second degree murder. Soon she retracted that plea, then admitted first degree murder, then again changed it back to a plea of second degree murder. Now she admitted the killing, but insisted she had simply been a pawn in Marchand's plot to kill his wife and said that she had done everything out of love for him.

After months of confusion, Jimerson was acquitted on February 28, 1931. Nancy Bowen, the women who had actually committed the fatal attack, pleaded guilty to reduced charges of first degree manslaughter and on March 13, 1931, was sentenced to a one to ten-year prison sentence. Because she already had been detained in jail for longer than the amount of the minimum sentence, she was allowed to go free.

# Winnie Ruth Judd

**Sharing an apartment with friends is often difficult, especially if they begin helping themselves to your belongings. However, as Agnes Ann LeRoi and Helwig Samuelson found out, if your roommate should decide that you are stealing their boyfriends then the payback can be horrifying.**

**When Winnie Ruth Judd, Agnes Ann LeRoi**, and Helwig Samuelson—three unmarried girls—decided to share an apartment in Phoenix, Arizona, in 1931, everything went well at first. Like many young women living with friends, they enjoyed each other's company, borrowed clothes, and swapped gossip. Sadly, the easy-going atmosphere wasn't to last. Winnie was somewhat promiscuous and brought a stream of men back to the apartment. Agnes and Helwig objected. The three women had fierce arguments, and Winnie began to believe that her friends were putting obstacles in her way because they wanted her boyfriends for themselves. As her rage and jealousy mounted, she became more and more convinced that Agnes and Helwig were sleeping with the men that rightfully belonged to her.

On October 16, 1931, she snapped, and furiously demanded why the pair kept ruining her relationships. In the circumstances her roommates did the worst thing they possibly could have: they laughed at Winnie. She then shot them both dead.

Working with remarkable presence of mind for a young woman who had just committed a double murder, Winnie immediately put a bullet through her own hand in order to be able to claim self-defense should she be caught. Then she set about disposing of the bodies. Her plan was to dump them into the ocean in her home state of California, and she packed the corpses of her friends into a large trunk for transport, then booked a ticket on a train. When a porter came to collect it he complained it was too heavy and demanded that she instead put "the medical books"—as she described the contents—into smaller cases. Winnie solved the problem by sawing the bodies into pieces.

Incredibly, the cases got as far as California without incident and remained at the station while Winnie fetched her brother to help her with them, telling him brazenly, "There are two bodies in these trunks and the less you know about it, the better off you are." Winnie's plan now began to unravel. A baggage clerk smelled the distinctive odor of rotting flesh coming from the cases, and suspected Winnie and her brother of being meat smugglers. He asked them to open the cases, but Winnie told him she didn't have the keys. Fearing that she was moments from discovery, she grabbed her brother's arm and walked away briskly. As the pair drove away, the clerk made a note of the car registration plate. Then he called the police, still thinking that the worst crime that had been committed was the transport of contraband meat. His mistake was soon corrected in the most horrific manner imaginable. Detectives broke into the cases to find the putrid rotting corpses of two young women.

The hunt was on for a murderer, and Winnie couldn't keep ahead of the law for long. The police traced her brother's car and, meanwhile, the wound in Winnie's hand had become infected. She was forced to attend a hospital and, her cover blown, was arrested.

In court, Winnie maintained her painfully concocted story of self-defense, telling the jury that Helwig had shot her first and that she had then wrestled the gun away from her assailant. The fact that Winnie was now armed hadn't deterred her roommates, and Agnes and Helwig both attacked her again. In fear for her life, Winnie had shot them both.

**BELOW:** Winnie Ruth Judd (centre), being returned to prison after one of her many escapes.

No one believed her. Winnie Judd was found guilty of the murders of Agnes Ann Le Roi and Helwig Samuelson and sentenced to death. But still she tried to evade justice. While in prison awaiting execution, Winnie's behavior convinced doctors that she was actually insane and not responsible for her crimes. At mental hearing, she put on a fine performance; pretending to hear voices, mumbling incoherently, and pulling at her hair and clothes. The death sentence was commuted to a life of imprisonment in the Arizona state mental institution. Winnie proved sane enough to manage to escape from the secure hospital several times, at one time staying on the run for seven years during which time she worked as a housekeeper. Winnie was finally released on December 22, 1971, 40 years after her deadly fit of jealousy.

# Thomas Andrew Keir

**The tale of Australian Thomas Andrew Keir is a confusing one, for while awaiting trial for the murder of his second wife, Rosalina Canonizado, police unearthed the remains of his first wife Jean beneath his home in New South Wales. While he was found not guilty of murdering Rosalina, his first wife came back to haunt him and, after various appeals, he would eventually serve time for her killing.**

**Keir married his first wife Jean in August 1984** when he was 26 and Jean was 18. Four years later, Keir claimed that his wife had run off with another man, leaving their three-year-old son behind. A few weeks after reporting his wife's disappearance, Keir met Rosalina Canonizado while in Sydney attending a family wedding. He divorced Jean on the grounds of desertion and married Rosalina in the Philippines in 1989. Then, on April 13, 1991, Rosalina was found murdered in the same house where Jean had once lived. She had been strangled with a lamp cord and then set on fire. Keir was charged with murder, the prosecution giving a substantial life insurance policy as his motive. But, believing Keir's claims that he was out shopping at the time of the murder, a jury found him not guilty on April 6, 1993. However, while Keir was awaiting trial in prison in 1991, police received information which led to them digging beneath Keir's house where they found fragments of human bone. DNA testing revealed them to belong to Jean Keir.

On September 17, 1999, Thomas Keir was found guilty of Jean Keir's murder in the New South Wales Supreme Court and sentenced to 24 years imprisonment comprising a minimum term of 18 years and an additional term of six years. The court was told Keir killed his 22-year-old wife in a jealous rage after discovering her infidelity. However, the trial judge did not mention Rosalina Canonizado's case during Keir's sentencing. Subsequently, on February 28, 2002, the New South Wales Criminal Court of Appeal revoked Keir's conviction on the grounds that the judge had misdirected the jury regarding the DNA evidence. At this first appeal the judge reduced Keir's sentence by two years to 22 years imprisonment with a non-parole period of 16 years.

A new trial commenced in July 2002 and on October 17 of that year, Keir was again found guilty of Jean's murder. He successfully appealed a second time because of misconduct on the part of members of the jury, but was once again found guilty of Jean's murder at a third trial in December 2004, and the previous sentence was upheld. The court heard that over a period of years Keir had threatened Jean that he would kill her if she left him or "messed around with somebody else." The day after killing his first wife, Keir "apparently coolly and calmly commenced an extensive course of deception designed to conceal the murder." He later dug up her remains and hid them elsewhere, but seven of Jean's bones were left behind and uncovered when police excavated the yard in 1991.

Keir has been decreed to be eligible for parole in 2014 because of time already served. His later conviction for the murder of his first wife would seem to cast doubt on the verdict of not guilty for the murder of Rosalina Canonizado, but perhaps it could be said that Jean had reached out from beyond the grave and exacted the justice owed to both of Thomas Keir's dead wives.

# Ralph Klassen

**Ralph Klassen's killing of his second wife caused outrage in Canada in the 1990s, not least because he received such a light sentence. The controversy that followed his trial would see a petition presented to the Canadian parliament in which 15,000 people demanded the provocation defense be abolished.**

**The 13-year marriage of Ralph and Susan Klassen** had long been a stormy one. They had already separated several times, and then reconciled, when they agreed to part for yet another trial separation of six months in October, 1995. Klassen left their Whitehorse home and moved to Alberta while his wife began finding an independent life for herself. In fact, she was relieved to be rid of her husband. His temper and jealousy had become increasingly difficult to live with and Susan found herself enjoying her newly peaceful life and freedom. So much so that when her husband began calling her later that month asking that they reconcile immediately rather than wait for the six months to end, she refused.

Suspecting that his wife was now involved with another man, Ralph Klassen returned to Whitehorse on November 1, and arrived at his old home demanding again that Susan take him back. Again, she refused him.

In the early morning hours of November 2, 1995, Ralph Klassen strangled his 36-year-old wife in the bed of their home, applying so much pressure to her neck that he sprained both his thumbs. He then took a pillowcase and tied it around Susan's neck, permanently cutting off the oxygen flow to her brain. There were no signs of a struggle.

When he was sure she was dead, Klassen wrote a brief note for his wife's supposed lover. It said, "I'm sorry I went into a jealous fit of rage. The image of you and my wife together made me insane." He then drove his car into a truck in a suicide attempt, but survived against the odds. When police arrived on the scene he confessed to killing his wife.

Klassen was charged with second degree murder, but used the Canadian provocation defense to have it dropped to manslaughter. The jury found him guilty on January 17, 1997. For the killing of his wife Ralph Klassen received a sentence of just five years imprisonment. The term was greeted with shock by the public. However, it was also established that he would be eligible for an early release in May, 2000, when only two-thirds of the light sentence had been served.

There was an immediate outcry. A week later more than 300 people marched through Whitehorse to protest and, also spurred on by the sentence, Klassen's first wife also came forward to tell how Klassen had repeatedly assaulted her during their marriage, on one occasion choking her. In response to the outrage on May 27, the Federal Justice Crown appealed against the lenient sentence arguing that it was "inadequate, given the aggravating factors of spousal violence and breach of trust." A month later three judges dismissed the appeal, saying that the five-year sentence was in line with those imposed in similar cases.

While the controversy raged on, and eventually culminated in an appeal to parliament that the law be revised so that others couldn't use the same defense in the future, Ralph Klassen's sentence remained unchanged. As suggested at his trial he was released from the William Head Institution, a medium-security federal penitentiary on Vancouver Island, in 2000.

# Ada Le Bouef & Dr. Thomas Dreher

**James Le Bouef was allowed to live only so long as he turned a blind eye to his wife's passionate liaison with his best friend. When he began to raise objections that threatened to end the affair his fate was sealed.**

**In the 1920s, Morgan City in Louisiana's** was a simply community of simply country folk. Set in the bayou country of swamps and creeks fed by the waters of the mighty Mississippi River, many Morgan City people lived by trading as frog catchers, trappers, moonshiner's, and alligator hunters. But James and Ada Le Boeuf were a cut above most folk in the area. In a time when electricity was moving from a luxury to a necessity for

**BELOW:** Lake Palourde, the beauty spot in southern Louisiana where Ada Le Bouef, Thomas Dreher and Jim Beadle dumped the body of Ada's husband.

every home, he was superintendent of the Morgan City Light and Power Company and a man of some standing in the small town.

The Le Bouefs had been long married, with five children, when Ada began suffering from terrible headaches that confined her to bed. Her worried husband immediately called his good friend Dr. Thomas Dreher to ease her pain. At first Le Bouef thought that Dreher was simply attending Ada so frequently out of concern for his wife, but as Ada's headaches began to strike more regularly with Dreher in attendance each time, it became obvious that it wasn't a dose of medicine the doctor was giving her. Nevertheless, Le Bouef didn't have the courage to face the scandal that would follow a confrontation of that kind in such a small town. He discreetly allowed them to continue with their liaison in the hope that it would fizzle out and things could get back to normal.

However, the affair couldn't escape the attention of others for long in such a small community, and the neighborhood was soon abuzz with rumors of adultery taking place at the Le Bouef house and anywhere else Ada and the Dreher could find to meet. An anonymous letter was sent to Dreher's wife, telling her, "Two nights ago there was a lady and a man in that empty shack in the bayou. One of them was Ada Le Boeuf and the other was your husband!" Someone else spread a story that Dreher and Ada had been spotted swimming naked together in the bayou.

James Le Boeuf had been prepared to keep quiet in order to keep his humiliation from becoming public knowledge, but now the secret was out he demanded that the affair stop straight away. But he underestimated the strength of the lovers' passion, and the steps they were prepared to take to preserve it" Le Boeuf's body was pulled out of the bayou in July 1927. He had been shot twice in the head.

The identity of his murderers was obvious, and the police swiftly arrested Ada and her lover. Soon after, they also brought a trapper of dubious reputation named Jim Beadle into custody. He was known to have held a grudge against James Le Boeuf.

All three were tried together at Franklin, Louisiana. Dreher's story was that Ada sent him a note asking him to get rid of her husband. It said that she would be rowing on the local lake with him on July 1, and that would be the time to strike. Dreher called on Beadle and they rowed out together. Dreher claimed it was Beadle who fired the two shots, but the trapper denied it, telling the court that the doctor shot James Le Bouef, after which he had "slit open Le Boeuf's stomach" so that the corpse would sink to the bottom and be hidden forever.

All three were found guilty of murder and conspiracy to commit murder. Dr. Thomas Dreher and Ada La Bouef were given death sentences and were hanged side by side on February 1, 1929. Jim Beadle was jailed for life for his part in the killing.

# Thomas Ley

**For some, a crime of passion is committed in a burst of terrible anger or jealousy, while for others the jealousy grows in their minds until it drives them literally insane. It was unfortunate for John McMain Mudie that he crossed the path of a man who was completely possessed by his own fevered suspicions.**

**The body of John Mudie was found in a chalk pit in Surrey**, England, on November 30, 1946. He had been beaten and hanged with a dirty rag stuffed in his mouth, then trussed and dumped. He had been a decent man in life; popular and jovial, he had served his country well during World War II and in peacetime had become a barman. His only crime was to take lodgings in a London house that was also shared by Maggie Brook, the long-term mistress of Thomas John Ley, a former Minister of Justice in New Zealand.

The police hunted down the killer quickly and efficiently. The identity card in Mudie's pocket led them straight to his lodgings, and their questions soon revealed a likely suspect, for Ley's terrifying jealousy was well known. And when one of the men who had helped him murder his victim turned Queen's Evidence, the whole story unraveled.

Despite the fact that Maggie Brook was a respectable woman, her lover was obsessed with his suspicions over her conduct. At some point or another he had accused her of sleeping with virtually every man she knew, including those who lodged at the same house. For some inexplicable reason though, he had come to focus his jealousy on Maudie, perhaps simply because Maudie's simple, likeable character was so different from his own dark nature.

Twisted by his suspicions, Ley hatched a plot to remove his rival and recruited carpenter Lawrence Smith and chauffeur John Buckingham to help. A woman friend, Lilian Bruce, was paid to play the role of

**OVERLEAF:** A 1947 photograph of murderer Thomas John Ley, a former Minister of Justice in New Zealand.

**BELOW:** The chalkpit at Woldingham in Surrey where the body of barman John Mudie was discovered in 1946.

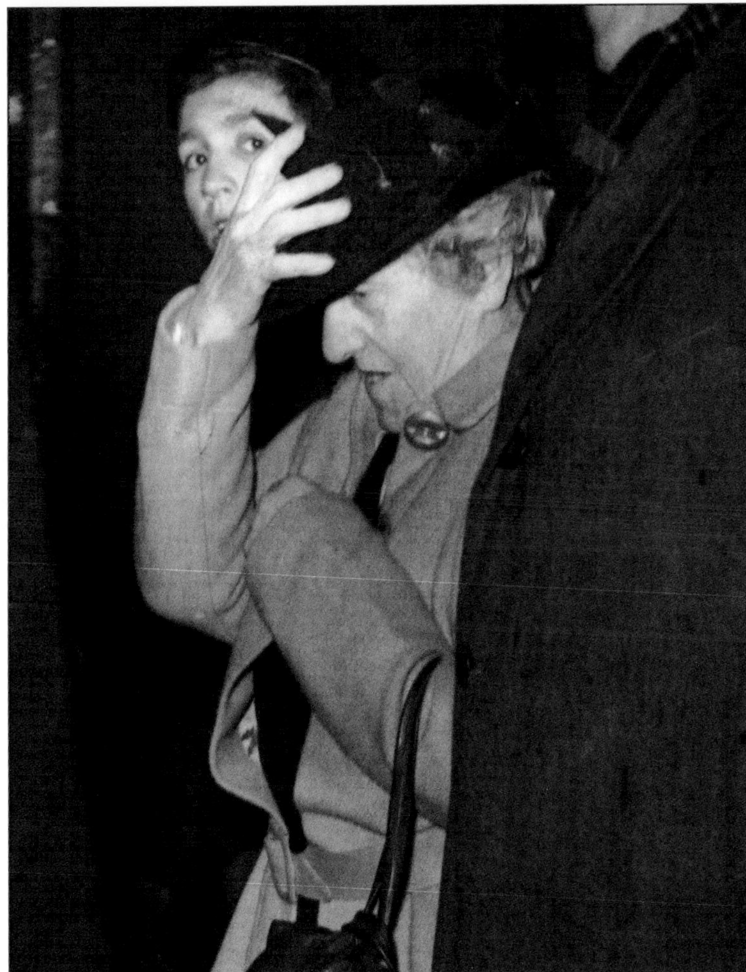

**LEFT:** Mrs Emily Ley, the wife Thomas John Ley, arriving at Waterloo Station from Australia, to attend her husband's trial.

**OVERLEAF:** John Buckingham being helped into his car by his son (left) after giving evidence at the Old Bailey, London, in the trial of Thomas John Ley

a wealthy woman who seemed to be attracted to Mudie and so lure him back to her home in a chauffer-driven car—with Buckingham at the wheel. The house they arrived at, however, was not hers, but Ley's. Once inside, Mudie was attacked by Ley and Smith, severely beaten, and hanged with a cord. Ley then handed Smith and Buckingham £200 cash each for their efforts—and for their silence.

When Buckingham heard about the discovery of John Mudie's body he went straight to the police. He had stayed outside with the car and had no knowledge that he had been part of a murder. All charges against him were dropped, and he later testified against Ley and Smith. Police also learned that the two men had been paid in one pound notes, the exact amount and denomination that had been withdrawn from Ley's bank that very day.

The four-day trial started on March 19, 1947, with both Ley and Smith pleading not guilty. Nevertheless, the case against them was unanswerable, and so dreadful was the crime against an innocent man that the death sentence was passed. Before he was hanged though, Ley was declared insane and given a reprieve. That presented a legal dilemma; if the man who organized such a brutal murder was not going to be executed, how could the man who had been paid to help face the death sentence? Smith was reprieved too and sentenced to life imprisonment. Within four months of his arrival at the top security mental institute of Broadmoor in Berkshire, Ley died of a brain haemorrhage.

# Ann Marie Linscott

**Fortunately for the wife of her lover, Ann Marie Linscott's plot to assassinate her was discovered before it could do any harm. Nevertheless, it is an interesting case and one that shows how crimes of passion might adapt to the digital age.**

**The age of the internet has resulted in many curious affairs.** Many people who would never otherwise have met have developed intense passions for each other in cyberspace and in numerous cases a liaison conducted in virtual reality has had a disastrous effect on real-life relationships. One such affair began in 2004 when Ann Marie Linscott met a man whose identity has never been revealed in an internet chat room. Ann Marie was 49, a wife, and mother to two teenage children, but thoughts of her family were far from her mind as the online lovers tapped out messages of lust on their keyboards.

Eventually, they managed to contrive a meeting. In 2005, the man involved was sent to a conference in Reno, Nevada. Ann Marie joined him there and at last their passion became physical. The brief sexual encounter only served to deepen their intimacy, and the pair continued the relationship by phone and email, the enforced separation serving only to fan the flames of passion, for Ann Marie especially. Although she and her lover managed to meet again, it was not enough for Ann Marie and she hatched a plot to make the man she adored single. It proved to be as stupid as it was potentially deadly.

In November 2007, three California residents were separately searching the website craigslist.com for job opportunities when they came across an advert that looked interesting. The job was described only as a "freelance" position and each of them asked for more information. They began exchanging emails with Ann Marie Linscott, who used an alias, and it soon became apparent that the freelance position was a crude code for a contract killer.

Linscott asked each of the three job applicants to "eradicate" a woman living in Butte County, California, and provided a description of the victim, her age, and the address where she worked. On two occasions she offered payment of $5,000 upon completion of the task. Realizing that she was deadly serious, all three of the jobseekers reported the mystery employer to the police.

Californian detectives quickly established the identity of the intended victim and discovered that she was married. Under questioning, the details of her husband's infidelity were revealed, and the trail finally led them to Ann Marie. Background checks on her revealed a list of irregularities: She had once taken out a restraining order on one of her colleagues, and he had responded in kind, claiming that she had made unwanted advances. She had also given false information on her resume, saying that she had worked as a massage therapist at a hospital that had never heard of her.

Linscott was arrested at her home in January 2008 and charged with perpetrating a murder-for-hire scheme. On February 4, 2009, she was found guilty and sentenced to 12 years and seven months in prison. The judge hearing the case condemned Linscott for showing no remorse and said the heavy sentence was to protect the public from people like her, and to deter anyone else who might be considering using the internet to recruit a killer. Strangely, her husband, John, supported her throughout.

# Denise Labbe & Jacques Algarron

**This crime of passion is unusual, and more sickening than most. It was not committed out of revenge or in the heat of the moment, but against a complete innocent whose mother had the misfortune to come under the spell of a philosophy student whose beliefs were nothing short of insane. He abused her love for him by asking her to prove it in the most vile way imaginable.**

**Denise Labbe's life had often been a struggle**, but she had worked hard to better herself. She was the daughter of a poor postman and after being orphaned at 13 had educated herself to the point where she was able to land a job as a secretary. She also allowed herself a little fun along the way, usually with the male students of her home town of Rennes, France, and by the time she reached 25, she had a toddler daughter called Catherine. Nevertheless, she was coping well with life's demands until she met a charismatic graduate of philosophy named Jacques Algarron. He was three years her junior and seduced her with the line he always used on women: "I offer you fervor." She was immediately bewitched by the complex and well-read young man and began a passionate affair with him.

Algarron was a great admirer philosophy that suggested the existence of "super humans" and told his new girlfriend that he believed they were a super couple. Unfortunately, his demented ideas quickly grew into an obsession. He needed Denise to prove that she was superior to other women and worthy of his love. The scheme Algarron hit upon should have told Denise that he was an extremely dangerous individual, but she was head over heels in love and couldn't bear the idea

ABOVE: Jacques Algarron, being escorted in a police car on the second day of his trial in Blois, France.

that she might lose him. Algarron read Denise a story in which a mother kills her child by another man to please her lover and told her how beautiful it was. She had to suffer, too, he said. The deluded Denise agreed, convinced by what she saw as Algarron's high intellect and advanced philosophy.

Her first attempt to kill Catherine wasn't successful. Appalled by the enormity of what she was about to do and disturbed by the appearance of a neighbor, Denise found that she could not drop her daughter from a window as planned. Her second went little better. Denise threw Catherine into a canal, only to be overwhelmed by her maternal instinct to protect her child. She summoned help, and the little girl was pulled out of the water by a passerby.

By now Algarron was becoming impatient and threatened to leave her if she did not carry out his orders. So, on November 8, 1954, she drowned Catherine in a washtub then telegraphed Algarron to tell him that she had done as asked. He later told a friend, "It takes courage to kill your own daughter."

The child's disappearance soon aroused suspicions among Denise's neighbors, and police were called in to question her. She confessed to the horrific crime, but told them that Algarron was to blame.

The thunder and lightning that accompanied the opening of the trial of Denise Labbe and Jacques Algarron was seen as a sign of their demonic possession. Both were found guilty of murder with Denise sentenced to life imprisonment and Algarron to 20 years. Algarron, however, had a final statement to the court and pompously stood to deliver it. "Certain monsters," he told the stunned people in the room, "are sacred because often the same qualities are found in a monster and in a saint." Like the horrendous crime he had incited Denise to commit, it was beyond anyone's comprehension.

# Adolph Luetgert

**The trial of Adolph Luetgert for the murder of his wife Louise in 1897 became one of the first in the United States to be carried out under the full glare of the media and with the nation eagerly awaiting every grisly new revelation. It was hardly surprising as the case had all the elements of a penny dreadful story: infidelity, violence, murder, and a particularly grisly method for deposing of the body.**

The trial of Adolph Luetgert for the murder of his wife Louise in 1897 became one of the first in the United States to be carried out under the full glare of the media and with the nation eagerly awaiting every grisly new revelation. It was hardly surprising as the case had all the elements of a penny dreadful story: infidelity, violence, murder, and a particularly grisly method for deposing of the body.

Like many of the marriages within these pages, Adolph and Louise Luetgerts' was not a happy one. He was the owner of a sausage factory and she was his second wife, but the fact that he was married did not stop him conducting numerous affairs and during their frequent arguments, during which Louise would implore her husband to stop sleeping with other women, Luetgert often became violent. In fact, neighbors once reported seeing Luetgert trying to strangle his wife, stopping only when he realized he was being watched.

On May 1, 1897, when her brother came looking for her, Luetgert admitted that Louise had disappeared. He claimed that she had left him and that he didn't know where she had gone, but her brother was suspicious. He informed the police who took Luetgert in for questioning, asking him why he had not reported her missing when the year before he had come to them for help when his dog disappeared. Luetgert maintained that he had hired a private detective to find his wife, fearing a scandal if his marital problems became public.

No one believed him and after a witness came forward to say they had seen Luetgert leading his wife into a back alley by his factory on April 24, a search for her body began. At first a nearby river was trawled, but when that proved fruitless the police turned their attentions to the factory itself and soon uncovered some gruesome evidence: fragments of human bone and a wedding ring with the initials "LL" in one of the vats. They also found a night watchman, who had unwittingly helped with the boiling up of Louise Luetgert and had been curious about the strange slime he had been asked to dispose of. He later testified that Luetgert had told him, "Don't say a word and I'll see you have a good job as long as you live."

The press went wild. Newspapers fought one another for scoops, people across the country claimed to have seen the missing woman alive, and each new clue led to fresh rounds of speculation about the crime. Meanwhile, sausage sales plummeted nationwide as rumors circulated that Luetgert had destroyed his wife's body in one of his factory's meat grinders. In fact, the rest of her body was never found and it is impossible to say what went on in the factory.

At Luetgert's trial, witnesses came forward to speak of his violent tendencies and letters from his various mistresses were read out. They suggested that Luetgert had promised to marry other women and share his fortune, though he was actually on the verge of bankruptcy. Through it all, Luetgert maintained his innocence, telling the jury that one day Louise would return to him. Despite his protestations, the evidence against him was overwhelming. Adolph Luetgert was found guilty of the murder of his wife and sentenced to life. He died in the Joliet State Penitentiary in 1899.

**BELOW:** Joliet State Penitentiary, in Illinois, where Adolph Luetgert served his life sentence for the murder of his wife.

# Harmohinder Kaur Sanghera

**When Sair Ali got married to his 17-year-old cousin, he didn't bother to trouble his existing lover with the news. But when she finally found out that he had been cheating on her with a new wife, Harmohinder's jealousy and anger drove her to a terrible revenge.**

**When Sair Ali got married to his 17-year-old cousin,** he didn't bother to trouble his existing lover with the news. But when she finally found out that he had been cheating on her with a new wife, Harmohinder's jealousy and anger drove her to a terrible revenge.

Harmohinder Kaur Sanghera and Sair Ali met in 2005 when she was 23, and he 25. Instantly attracted to one another they began a passionate affair, kept secret to avoid scandal among their respective communities—Harmohinder was a Sikh, Ali came from a strict Muslim family. However, completely unbeknown to Harmohinder, her lover was already betrothed to his cousin Sana, and when they were married in Pakistan Ali still did not confess.

Nevertheless, Harmohinder's suspicions were aroused when Ali's passion for seemed to cool. They no longer met so often and when they did, he seemed distant. The reason, she was later to discover, was not only did Ali have a wife but she was already four month's pregnant.

Furious that the man she loved could keep such an enormous secret from her, Harmohinder decided that if her own happiness was to be destroyed, then Ali's would be too. She told a friend that the following day she intended to confront Sana with the truth about her husband's adulterous affair and then end the relationship with him for good. But over the next 24 hours she appears to have changed her plan.

Harmohinder drove to the couple's home in Bury, Lancashire, armed with a knife and stabbed Sana to death in a frenzied attack as she lay in her bedroom. Examiners would later find 43 knife wounds on the body, among which was a deep abdomen wound that had obviously been intended to destroy the 11-week foetus of Sana's baby boy. Harmohinder then calmly climbed through a kitchen window, secured the house, and drove back to her home in Birmingham.

Like many first-time murderers, Harmohinder was quickly discovered. Her footprints were found at the scene, and proof that she had travelled to Birmingham that day was easily gathered from CCTV cameras that lined the roads she had used. She was found guilty of murder in November 2007 and sentenced to life, to serve a minimum of 14 years.

Nevertheless, Harmohinder's revenge had found its target. The cheating Sair Ali lost both his wife and child. Although no one could ever deserve the punishment that Harmohinder meted out, Ali must have known that if his own behavior had been different the crime might well have been averted. As he later said, "No one can sleep. We all have nightmares. We cannot stay in the house now. No one can go into Sana's bedroom; the door is always closed. Her clothes still hang in her wardrobe. We can't face it yet and don't feel we ever can."

# Larissa Schuster

**Since dubbed the "Mad Chem Chick" by the press at the time of her arrest Larissa Schuster seemed the least likely of murderers. Stout, bottle blonde, and 42 years old, she was a successful businesswoman and devoted mother. The method she chose to despatch her husband was so sickening that it shocked the United States. Her story is a complex one but perfectly illustrates what can happen when love turns to ashes.**

**Larissa Schuster's background gave no hints that one day she would become a murderer**. She was born on a farm in Missouri and raised by parents who taught her strong Christian values. She was, as a court was to hear many years later, a "happy and normal child" with a love of animals and people.

At college, Schuster appears to have been a popular A-grade student and a star baseball player. After learning to drive she became a volunteer hospital worker. If there was a flaw in her character it was that she had expectations of others that sometimes could not be fulfilled, expectations that saw her first serious relationship end disastrously.

**BELOW:** Larissa Schuster listening to evidence being given at a hearing in a Los Angeles County courthouse during her trial for the murder of her husband.

Despite the painful break-up with her first boyfriend, Larissa pulled herself together and while still at college fell in love again, this time with a young man called Tim Schuster, who she met and married shortly before graduating with honors. The couple set out on a married life that was full of promise. He was a registered nurse, she a bright graduate quickly taken on to perform research for the pesticide industry by ABC Laboratories in Columbia, Missouri. In 1985, they were blessed with a daughter, Kristin, and four years later Larissa was offered the job of laboratory manager for the Pan Am airline in California. The family moved to Fresno, California, and in 1990 Larissa gave birth to their son, Tyler.

To the outside world Tim and Larissa's family life looked like the fulfilment of the American dream; they were comfortably off and regular churchgoers with a wide circle of friends. If Larissa had suffered from a lack of self-confidence in her younger years, success at work had given her a new poise. But behind closed doors, as is so often the case, the relationship was not all it seemed. Over the years, Tim Schuster had gradually begun treating his wife with more and more contempt. He belittled her efforts at her job and constantly reminded her of her poor, rural upbringing. The couple bickered and argued often, and though beneath it all Larissa still loved her husband, their house had a constant atmosphere of tension and mistrust. In court, she would later describe her home life thus: "Everything seemed fine on the surface; trying to do good and admirable things, but the problem was the interior of the marriage. It was surviving but still had problems."

In fact, the marriage was breaking down fast. The Schusters' sex life had dwindled and, unhappy at home, Larissa threw herself into work. Often tired and irritable as well as suffering

ABOVE: Shirley Schuster, mother of murder victim Timothy Schuster, hugging Clovis Police detective Larry Kirkhart, outside superior court, before a verdict was read in James Fagone's trial for the murder of her son.

from the constant strain of a difficult marriage, she tried to maintain some kind of order in the house by being a strict disciplinarian with the children. In turn, they developed behavior problems, something Larissa had to deal with on her own. Kristin was sent off to live with her grandparents in Missouri in a bid to give her a more settled home life.

Amazingly, in this pressured environment the Schuster's marriage struggled on for another 12 years, during which time Larissa invested much of her emotional energies into work. Eventually, she opened her own business, Central California Research Laboratories, and came to be respected as one of the top chemists in the country. Nevertheless, the unhealthy marriage had become increasingly poisonous. By now the Schusters could not even look at each other, and Larissa confided in a friend that she genuinely hated her husband. Something had to give, and Larissa finally asked Tim for a divorce.

To her surprise, he refused to even acknowledge the request, let alone move out of the family home, and the marriage limped on until Larissa noticed that her husband had started keeping a journal. Her curiosity was aroused and she sneaked a look one night to find that Tim had been writing damning entries about her emotional state and inability to care for the children or her business. He had also noted actions that could be

**LEFT:** A handcuffed James Fagone being led from court after a guilty verdict was read in his trial.

interpreted as signs of mental problems. Larissa jumped to the obvious conclusion—her business was doing well and Tim was preparing to wage a bitter divorce battle to take the children and as much money as possible.

After more angry scenes, Tim finally left the family home in July 2002. He was awarded custody of their son and took away every stick of furniture and every possession while Larissa was away visiting her parents and Kristin. By now, her mental state had begun to unravel. All the love she had once felt turned to a bitter loathing. She began making vicious, angry calls to her husband, up to eight times a day, calling him names, mocking his sexual performance, and telling him that he was a terrible father to their children.

The divorce dragged on. A year later the couple were still fighting over their share in Larissa's business, with Tim wanting a million dollars as a settlement. The emotional turmoil was also taking a toll on their children. In an attempt to find a little peace for them and herself, she took Tyler to visit his sister and grandparents in Missouri. Tim Schuster retaliated by calling the police and accusing his wife of kidnapping their son.

In the middle of all this confusion Larissa had found a friend and confidante. James Fagone was a young laboratory assistant. Lazy, lacking in ambition, and with a variety of personal problems of his own, it is probably a sign of her state of mind that Larissa didn't recognize immediately that he was a deeply disturbed individual. Nevertheless, he proved useful and was often at her house clearing the yard, walking the family dog, and generally helping out. Larissa found that she could

ABOVE: Judge Wayne Ellison speaking during the murder trial of Larissa Schuster in a Los Angeles County courthouse.

talk to the young man and often, of course, their conversations revolved around her problems with the divorce and her hatred of her husband. Fagone assured her of his own disgust at Tim Schuster and promised to help whatever the circumstances.

What finally caused Larissa to snap was a fairly trivial incident by the standards of her acrimonious marriage and divorce. She wanted to take Tyler to Disneyland and then on a visit to Missouri. Tim scuppered it. It proved to be the final straw. Now, Larissa just wanted her husband dead.

In the early hours of July 10, 2003, Fagone and Larissa went to Tim's home and fired a stun gun at him as he opened the door. They then dragged him through the house, held a chloroform-soaked rag to his mouth, and tied him up before loading him into a truck and driving him to Larissa's house. What happened next outraged the court and the American public. While still alive, Tim Schuster was shoved head-first into a 55-gallon plastic barrel, then Larissa and her accomplice poured hydrochloric acid over him and sealed the barrel.

Two days later Fagone and Larissa drove the barrel to her Fresno business premises. She poured in more acid, but had trouble resealing the lid so she used a handsaw to cut off her husband's feet. However, Larissa knew that the incriminating barrel couldn't remain somewhere so obvious. She organized a storage unit and called her friend to ask him to remove it, but by that time even the deranged Fagone had had enough by now and fled the area.

Police were alerted to Tim Schuster's disappearance when the normally obsessively punctual man failed to turn up for appointments. A search of his home quickly established that something was amiss. There was no sign of Tim, but his wallet and mobile phone remained in the house. Further enquiries led to interviews with staff at Larissa's laboratory. Investigators heard of the hatred between the couple, their multi-million dollar divorce, the custody battle, and how Larissa had often been heard to say that she wished her husband was dead. Larissa immediately became the prime suspect.

While it was already obvious to the police that they had found their killer, investigations continued. At the laboratory, staff told of how Larissa had joked that her husband's body might fit into the 55-gallon barrel. And when they went to show it to officers were surprised to find it had vanished. Another employee told them that Larissa had asked him to rent a truck and a storage unit in his name so that she might hide some property from her husband until the divorce was final. When she had returned the truck, the employee noticed blood on one of Larissa's shoes.

Over the next couple of days, police searched Larissa Schuster's home, her offices and laboratory, and the self-storage unit. They unearthed several items including blond wigs and bloody tennis shoes from Schuster's home; and Fagone's time sheets, chemical order invoices, saws, and a mop and bucket from the business. And when they opened the self-storage unit they found what remained of Tim Schuster. Partially dismembered and decomposing, the corpse was later described as "intact from only the belt buckle down."

Police arrested Fagone on July 15, 2003, and Schuster the next day. Three days later, detectives searched Fagone's home and seized receipts for a stun gun and a 14-inch cable tie, bank statements, folding buck knife, and computer equipment.

Under questioning, it immediately became apparent that Larissa's mental state was completely breaking down. One moment she expressed sickness at the atrocity she had committed on the man she once loved, the next she was desperate not to let Tyler down by missing the promised trip to Disneyland.

Fagone and Schuster first appeared in court on September 29, 2003. Then followed another hearing at Fresno County Court where the couple pleaded innocent to charges of murder with special circumstances—torture, murder during a kidnapping, lying in wait to commit murder, and murder for financial gain. The Fresno County District Attorney's Office later added a fifth special circumstance—that the pair murdered Timothy Schuster during a burglary. If convicted of the murder and any of the special circumstances, the law could impose the death penalty.

While the killers awaited trial in jail, the police and lawyers took almost three years to carefully compile their evidence and prepare for court. The case of James Fagone, by now aged 25, finally came before a judge on November 25, 2006, at Fresno County Court. The prosecution had prepared well and a judgement was reached quickly. His guilty verdict was read out on December 11. Fagone was given life imprisonment with no chance of parole on February 20, 2007. On hearing the sentence he muttered, "I humbly ask the court for your forgiveness."

The trial of Larissa Schuster began at Los Angeles County Court on October 15, 2007. Roger Nuttall, her defense lawyer, attempted to paint Larissa as a victim of circumstances, a woman who had tried her best to maintain order amid terrible emotional stress, and eventually failed. He described her as "a very committed mother, talented individual, and a very lovely human being." The prosecution, however, argued that Schuster was a domineering woman who repeatedly made threats against her husband and that Fagone had only become her accomplice because she intimidated him. Nuttall responded by repeatedly questioning the validity of Fagone's evidence.

Schuster's case lasted longer than that of her accomplice. Nevertheless, she was finally found guilty in December 2007 and, like Fagone, was sentenced to life without parole on May 16, 2008. Judge Wayne Ellison told her that her attorneys were to be thanked for saving her life. He commented, "This is the kind of case in which the jury may have imposed the death penalty, and this court might have upheld the imposition of that penalty. In the light of everything Mr Nuttall has said, it is true to say, he saved your life."

# Carolyn Warmus

A wealthy, if unhappy, family life gave Carolyn Warmus a sense of entitlement from an early age. Later, it would begin to show in bizarre behavior if one of her many affairs didn't go exactly as she expected; behavior that would come to a tragic climax when her latest married lover dumped her.

Carolyn Warmus was born in January 1964 and grew up in Birmingham, Michigan, a rich suburb of Detroit. Her parents divorced when she was just eight years old and by the time she began attending the University of Michigan it was obvious to those who came close to her that she had psychological problems. She seemed desperate for physical and emotional contact, but one by one all of her relationships broke down because of her possessiveness. Finally, one former boyfriend, Paul Laven, was forced to take out a restraining order to keep Carolyn away from him. The obsessive behavior continued when Carolyn moved to New York, where she hired a private detective to follow a married bartender who had also had the nerve to end their relationship.

Despite her emotional problems, Carolyn eventually earned a master's degree in elementary education from Columbia University and landed a job in September 1987, at the Greenville Elementary in Scarsdale, New

**OVERLEAF:** The two-story Scarsdale apartment complex where murderer Carolyn Warmus allegedly shot her lover's wife before meeting him for sex in a parking lot.

**BELOW:** High school yearbook picture of future murderer Carolyn Warmus (center) who would kill her lover's wife eight years later.

66

York. There, she met Paul Solomon, a fifth grade teacher who was soon to become yet another married lover. With no knowledge of Carolyn's previous behavior, Solomon badly misjudged her, introducing her to his wife Betty Jeanne and their daughter Kristan. Before long Carolyn was almost part of the family, becoming a big sister figure to Kristan whom she showered with expensive presents. Behind the scenes though, Carolyn was sleeping with Solomon and her resentment of his seemingly perfect, happy family life was growing.

During the early evening of January 15, 1989, a New York Telephone operator answered a call from a woman who was clearly in fear for her life. When it was suddenly disconnected, the operator immediately contacted the police. However, they were unable to trace the call, though it soon became apparent who had made it. When Paul Solomon returned home that night he discovered his wife's body. She had been beaten around the head with a gun and then shot nine times in her back and legs.

Detectives immediately suspected that Solomon had murdered his wife himself, but he was able to give credible alibis, including having spent part of the evening with Carolyn. The illicit relationship now came to an end. Solomon told Carolyn that he no longer wanted to see her and was soon involved with another woman, Barbara Ballor. It was this new relationship that pointed police in Carolyn's direction. She was soon back to her old ways, pursuing Solomon and his new girlfriend and attempting to split them up. The increasingly suspicious police also learned that she had purchased a .25 caliber Beretta pistol just before Betty Jeanne had been murdered. Further investigations showed that on the day of the killing, a call had been made from Carolyn's home to a sports shop, where she later arrived to buy ammunition. With enough evidence to charge her for murder, the police moved quickly to arrest her.

The trial of Carolyn Warmus began on January 14, 1991, and from the outset she did little to court public sympathy. The tight outfits she wore accentuated her figure, and the New York press dubbed her Sex Tigress, A Woman Possessed, and the Black Widow. Nevertheless, the trial dragged on for months before the jury finally announced that it was unable to reach a unanimous verdict. On April 27, 1991, the judge announced a mistrial.

At the second trial, which began in January 1992, a new piece of evidence was presented: a blood-soaked woollen glove that had been found at the murder scene. It was shown to have belonged to Carolyn, and this time the jury was convinced of her guilt. On June 26, 1992, Judge John Carey told the court that Carolyn Warmus had committed "a hideous act, a most extreme, illegal, and wanton murder" and gave her a sentence that matched the severity of the crime: 25 years to life in prison.

# Mary Eleanor Wheeler Pearcey

**With an auburn-haired beauty so fine that even her hangman would remark that she was the most beautiful woman he had ever executed, Mary Eleanor Wheeler Pearcey, left a trail of broken hearts behind her. But when her own was shattered, she tried to mend it by killing the family of her lover.**

**Born in 1866**, Mary Eleanor Wheeler was no stranger to unhappiness from an early age. Her father was a robber and murderer, and when he was hanged for his crimes Mary attempted suicide. She failed and soon after that her family moved to London where it seems she tried to heal her emotional pain in the beds of a string of men.

The first was Charles Pearcey, whom Mary met when she was just 16. So smitten was Mary with him that she took his last name even though they never actually married. But despite the love that grew between them, Mary found it difficult not to flaunt her charms elsewhere, and Pearcey left her when he found out that she had been sleeping with married, self-made businessman Charles Creighton. For a while Creighton kept Mary as his mistress, but her wandering eye was soon caught by another—a young man named Frank Hogg who worked at his family's grocery store.

This time it looked as though one of Mary's relationships might last the distance. She fell deeply in love with Hogg, and he with her, but again the relationship was wrecked by infidelity. This time though it was not Mary who cheated. Hogg had been sleeping with a girl called Phoebe Styles. When she fell pregnant his family insisted he marry her. Mary was devastated, but when Hogg offered to move away to spare her feelings she told him that she would prefer he stayed close to her than suffer the pain of never seeing him again.

Unsurprisingly, Hogg's marriage did nothing to cool his and Mary's passion for one another and they were soon back in each other's arms, while Mary also began seeing Charles Creighton again. She also took an interest in her lover's new wife and tried to befriend Phoebe, though it appears that she was instinctively wary of Mary. On one occasion she refused Mary's invitation to visit a seaside house, explaining to her husband that "no one would think to look for me in a big, empty house."

On October 24, 1890, Mary sent an invitation by messenger boy to her lover's wife and 18-month-old baby Tiggie; this time to take tea with her. Phoebe accepted and wrote a brief note for Hogg so that he would not worry, simply saying, "Shall not be gone long." She then pushed the baby round to Mary's apartment in a pram.

The body of Phoebe Hogg was discovered on the heath at Hampstead in north London. The man who found her later confessed to stealing her wedding ring and selling it for food before finding a policeman. A doctor who examined the corpse noted that Phoebe's throat was slashed from left to right, and that the cut was so deep her head had been nearly severed from her body. Newspaper reports assumed the murderer was a man because of the force used.

The following day, Saturday, 26th October, baby Tiggie was found on waste ground. Her only wound was a scratch on her forehead most likely caused by being dumped, but she was also dead. The pram was found some miles away, blood soaked and missing a bolt. The medical examiner could not determine if the baby suffocated under the weight of its dead mother, or if it died from exposure.

During Mary's trial, the court was packed with middle-class ladies. Her story had captivated numerous wives and mistresses who felt sympathy toward a wronged woman even though an innocent woman and tiny child had been the victims of her terrible revenge. Despite their support and her claims of innocence, Mary was sentenced to hang. In a very odd twist of fate, her execution, on December 23, 1890, was carried out by a man called James Berry who was the assistant to the man who had hanged her father at St. Albans some 14 years earlier.

Mary Eleanor Wheeler Pearcey was buried at Newgate Prison in an unmarked grave. While never confessing to the murders and saying the evidence against her was false, she said the sentence was just. She also left a cryptic note with her solicitor that read, "MEWP. Did not betray. MEW." No one knows what it means, though it has been suggested it was a note meant for a husband from a secret marriage.

# Elizabeth Workman

**Like many women before and after her, Elizabeth Workman snapped after enduring years of abuse from her husband. What makes her case more notable is that despite public support and the wishes of the jury, she still went to her death.**

**Elizabeth and James Workman** were among a wave of immigrants who landed in Canada in the mid-19th century looking for a better quality of life. They came from Scotland, and Elizabeth was in her 20s, about 30 years younger than her husband who also brought with them his daughter Mary from a previous marriage. Sadly, they did not find the better life that they had hoped for in a new country. Poverty forced the family to live in a two-room apartment, in which Elizabeth soon gave birth to their son.

Elizabeth's miseries were made worse by the realization that she had married a drunken bully. Although she refused to criticize her husband, she often ran to the neighbors to hide from his vicious tongue and fists. One of those who gave her shelter was Samuel Butler, a black man who owned a small barber shop. A charitable man, Butler tried to help the struggling family by offering Elizabeth a job doing his laundery and cleaning the shop.

Elizabeth and Butler's friendship was soon noted by the town gossips and rumors began to fly that the pair were having a love affair, a relationship that would have been taboo at that time. The tittle-tattle inevitably reached the ears of James Workman, and on October 24, 1872, while Elizabeth was scrubbing the floor at Butler's barber shop, her husband arrived with their little boy. Obviously the worse for drink, James demanded that his wife return home. When Elizabeth refused, Workman made to grab her, but Butler intervened. Elizabeth was so furious that she beat her husband with a mop handle. However, her anger was not to end there.

As the court would later hear, the next morning an upstairs neighbor saw Butler leaving the Workmans' rooms. James Workman was in bed recovering from the beating his wife had given him, but still he constantly berated and abused Elizabeth until—as she later confessed—she could take no more. She beat him on and off for two hours until one heavy blow rendered her husband unconscious—for good.

Later that day, Elizabeth called on another neighbor, David Patterson, as she was concerned about her husband. But it was too late for him. At first Patterson said Workman had died in his arms but then he changed his story to say he was dead when he got there, and that the body looked suspiciously as if it had been washed clean of blood.

The postmortem examination was conducted on the following Sunday morning. James Workman's body was recorded as being malnourished and—in the coroner's view—bruises and abrasions on his legs were consistent with having been bound with a rope. Other bruises suggested that he had received between 20 and 30 blows from a blunt object. The killing blow, however, had been made by a "sharp cutting instrument" near the left temple. Two butcher's tools were found in the home that could have caused it.

Elizabeth was quickly arrested but denied having anything to do with her husband's murder, saying he had died of natural causes. She also staunchly defended Samuel Butler, denying he had anything to do with the death. Her trial lasted just two days, during which she heard a flood of evidence against her, ranging from absurd and irrelevant accusations that she was "not very kind" to witnesses declaring that although James Workman had verbally abused his wife regularly, he had never actually been seen to hit her. The court also heard suggestions of an improper relationship between Elizabeth and Samuel Butler.

The judge finally swayed the verdict. Although the jury had sympathy for Elizabeth and did not want to convict her for murder, the judge's conclusion was that there was strong circumstantial evidence against her and he recommended that the jury decided accordingly. Sure enough the jury returned a guilty verdict against Elizabeth while Samuel Butler was acquitted through lack of evidence.

Elizabeth Workman spent three months in prison before her execution on June 19, 1873. The reprieve she waited for never came despite growing public support. She walked to the gallows clutching a bunch of flowers. She was the only woman ever to be executed by hanging in Canadian history. A later report noted, "The crucial reason that Elizabeth Workman was allowed to hang was that the judge's negative characterization was uncontested at the trial by the defense. Elizabeth Workman, a poor, marginalized, working-class woman was ill-served by a judicial system that accorded her little regard. Specifically, no real effort was made to defend her."

# Picture Credits

**Getty Images**
8 Universal Pictures
9 (top) J. David Ake/AFP
10 POOL/AFP
11 (top) J. David Ake/AFP
15 Justin Sullivan
21, 22, 25 David Goddard
27, 28, 29 Topical Press Agency
30, 31, 32, 34 Edward Gooch
35, 36 Topical Press Agency
39 W. G. Phillips/Topical Press Agency
45, 46 Keystone
47 Bentley Archive/Popperfoto
50 Evening Standard
66, 67, 75 Brian Miller/Time Life Pictures
77, 78, 79, 80 Keystone/Hulton Archive
84 Chicago History Museum
91, 92 Michael Abramson/Time Life Pictures

**iStock**
4 iStockphoto.com/Terraxplorer
6 iStockphoto.com/davidmartyn

**Press Association**
6 (left), 9 (bottom), 11 (bottom), 41 (both), 42, 43, 44, 49, 53, 55, 57, 61 (both), 63, 72, 82, 86, 87, 88, 89.

**TopFoto**
13, 14 The Granger Collection

Every effort has been made to trace the ownership of copyrighted material and to secure permission from copyright holders. In the event of any question arising as to the use of any material, we will be pleased to make necessary corrections in future printings.

TRUE CRIMES

# UNDYING LOVE

igloo

igloo

This edition published in 2010
by Igloo Books Ltd
Cottage Farm
Sywell
NN6 0BJ

www.igloo-books.com



A copy of the British Library Cataloguing-in-Publication Data is available from the British Library.

10 9 8 7 6 5 4 3 2 1

ISBN 978-0-85734-397-0

Printed and Manufactured in China

# Contents

# Millicent Adams

**The case of Millicent Adams is a classic example of what can happen when a woman in love is treated with contempt by her lover. What is unusual about it is that even though Millicent freely admitted killing Axel Schmidt, her sentence was as light as the court could possibly impose while still seeming to punish her.**

**The daughter of a wealthy and respected Philadelphia family**, the misfortunes of Millicent Adams began at Bryn Mawr University in the early 1960s where she met and fell in love with fellow student Axel Schmidt. Although he was studying to be an engineer, it occurred to Schmidt that a faster route to the wealth and the glittering social life he dreamed of might be through marriage, and he tirelessly courted Millicent until another girl came along whose family was even more wealthy and prominent than hers. With richer pickings on offer, Schmidt quickly dumped Millicent. As she later told police, she had been so hurt that she just wanted to kill herself.

**BELOW:** A Smith And Wesson Ladysmith .22 revolver, similar to the one used by Millicent Adams.

In preparation for her suicide Millicent bought a large St. Bernard dog, then took it to an unused room in her parents' mansion and shot it with a .22 caliber Smith & Wesson pistol. She explained during questioning that she wanted to be sure that it worked when she turned it upon herself. But it wasn't Millicent that ended up dead. With the promise of farewell sex in the air, she lured Schmidt to her home and after inviting him into her bed fired a single bullet and killed him. If she had been thinking about suicide before, she seemed to have forgotten about it now, for she didn't shoot herself after all. It may have been the knowledge that she was carrying Schmidt's child which stopped her pulling the trigger.

At her trial, Millicent's defense argued that she had acted in a moment of insanity caused by her lover's cold treatment of her. The court agreed that she should be allowed to plead guilty to manslaughter and not murder and, when she was pronounced guilty, gave her a ten-year probational sentence on condition that she admitted herself to a mental health institution.

Millicent gave birth to a baby daughter, Lisa, soon after. The child was taken away from Millicent though she was still given regular access. After three years under the care of mental health doctors, Millicent was deemed to be rehabilitated and released from detention. Disowned by her parents, Millicent Adams moved to build a new life on the West Coast.

# Antonio Agostini

**The case that became infamous as the "Pyjama Girl" murder was surrounded by mystery and took Australian police nearly 10 years to solve. The jealous husband, who eventually served time for Linda Agostini's death never fully revealed what happened that day, but it seems likely his passions were inflamed by her cheating and he set out to bring a murderous end to his unhappy marriage.**

Italian immigrant Antonio Agostini married Linda Platt in 1930, and the couple settled in Melbourne, Australia. But their marriage wasn't a partnership of mutual support. Agostini worked at odd jobs to raise money, while Linda spent her days drinking and entertaining a string of lovers until suddenly, she disappeared. The last time anyone saw Linda Agostini alive was at her home in August 1934.

When asked about his missing wife, Agostini said that she had run away with one of her boyfriends, but before long a farmer discovered the body of a woman in a culvert between Melbourne and Sydney. She had been savagely beaten in her last moments before being shot through the head, then the corpse had been burned. Little was left to identify her from save the yellow silk pyjamas she had been wearing.

**RIGHT:** Linda Agostini was born in Forest Hill, London, in 1905. She moved to New Zealand at the age of 19 after a failed romance. In 1927, Platt moved on again to Sydney, Australia.

At first, police believed the body to be that of Mrs Anna Philomena Coots who had gone missing at the same time. Even Linda's mother could not confirm the mutilated body was that of her daughter but she wasn't told about the pyjamas that later proved to be a crucial piece of evidence. The case was closed and might have remained so were it not for a policeman whose wife had been a friend of Linda's. He was certain that the body was hers and set about trying to prove it. Finally, Linda's mother was shown a photograph of the pyjamas the murdered woman had been wearing and identified them as a set that she had given to Linda as a wedding gift. She also told police again that Agostini had mistreated her daughter. Linda was identified through dental records, and Agostini was arrested in 1944.

Under interrogation, he admitted to killing his wife 10 years earlier, but said it was not intentional. He told police that he and Linda had both got drunk on August 28, 1934, and that she had accused him of having an affair with a woman at the restaurant where he worked. Agostini said Linda had been drunkenly waving a gun around and when it went off by accident she had been shot. It was obviously a tissue of lies. Further examination of Linda's body revealed that her brutal head wounds had been inflicted before she was shot and that it one of these was that killed her, not a bullet. Incredibly, Agostini also maintained that he had no idea how her body had come to be burned and suggested that someone else must have stumbled across her corpse and set fire to it.

Agostini went on trial on June 9, 1944, charged with his wife's murder. But the charge was reduced to manslaughter, and he was sentenced to six years' hard labor. He was released in 1950 and returned to Italy.

# Edward Charles Allaway

**Edward Allaway had long shown all the symptoms of paranoia schizophrenia, but he was a quiet man who kept himself to himself and few suspected how deep his psychological problems ran except the women he was married to. But when his second wife left him, his weak grip on sanity broke and he went on a killing spree that left nine people dead.**

**Allaway was diagnosed as a paranoid schizophrenic** during his first marriage to a woman named Carol and though he once received a month-long course of electric-shock therapy it did little to help. The delusions continued and were particularly vivid. Carol, he thought, was not only sleeping around but posing for pornographic photos behind his back. The fact that she remarried within days of the couple's divorce being finalized did nothing to stem his suspicions or alleviate his mental condition.

Nevertheless, Allaway married again within a few months of moving south to Orange County, California, in 1973, and he and his new wife Bonnie took a long, cross-country camping trip, living a hand-to-mouth existence and taking work wherever they could find it. Eventually, they returned to Orange County and Allaway's sister managed to secure her brother a custodial job in the library of California State University, Fullerton.

All of Allaway's old symptoms were by now beginning to re-assert themselves, and were chillingly similar to those he had had before. Like with his first marriage, Allaway was certain that Bonnie had begun sleeping with other men and also that she was appearing in pornographic films made by employees of the library where he worked. He also began verbally abusing his co-workers as well as becoming increasingly prejudiced toward African and Hispanic Americans. At home his violent streak became more pronounced. He was insanely jealous and threatened to slash Bonnie's face with a pen knife if he caught her cheating. It was more than she could bear. Bonnie left.

**ABOVE:** A memorial grove of seven pine trees that honors the seven people killed by Edward Allaway on July 12, 1976, in the library of California State University.

In a towering rage of jealousy, Allaway snapped. But where a more sane man might have tried to take revenge on his wife, he just wanted to inflict some of the pain he was feeling, indiscriminately. On July 12, 1976, 37-year-old Edward Allaway walked into the library at California State University armed with a .22 caliber rifle and fired. As he roamed the halls, the psychotic gunman shot nine people, killing seven. He then drove to the nearby hotel where his wife worked, called the police, and quietly surrendered.

In 1977, Allaway was convicted of murder, but found not guilty by reason of insanity. Although there was an attempt in 2001 to reintroduce him to society, it was overruled by a judge in 2003 who said that Allaway should not be released from the Patton State Hospital in San Bernardino County.

# Henriette Caillaux

**Henriette Caillaux was discovered by shocked staff at the busy office of Le Figaro newspaper in Paris standing over the dead body of her victim. The corpse of the paper's editor, Gaston Calmette, was riddled with bullets and in her hand Madame Caillaux held a smoking gun. Even so, Caillaux eventually walked free, having befuddled a jury with a mixture of psychology and pure theater.**

**While crimes of passion may occur in all societies around the world**, the French seem to have a certain flair for them, and have even made laws governing how a *crime passionel* should be judged. Even so, the case of Henriette Caillaux was a complicated one. Although the victim of her murderous fury was an old lover, their affair had been over for years and would have remained forever buried if Henriette had not gone on to marry Joseph Caillaux, who would become the French Finance Minister. Her former beau, Calmette, meanwhile became editor of Le Figaro, one of France's leading newspapers.

Henriette's rage was sparked when Le Figaro began lampooning her husband in a series of article and cartoons published in the newspaper and reached boiling point when she and the Finance Minister were further humiliated. Calmette had kept some letters from his days as Henriette's swain and they included a love letter from Caillaux written to Henriette 13 years previously when she was also his mistress.

Wearing a fur coat over a gown and with her hands tucked in a muff Madame Caillaux arrived at Le Figaro's offices during the early evening of March 16, 1914. As the wife of the Finance Minister and a woman of some standing, she was immediately ushered in to see the Calmette. Standing before the editor, Henriette asked a single question: "You know why I have come?" Caillaux barely had time to answer "Not at all Madame", before his old flame pulled a gun from her muff and shot him six times. Newspaper staff immediately poured into the office and attempted to seize the murderer. With French haughtiness, Henriette Caillaux shouted "Do not touch me. I am a lady!"

**RIGHT:** Gaston Calmette, the editor of Le Figaro, who was shot and killed by Henriette Caillaux.

Today, the result of the trial would certainly be a forgone conclusion, and even then the future looked bleak for Henriette. But, as Calmette had already discovered, she was a woman of considerable mettle who it was unwise to underestimate. French courts were notoriously sympathetic toward crimes of passion and she was determined to use that in her favor, even though she and Calmette had not been lovers for years. Appointing Fernand Labori, one of France's most

**BELOW:** Henriette Caillaux, in a photograph taken during the same year as her trial for the murder of Gaston Calmette.

**LEFT:** Fernand Labori, the counsel for the defence in the murder trial of Henriette Caillaux.

celebrated lawyers, to defend her, Henriette Caillaux went into court with every possible argument prepared. The jury heard Labori criticize the 1804 Napoleonic Code that discriminated against women then argue that a woman must be expected to vent her passionate feelings.

Henriette herself performed amazingly on the witness stand, managing to present herself as a highly romantic woman at the mercy of her emotions while offering scientific research that showed how the nervous system and unconscious mind could make people capable of terrible actions under extreme pressure. Henriette's entire defense was intended to make her appear a heroine of uncontrollable passion to the jury, and a victim of psychological laws to the experts. In popular opinion women of ungovernable passions were to be viewed sympathetically—such strength of feeling was even desirable—while temporary insanity placed her beyond the law.

It worked like a charm. After a seven-day trial in the Cour d'Assises in Paris, Henriette Caillaux walked free. After less than an hour of deliberations, the all-male jury decided the homicide was committed without premeditation or criminal intent. The jurors accepted her testimony that when she pulled the trigger, she was a temporary victim of (as Labori put it) "unbridled female passions."

# Yvonne Chevallier

**The term *crime passionnel* could have been invented for Yvonne Chevallier. Hers was a rags-to-riches story that had all the ingredients for a fairy-tale ending, for it wasn't the money or respect that mattered to Yvonne; it was the dashing hero she had married. So when her adored husband became involved with another woman her life was shattered.**

**At 24 years old, Yvonne was working as a midwife** at a hospital in Orleans, France. The daughter of a peasant family, she had little money and was uneducated, unworldly, and very shy—quite the opposite to the intelligent and ambitious doctor Pierre Chevallier, who was from an excellent family.

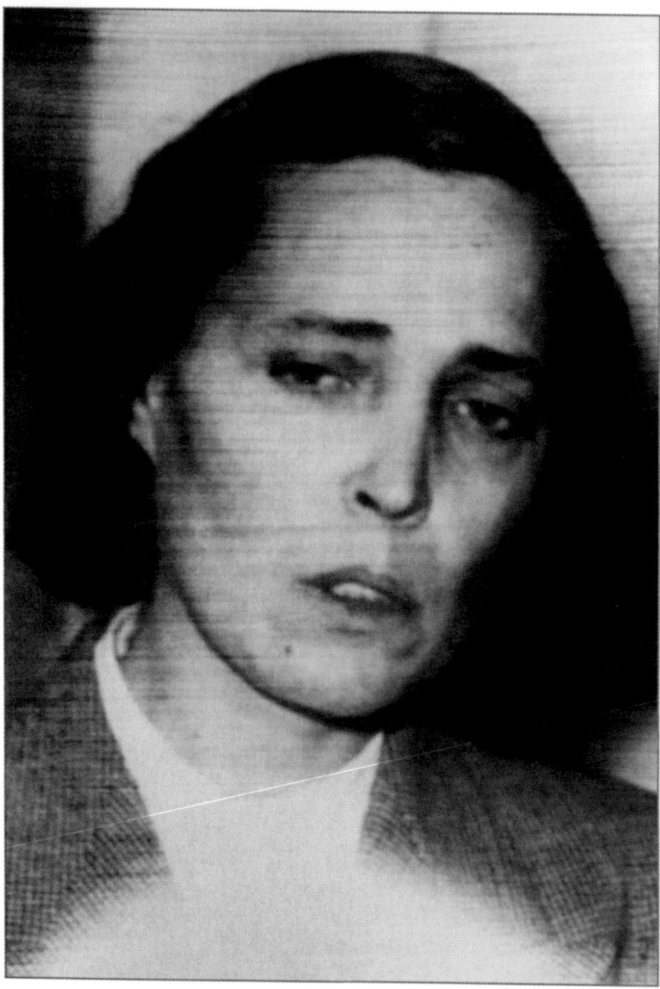

**ABOVE:** Yvonne Chevallier, pictured during her trial for the murder of her husband Pierre.

Nevertheless, he was only two years older than her and the attraction between them was instant and intense.

Just a few weeks after they met, in 1937, she had moved into his apartment, where Chevalier's unquenchable desire for Yvonne meant that much of their free time was spent between the sheets. Chevalier's family strongly disapproved of the relationship with a mere peasant girl, but he ignored their protests. When war broke out in 1939 he became an even greater hero in Yvonne's eyes, and those of many others. He served as a medical officer with the French Army, saving lives at the front line. While on leave—and with none of Chevallier's family present—the passionate couple married in 1939.

When France was overrun by Germany a few months later, Chevallier became the head of the local Resistance movement. As the Germans retreated in 1944, Chevallier became an even greater hero. He led Resistance forces against the Germans and drove them from Orleans. On a wave of public acclaim Chevallier was elected mayor of the city the same year.

That was the first step on what would become a high-profile political career. As mayor, Chevallier organized the reconstruction of the city—a challenge that won him further praise when it was officially declared the best rebuilt city in France. He became parliamentary representative for Orleans in 1951, and from now on affairs of state would mean he spent much of his time in Paris.

Meanwhile, the sweet and shy Yvonne remained in the background. She bore Pierre two sons who became good friends with the children of wealthy neighbor Leon Perreau and his wife Jeanne. And while the children played, Yvonne became close to the couple, recognizing in them a pair who were as mismatched, but happy, as she and Chevallier. What Perreau lacked in physical attributes—he was short, fat and bald—he made up with his personal charm, and his success as owner of Orleans' most prestigious department stores, Jeanne was 15 years younger than her husband and a red-headed, spirited beauty who easily held her own in the political and social circles that made Yvonne feel so ill at ease.

**BELOW:** Pierre Chevallier, in a photograph taken just a year before he was killed.

Unfortunately, the state's affairs weren't the only ones that Pierre Chevallier was attending to. Ironically, unlike their both married couples, he and Jeanne were a perfect match and they were soon deeply infatuated with each other.

Even before she found out, Yvonne was displaying symptoms of a breakdown. Anxious over a husband who was so frequently far away, she smoked incessantly, drank endless cups of strong, black coffee, and was becoming increasingly reliant on the amphetamine and barbiturate drugs her doctor prescribed. It wasn't long before her intuition told her that her marriage had started to fall apart, and it was confirmed when one of her sons fell sick. She brought him into bed with her so that she could comfort him during the night, and Chevallier moved to a couch in his office. But when the boy recovered, her husband refused to move back into the marital bed. Where once he had been insatiable in his lust for Yvonne, now he would not touch her. She visited beauty salons and *haute couture* shops and even began trying to understand his political world in an attempt to win back his affections, but nothing worked. She was rejected and alone; her hero had now become her tormentor.

Her devastation became complete when she received an anonymous letter that explained her husband's new coldness. It told her that Chevallier was having an affair. This was confirmed when an increasingly distressed Yvonne discovered a letter

**ABOVE:** Yvonne Chevallier appearing in the dock at the Reims Court of Assizes charged with the murder of her husband Pierre.

in one of her husband's jackets. It was addressed to "Dear Pierre" and went on to say, "Without you, life would have no beauty or meaning for me." The note was signed "Jeanne." A confrontation with her husband was at first met with furious denials, then confession, and then a demand for a divorce so he could be free to marry Jeanne. Chevallier told his wife, "As far as I am concerned you are a free woman. Take a lover because I will never make love to you again."

In desperation, Yvonne turned to Leon Perreau, hoping with his help to break the lovers up. If the affair continued, she explained to him, she might kill herself from grief. Perreau's response was a shrug. He already knew about the affair and had accepted the humiliation of being a mari complaisant—compliant husband. Next, Yvonne visited the National Assembly to find her husband and beg him again to give Jeanne up. She was turned away, and Chevallier left to take a vacation with his lover, but not before telling his wife she was a "cow."

At first, Yvonne attempted suicide with poison, but it only made her ill. Then she obtained a firearms license and bought a Mab 7.65mm, a French-made semi-automatic with a nine-round magazine. It was the perfect weapon she later said, "to kill without any doubts."

On August 11, 1951, Pierre Chevallier returned to the family home to collect the last of his clothes and belongings. Imploring him to stay, Yvonne followed him to their sons' bedroom and watched as he kissed them both goodbye. The heartbreak of watching him say farewell to his children was overwhelming. Yvonne fell to her knees clutching at her husband's legs while he snarled at her to keep her hands off the Under Secretary of State. Then Yvonne ran to grab the gun she had bought earlier screaming that would shoot herself. Chevallier made an obscene gesture and sneered, "Do it then. But only when I have left." They were the last words he ever spoke. Yvonne fired randomly at her husband, shooting him in the forehead, leg, chest, and face. He fell dead to the floor with Yvonne crouched over him. Only thoughts of her children prevented her from turning the gun on herself. As she stood up, the gun accidentally went off again sending a final bullet into Chevallier's back.

When the news of his murder at the hands of his wife became public the response was outrage. Although Yvonne knew what a vile man her husband had become, to the rest of France he was a revered politician and a national hero. So intense were emotions in Orleans that it was decided Yvonne's court hearing should take place some distance away, where passions were running slightly cooler.

However, by the time the trial began on November 5, 1952, the public's sympathy had started to come round to Yvonne. Tales of her husband's infidelity were well publicized and the frail and lost woman with her white face and gaunt appearance was a sight to melt the hardest of hearts. As one journalist would later write, "The French press went crazy, throwing caution to the wind with police reporters, court reporters, sob sisters, psychiatrists, novelists, the works. The French felt they invented the crime passionnel. They were determined to leave nothing unsaid and they left nothing unsaid. The whole country was outraged, or outraged that anyone would be outraged."

As each new detail of the case came to light support for Yvonne grew. By the time Jeanne Perreau came to give evidence she was hissed in court while confessing that her affair with Pierre Chevallier had gone on for five years. Her arrogant declaration that, "Love does not make one ashamed. I believe that for love one is never punished," caused such a stir that she was asked to leave. Leon Perreau, meanwhile, became a figure of contempt for his acceptance of his wife's infidelity. He even spoke calmly of how Pierre Chevallier was the favorite of all his wife's lovers and shared her bed on average three times a week.

When Yvonne herself took the stand public sympathy became total. After hearing of how deeply she had loved her husband and how she had fallen at his feet to try and prevent him leaving, only to receive a rude gesture in return, even the prosecuting counsel said that the death penalty in this case was not appropriate, calling instead for just a two-year prison sentence.

The jury took less than an hour to reach its verdict. Yvonne was acquitted. The Catholic Church later granted her absolution for the killing, but gentle, sensitive Yvonne could not absolve herself so easily. She took her sons to live in one of France's notorious mosquito-infested colonies in French Guiana, West Africa—a place that had once been a penal colony and was now described as a tropical hell. A desolate community of people still lived there and Yvonne returned to her work as a midwife among them.

# Vincent Ciucci

**Although 36-year-old Vincent Ciucci dreamed of a happy life with the woman he intended to marry, his existing wife and children stood in the way. However, he wasn't about to let his existing responsibilities scotch his dreams so he came up with a vile plan that would free him to begin afresh and also allow him to collect insurance money on his wife's death.**

**On December 5, 1953,** Vincent Ciucci chloroformed his wife Anne and their three children and then shot each one in the head. He then set fire to his Chicago apartment behind the grocery store he owned to make it look like they had died in the flames. Thinking it would put him beyond suspicion, the grocer stayed in the house and when the fire department team arrived, Ciucci made a great show of stumbling out of the smoke-filled apartment, choking and begging for his family to be rescued. He had wrongly assumed that if their bodies were burned, the bullet wounds would be impossible to see.

It was a bungled attempt to disguise a murder. After they had retrieved the bodies, the police quickly realized that this was no ordinary house fire and took Ciucci in for questioning. He denied everything, saying '"I admit that I am a gambler and I like to fool around with women. But I wouldn't do anything like that. How could a man kill his own children? He would have to kill himself instead." Becoming more desperate he then concocted a story that mysterious intruders had entered his apartment and shot his family before putting a torch to the building. Incredibly, he claimed that he would not have heard the four shots because he was a heavy sleeper.

Ciucci was charged with the four murders and stood trial three times before he was finally brought to justice. At the first two, he was found guilty of first degree murder of his wife and two of their children. At the third he was also found guilty of the first degree murder of the third child. His defense counsel's pleas for clemency fell upon deaf ears, and Ciucci became the last man to die in the electric chair in Chicago on March 23, 1962. The execution took place at one minute past midnight and was witnessed by nearly 30 people including journalists.

# William Corder

**William Corder was more than happy to indulge in a sexual dalliance with Maria Marten, as others had done before him, but he hated the idea of marrying her. Instead, he arranged to elope with her, and when she met him on the night they planned to run away, he shot her.**

**The gruesome story of William Corder and Maria Marten** would later become known as "The Red Barn Murder" and began in the little village of Polstead in Suffolk, England, in the early 19th century when she was 24 and he was just 22.

Maria already had two illegitimate children by former lovers by the time she and Corder, the son of a farmer, became involved and quickly became pregnant with another. With his attempts to keep their relationship secret now rendered useless by her swelling belly, Corder said he would marry her, but kept putting it off. When the baby died (amid rumors that it had been murdered), he decided that he no longer owed Maria the wedding she craved. Nevertheless, she continued to badger him.

In the late spring of 1827, after several more postponements on Corder's part, the couple arranged

**RIGHT:** An early-19th century illustration of William Corder, the perpetrator of the notorious "Red Barn Murder."

to meet at the Red Barn, close to Maria's house, so they could elope. Although there was no real reason for them to run away together, Corder claimed he had heard that the parish officers were going to prosecute Maria for having bastard children. Maria Marten was never seen alive again.

Corder disappeared from the village for a time, but later returned to say he and Maria were now happily living in Ipswich. He also said he could not yet bring her back as his wife for fear of the anger of his friends and relatives. Already though, the village folk were suspicious, and the pressure on Corder to produce his wife eventually forced him to leave the area again. Now he wrote letters to her family claiming they were living on the Isle of Wight, and gave various excuses for the fact that she had not contacted them.

Suspicion continued to grow, and on April 19, 1828, Maria's stepmother persuaded her husband to go to the Red Barn and dig in one of the grain storage bins. He quickly uncovered the remains of his daughter buried in a sack. Maria's body was badly decomposed but was identified, by her sister Ann, from her hair, clothing, and a missing tooth. Corder's green handkerchief was discovered around her neck. Although it was obvious that there had been foul play, it was difficult to establish the exact cause of Maria's death. It was initially thought that a sharp instrument—possibly Corder's short sword—had been plunged into her eye, but this wound could also have been caused by her father's spade when he was exhuming the body. The handkerchief at her throat suggested strangulation while other wounds suggested she had been shot.

Corder was tracked down to Brentford, Middlesex, where he was running a boarding house with a woman he had married. The police charged him with

**BELOW:** William Corder being executed at the gallows in Bury St. Edmunds, Suffolk, on August 11, 1828.

**BELOW:** A contemporary pamphlet containing details of the "horrid murder" of Maria Marten by her lover William Corder.

THE MURDER OF

MARIA MARTEN

IN THE RED BARN AT POLSTED.

Containing the whole Account of the horrid Murder,

COMMITTED BY HER LOVER AND SEDUCER WILLIAM CORDER.

Which was revealed in a Dream by her Mother, and also a graphic

ACCOUNT OF HIS CONFESSION AND EXECUTION

R. MARCH & CO., ST. JAMES'S WALK, CLERKENWELL.

"murdering Maria Marten, by feloniously and willfully shooting her with a pistol through the body, and likewise stabbing her with a dagger." And in order to be sure of a conviction eight other charges were brought against Corder, including one of forgery.

Corder's trial started on August 7, 1828, at Shire Hall, Bury St. Edmunds. The court was so swamped with hopeful spectators that admittance was by ticket only. Finally standing before a judge, Corder pleaded not guilty to the murder of Maria Marten. He admitted being in the barn with Maria but said he had left after they argued. He claimed that while he was walking away he heard a shot, ran back to the barn, and found Maria dead with one of his pistols beside her.

It took the jury just 35 minutes to return with a guilty verdict. He was sentenced to hang and afterward be dissected. Corder spent the next three days in prison agonising over whether to confess to the crime and make a clean breast of his sins before God and after several meetings with the prison chaplain, entreaties from his wife, and pleas from both his warder and the governor of the prison, he finally gave a different story. While he still hotly denied stabbing Maria, he now said he had accidentally shot her in the eye as she changed into her traveling clothes.

Corder was hanged in Bury St. Edmunds on August 11, 1828, in front of a large crowd. One newspaper claimed there were 7,000 spectators, another as many as 20,000. His body was later used to demonstrate the workings of the nervous system to medical students.

# Pauline Dubuisson

**As little as she valued the faithful young man who adored her while they were together, Pauline Dubuisson was determined that he wouldn't find happiness. If she couldn't have him, then no-one could.**

**A young woman who was used to having everything she wanted**, Pauline Dubuisson clearly didn't have much time for morality. During World War II, the young Frenchwoman had become the mistress of an enemy German Army officer when she was just 17 years old, and when she enrolled as a medical student at the French University of Lille after the war, she soon showed just as little regard for right and wrong.

At university in 1946, she met a charming and gentle-natured fellow student, Felix Bailly, and the two began a relationship. But during the stormy three years they were together, Pauline was anything but faithful. Smitten by his wild lover, Bailly proposed to her again and again and—just as frequently—Pauline turned him down and cheated on him.

Emotionally drained and heartsick, Bailly eventually came to the end of his tether. Leaving the wanton Pauline and Lille behind, he went to continue his studies in Paris where he soon met the beautiful Monique Lombard, a woman deserving of Bailly's love and who returned it fully. Finally happy, Bailly became engaged to Monique at the end of 1950.

Back in Lille, Pauline was furious when she heard the news. Although she had cared little for Bailly when she had the chance, she was the kind of woman who believed that she could treat men as her playthings and wasn't used to losing a lover to another woman. Her pride demanded that she win him back. But the tables were turned. The man who would have once done anything to win her love now rejected Pauline's advances, telling her that he was blissfully happy. His fiancée was the love of his life.

With venom in her heart, Pauline returned to Lille where she spent some money she had been given as a birthday gift on a .25 caliber automatic pistol. She then wrote a letter saying she intended to kill Bailly after which she would commit suicide. The note was soon found by Pauline's landlady who quickly sent a warning to Bailly. When Pauline arrived in Paris, Bailly refused to let her into his apartment, insisting that anything she wished to say to him could be said in public at a café. Having arranged a meeting, he duly arrived with a friend to protect him.

Pauline never turned up. But she was watching as he returned home. Soon after, Bailly answered a knock at his door, believing it to be another friend who was arriving to watch over him. Pauline raised the gun and fired three times. She then turned it upon herself and pulled the trigger. But the gun jammed. An attempt to gas herself also failed when a neighbor arrived to investigate the gun shots. Pauline was arrested and sent to jail to await trial. While there she would hear that the shame brought upon him by her actions had caused her father to write in sympathy to Bailly's family and then poison himself.

After attempting to slash her wrists the day before her trial began, Pauline Dubuisson was finally brought before a court in November 1952. Her lawyer attempted to soften the jury by using the old French defense that hers had been a crime passionnel. The jury found it unconvincing: her relationship with Bailly had ended 18 months before she murdered him. The suicide attempts were also seen as dramatic grabs at sympathy, and the court heard exactly how wayward Pauline's lifestyle was. She had kept a journal of all her lovers' performances, including Bailly's, and they were read out. When Monique Lombard took the stand, her good-nature and calm serenity left the jury with no doubt that the vicious and manipulative Pauline had been seething with rage at losing a lover to a woman so obviously superior to her.

Fortunately for her—and many said that it was more than she deserved—Pauline Dubuisson was found guilty of murder, but without premeditation. As a result, she escaped execution, but received a sentence of life imprisonment.

# Frances Hall, Henry Carpender & Willie Stevens

**It is most likely that this bloody and shocking double murder was instigated by a scorned wife who was all too aware that the infidelity of her minister husband was common knowledge. However, while some murderers successfully appeal to the sympathy of the court and others are set free through lack of evidence, Mrs Hall and her partners in crime appear to have spread enough confusion for the case against them to be completely botched.**

The bodies of the Reverend Edward Wheeler Hall and his mistress, Mrs Eleanor Mills, were found laying side by side on September 16, 1922. She wore a red-spotted blue dress and black stockings as well as a blood soaked silk scarf around her neck. Her left hand rested on the knee of the Reverend Hall while his right arm was under her shoulder. Propped up against one of his shoes was a business card and all around were shreds of torn up letters. When pieced together one read: "Oh, honey. I am fiery today. Burning flaming love." Hall been shot once over the right ear. Eleanor had been shot three times in the right temple, under the right eye, and also over the right ear. In what could only have been a furious personal revenge, the choir singer's tongue had been cut out after she was shot and her larynx removed. It looked like a classic crime of passion.

Reverend Hall had been the pastor of the Episcopal Church of St. John the Evangelist in New Jersey; Eleanor Mills a singer in the church choir. Both were married. Hall's wife was Frances Noel Stevens, heiress to a sum from the Johnson & Johnson Company while Eleanor's husband James was sexton at St. John's. There were few people in the parish who didn't know about the affair. Hall and Eleanor had been involved for four years and a neighbor later told how the couple met every afternoon at Mills' house.

It was nothing out of the ordinary then, when Eleanor telephoned the Hall house on the evening of September 14. Both the maid and Mrs Hall herself would later testify that Eleanor had called the reverend about a medical bill, and that he had left the house on the pretext of discussing it with her shortly after. However, it was no ordinary evening. After years of illicit meetings and secret passion Eleanor and Mills had finally decided to elope.

At the Mills' house, Eleanor told her husband that she was going to call Reverend Hall soon after dinner. When she returned she said that she was going to the church and there was a slight scene, during which she scornfully told Mills to follow her if he dared. It was the last time that Eleanor would be seen alive. The worried Mills waited until 11pm then went to look for her at the church. Finding nothing, he returned at 2am. Again, there was no sign of the lovers.

When he went to work at the church the next morning, he asked Mrs Hall if she thought their spouses had eloped. She told him that she thought they were dead. At around the same time, Mrs Hall's brother, Willie Stevens, told the maid, Louise Geist, that "something terrible" had happened during the night. Strangely, the bodies had yet to be discovered.

That changed the next day, and the police quickly took four suspects in for questioning: Frances Hall, Stevens, another of Frances' brothers named Henry (who was known to be an excellent marksman), and her cousin, Henry Carpender. Not long afterward, Hall, Carpender, and Willie Stevens were all charged with the murder of Reverend Hall and Eleanor.

The court hearing that followed was confused and mismanaged from the start and was eventually dropped for lack of evidence. But a few years later evidence that the defendants had perverted the course of justice began to emerge. In 1926, Geist's estranged husband claimed that his wife had received $5,000 from the Hall

family. He said that the maid had learned that Reverend Hall planned to elope and had forewarned his wife. The money was a payment to ensure her silence. Later, a state trooper who had been on the investigative team also claimed that Carpender had paid him to leave the state.

**ABOVE:** Two New Jersey State policemen (center), with two traffic policemen, waiting to escort a witness to The Hall-Mills Murder Trial, 1926.

A new court case also brought forward a compelling witness. Mrs Jane Gibson (also known as "The Pig

**ABOVE:** Willie Stevens on the witness stand during the trial in which he was jointly accused of the murder of Reverend Edward Hall and Eleanor Mills.

Woman," because she owned a pig farm) testified that she had witnessed the killings. She identified Carpender as the shooter, and told that he had been at the scene with Frances Hall and Willie Stevens. Gibson claimed to have returned to the bodies after the murder and had then seen Mrs Hall crying over her husband's dead body. Nevertheless, her testimony was ignored because she had given quite a different account in 1922. Despite a fingerprint on the business card left at the murder scene belonging to Willie Stevens, all three defendants were finally found not guilty on December 3, 1926. Some observers said the jury's verdict was a gesture of defiance to a Jersey City prosecution counsel who had called them "country bumpkins."

# Gavin Hall

**When hospital radiographer Gavin Hall found messages on his wife's computer that detailed a sordid affair it sent him into a catastrophic mental breakdown that ended in tragedy. But while his unfaithful wife escaped his murderous intentions, their three-year-old daughter did not.**

**One evening in October 2005**, Gavin Hall's 31-year-old wife Joanne thoughtlessly forgot to switch off the computer. And when her husband came to look at it, the double life she had been leading was revealed before his disbelieving eyes.

Joanne had joined a sex contact web site for married people. A distraught Hall discovered that his wife saw herself as "an incredibly bored married woman" and "an easy lay." There were messages, too, from her lover; a 45-year-old married district judge called James Muir-Little. His profile said that he was a "38-year-old non-smoker" who had "a very active imagination and I think about sex all the time."

As Hall read the messages they had swapped, it became obvious that the pair were already involved in a highly sexual relationship. They had swapped naked photographs of themselves and described in graphic detail the sexual acts they would like to indulge in. The judge had also suggested setting up a sexual threesome.

When confronted, Joanne admitted the fling, but told Hall that it was over. She was lying. As her husband's mental state deteriorated she continued her liaison with Muir-Little all the while reassuring Hall that he had nothing to worry about.

Eventually, Hall's mental state had reached a point where he could no longer work, and he took sick leave due to personal problems. Now, he broke down completely. Suicide, he thought, was the only answer to his mental anguish and he also decided that his and Joanne's daughter Amelia—or Millie as the family called her—should die too. As he later explained to the court, the little girl had told him repeatedly that she wanted to "come with Daddy."

On November 29, 2005, Gavin Hall fed Amelia anti-depressant pills to make her drowsy. Father and daughter said farewell—"like Romeo and Juliet" as he later described it—before he smothered her with a rag soaked in chloroform.

Although Hall later told a court he had no memory of the night, he then sent lengthy text messages to his wife and her lover. One, sent to Joanne at 2.57am, said, "I loved you. Millie asked to stay with me. I've dealt with your deceit for two months, now you have the rest of your life to deal with the consequences." Shortly before 4am he again texted his wife. This time the message read, "Goodbye, Millie sends her love. She died at 3.32am. Love till death us do part I said and this is what I meant."

He then dosed himself with the chloroform and slashed his wrists. Millie died just two days before her fourth birthday. Her mother Joanne found her under a duvet on the living room floor that morning.

Hall's attempt at suicide was unsuccessful though. He was convicted of murder in November 2006 after a six-day trial and told by the judge he would serve a minimum of 15 years in prison.

# Muhammed & Ahmed Hanif

**The 14-year affair of Arshad Mahmood and Zahida Hanif might have gone on undetected for much longer had Arshad not decided to use his lover's passion for him to extort money from her. When her family found out, their revenge was terrible.**

**Doorman Arshad Mahmood's secret relationship with the married Zahida Hanif** had begun in the early 1990s when he was in his late 20s. Although he was a cousin of her husband, Muhammed, for years the couple met for sex sessions without arousing suspicion until an argument over money started between Muhammed and his wife's lover. Arshad had recently helped Muhammed's younger brother Ahmed come to the United States from Pakistan, and thought he was owed $20,000 for his trouble. Muhammed disagreed. Arshad also disliked the fact that Ahmed was now living with the Hanifs, making meetings with his mistress more difficult. Blackmail, he decided, was the perfect answer to his problems.

During a particularly steamy session with Zahida, Arshad had filmed himself and his mistress making love. Now he threatened to show it to her husband if Zahida didn't give him the $20,000 he deserved and make sure that Ahmed was evicted. For months the petrified, unfaithful Zahida struggled to meet his demands, but eventually the strain became too much for her to bear. She broke down and confessed all to her husband.

Muhammed decided that rather than go to the police, the matter was best kept within the family and enlisted his young brother to help punish the blackmailing doorman.

The two men grabbed Arshad when he arrived at his cousin's home after work, smashed him in the face with a metal pipe and strangled him with their hands and scarves. They then put the body in Muhammed's car, tearing his clothes, and removing all his possessions to make it look like a robbery, before dumping him on 54th Avenue near his Elmhurst home. Unfortunately for the killers, police found the explicit video in Arshad's work locker on June 9, 2005, and the whole case began to unravel. Muhammed and Ahmed were quickly arrested and charged with murder, though they appeared to have no remorse for their crime. A police spokesman later said, "They were kind of proud of it. They were joking around."

By the end of the month both men had been convicted and had begun their long sentences. Muhammed was found guilty of manslaughter and sentenced to 18 years in prison, while Ahmed got 21 years. At the trial, Robana Mahmood—Arshad's daughter—made it clear who she thought was to blame. Pointing to Zahida Hanif, she said "You all did it because she said so."

# Jean Harris

**When respected school principal Jean Harris met a man she liked and admired, murder was the last thing on her intelligent mind. But over years of betrayal and disappointment, love can turn even the most sensible of people into vengeful killers.**

**At 42, Jean Harris was a divorced and rather shy woman** who was well-respected by her friends and colleagues at school. She was also not unusual in hoping that she might again find love in middle age, and at a dinner party in 1966 Jean thought she might have finally met a man who could make her happy. Dr. Herman Tarnower was a brilliant researcher at the Scarsdale Medical Center and would later earn himself a certain amount of fame on the publication of the successful book, The Scarsdale Diet. There was an instant chemistry between the pair and they began dating. Soon, Jean was deeply in love with Tarnower.

But he was not the type of man to be satisfied with a single lover, especially after he became something of a celebrity. Over the course of the 14-year relationship, he cheated again and again. Jean, who had never been very confident, turned a blind eye while her self-esteem sank with every new revelation.

The situation came to a head in 1980 when Tarnower began a sexual liaison with Lynne Tryforos, who worked as a receptionist at the medical center. Jean feared that there was something between her long-term partner and the receptionist that went beyond his usual flings and became certain that she was about to lose Tarnower for good. On March 10, she wrote a ten-page letter to her lover, revealing all her insecurities and expressing her own self-loathing for having become so desperately needy. With the attention to detail that might be expected of a highly organized school principal she also finalized her will. Then she drove to Tarnower's home and would later claim that the gun she took with her was intended for her own suicide.

ABOVE: Jean Harris, photographed just hours before being found guilty of murdering her lover, Dr. Herman Tarnower.

Jean said that she had fully expected her final pleas for love to be fruitless and wanted only to take her own life. But when she reached her lover's apartment the sight of Lynne Tryforos's lingerie in Tarnower's bedroom sent her into a rage and she shot her lover four times at point blank range.

Jean was arrested and charged with second degree murder. Released on $40,000 bail she then admitted herself to a psychiatric hospital. When her case came to court, on November 21, 1980, she pleaded not guilty to murder, insisting that the gun had gone off accidentally as Tarnower tried to wrestle it away from her. It was an obvious deception and courtroom observers at the time asked why her defense attorney had not pleaded that the murder was committed while Jean was in a state of extreme emotional disturbance with a view to her being convicted of the lesser charge of manslaughter. That, however, is exactly what her defense counsel had wanted. She refused.

After a 14-week trial, Jean was found guilty of murder and sent to the Bedford Hills Correctional Facility in Westchester County, New York, for the minimum of 15 years to life. Numerous appeals followed the conviction, but the higher courts all agreed that she had received a fair trial. She served 12 years of her sentence and was finally pardoned in December 1992.

# Tony Mancini

**In one of the most macabre murder cases of the early 20th century, petty criminal Tony Mancini was accused of killing his lover, Violet Kaye. But despite her decomposing remains being found in a chest that he had been using as a coffee table, Mancini was still acquitted. While there may be strong suspicions that the jury reached the wrong verdict in many other cases, in this one it is certain that they did. Years later, Mancini later made a deathbed confession.**

The 42-year-old Violet and her 25-year-old lover inhabited a shady underworld of drugs, drink, and petty crime in Brighton, on Britain's south coast. She was a prostitute, and he worked occasionally as a waiter or at the door of a nightclub. Fuelled by their debilitating addictions and the difference in their ages, the couple's relationship was stormy, and jealousy boiled over on May 10, 1934. Violet had seen Mancini flirting with a teenage waitress at the Skylark Café, and witnesses later testified that an argument was already in progress by the time they returned to their lodgings.

That was the last time Violet would be seen alive. For nearly two months her body stayed in a trunk at the bottom of Mancini's bed. Although it smelled repulsive and fluids soon began to leak from it, Mancini simply threw a cloth over it and used it as a coffee table.

Meanwhile, he tried to cover his tracks by telling those who knew Violet that she had gone away for a while. He also sent a telegram to Violet's sister telling her the same. However, Violet's many prostitute friends became suspicious and reported her missing to the police. They immediately questioned Mancini, who panicked and went on the run. This was enough to prompt a police search and on July 18, they entered his lodgings. The first thing

**LEFT:** Violet Kaye, seen in a photograph from 1933, a year before her death.

that hit them was the smell, which led them straight to the grisly "coffee table" at the end of Mancini's bed.

The police eventually caught up with Mancini in London. He was arrested and faced a jury in December, 1934. Over the course of the five day trial the prosecution focused on the fact that Kaye had died from a fatal blow to the head and the gruesome coffee table Mancini kept at his lodgings. Who else but a murderer could live with a decaying body, they asked the jury. A handwriting expert was also brought in and confirmed the handwriting on the form for the telegram sent to Violet's sister matched that on menus Mancini had written at the Skylark Café. One witness, Doris Saville, said Mancini had asked her to provide a false alibi. Others—former friends of Mancini—claimed he boasted in the days after the murder of giving his "missus" the "biggest hiding of her life."

When the turn came for the case for the defense to be made, Mancini's counsel told the court of Violet's dubious drunken character, her jealousy, and—most crucially—her work as a prostitute. It was argued that Mancini had discovered her body at her flat and assumed she had been killed by a client. On the witness stand Mancini said he had panicked. He thought that because of his past criminal record the police would not believe his story and had put her body in a trunk then taken it with him when he moved to new lodgings.

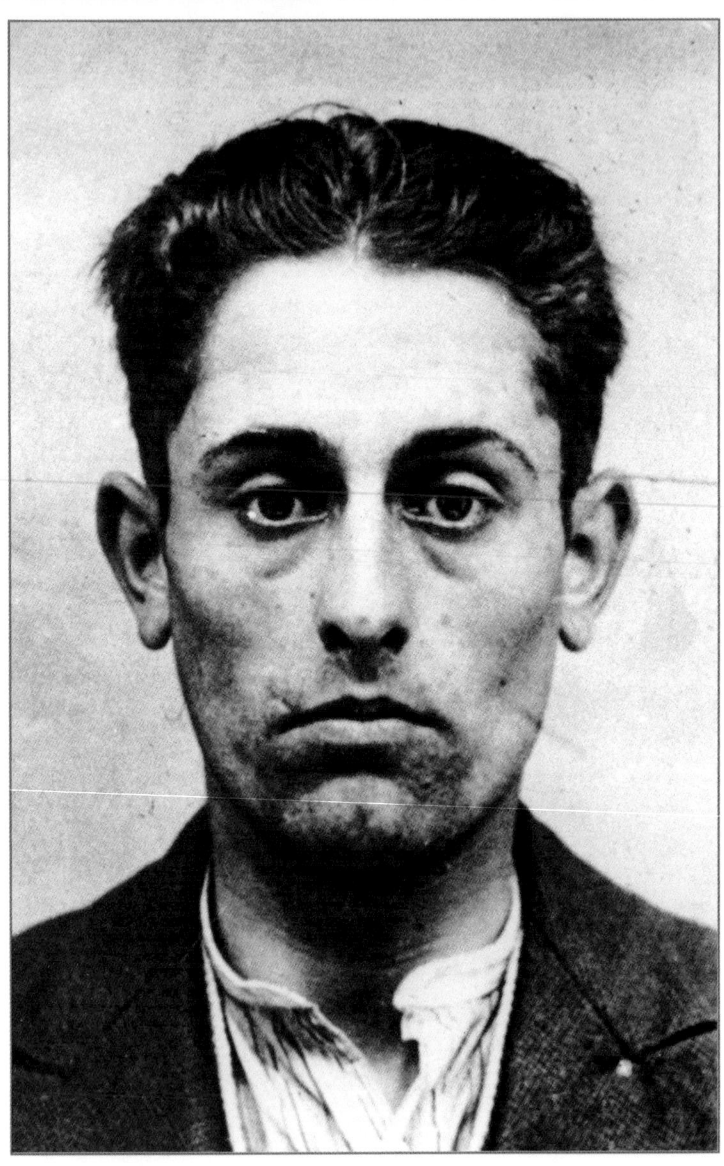

**ABOVE:** Tony Mancini, the petty criminal who only admitted to murder on his deathbed.

**ABOVE:** Tony Mancini leaving Lee Road Police Station, London, in a police car on the day of his arrest for the murder of Violet Kaye.

Slowly, the prosecution case began to fall apart. Blood-stained clothing that had been shown as evidence was proved to have been bought after Violet's death and the defense also told the jury that her body contained morphine. It was possible, they argued, that she had had fallen over while high on drugs and hit her head. In spite of their reputation as an argumentative couple, a number of witnesses also confirmed that Mancini and Violet had seemed contented. Mancini told the court he had loved his Violet even though she was a "loose woman."

After deliberating for two and quarter hours, the jury returned a verdict of not guilty and Tony Mancini

**LEFT:** The bedroom of 47, Kemp Street, Brighton, where the body of Violet Kaye was found: The trunk that contained her remains can be seen in the foreground.

walked free. For the next 42 years though, his conscience plagued him, and in 1976, shortly before he died Mancini told a Sunday newspaper how Violet had died. During a blazing row she had attacked him with the hammer he used to break coal for the fire. He had wrestled it from her, but when she had demanded it back, he threw it at her, hitting her on the left temple and killing her.

# Marie-Madeleine-Marguerite, Marquise de Brinvilliers

**The eldest of five children, Marie-Madeleine-Marguerite was born into an aristocratic French family. Despite her nobility and good breeding, passion turned her into a monster; a serial murderer whose exploits would later inspired poet Robert Browning (*The Poisoner*) and several authors, including Alexandre Dumas (*The Marquise de Brinvilliers*) and Arthur Conan Doyle (*The Leather Funnel*).**

**The daughter of Viscount Antoine Dreux d'Aubray,** a civil lieutenant of Paris, Marie-Madeleine-Marguerite submitted to an arranged marriage in 1651 at the age of 21. This was normal among the French aristocracy at the time, and the bride's her feelings on the matter were seldom taken into account. Unsurprisingly, Marie soon became deeply dissatisfied with her new husband, Antoine Gobelin de Brinvilliers. In addition to being a womanizer and gambler, de Brinvilliers all but ignored his wife, leaving her at the whim of temptation. It was close at hand: Chevalier Jean-Baptiste de Sainte-Croix was an army captain and friend of her father. The pair were soon locked in a passionate affair.

While her husband's illicit liaisons were well known in certain circles, her father was furious upon discovering his daughter was also having an affair. The fact that her lover was a family friend enraged him even further. Marie was forbidden to see her lover again, and in 1663 her father had Sainte-Croix thrown into to the Bastille prison in Paris.

Wrenched apart from the one man who had cared for her, Marie's passion turned to bitter hatred and a lust for revenge. When Sainte-Croix was eventually released, she ignored her father's order and was reunited with her lover. As chance would have it, he had learned the art of poisoning during his imprisonment. It was a skill the couple intended to make full use of as they plotted to take revenge on his lover's father, while at the same time ensuring Marie's inheritance. With the assistance of one of the royal apothecaries to the court of King Louis XIV, Sainte-Croix obtained tasteless but lethal potions, which Marie fed to her father. In 1666, he became her first victim.

Having killed once, it seems that Marie found it easy to do so again. Having quickly spent her way through her portion of her father's wealth, she turned her murderous attentions to the rest of her family. Her elder brother died in 1670, followed by her younger brother, and then her sister and sister-in-law. Of course, she also attempted to rid herself of an unwanted husband, but he proved stubbornly difficult to kill, though from now on he would be prone to mysterious illnesses.

Perhaps in an effort to find a potion that would finish him off, Marie worked to perfect her poison techniques on sick people in a local hospital. While visiting them under the pretext of being charitable, she killed as many as 50.

Her crimes were discovered in 1672. When Sainte-Croix died that year, his wife opened a box that he had told her was to be delivered, to his mistress. Inside were poisons and papers that made it clear the pair had been on a murder spree.

Marie immediately went on the run, but was arrested in Liege. Under interrogation, she threatened, "Half the people of quality are involved in this sort of thing, and I could ruin them if I were to talk." But whatever secrets she knew, Marie took them to her grave. The once haughty aristocrat was brutally tortured, her jailers mainly employing what was known as "the water cure," in which she was forced to drink 16 pints of water. But no further information was forthcoming. Tried in Paris in 1676, Marie was found guilty and executed, her body and severed head being thrown onto a fire.

**RIGHT:** Alexandre Dumas, whose *The Marquise de Brinvilliers* was inspired by the exploits of Marie-Madeleine-Marguerite.

# Francesco Matta

**First loves are notoriously difficult to forget. Those days of innocent youth coupled with the first stirrings of sexual excitement leave indelible memories and, sometimes, every relationship that comes after is compared to the one left behind. When Susan Matta stumbled across her first boyfriend on the internet site Friends Reunited all those old memories came flooding back and she again fell deeply in love. But the happiness she though she had found came at a price her husband was unwilling to pay.**

**Having been divorced,** Susan thought she had finally found the man of her dreams when she met Italian Francesco Matta, who ran a successful restaurant in Devon, England, in 1999. Matta's own marriage had also been annulled, and the two wed in 2003, after which they moved to Matta's home town of Caligari,

Sardinia, to begin a new life running a business leasing villas to vacationers.

All was going well until Susan posted adverts for the couple's villas on the Friends Reunited site in 2004. They caught the eye of Stephen Keen who had been Susan's first boyfriend 35 years before when she was 14 and he was 16. He was now a flight lieutenant with the RAF and married with two children, but immediately contacted her. She was delighted to hear from her old flame and as email after email arrived in their inboxes they rediscovered their old bonds. When Keen's wife Doreen discovered what had been going on she wrote to Susan, demanding that she leave her husband alone, but it was too late: the couple had fallen in love.

In February 2006, Susan traveled back to Britain to see her long-lost love and by the end of the trip both were certain that they wanted to make up for all the lost years and live together on a permanent basis. In April that year, Susan wrote a letter to Matta telling him about Stephen. Her distraught husband called to beg her to return, but she simply kept repeating the words, "I'm so sorry."

Matta couldn't let go of the woman he loved though. As Susan and Keen set up home together in Tiverton, Devon, he sent a stream of text messages telling Susan how much he loved her and begging her to end the affair. And when his wife refused he eventually tracked down her new address.

On July 6, 2006, Matta arrived in Devon in a hired van. When Keen answered the door his lover's husband stormed in shouting, "I thought you were an officer and a gentleman." He then said he had a hired a mafia hit man to kill Keen, and that the couple would have to pay £50,000 for him to call him off. As Keen picked up the phone to call the police, Matta lunged at him with a knife, stabbing him four times in the throat. Susan cradled her lover as he lay dying on the floor.

**BELOW:** The Friends Reunited website where Susan Matta got back in touch with her first love, Stephen Keen.

When the police arrived Matta told them calmly, "I came here to kill the man. I have done what I had to do." Turning to Susan, he continued, "My life is over. Now you will suffer as I am suffering." And as he was led away, he told his wife "I love you."

Francesco Matta was tried for murder at Exeter Crown Court in October 2007. He pleaded not guilty. The jury heard that while he accepted that he had killed Stephen Keen, he felt he should be convicted of manslaughter on the grounds of diminished responsibility. After several days of deliberation, the jury failed to reach a majority verdict and a retrial was ordered. On April 18, 2008, the jury at a second trial had no such difficulties. They found him guilty of murder, and Matta was sentenced to serve a minimum of 11 years before being eligible for parole.

# Florence Maybrick

**The marriage of Virginian beauty Florence Elizabeth Chandler to British cotton broker James Maybrick would later become littered with betrayals and despair, but at first they seemed happy. Despite the 23 year difference in their ages—Maybrick was 42, Florence just 19—they married in London in July 1881, soon after meeting on the White Star liner *Baltic* during an Atlantic crossing.**

**The newlyweds split their time between homes in Virginia** and the grand Battlecrease House in the Liverpool suburb of Airbrush and appeared to lead a happy life. The marriage was quickly blessed with a son, James, and after the couple settled permanently in Liverpool a daughter, Gladys Evelyn, followed. Meanwhile Maybrick and his vivacious young wife enjoyed a swirl of social engagements and mixed in the best society. Theirs seemed a perfect life.

But as is so often the case, behind closed doors the reality of their relationship was very different. Maybrick was a hypochondriac and had begun regularly taking the poison arsenic, the one cure he felt would relieve his imagined illnesses. And the trappings of wealth were not all they seemed, either. The couple had lived beyond their means and financial disaster loomed. In an effort to stave it off, Maybrick quietly made attempts to save money. Florence was given a small allowance on which she not only had to survive herself, but from which she was expected to pay the wages of five servants and all the household bills.

The marriage began to crack, but further humiliations were in store for Florence. The young wife, so pretty and spirited, now found out that her husband had been keeping a string of mistresses, one of whom had borne him five children. In those Victorian times there was little Florence could do except keep up the lie that all was well for friends and associates while fuming in private. Her perfect life of love and wealth lay in tatters.

The emotional strain must have been torture, as Florence tried to cope with an arsenic-addled, unstable, philandering husband under the threat of financial ruin. It is perhaps no great surprise then that when temptation arrived, Florence gave in quickly, seeking solace—and revenge—first in the arms of one her husband's brothers and then with a man named Alfred Brierley. The latter had been a guest at one of the Maybrick's popular dance evenings, which they continued to hold in order to keep up appearances. Florence became quickly besotted with him. Young, attractive, and healthy, Brierley was everything her husband was not.

Sad at home, and thinking herself deeply in love, Florence threw caution to the wind and booked a room at Flatman's Hotel in London under the name of Mr and Mrs Thomas Maybrick for herself and her new lover. Telling her husband that she was visiting a sick aunt for a few days, Florence joined Brierley at the hotel, and together they enjoyed several days of illicit pleasure. For the unfortunate Florence though, even this tryst was to be tainted with disaster and betrayal. Before they parted, Brierly confessed that he had fallen for another woman. As she later recalled, "He said he could not marry me and that rather than face the disgrace of discovery he would blow his brains out. I then had such revulsion of feeling I said we must end our intimacy at once."

**BELOW:** Liverpool cotton merchant James Maybrick, who died from arsenic poisoning.

Meanwhile, in her eagerness to be with Brierly, Florence had forgotten that the hotel was a regular haunt of her husband's cotton-trading associates. It didn't take long for news of his wife's adultery to reach Maybrick's ears, and in those hypocritical times his fury wasn't lessened by guilt over his own frequent betrayals.

It seems that Florence soon got over her problem with Brierley. Soon after Maybrick saw his wife talking to her lover at the 1889 Grand National horse race at the Aintree course near Liverpool. And the romantic pair displayed every sign of be a happy couple. Humiliated and enraged, Maybrick tore into his wife when the couple returned home to Battlecrease House and a loud and violent row ensued. Maybrick punched his wife and ripped her dress. As she staggered away, he threatened divorce before storming out of the house—presumably into the arms of one of his mistresses.

Servants later reported that after the argument Florence appeared unusually calm. Serene even. One maid also recollected that it was at this time she had noticed that Mrs Maybrick had begun soaking large quantities of flypapers in arsenic in her room. These she had purchased during two visits to the local chemists. Florence

ABOVE: Florence Maybrick making her statement to the Liverpool Court during her trial for the murder of her husband James Maybrick.

assured the maid that she had heard that the resulting mixture made an excellent treatment for the skin and ensured a pale complexion.

If Florence's mental state was already crumbling, the next calamity to befall her may have finally pushed her over the edge. She visited Brierley again, hoping to win back his affections after their tender moments at Aintree, but the young man told her that their affair was over for good.

James Maybrick became ill—quite genuinely this time—on the morning of April 27th – just over a month after his row with Florence. A Dr. Humphreys was quickly called to Battlecrease House, but could find no obvious cause for his patient's symptoms of

ABOVE: Portraits of Florence and James Maybrick taken from an 1889 edition of the British illustrated newspaper The Graphic.

vomiting, numbness in his limbs, and shivering. Vexed by Florence's revelation that her husband had been taking arsenic and strychnine and Maybrick's fevered denials, the doctor diagnosed chronic dyspepsia and left, hoping that this was just another instance of Maybrick's hypochondria.

Maybrick did not recover. Two days after the doctor's first visit Florence again bought flypapers at the local chemist, and soon after her husband's condition deteriorated. Still perplexed, Dr. Humphreys prescribed the Victorian cure-all tincture of white arsenic and carbonate of potash.

The previously popular Mrs Maybrick had by now become the subject of scandalous gossip. Word of the couple's sexually tangled lives had leaked out and it had become common knowledge that Florence was desperately unhappy in her marriage. The ever-fickle Brierley now also reappeared on the scene and, with neither he nor Florence making much effort at secrecy, it soon became widely believed that Florence was poisoning Maybrick in order to marry her young lover. Suspicions were further aroused when the Maybrick's nanny, Alice, intercepted a letter from Florence to her reinstated lover. Dated May 8, it read, "Dearest, since my return I have been nursing my M day and night. He is sick unto death."

The nanny passed the letter to Maybrick's brother Edwin, who in turn showed it to another brother, Michael. Together they rushed to Battlecrease House and promptly gave orders that Florence was not to be left alone in her husband's room. Nevertheless, her suspicious behavior continued. One servant later told police that Florence had been seen replacing the medicine in her husband's bottle with a different liquid, while another overheard Maybrick gasping out an accusation of poisoning to his wife.

James Maybrick died on May 11. The circumstances of his death were found to be suspicious and an immediate postmortem was called for. It revealed that Maybrick had been swallowing a particularly toxic irritant such as arsenic. On hearing the results, Florence fainted away and was taken to her own bed, where she would remain for several days, listening as the police searched her home for evidence of a crime.

They found letters from Brierley and enough arsenic to kill as many as 50 people. But what appeared to be an open and shut case was complicated by other evidence. Maybrick had been buying an arsenic-based tonic on a regular basis for 18 months and appeared to be long-term user. Nevertheless, Florence was arrested on suspicion of murder.

On July 31, 1889, she appeared at Liverpool Crown Court before Justice James Fitzjames Stephen charged with murder. Her defence put forward the argument that Maybrick's addiction to arsenic and other similar drugs meant that large traces of the poisons would be found in his body. Regular intake would have a cumulative affect, Florence's lawyers argued. Further, though Florence's marriage had been all but over, she had little motive for murdering her husband. The financial provision Maybrick had made for her and the children in his will was small, and Florence would have been better off legally separated from him.

It was undoubtedly a strong case, and perhaps that was just as Florence planned. However, it was not strong enough to convince the jury. In the end, it was Florence's last letter to her lover that condemned her. She had hinted that Maybrick would not live through his latest attack of illness, and it looked as though she was predicting his death with certain knowledge that it would soon arrive. It is also likely that Florence's adultery played a part in setting the disapproving Victorian jury against her.

Without her husband or her lover, who had fled to escape the scandal, Florence Maybrick was found guilty of murder on August 7, 1889, after the jury had deliberated for just 38 minutes. She was sentenced to death, and an execution set for August 26. However, many people in both Britain and America believed that the evidence against Florence was too slight to warrant capital punishment, and petitions flooded in. Just three days before Florence schedule's execution, news came from the Home Office that her sentence should be changed to life imprisonment. Her life may have been saved, but it was much less than a full pardon. The Home Secretary declared, "The evidence clearly establishes that Mrs Maybrick administered poison to her husband with intent to murder, but there is ground for reasonable doubt whether the arsenic so administered was in fact the cause of his death." His was to be the last word. No court of appeal existed at that time, and Florence Maybrick was taken down to serve 14 years in prison.

She was released in 1904 and returned to America where she wrote a book, *My Fifteen Lost Years*, and then became a recluse living in a remote cabin. She never saw her children again and died alone on October 23, 1941. Among her few possessions was a family Bible. Pressed between its pages was a scrap of paper bearing directions in faded ink of how soaking flypapers in certain substances made a useful beauty treatment.

# Ruby McCollum

**The murder of senator-elect Dr LeRoy Adams by African-American Ruby McCollum is not notable for being an out of the ordinary crime of passion. What makes it stomach-turning is the treatment that Ruby received purely because she was black.**

**Senator-elect Dr LeRoy Adams of Live Oak, Florida,** was not a pleasant man. Although married, he kept a mistress and would later be revealed as a thief and fraudster. But one lover wasn't enough for him. Adams also forced his sexual attentions on Ruby McCollum, who was already a wife and mother.

Theirs was not so much an affair as an exercise of his power over her, and time and again she submitted to his sexual demands, eventually giving birth to a child she insisted was the doctor's.

When she fell pregnant for a second time, it tipped her over the edge. She asked Adams to arrange a termination, and he refused, telling her to keep the baby though offering no financial support. On the morning of August 3, 1952, Ruby shot and killed Adams at his office.

The jury at Ruby's trial was made up of white men and from the start it was obvious that she was not going to get a fair hearing. The court simply did not want to know about an African-American woman having an affair with a powerful married white man. Neither were they interested in the fact that she had begged him to arrange the abortion of their second child and been turned down. They also turned a deaf ear to the fact that Adams had another mistress. As far as they were concerned a black woman who killed a white man deserved the full penalty of the law, and the circumstances were irrelevant. Ruby was duly convicted of first degree murder on December 20, 1952, and sentenced to death.

Fortunately for her, the judge had made a significant mistake. He had not been present during the jury's inspection of the crime scene, and on July 20, 1954, the Florida Supreme Court declared the trial invalid and overturned Ruby's sentence.

At a retrial, Ruby pleased insanity. Court-appointed physicians declared her mentally incompetent and she was incarcerated for 20 years in the Florida State Hospital for mental patients at Chattahoochee. She served the full term.

After her first conviction, Ruby's plight was followed in a series of articles written for the Pittsburgh Courier by journalist Zora Neale Hurston. Entitled *The Life Story of Ruby McCollum*, the pieces ran during the early months of 1953. They put forward the case that Ruby's trial sounded the death knell for "paramour rights" in the south of the United States. The presumed right of a white man to take a black woman as his concubine was finally at an end.

Ruby, the tragic victim of pre-civil rights America, died of a stroke on May 23, 1992, at the New Horizon Rehabilitation Center. She was 82.

# Charlotte McHugh

**Dull-witted, lazy, and promiscuous, Charlotte had the good fortune to marry a man who worked hard to keep her and their children. Sadly, she saw her hard-working husband only as a meal ticket and—when she fell in love with a romantic gypsy—the husband became an obstacle.**

**Charlotte McHugh was born in Ireland** in the early 20th century and by the time she had grown in to a young woman it was obvious that she enjoyed flirting and tempting men far more than working. Nevertheless, her sexual allure snared her a husband; a soldier named Frederick Bryant. They married when he was 25, and she 19, and moved to the rural English county of Somerset in the early 1920s. There, Charlotte would eventually give birth to five children, though there were always doubts about how many Bryant had fathered. Even so, he did his best to house and feed his idle, cheating wife and the growing number of children that filled the house. In 1925, Bryant was given a job as a farm laborer in Over Compton, near Yeovil, Dorset. Along with a small wage, Bryant was also given use of a cottage as part of his earnings.

While her husband worked hard, Charlotte existed only for pleasure. Numerous men were only too pleased to satisfy her sexual cravings, and some of them were even tempted into her marital bed while Bryant was out in the fields. Among her lovers was a gypsy horse-dealer named Leonard Parsons to whom Charlotte was particularly attracted. On the pretext of earning a little extra money for the family, she installed him in the house as a lodger in 1933 and when he wasn't out on the open road or with his own wife and four children, the affair flourished.

Having gotten away with so much for so long, and now deeply infatuated with her gypsy lover, Charlotte threw caution to the winds. She now paraded Parsons around the local village on her arm as if he were her husband and not Bryant, and made no secret at all of her passionate, and carnal, love for him.

The conservative rural community was shocked. Charlotte's behavior cost her husband his job, and the couple were forced to leave their cottage and move to Coombe, near Sherbourne. Charlotte did not give up Parsons, however. She was determined to have him at any cost, and the best solution she could think of was to remove her husband from the scene permanently.

In May of 1935, Bryant became ill with stomach pains. The doctor did not suspect poison and diagnosed gastroenteritis and he recovered, only to fall ill again on December 11. He was obviously a sturdy man for once again he survived the poisoning. Eleven days later though his mysterious stomach pains returned, and this time Charlotte had upped the dose. Bryant became violently ill and died within hours. When his body was examined, four grains of undissolved arsenic were found in his stomach.

The police searched the Bryant's home where the ever-lazy Charlotte hadn't even bothered to conceal her crime properly. A tin that had contained arsenical weed killer was found in a pile of rubbish and traces of arsenic were discovered on shelves in the house and in one of her coat pockets.

Charlotte Bryant was arrested on February 10, 1936, and charged with the murder of her husband. Her trial opened at Dorset Assizes, Dorchester, in front of Mr Justice MacNaghten, on Wednesday May 27, 1936, and it was reported that the unintelligent Charlotte seemed barely able to follow the proceedings. During her defense she protested that she had been on very good terms with her husband, but numerous witnesses drew a more accurate picture of her marriage for the jury and on May 30, 1936, Charlotte was found guilty of murder and sentenced to hang. She was executed, aged just 33, at Exeter Prison on July 15.

# Candy Montgomery

**Candy Montgomery's savage axe attack on the wife of her former sex partner left two children motherless. There was no question that someone else might have committed the terrible crime; Candy admitted it, but the jury was convinced by her claims of a psychological disorder and, amazingly, she was allowed to walk free.**

**Unlike many people who find themselves caught up in extramarital affairs,** Candy Montgomery was not swept off her feet in raw passion but deliberately set out to find a lover. The Texas housewife was bored with her husband of seven years and wanted some excitement. In her own words, she said she was looking for "fireworks'. The man she chose was computer software engineer Allan Gore whom Candy met at a church volleyball game. Soon afterward, she pulled Gore aside and asked him straight out if he was interested in having an affair. It would be dangerous as both Candy and Gore's families attended the same Methodist church , but the two reached an agreement: they would sleep with each other, but make sure not to fall in love. On December 12, 1978, Candy and Gore met for their first sexual encounter. It did not produce the fireworks that she had been hoping for and Gore, too, was unenthusiastic. They tried again on numerous occasions, but after 10 months the affair fizzled out.

On June 13, 1980, Gore kissed his wife Betty goodbye and left home for a business trip to Minnesota. Betty had their baby daughter, Bethany, at home, and their other child—six-year-old Alisa—stayed with the Montgomerys, with whose daughter, Jenny, she had become good friends. Gore spoke to Betty again just before his flight departed, but he became concerned when she failed to answer his frequent phone calls later that afternoon. He began phoning friends and neighbors, asking whether they had heard from Betty. One of them, Richard Parker, went to the door and called for Betty, but saw nothing. He told Gore that he had found nothing amiss.

Next, Gore called the Montgomery home to check on Alisa. Candy said she had visited the Gore's house at 10am during a quick break from Bible School. Betty was fine, Candy insisted. But by the evening, with his calls still going unanswered, Gore was becoming increasingly frantic. From his hotel room in St. Paul, he called neighbors again and pressed them to go inside.

Parker returned to the house with two other men. The front door was unlocked and, this time, they went inside. Parker immediately heard whimpers. He followed the sound and found little Bethany in a bedroom. The men then noticed crimson smears on an upright freezer in a utility room adjacent to the garage. They peeked around the corner, and there on the vinyl floor lay the body of Betty Gore. Her yellow top and pink shorts were soaked red, and blood had pooled and congealed beneath her body. The men's attention was drawn to the right side of her face, which had been disfigured by what appeared to be a large gunshot exit wound. Her left eye stared blankly into the distance.

Almost immediately, the telephone began ringing. It was Gore. Parker gave him the bad news, saying, "The baby is fine. But Betty's dead. She's been shot. It looks a like a suicide."

It wasn't suicide, and it wasn't a gunshot wound either, as the police discovered. Under questioning, Gore at first denied ever cheating on his wife. Then he admitted his affair with Candy Montgomery, whose bloody fingerprint had been left at the murder scene. Candy was taken in and soon crumbled during interrogation. In her version of events Candy told detectives that Betty Gore had confronted her about her affair and on learning the truth had come at Candy with an axe. Candy was hit but not badly. She grabbed the axe from her friend's hands and in a blind frenzy swung it at Betty's face, not once but dozens of times.

During the trial, Candy's defense team told the jury that she suffered psychological problems that stemmed from a troubled childhood. It was also said that she had an aversion to blood, the sight of which brought on violent feelings. The defense's final argument was that Candy acted in self-defense when Betty attacked her. It was enough for the jury, if not for observers at the court. A verdict of not guilty was pronounced, and Candy was set free with cries of "murderer" ringing in her ears. A newspaper summed up popular feeling with the headline, "Woman Hacked 41 Times in Self-Defense, Jury Rules.

# Alice & Thomas Morsby

**Although she adopted the surname of her lover, Alice Morsby was actually the wife of Thomas Ardern, the mayor of Faversham, in the English county of Kent. In 1550, Arden was murdered by Alice who wanted to inherit his fortune and begin a new life with the man she adored.**

The household arrangements of Thomas Ardern and his wife were more than a little unconventional for their time in Tudor England. That fact that Ardern had married Alice for her connections and money rather than love was not so remarkable, but he appears to have been either an unusually understanding man or totally in thrall to his tempestuous wife. He did not object when Alice took Thomas Morsby, a young tailor, to her bed and even appears to have been on excellent terms with his wife's lover. The mayor often invited Morsby to stay at the family home while he was away on business and enjoyed Morsby's company at the gaming table when he was at home. The official record of the case says that Alice "did not only keep Moresby carnally in her own house, but also fed him with delicate meats and sumptuous apparel, all which things Ardern did know well and willfully did permit."

Although she enjoyed the almost constant attentions of her lover, Alice was still dissatisfied. She objected to being one man's wife and another man's mistress. In 1550, after years of a dull marriage and desperate to be free of the husband whose very existence prevented her from marrying Moresby, Alice decided Ardern had to die. The first attempts of the fledgling murderess involved a poisoned crucifix and poisoned pictures. These weapons failed.

Next, Alice appealed to her lover for help. While Morsby refused to initiate the murder himself he gave in to Alice's demands and together they plotted Ardern's demise. Others were taken into their confidence: their servants Michael Saunderson and Elizabeth Stafford, Moresby's sister Cecily, and two men of the town, John Green and George Bradshaw. The latter was dispatched to Calais, France, with a mission to find willing assassins. He returned with two cut-throats called Loosebagg and Black Will.

As was their custom, Mayor Ardern and Thomas Morsby were sitting at the gaming table when the murderers struck. Black Will had been hidden in the house by Alice. The hired killer rushed into the room, threw a handkerchief around Ardern's neck, and strangled him. As the mayor's life faded, Morsby took up an iron and crushed his skull then brutally cut his love rival's throat.

The murderers, Moresby's sister, and the servants dragged the body to a nearby field. Black Will was paid the sum of eight pounds and immediately disappeared with his accomplice, Loosebagg. But the inept killers had failed to notice it was snowing and did not even bury the body. The next day Ardern's corpse was discovered, and investigators had no difficulty tracing footprints and bloodstains across the field back to the house. Everyone involved in the murder, with the exception of Loosebagg, who was never found, and John Green, were arrested, tried, and found guilty. Alice and her maid Elizabeth were burned alive at Canterbury on March 14, 1551. Morsby and his sister were hanged at Smithfield in London. George Bradshaw was hung in chains at Faversham. Black Will was burned on a scaffold. John Green was later apprehended in Cornwall and was returned to Faversham where he was also hanged in chains.

# Augusta Nack and Martin Thorn

**The 36-year-old Augusta Nack was an unlicensed midwife who also ran a boarding house—appropriately in Hell's Kitchen, New York City. A married woman, her husband had long since tired of her and after he departed Augusta took numerous lovers. The latest and most regular was German masseur Willie Guldensuppe, though when he went away on a trip, she could not resist the opportunity to introduce a little variety in her bed. Augusta decided that one of her lodgers, the youthful Martin Thorn, would suit her just fine.**

**Unfortunately for the couple,** Guldensuppe returned unexpectedly in the middle of Augusta's seduction scene. Driven to a mad rage by seeing his lover in a state of undress and in the arms of another man, the German furiously attacked Thorn. Beaten half to death, the barber was hospitalized.

While he slowly recovered, Thorn's thoughts turned to revenge: On June 26, 1897, parts of Willie Guldensuppe began bobbing to the surface of New York's East River wrapped in distinctive red and gold oilcloth decorated with flowers. His upper torso and arms were found in one part of the river, his lower torso in another, and his legs in yet another. The head, which—as the court later heard—had been coated in plaster, was missing. But as the coroners worked to piece the body together, they noticed another small part wasn't there: a four-inch square of skin had been cut from the corpse's chest. It would play a crucial part in identifying the body for investigations eventually led to the Turkish baths where Guldensuppe had worked, and his colleagues were able to identify the body from an abscess on one finger as well as telling investigators that the German had had a tattoo in exactly the place the flesh was missing.

**BELOW:** William Randolph Hearst, the press magnate whose reporters helped to reveal the sordid details of the murder of Willie Guldensupper.

Meanwhile, the press were covering the case avidly. Sensing a sensational story, the newspaper magnate William Randolph Hearst assigned a large group of reporters from his Journal newspaper to the case, and soon they were making breakthroughs. First, they found Augusta, who oozed guilt when the pack of reporters quizzed her. She had withdrawn a large amount of cash from her bank account and had made enquiries about leaving for Europe on a steamship. The journalists also discovered where the oilskin had been bought, and by whom. Thorn was arrested soon afterward as he tried to slip across the border into Canada.

While Thorn denied everything, Augusta confessed under questioning. She told police that she had become tired of her German lover's numerous affairs while demanding that she remain faithful and that she had lured Guldensuppe to a farm cottage on the promise of sex. It was there that Thorn had taken his own bloody revenge. Hearst's reporters soon tracked down the Long Island farm where the owner said a couple matching Thorn and Augusta's description had rented a cabin.

The farmer said he had noticed how all his ducks had suddenly turned pink while they had stayed there! They had been bathing in wastewater flowing from a pipe connected to the cottage. It was later discovered that Thorn had shot Guldensuppe, stabbed him, and cut him up in the bathtub.

So graphic were the details of the murder that during the trial a sensitive juror fainted. Augusta and her young lover were both convicted of murder, but while Augusta was sentenced to 15 years (serving nine) in Auburn Prison, Thorn met his death in the electric chair on August 1, 1898, at Sing Sing.

# Fernado Ortega

**A short and simple story, the case of Fernado Ortega perfectly captures the despair that accompanies humiliation and rejection. His was a sad, but typical, crime of passion.**

Garage owner Fernado Ortega of Guadalajara, Mexico, knew he could never have the woman he desired. She was beautiful, while he was hunchbacked and ugly. They met in 1972 when Maria Pineda became Ortega's nurse, administering injections and generally caring for her patient who suffered from chronic tuberculosis alongside his physical deformity. And as the weeks passed Ortega's attraction to the pretty woman grew into an love.

That Maria did not return his feelings was obvious, but still he tried to explain how he felt. When she rejected him, Ortega's love turned to despair and desolation at his own physical shortcomings. Perhaps we could have felt pity for him, but for the fact that Ortega decided that if he could not have Maria then he could not bear for her to be happy with anyone else. At knifepoint he forced her to drink deadly cyanide and laid her expiring body on his bed. As she lay dying, Ortega then he drank from the bottle himself and lay down beside her to await death.

The horrific scene was discovered by Francisco Pineda, a car mechanic who worked for Ortega and who—tragically—was also Maria's stepfather. His first thought was that Ortega had overpowered her so that he might rape her, but though Maria's skirt had slipped up to her thighs, Ortega had not wanted to violate the woman he loved. There was no sign that he had sexually abused her at all.

# Pauline Yvonne Parker & Juliet Marion Hulme

**The case of two teenage lesbian lovers who murdered one of their parents shocked New Zealand in the mid-1950s. The two girls were so desperate not to be parted from one another that they were prepared to kill to stop it happening.**

ABOVE: Juliet Marion Hulme (left) and her friend Pauline Yvonne Parker after being remanded in custody charged with the murder of Pauline's mother Honara Mary Parker.

Pauline Parker and Juliet Hulme came from different worlds. Pauline's father managed a fish shop while her mother, Honora Mary Parker, took in lodgers to make ends meet; Juliet's father was a famous British physicist and her mother a marriage counselor. Nevertheless, the two young girls were drawn to each other, perhaps due to their similarities in temperament. Pauline's education had not been of the highest standard, but she was a gifted and imaginative writer, and Juliet was deeply sensitive to the point of being psychologically fragile.

Over time, what started out as a friendship became much, much more. The two adolescent girls—Pauline was 15, Juliet 16—began to explore their sexuality with one another and quickly became passionate lovers. As Juliet would later say, when they were together it was "better than heaven." Unfortunately, events were conspiring to bring their relationship to an end. Juliet's marriage-counselor mother divorced her father, and the young girl was deeply traumatized when she caught her mother in bed with a new man. Soon after, her father announced that he was returning to Britain to take up a new post, and Juliet would be sent to live with relatives in South Africa where it was hoped her health would improve.

Both girls were devastated at the idea of being separated, but Honora Parker made no secret of her relief. She had grown suspicious of their friendship and the strange hold Juliet had over her daughter, so when Pauline begged to be allowed to go to South Africa too, she refused. In doing so she became the focus of the girls' frustration and anger. If Pauline was orphaned, they reasoned, there would be no-one to stop her joining Juliet in South Africa. As Pauline wrote in her diary on February 13, 1954, "Why could mother not die? Dozens of people are dying, thousands are dying every day. So why not mother and father too?" It would be one of the many diary entries that eventually helped convict her.

On June 22, not long before Juliet was due to leave, Honora Parker took the two girls to Victoria Park for tea and cakes. After the treat, the three strolled in the park and when they reached a secluded spot, Mrs Parker bent over to pick up a stone that had attracted her attention. As she did a stocking loaded with a brick crashed into her skull. Over and over, the teenage girls took it in turns to beat Pauline's mother to death. And when they were sure that she was gone, they ran back to the tea kiosk, screaming for help and crying, "Mummy's been hurt."

Police found the stocking and brick close by Honora Parker's body and the two girls were arrested. Both admitted that they had they had helped in the grisly task of killing Mrs Parker, and both were found equally responsible. After a sensational trial unlike any New Zealand had ever seen, the two girls were found guilty of murder on August 29, 1954, and—in view of their ages—sentenced to five years in prison each with the added condition that when they were released they could never see each other again.

**ABOVE:** A New Zealand police mug shot of Pauline Parker, who was convicted with her best friend Juliet Hulme for the murder of her mother in 1954.

# Alpna Patel

**When Alpna Patel was married to a man she hardly knew, she didn't realize that along with a husband she would be getting a father-in-law who wanted to control every detail of her life. When she was forced to sleep in his basement while her new husband worked 500 miles away, she became desperate to get out of her appalling situation.**

**Alpna was 29 and her soon-to-be husband 26** when their marriage was arranged for them in 1998. Although they were both American, their families stuck rigidly to the rules of their homeland's culture and during the "courtship" the couple were strictly chaperoned during meetings and the brief dates they were allowed. The traditional wedding was an extravagant affair and afterward the couple, finally alone together, went to Disneyworld to enjoy a honeymoon during which they could get to know each other. As

**LEFT:** This wedding photo of Alpna Patel with her husband Viresh Patel was introduced as evidence during her trial for his murder.

Viresh Patel would now begin to discover, his new wife had a reputation for being "moody" and "temperamental."

It didn't take long for the marriage to begin to disintegrate. Back home from their brief vacation, Alpna found that her new father-in-law had strong ideas about how the young couple's lives should be run and as head of the family he was determined to implement them. Alpna was allowed to continue her work as a dentist at a local hospital in Buffalo, New York, but was told she had to live in the basement of her in-laws house and now needed to submit to her father-in-law's will in all aspects of her life. She even needed to seek his permission before going out with friends. Her husband, meanwhile, was to continue as a surgical resident in Baltimore, where he had an apartment that would become their married home on the occasions they spent time together.

For Alpna, the situation was intolerable and in March 1999, it came to a head. When her husband made a brief appearance at his parents' house, Alpna confronted him and a vicious argument was overheard by Viresh's sister. A day later a scowling Alpna argued with him again in the driveway. On March 23, 1999, Alpna Patel dropped another sister-in-law, Beena, off at school. As a court would later hear she seemed in a good mood and was even "giggly." She made no mentions of her plans for the rest of the day, but after Beena was delivered to school, she drove to the airport and took a plane to Baltimore.

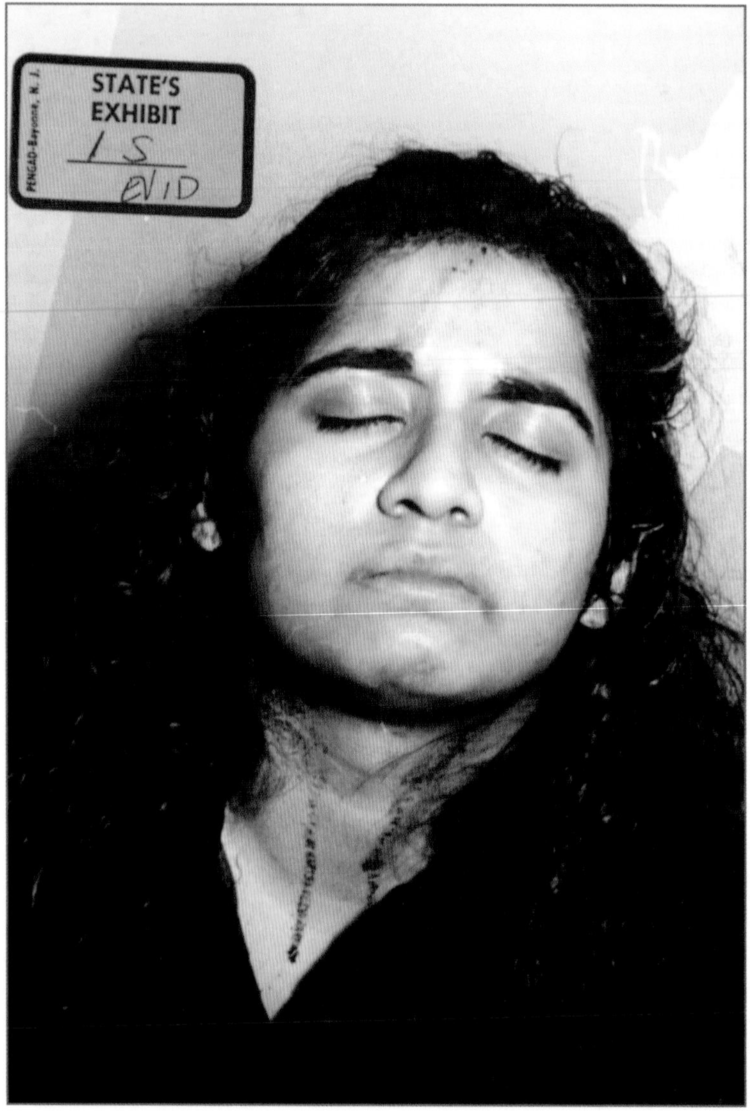


**BELOW:** A photo of Alpna Patel, 26, taken by Baltimore police after she was brought to the police station for questioning in connection with the murder of her husband.

When Baltimore police arrived at the Patels' one bedroom apartment the next day, they found Alpna sitting at the kitchen table—she was covered in blood. In the bedroom was the body of her husband, his jugular and carotid artery slashed with a knife that had been part of a set given to the couple as a wedding gift.

In court Alpna Patel claimed the killing had been self defense, stating that she and her husband had discussed the problems with their marriage, after which they had decided to sleep on it. She had awoken two hours later to find Viresh straddling her and pointing a black-handled steak knife at her chest. She told the court that she had managed to knock him off her and in the ensuing struggle for the knife, her husband was killed.

Alpna was acquitted of first degree murder at her first trial and the jury could not agree on the charge of second degree murder. At a second trial, in September 2000 she was given a three-year sentence for manslaughter. She served 13 months and was given credit for three more spent in custody during the trial. She was released in February 2002.

**ABOVE:** Alpna Patel (right) with assistant attorney Lynn Williamson walking from court in Baltimore, during her trial.

# Nan Patterson

**Sex, adultery, and blackmail—the sensational 1905 murder trials of the beautiful young dancer and performer Nan Patterson had it all. And though the evidence against her was overwhelming, still she walked free, saved from the death penalty by her looks and an air of innocence that came easily to a professional actress.**

**The wealthy bookmaker Caesar Young** died of a gunshot wound in the back of a horse-drawn hansom cab on the way to meet his wife at the New York docks where the couple were due to take a ship, bound for an extended tour of Europe. With him was another passenger; Nan Patterson, a young actress with whom Young had been conducting an illicit two-year affair. The lovers had met to say their farewells before

Young's departure. They had also marked the occasion with a drinking spree.

As the only other person in the cab, Nan was arrested immediately, and it looked to prosecutors like an open and shut case. But when the case came to court and the details of the affair began trickling out, the press went wild and public support quickly surged around the actress. Nan Patterson, it was reported, had met Young two years earlier on a train to California. Despite her youth she was already married, as was he, but Nan was dazzled by the rich older man and the pair embarked on a passionate affair. As time went on Young gave Nan the money to divorce her husband, promising that he, too, would soon split from his wife. While she waited, he lavished his young mistress with expensive gifts and money. As is so often the case though, Young's divorce never materialized, and documentary evidence was produced that showed Nan had recently begun trying to blackmail her sugar daddy. Matters had come to a head in the back of the cab, and ended with Young slumped dead in his seat.

Nan denied all charges, testifying that Young had killed himself because she had ended their relationship, but the evidence continued to mount. The jury heard that on the day of Young's death, Nan's brother had pawned jewelry and used the cash to buy a gun. Still, the actress protested her innocence. The trial ended with a hung jury.

A second trial was convened with the press again feeding an insatiable public hunger for every tiny detail. The sheer volume of sympathetic, colorful newspaper articles meant that the public remained staunchly on the side of the accused. Nan maintained her plea of not guilty and she and her defense team played on her youth and saintly appearance for all it was worth. Her lawyer at one point declared, "What is there against this girl? She went on the stage, but it was to make an honest living. She met Young when she was but 19 years old. Who was the stronger of the pair?" When the trial ended, the New York Times reported that the closing scenes were "arousing public interest to a degree almost unprecedented in the history of criminal cases in New York."

The trial ended on June 3, 1905, with another hung jury unable to agree a verdict. Nan Patterson spent nearly a year in jail while legal discussions rambled on and talk of a third trial fizzled out. In the end it was felt that in another trial, any jury would base its decision on newspaper reports even though the evidence against her was so strong. Eventually, a court set her free. Nan walked out of the building to be welcomed by a cheering throng of supporters.

# Queen Elizabeth I & Sir Robert Dudley

**Queen Elizabeth I never married and is remembered by history as the Virgin Queen—the root of the name Virginia, which was named in her honor. However, the reality was very different. Although it remains unproven, the Queen is thought to have taken Sir Robert Dudley as a lover and conspired with him to murder his wife. The evidence against them is circumstantial but compelling.**

**Queen Elizabeth I never married and is remembered by history as the Virgin Queen**—the root of the name Virginia, which was named in her honor. However, the reality was very different. Although it remains unproven, the Queen is thought to have taken Sir Robert Dudley as a lover and conspired with him to murder his wife. The evidence against them is circumstantial but compelling.

ABOVE: An 1879 painting by William Frederick Yeames depicting the death of Amy Robsart.

It is beyond doubt that Sir Robert Dudley was a philanderer and fiercely ambitious, yet his love for Queen Elizabeth appears to have been genuine. He was her constant companion and confidant for more than 30 years. After the death of his wife, Amy Robsart, he turned down numerous offers of marriage, including to a number of foreign princesses and one to Mary, Queen of Scots, which could have placed him on the thrones of both England and Scotland. All this he sacrificed in order to remain by his queen's side. For her part, Elizabeth heaped honors and riches upon her favorite companion. Indeed, the court of the day was inflamed with gossip regarding the pair, and it was widely believed that there was an love affair between them and that they would be married if and when Amy died.

Amy was the fly in the ointment of the Dudley's love for the queen. Although theirs appears to have been a love match, made when Amy was just 18, Dudley and his wife had been leading separate lives since Elizabeth I had come to the throne, and Dudley began to spend more time at court.

On September 4, 1560, the Queen had a strange—and rather suspicious—conversation with the Spanish ambassador during which she said that Amy Robsart was "dead or nearly so." In fact, it was widely known that Amy had a "malady in one of her breasts," which was possibly cancer. Nevertheless, it is suspicious that only four days later Amy was indeed dead. On September 8, she allowed all

her servants to take the day off to go to Abingdon Fair in Oxfordshire. When they returned, they found her at the foot of the stairs with a fractured skull.

While her death was officially deemed to have been a tragic accident, whispers soon circulated. There was a belief that Dudley and the Queen had organized Amy's murder between them; a belief that was strengthened when one of Dudley's staff was reported to have been part of the plot. It is possible, however, that such rumors were started for political reasons. There were some members of the royal court whose interests would have damaged by a marriage between Dudley and the queen. If so, the rumor-mongers won the day. Perhaps fearing to further inflame the scandal, Elizabeth and Dudley never married.

**LEFT:** A painting of Queen Elizabeth I of England by Flemish artist Steven van der Meulen.

**RIGHT:** A picture of Robert Dudley, Earl of Leicester, from around the time of Amy Robsart's suspicious death.

# James Stewart Ramage

**Fearing a violent reaction from a husband who had a history of lashing out when crossed, Julie Ramage made a careful plan to leave him as gently as possible, but she was only delaying the inevitable. Fourteen months later he took her body out to Australia's Kings Lake National Park and buried it.**

**To all appearances James and Julie Ramage** had a perfectly normal middle-class family life. They owned a beautiful home in Melbourne, Australia, as well as a holiday house and the three cars in the garage, and had a very healthy bank balance. But Julie lived in fear of her 43-year-old husband and told friends that he might "lose it" one day. Nevertheless, keen to provide a stable family environment for their children, she endured his temper and occasional outbursts of violence for 20 years before finally deciding to leave.

In order to let him down gently Julie enlisted the help of friends and family. Avoiding a face-to-face confrontation, she left the family home while he was on a business trip abroad, leaving him with a letter that suggested they might get back together after a while. As she explained to friends, he was not ready to face the truth. The letter was a moving appeal for peace between them. She wrote, "If you do care for me, please let me go without a horrible fight, for the kids' sake. Let's prove to them that we are better than all the other separated couples that we know. I could hate you so much for some of the things you have done and said to me over the years, but I also understand that you are a good person and that you work hard and, most importantly, that you love our kids very much."

However, Julie had no intention of ever going back to her husband and before long had met a new man, Laurence Webb. Meanwhile, James Ramage seethed with anger at the desertion. On July 21, 2003, the violent confrontation that Julie had worked so hard to avoid exploded. Having regained her confidence and made furious during and argument, Julie told her husband that sex with him had repulsed her and that she should have left him 10 years earlier.

Ramage's response was terrible. He strangled his wife then put her body in his car, packed a change of clothes, and gathered up Julie's handbag and mobile. He then drove out to Kings Lake National Park and on the way called his wife's work and mobile numbers as if he were looking for her. At the park Ramage dug a hole and put Julie's body in it, then covered the newly turned soil with branches and bracken. A few meters away he dug a second hole, where he buried incriminating evidence, including the bedding that he had used to wrap her body.

Julie's disappearance didn't go unnoticed for long, and Ramage's long history of violence and the calls he had made after killing his wife immediately brought him under suspicion. Nevertheless, at his trial—which began on December 9, 2004, at Victoria's Supreme Court—he made full use of Julie's own outburst of temper to claim that he had been provoked. Although the prosecution argued that she would have been too afraid of Ramage to actually speak to him in that way, after 20 years of taking his verbal and physical abuse, Julie's alleged final snap of anger at her husband saved him from a murder charge. The jury found that he should be convicted of manslaughter. The judge, however, did not appear to be quite so convinced. Sentencing Ramage to a maximum 11 years in prison, Justice Robert Osborn said, "The killing was done with murderous intent and savage brutality and where, although the jury has accepted the reasonable possibility of provocation, it is apparent that such provocation was not objectively extreme."

Julie Ramage's mother, Patricia Garrett, perhaps summed it up best. Describing her son-in-law's prison sentence as pathetic, she said, "Any woman that's in a relationship where she feels threatened, I tell her not to stay for the sake of the children. Get out. My daughter stayed for the children, and she's paid the ultimate price. She's dead."

# Dr. Buck Ruxton

**The murder of Isabella Ruxton at the hands of her common-law husband was a classic crime of passion. Incensed at her cheating on him, Ruxton strangled and stabbed his wife to death, then turned his killing fury on a maid who had the misfortune to walk in and witness the act. The only thing missing was Isabella's guilt, for she was a faithful wife and completely innocent of the accusations he made against her.**

**A doctor of Persian ancestry,** Buck Ruxton's jealousy of his wife was common knowledge among their circle of friend and acquaintances in Lancaster, England. In fact, he had become so suspicious of Isabella that when she took a trip to Edinburgh with some friends he secretly followed her, certain that she

**ABOVE:** Dr Buck Ruxton, who was convicted of the murder of his wife, Isabella Ruxton, and his housemaid, Mary Jane Rogerson at his home in Lancaster.

was having an affair with a man called Robert Edmonson who was among the group. But while his snooping didn't turn up a single scrap of evidence against her, the facts did nothing to quench the fury that was boiling within him as he followed his wife from one hotel to another, sure that she was sharing Edmonson's bed.

Isabella returned home to find her husband waiting for her. By now he had worked himself into such a passion that violence took possession of him. He grabbed at his wife, strangled her into unconsciousness, and then stabbed her to death. During the struggle a maid, Mary Rogerson, heard Isabella's screams for help and she rushed to help, only to find Ruxton standing over the body of his wife. He immediately knew that if he were to escape punishment then Mary would have to die too and he quickly dispatched her in the same way. Then, Dr Ruxton set about concealing his crime. First he had to deal with the bodies. On September 15, 1935, two severed heads and assorted dismembered limbs were found wrapped up in copies of the Sunday Graphic newspaper.

When Mary Rogerson's parents asked after her, Ruxton told them that their rather plain and single daughter had fallen pregnant and his wife had taken her away to have an abortion. They didn't believe him and reported her missing. Meanwhile, friends and neighbors had also begun to question why Isabella Ruxton had suddenly vanished. Ruxton was well known for his temper and jealousy and the rumor that he was responsible for the killings spread like wildfire. In desperation, and eager to throw detectives off his scent, Ruxton presented himself at the police station and begged for their help in finding his wife.

Unfortunately for Ruxton, he was already the prime suspect. The new forensic sciences of fingerprinting and super-imposure (where a photograph of a victim is matched to a skull) had allowed police to identify the victims, now all they needed was the evidence to convict Ruxton. They found it in the testimony of Ruxton's cleaner, who told them that on the day the two women went missing she had arrived at the house to find it in disarray with blood-stained carpets.

Ruxton was arrested on October 13, 1935, and tried at Manchester Assizes in March 1936. The jury took just over an hour to find him guilty of murder. Although a petition to have his sentence commuted was signed by 10,000 people it failed and he was hanged at Strangeways Prison in Manchester, on May 12, 1936. A few days later his signed confession was published. It read, "I killed Mrs. Ruxton in a fit of temper because I thought she had been with a man. I was mad at the time. Mary Rogerson was present at the time. I had to kill her."

# O. J. Simpson

It was the trial of the century, possibly the most famous and widely followed courtroom drama ever witnessed. And at first it seemed an open and shut case: the celebrity suspect had been watched on televisions around the world apparently fleeing justice, motive was clear, and crucial evidence had been found in the shape of an incriminating glove. All the elements of an obvious crime of passion were in place. And yet the former football star, O. J. Simpson was acquitted of the charge of murdering his ex-wife Nicole Brown Simpson and her friend Ronald Goldman. He walked free in 1995 after the longest trial in Californian history.

**The drama began at 11.40pm on June 12, 1994.** The barking of Nicole Simpson's pet dog alerted neighbors that something was amiss and the police were called to her Brentwood, Los Angeles, home. What they found there was truly shocking. While her two young children— Sydney, 8, and Justin, 5—slept upstairs, Nicole and her friend Ronald Goldman had been brutally slain. Nicole had been stabbed many times through the throat; the wounds so ferocious she was almost decapitated. Goldman had minor wounds to his body as well as fatal slashes, suggesting the murderer had played with his or her victim before finally despatching him. The police put the time of the double murder at between 10.15 and 10.40pm.

It did not take long for investigators to name Nicole's ex-husband, the football star O. J. Simpson, as the prime suspect, and an appeal went out for him to turn himself in while a huge crowd of reporters gathered at the police station. Instead, Simpson responded by sending a letter, which his lawyer read out. It said, "First everyone understand I had nothing to do with Nicole's murder… Don't feel sorry for me. I've had a great life." It followed by naming Simpson's partner at the time Playboy Playmate Traci Adell as an alibi.

The hunt was on. Police tracked calls from a cell phone in Simpson's van in Orange County and, later, a patrol car spotted a white Ford Bronco being driven by Simpson's friend, Al Cowlings, headed south on Interstate 405. Cowlings yelled that Simpson was pointing a gun at his own head. The officer kept his

**RIGHT:** O. J. Simpson accompanying his children, Sydney and Justin, at the funeral service for his ex-wife, Nicole Simpson.

distance, but followed the vehicle, which was traveling at just 35 miles an hour. For some time a Los Angeles KCBS News Service helicopter had exclusive coverage of the chase, and it was soon joined by nearly a dozen others. Already, the case had become a media circus.

One radio station contacted Simpson's former coach, John McKay, who went live on air to beg Simpson to give himself up. Meanwhile, thousands of curious spectators thronged overpass roads along the route waiting to catch a glimpse of the rolling crime scene. By this time, a staggering 95 million people around the world were watching on TV.

The 50-mile chase ended at 8.00pm outside Simpson's Brentwood home, and Simpson was allowed

**ABOVE:** Police cars pursuing the Ford Bronco (white, right) driven by Al Cowlings, carrying fugitive murder suspect O. J. Simpson.

to go inside before his attorney, Robert Shapiro, arrived and suggested Simpson turn himself in.

There was more drama to come, and it began to unfold rapidly. A grand jury, called to determine whether to indict Simpson for the two murders, was dismissed two days later when it was considered that the media frenzy would prejudice its decision. Then a man who might have been a key witness was dismissed after selling his story to the newspapers. Jose Camacho, a knife salesman at Ross Cutlery, claimed that had he sold Simpson a 15-inch German knife similar to the

**ABOVE:** Los Angeles Police Detective Tom Lange (left) pointing to pictures of the trail of blood at Nicole Brown Simpson's condominium where she and her friend Ron Goldman were murdered, during testimony in the O. J. Simpson murder trial.

**LEFT:** O. J. Simpson reacting as a coroner describes the autopsy report on Nicole Brown Simpson in court in 1995.

murder weapon three weeks before the fatal attacks. A female witness who claimed she saw Simpson driving away from Nicole's home on the night of the murders was forbidden to give evidence for the same reason. Nevertheless, after a week-long court hearing, a California Superior Court judge ruled on July 7, that there was ample evidence to try Simpson. At his second court appearance, on July 23, Simpson stated, "Absolutely, one hundred percent, not guilty."

Amid a welter of media attention, the trial began on January 25, 1995. Los Angeles County prosecutor Christopher Darden stated that Simpson had killed his ex-wife in a jealous rage and opened the case by playing an emergency 911 call made by Nicole Brown Simpson on January 1, 1989. The jury heard Nicole crying out that Simpson was going to attack her, while her husband could be heard shouting threateningly at her in the background.

The prosecution continued to produce what seemed like damning evidence: Simpson had a history of violence toward his wife and dozens of expert witnesses testified that DNA, fingerprints, blood, and shoe prints clearly placed Simpson at the scene of the crime. All evidence, it was alleged, pointed to a murder during which Simpson had forced Nicole to the ground, grabbed her hair to pull her head back, put his foot on her back, and slit her throat as she lay face down on the ground. A trail of blood spots had been identified leading from Nicole's house to Simpson's Bronco and his own home on Rockingham Drive.

While this evidence alone looked convincing, even more was produced. Simpson had last been seen in public on the night of the murders at 9.36pm when he returned to his house with Brian "Kato" Kaelin, a bit-part actor, after which they had eaten at a nearby McDonald's. Simpson was not seen again until 10.54pm when he got into a limousine and went to LAX Airport to fly to Chicago. During the time the murders took place no alibi could be given. Simpson had also been spotted driving the Bronco to and from the scene during the time both prosecution and defence agreed the murder had been committed. The driver of the limo the accused would later take to the airport reported that he had arrived at Simpson's home around 10.30pm and rung the doorbell, but got no answer. He then saw Simpson come home about 15 minutes' later. At first Simpson's excuse for not answering the bell was that he had overslept. Another witness, a neighbor, said he heard "three loud thumps" and went out to investigate. The two men both said they had seen Simpson outside, looking agitated. Further evidence showed that DNA samples from

**BELOW:** Prosecutor Brain Kelberg points to a chart showing where wounds were inflicted on murder victim Ronald Goldman in the O. J. Simpson murder trial.

**ABOVE:** O. J. Simpson showing the jury a new pair of Aris extra-large gloves, similar to those found at the crime scene.

bloody footprints leading away from the bodies and from the back gate of the condominium matched Simpson's blood.

Although no actual murder weapon had been found, and no further witnesses had come forward save those who had earlier been dismissed, the prosecution was confident of a conviction.

Now it was the turn of Simpson's top-flight defence team, which had been described by the press as a "Dream Team." It comprised lawyers F. Lee Bailey, Robert Shapiro, Alan Dershowitz, Robert Kardashian, Gerald Uelmen (a law professor at Santa Clara University), Carl E. Douglas, and Cochran, as well as Peter Neufeld and Barry Scheck, two attorneys specializing in DNA evidence. They swiftly set out to destroy the evidence, alleging that Simpson was the victim of police fraud and that "sloppy internal procedures" had contaminated the DNA evidence.

Further to this, they claimed that Simpson had not left his house that evening, but had been busy packing for his trip to Chicago, save for a short break during which he had gone outside to hit golf balls into a children's sandpit in the front garden—hence the three loud thumps on the wall of the neighbor's bungalow. The Spanish-speaking housekeeper of another neighbor testified that she had seen Simpson's car parked outside his house at the time of the murders. When challenged, however, she said she could not be sure of the exact time she had seen the car. But adding weight to the defence was the evidence of an airport check-in clerk who said Simpson appeared perfectly normal at LAX airport on the night of the murders.

The defence also suggested that Simpson was not physically capable of carrying out the murders; Ronald Goldman was a fit young man who had put up a fierce struggle against his attacker while Simpson had chronic arthritis. To counter this, one of the prosecuting team, Marcia Clark, showed an exercise video that Simpson made two years earlier.

The most famous piece of evidence was till to come though: a glove carrying traces of Goldman's DNA that had been found at Simpson's house. Cochran goaded

**BELOW:** O. J. Simpson reacting to the not guilty verdict at his criminal trial for the murders of his ex-wife and Ron Goldman.

an assistant prosecutor into asking Simpson to put the glove on. It appeared too tight, prompting Gerald Uelman to tell the jury, "If it doesn't fit, you must acquit." Police had planted the glove in Simpson's house, they claimed. Prosecutor Darden would refute that Simpson was framed in his closing arguments, pointing out that police had visited his house eight times on domestic violence calls without arresting him before eventually citing him for abuse in 1989.

Ripples from the Simpson case were felt far and wide during the trial, and stirred racial tension between black communities in which many thought Simpson a victim of injustice and white communities where a majority believed he was guilty. It also caused a storm of argument over media coverage of trials.

Following a trial of over eight months the not guilty verdict was returned by a majority African American jury at 10.00am on October 3, 1995. After long months of hearing the evidence they deliberated over the decision for just four hours. In all, 150 witnesses had given testimony and media coverage was unprecedented throughout. Simpson's defence was said to have cost between three and six million dollars.

**ABOVE:** Lou Brown (left) and Juditha Brown (right), the parents of Nicole Brown Simpson, with their attorney John Kelley (centre) outside the Santa Monica, California, courthouse, following the guilty verdicts in the O.J Simpson wrongful death civil trial.

Nevertheless, there were still more dramas and revelations to come. In post-trial interviews a few jurors said that they believed Simpson probably committed the murders, but that the prosecution had bungled the case. Three of them later published a book called Madam Foreman, in which they described how police errors, not race, led to their verdict, and that they considered prosecutor Darden to be a "token black" assigned to the case. A year later, both the Brown and Goldman families sued Simpson for damages in a civil trial. On February 5, 1997, the jury unanimously found there was sufficient evidence to find Simpson liable for damages in the wrongful death of Goldman and battery of Brown. In its conclusions, the jury effectively found Simpson liable for the death of his ex-wife and Ron Goldman, although the burden of proof is lower in civil cases than in criminal ones. Yet another indication that Simpson's acquittal may have been a miscarriage of justice came in September 2004, when porn star Jennifer Peace came forward claiming that she was Al Cowlings' girlfriend and that Cowlings—who had been in the car with Simpson during the famous chase—had told her that Simpson confessed his guilt. In 2008, Mike Gilbert released his book *How I Helped O. J. Get Away with Murder*, which told how Simpson had also confessed to him.

# Yvonne Sleightholme

**At first glance the killing of Jayne Smith by a former girlfriend of her husband appears to be a straightforward case of a murder committed by an unbalanced woman in a frenzy of jealousy. However, Yvonne Sleightholme has always maintained her innocence and after she was convicted evidence came to light that suggests there may be a shred of truth to her claims. Nevertheless, she served six years more in prison than the judge at her trial recommended.**

**Yvonne Sleightholme, a doctor's receptionist**, met William Smith at a disco nightclub in Yorkshire 1979, and the two began a relationship soon after. But while they talked of weddings Smith began to have doubts about his girlfriend and, growing weary of her controlling nature, he eventually finished with her. Yvonne took it badly and lied that she was dying of leukemia. Out of sympathy Smith briefly took her back, but it soon became obvious that there was nothing physically wrong with Yvonne and meanwhile he had met Jayne, who he would later marry. The relationship with Yvonne ended once again.

On December 12, 1989, the body of Jayne Smith was found in the yard of the couple's farm at Salton in the Yorkshire Dales, England. It looked like an attempted rape gone wrong; her clothes were in disarray and her body scratched. She had died of a gunshot wound fired at point blank range into the back of her head. There was a strange irregularity about the killing though, and one that would lead straight back to Yvonne Sleightholme. Jayne's attacker had taken the trouble to remove her wedding ring. It spoke of a murder committed out of jealousy rather than lust.

At her trial in May 1991, Yvonne claimed she had been at the farm on the night of the murder, but had had nothing to do with it. Mr Justice Waite, prosecuting, argued that after her fiancé had broken off their engagement and later married another woman, the already unstable Sleightholme had been twisted by envy and "wrought upon the newly-married couple a terrible revenge." The jury was convinced. Yvonne was found guilty of murder and sentenced to life in prison, with a recommendation that she should serve at least ten years.

Several years later, Yvonne's supporters came up with new evidence that seemed to cast doubt on the court's decision. A bloody handprint had been found in her car, but it was too large to have been made by her. Nevertheless, Yvonne's hopes of taking her case back to the Court of Appeal were dashed when judges threw out the application. Still she protested that she was innocent and, in January 2002, gave an interview to the local evening paper from Styal Prison in Cheshire. She told the reporter that she would never admit to killing Jayne Smith, saying, "I value the truth more than anything... I didn't do it, and nothing—not even the chance of freedom—will make me lie and say I did it. I was not responsible for that terrible murder."

In March 2003, the Yorkshire Evening Post newspaper revealed it had obtained documents proving Sleightholme had been an exemplary prisoner, and that she was not, as had been claimed, likely to commit another violent act. The editor wrote to the parole board, asking for it to look again at the application, and Ryedale member of Parliament John Greenway passed the documents on to a government minister. The following month, the then Home Secretary David Blunkett referred the case back to the board for a fresh review. Following this, Sleightholme was transferred to an open prison, Askham Grange near York, finally being released in December 2005 after 16 years in prison.

**BELOW:** Yvonne Sleightholme being helped into Leeds Crown Court, to face charges for the murder of Jayne Smith.

# Pam Smart and Billy Flynn

**Pam Smart began a fling with one of the boys at the school where she worked in order to get back at her cheating husband and never expected to fall in love with a 16-year-old boy. When she did, she conspired with her lover to remove the man who stood in the way of their future together. She should have remembered that it is impossible to keep secrets in the classroom.**

**The marriage of Pam Smart and her insurance salesman husband Greg** was already rocky by the time that he came back from a business trip and confessed that he had had a one-night stand while he was away. Pam was furious and determined to level the score with him. She was 21 and attractive, and had always had a certain sexual allure. It was obvious that William Flynn, one of the boys at the school where she worked, had long had a crush on her, so Pam set out to teach the young student a few things he would never have learned in the classroom while taking revenge on her cheating husband.

Pam and Flynn were soon having sex whenever they could and at some point Pam realized that what had started out as a casual thing had become much, much more. Now she constantly craved the attentions of her teenage lover and was deeply infatuated with him. She wanted Flynn so much more than she wanted Greg Smart, but instead of a lengthy divorce, her thoughts turned to getting Smart out of the way a little more speedily.

She confided in Flynn and at first the boy was shocked by her plan, but his older lover was persuasive and soon he had agreed to what looked like a foolproof murder plot. He recruited two of his best friends, Pete Randall and Vance Lattime, to help and another, Raymond Fowler, would go along with them just for the ride. On May 1, 1990, having been married for less than a year, Pam was at a school meeting, which gave her a perfect alibi. Greg Smart was at their home Derry, New

**LEFT:** Pamela Smart on the witness stand during her trial at Rockingham County Superior Court in Exeter, New Hampshire.

**ABOVE:** Vance Lattime giving evidence against Pam Smart in Rockingham County Superior Court in Exeter, New Hampshire.

Hampshire, when the boys entered the house, shot him in the head, and quickly made the scene look like a badly botched burglary. On returning home, Pam discovered the body and—pretending to be devastated—called in the police.

But teenage boys are never very discreet. Randall and Lattime were overheard talking about the killing and another pupil, Cecelia Pierce went to the police. She agreed to co-operate with them and made recorded phone calls in which she encouraged Pam to give details of the murder plot.

Hers was not the only accusation the police heard. Flynn told a friend that he shot Greg Smart because he beat his wife and gossip and rumor spread like wildfire in the schoolyard. The police department received an anonymous phone call informing them that "the school teacher was sleeping with one of the boys and she staged the whole thing." The caller mentioned all three boys involved in the killing by their first names. Flynn, Randall, and Lattime were arrested on June 11, 1990. Flynn was charged with first degree murder, the other two with being accomplices to first degree murder. Pam Smart was arrested at work on August 1, 1990 with the officer, Dan Pelletier telling her, "Well Pam, I've got good news and I've got bad news. The good news is we've solved the murder of your husband. The bad news is you're under arrest."

The trial of Pam Smart and the three boys began on March 5, 1991. With its ingredients of a young attractive woman involved with the murder of her husband after seducing a teenage student, it attracted

**BELOW:** William Flynn appearing at Rockingham Superior Court in Brentwood, New Hampshire in 2008. Flynn, was seeking a sentence reduction.

huge media attention. The jury went out on May 20 and deliberated for 13 hours before finding Pam guilty on three counts; conspiracy to commit murder, accomplice to a murder, and tampering with a witness. She was sentenced to life imprisonment. Flynn and Randall each received 40 years with a parole review in 2018. Lattime was sentenced to 30 years, but released in 2006. Fowler also received a prison sentence, later extended because of a parole violation. He was eventually released in 2005.

# Madeleine Smith

**The 19th century is notorious for its strictly enforced morality, particularly when it concerned the behavior of wealthy young women. The slightest sin could permanently ruin a girl's reputation, bring shame on the family, and wreck her hopes of a good marriage. And for a girl to lose her virginity out of wedlock was the ultimate crime, so for 19-year-old Madeleine Smith the threat of a previous sexual dalliance being revealed to her family and new fiancé was a peril worth killing to prevent.**

**Madeleine was the daughter of a prosperous Scottish architect** and enjoyed all the trappings of her father's wealth; a busy social life in her native Glasgow as well as a large country home. Unfortunately, her carefree lifestyle would come to an abrupt end. It began when friends introduced her to a dashing young Frenchman in the street. Pierre Emile L'Angelier was an apprentice nurseryman staying in Glasgow and immediately caught Madeleine's eye. The young girl was overwhelmed by her new passion and began to meet L'Angelier in secret whenever it could be arranged, and when a meeting was impossible she poured out her feelings in letters, addressing them to "my own darling husband."

Their love was chaste for months, and could later have been explained away as a girlish crush had this continued. But that was to change during an unchaperoned visit to the family house in the country that Madeleine managed to arrange. In secret, L'Angelier followed his wealthy young love, and with her parents absent their desire for each other could be contained no longer. Afterward, she wrote another of her gushing letters to L'Angelier, telling him, "If we did wrong last night it was in the excitement of our love." The couple became unofficially engaged.

In those days when a young woman's conduct was watched carefully, it was inevitable that Madeleine would eventually be found out. Sure enough, her parents soon became aware of their daughter's illicit affair with a mere apprentice. Although Madeleine managed to keep from them the information about the loss of her virginity, they were shocked and instantly ordered an end to the affair. And it seems that Madeleine had become bored of her lover anyway, and certainly didn't waste any time pining for him. Soon after, she was introduced to a wealthy bachelor named William Harper Minnoch. There was an instant attraction between the two of them, and this time Madeleine was given her parents' blessing for what, after all, was a much better match. The only fly in Madeleine's ointment was her former beau.

L'Angelier had kept all of Madeleine's letters, which contained unmistakable references to the fact that she had surrendered her virginity to him. Knowing how devastating these would be if they ever became public knowledge, she wrote to him, begging that the letters be returned so that she could destroy them. The spurned L'Angelier had other ideas however. Instead, he threatened to reveal all to Madeleine's father unless she honored her promise to marry him.

Her response was to hatch a plot that would forever silence the man who had the power to ruin her reputation and with it her future happiness. Not long after, a woman was seen in a shop buying arsenic. She signed for the poison in the name of M. H. Smith. Meanwhile, Madeleine had continued writing to L'Angelier and lulled him with sweet words and protestations of undying love. Soon, she had managed to arrange another meeting, smuggling the young man into the basement of the family's Glasgow home. During the visit she kept up the appearance of a young girl still in love, while serving her blackmailer cocoa laced with arsenic.

Madeleine played her part so well that L'Angelier suspected nothing when he became ill soon after their meeting. As soon as he was able, he returned to Madeleine's basement. And a second cup of cocoa. This one would prove fatal. Within hours, L'Angelier fell gravely ill and in less than a day, he was dead. His doctor, mystified at L'Angelier's symptoms, ordered a postmortem that revealed 87 grains of arsenic still in his patient's stomach. It did not take the police long to discover a bundle of Madeleine's letters at L'Angelier's lodgings, and the tale they told gave investigating officers a prime suspect for the murder. Madeleine was arrested on March 31, 1857. She stood trial soon after.

Her defense told the jury that Madeleine had bought arsenic to use as rat poison and maintained that L'Angelier had often taken arsenic himself for health reasons. It was a flimsy argument and all evidence pointed to her having murdered her former lover. Nevertheless, it was deemed circumstantial, and not enough to convict her. Instead, a verdict of "not proven" was given, which in Scottish courts means that the jury does not believe the accused to be innocent, though the prosecution has failed to make a strong enough case. Fortunately for Madeleine what would have been a key witness—a person who had seen her together with a male companion on the night of the poisoning—was not allowed to testify. They had come forward too late and the trial had already started. Madeleine walked free from the court, but was widely believed to be guilty of murder. Her engagement to William Minnoch came to an abrupt end, and instead she married George Wardle before leaving Scotland—and the scandal—behind for good.

**BELOW:** A contemporary illustration of Madeleine Smith, from around the time of her trial for the murder of her former lover Pierre Emile L'Anglier.

# Susan Smith

However grisly and twisted the murder, most of us can understand how a thwarted love or systematic abuse might lead someone to a killing rage. Susan Smith's crime though, went far beyond that. It is one thing to murder a cheating lover, but to take the lives of your own children is on a level of horror all its own.

The crime of three-year-old Michael and his 14-month-old brother Alex was that they came between their mother and the man she wanted to be with. Recently divorced, struggling to cope, and becoming deeper in debt with every month that passed, 23-year-old Susan Smith was desperate for the security that her relationship with Tom Findlay might bring. He, however, was not ready to step into a ready-made family and wrote to tell her that though he cared deeply for her, he was just not ready for the responsibility. As he would later strenuously point out, at no point did he make any suggestion that Susan should somehow get rid of her children.

Nevertheless, that is exactly what Susan decided she needed to do. Although she might have given them over to the custody of their father, instead she strapped them into the back of her car, took the emergency

**BELOW:** Police mug shots of Susan Smith released by the South Carolina Department of Corrections after her arrest in 1994.

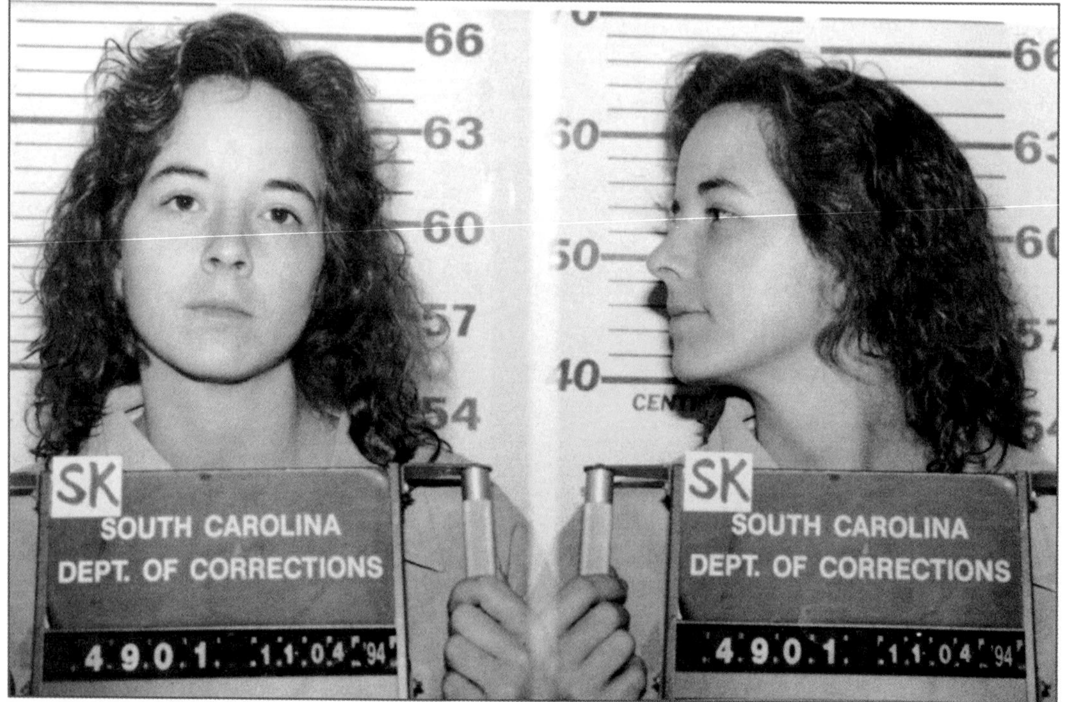

brake off, and let it roll downhill and into a lake where the two boys drowned.

At about 9.15pm on October 25, 1994, the police took a call from a hysterical woman. Smith told them that she had been driving her two children home in Union, South Carolina, when a young black man had forced his way into the car while she was stopped at a red light. At gunpoint, he demanded Smith drive off and then pushed her out of the car a few miles down the road, before driving away with her two boys still strapped into the back seat.

A huge manhunt immediately swept into operation and the eyes of America fastened on the devastated young woman. But the television appeals of Smith and

**ABOVE:** A shrine at John D. Long Lake, South Carolina, featuring toys and pictures of Michael and Alex Smith, who were murdered by their mother Susan.

her estranged husband David produced no results, and the search, too, was a failure. Puzzled by the lack of success, nine days after the boys had gone missing the police again questioned Smith to see if there might be some detail not yet mentioned which might help them. This time she broke down and confessed to her terrible crime. Police divers were sent to search the lake and quickly found her Mazda not far beneath the surface, with her sons dead in the back. Smith was charged with first degree murder.

The trial of Susan Smith began amid a whirl of media attention on July 18, 1995. It was to become one of the most avidly followed and harrowing court cases the United States has ever witnessed. From the start the prosecution were determined that the jury understood the severity of the crime, and the details heard in court were shocking. One diver recalled the moment that he had shone his flashlight at the car and through the murky water had seen "a small hand against the glass." Lawyers defending Smith argued that it was not murder, but a suicide attempt gone awry. Rejected by the man she had hoped might turn her life around, they told the jury that Smith had wanted to take her own life along with her sons'. They also painted a detailed picture of Susan's life up to that point—the alcoholic father who had committed suicide, the sexual abuse she had suffered as a child, and the desolation she carried with her every day.

It was a powerful defense and in her closing speech, Judge Judy Clarke asked the jury to show mercy toward Smith, telling them that she had made the decision "with a confused mind and a heart that has no hope." Nevertheless, the sheer horror of Smith's crime was more powerful. On July 28, 1995, she was found guilty of the murder of her two sons. Her sentence was life, with no possibility of parole until 2025.

# Paul Snider

**To marry a woman who turns heads whenever she walks into a room can be difficult for an insecure man. For Paul Snider, whose wife was Playmate of the Year in *Playboy* magazine, the attention she received was more than enough to turn him mad with jealousy, and when she divorced him and became involved with one of Hollywood's great directors, his envy became a killing rage.**

Dorothy Stratten was plain Dorothy Hoogstratten when Paul Snider walked into the Dairy Queen in Vancouver, Canada, where she worked in 1977. She was stunningly beautiful and he was a man on the up. After seducing her, Snider began taking sexy photos of his lover and eventually managed to get them published in the men's magazine *Playboy*. Dorothy's sex appeal did not go unnoticed, and soon the couple were invited to join in the fun at *Playboy* founder Hugh Hefner's "Playboy Mansion." At first Snider was happy for Dorothy to indulge in sexual frolics with the other guests; it was good for her career—and for his bank balance. But Snider hadn't stopped to consider how attached he had become to Dorothy. As he realized that he had fallen in love with her so his jealousy grew.

The couple married in Las Vegas in June 1979. In August, Dorothy was Playmate of the Month. Dorothy was 20 and Snider, 29. At the time, Snider's new wife told friends that she couldn't imagine being with anyone but Paul. However, Snider was now obsessed with Dorothy's career and was increasingly controlling. He forbade her to drink coffee, because it would stain her teeth, and it is rumored that he also poisoned her pet dog because he was jealous of it. Dorothy couldn't ignore his erratic behavior for long, and the marriage crumbled. After a year if marriage they filed for divorce. Life in 1980 was good for Dorothy—she was Playmate of the Year. Free of the man who thought he had discovered her, she began seeing film director Peter Bogdanovich then moved into his Bel Air home.

Snider had lost both the woman he loved and the key to success and riches. He took a distinctly sinister turn. He hired a private investigator to follow Dorothy.

On the morning of August 14, 1980, Dorothy agreed to meet Snider at the apartment they once shared. She arrived with a large handbag containing $1,000 to pay off her ex-husband. It was around 11pm that the private investigator finally got an answer from the numerous phone calls he made to the apartment. He told one of the women who lodged with Snider that he had been trying the number all day and asked her to check on her landlord. When she did, she found Dorothy lying across Snider's waterbed, dead from a bullet would. She was missing the tip of her left index finger, blown off as she tried to protect her face.

Close by was the body of Snider. He had shot himself. Examination of the scene revealed that Dorothy had been sexually brutalized both before and after she died. She was cremated and buried on August 19, at Westwood Memorial Park.

**BELOW:** Playboy Playmate Dorothy Stratten in May 1980.

# Dr. James Howard Snook

**For three years the wealthy and successful Dr. James Snook met his young lover several times a week in the rooms he rented so that they might have a comfortable place to have sex. But somewhere their relationship went awry. What started out as a purely physical affair ended with Theora Hix laying dead in a patch of weeds, battered with a hammer and her throat slit.**

**Doctor Snook was successful and confident man** to whom life had been kind. He was a professor of Veterinary Medicine at the Ohio State University in Columbus and a respected horse surgeon. He had also won two Olympic gold medals for pistol shooting and enjoyed the love of his devoted wife Helen and their baby daughter. And in June 1926, soon after giving 21-year-old medical student Theora Hix a lift to the university, he also had a fresh and attractive young sexual partner. After spending a day at work, Snook visited Theora in the rooms he rented. The couple would make love in the early evenings then the doctor would return home to his wife. As Snook would later testify, neither he nor Theora were in love, the relationship was purely sexual. For a relationship that was all about sex though, something was amiss. Theora taunted her older lover about his sexual performance and even went so far as to recommend books he might read to improve his technique.

Nevertheless, the relationship continued. On one occasion, after a break-in at her university room, Snook gave Theora a Remington Derringer pistol for protection, and the two began going to the New York Central Rifle Range on the outskirts of Columbus to practise. It was here that two 16-year-old boys discovered her body on June 16, 1929. She had been beaten around the head and her throat was cut. The body was soon identified; Theora's roommates had already reported her missing and when her photograph appeared in the local newspaper, Mrs Margaret Smalley recognized Theora as the young "wife" of a man called Howard Snook who rented the room from her.

When Snook was arrested, police found blood inside his car, on the clothing he wore the night of the murder, on his ball-peen hammer, and on his pocket knife. He had tried to clean everything, but enough traces remained to declare his guilt.

Exactly why Snook's passions were roused to the point where a previously law-abiding man would beat a young woman to death will never be known. The only testimony we have is Snook's, and he had good reason to construct a story that would help the jury see him as a victim of a jealous lover's threats. In fact at his trial, Snook testified that he and Theora had driven to a local country club to make love. Once they arrived, she had told him that she wanted to go "some place where I can scream," and Snook had taken her on to the New York Central shooting range.

Snook then told Theora that he then had to go as he was due to visit his mother. At this point, he said, Theora became angry shouting, "Damn your mother. I don't care about your mother. Damn Mrs Snook. I'm going to kill her and get her out of the way." Snook said she then continued to threaten his family, even saying she would kill his daughter. He went on to testify that she had grabbed open his trousers and began to bite and pull at him. In fear for his safety and for his family's lives, Snook said he grabbed the ball-peen hammer from his kit in the back of the car and hit her with it. Theora then screamed, "Damn you, I will kill you too." According to Snook, she began digging through her purse. Afraid that she was looking for the Derringer pistol, he hit her on the head with the hammer several times until she fell to the ground.

We should approach this tale with caution, for Snook's explanation of Theora's cut throat changed over time. At first he said he did not know how her neck had come to be cut open, but it was pointed out to him that it had been cut so precisely that only someone experienced in anatomy and surgery—such as a veterinarian—could have done it. He then said that he had cut her throat because he did not want to see her suffer from the head wounds.

On August 14, 1929, Snook was found guilty of first degree murder and sentenced to death in the Ohio Penitentiary's electric chair. Before the day of his execution arrived, his story changed again. Snook supposedly confessed to a warden that the murder had been premeditated. After several attempts to obtain a new trial or change the verdict to manslaughter or second degree murder, Snook was executed on February 28, 1930.

# Ruth Snyder

**Ruth Snyder led a double life: To her husband she was a doting wife and mother, and to her lover she was a domineering sexual mistress. But dissatisfaction, coupled with a good helping of greed, would lead her and her lover to try and make her double life a single life.**

**At the age of 20,** in 1895, Ruth Sorensen was an attractive and charming young operator at a New York City telephone exchange where one bungled call changed her life and set in motion a train of events that would eventually lead to murder. The call was between a man named Albert Schneider, who was the art editor of a magazine called *Motor Boat*, and his client. Ruth was so sincere and appealing in her apology for having messed it up that Schneider offered her a job as a

**RIGHT:** A photograph of Ruth Snyder taken in 1927, the year that she murdered her husband.

secretary on the magazine. Before a year had passed they were married, and afterward changed their names to Snyder to avert some of the anti-German feeling that was then common.

Seemingly a perfect suburban couple, their home on Long Island soon welcomed the arrival of a baby, and Ruth sank all her energies into being as good a mother and wife she could be. And for a while she enjoyed it. Her husband, however, was not so happy. He was domineering, prone to outbursts of temper, and found domestic life boring. The two began to lead separate lives, neither questioning the other about where they were or with whom.

Young, attractive, and all but deserted by her husband, Ruth invited her mother to move into the house, and with a permanent babysitter on call, began a series of affairs, the most serious of which was with corset salesman Henry Judd Gray. Theirs was an unusual sexual relationship, with Ruth now taking on the dominant role and Gray enjoying subservience. The two would later be labelled by the press "Granite Woman and Putty Man."

The only thing that stood in the way of Ruth's total freedom was her husband and the money he brought in to support her and the baby. However, Ruth soon came up with a plan to solve both problems.

Back in her role as the concerned wife, Ruth persuaded her husband to purchase a life insurance policy and with the assistance of an agent (who was subsequently imprisoned for forgery) she signed an additional $48,000 policy that paid extra if an unexpected act of violence killed the victim. She then made a series of botched attempts to kill Snyder, all of which he survived.

But on March 20, 1927, with the help of Gray, Ruth finally succeeded. When Snyder was safely asleep in bed, the couple sneaked into his room, smashed his head, garroted him, and stuffed his nose full of chloroform-soaked rags. They then made a hasty attempt to make it look like the Snyders had been victims of a burglary gone wrong. Ruth got Gray to tie up her ankles and wrists, but managed to "break free" to raise the alarm while her lover fled the scene.

It didn't take detectives long to unpick the lies. Ruth was betrayed by many small clues. The police wondered why when she had undone her wrists she had not untied her ankles as well. And whoever had attacked Albert had gone out of their way to kill him, which didn't fit into the pattern of a burglary. Finally, property that Ruth said had been stolen started turning up in odd places around the house. Then detectives came across a letter signed "J.G." Snyder tried to convince them the initials were those of a young woman that her husband had once dated, but a flip through Ruth's address book revealed the names of a total of 28 men. One was Judd Gray.

Eventually though it was Ruth who declared her guilt. When the police took her in for questioning and told her that they already had Gray in custody and that he had confessed everything. She crumbled and the whole story spilled out. In fact, it was a standard police trick. At that time they hadn't even caught up with Gray though he was arrested at a hotel in Syracuse later that night.

Both Judd Gray and Ruth Snyder were charged with murder, and the case went to trial on April 18, 1927. Each tried to blame the other for the murder, but the jury found both guilty and they were sentenced to death. They were executed on January 12, 1928. Ruth Snyder would later achieve a degree of grim fame after a reporter took a picture of her dying in the electric chair with a miniature camera strapped to his ankle.

# George Stoner

**A difference in age is no barrier to love, as Alma Rattenbury found out when she advertised for a boy to help around the home she shared with her husband. She would also find out that the young are just as prone as their elders to jealousy.**

**No stranger to scandal**, 39-year-old Alma Rattenbury and her 67-year-old husband Francis had been forced to flee their home in Canada by wagging tongues. He had been married when he began his affair with Alma and, soon after, asked his wife for a divorce. When she refused, he simply moved his mistress into the family home until eventually his wife agreed to part. Inevitably, the details of this scheme to force an innocent woman into divorce became public knowledge and the criticism of Alma and Rattenbury was so great that they crossed the Atlantic to seek a quiet life in Bournemouth, England.

Unfortunately, a quiet life was not what they found. The couple bought a large house and moved in with Alma's thirteen-year-old son Christopher from an earlier marriage, and the couple's six-year-old son John. They soon found that a little extra help would be needed to run the house, and Alma placed a notice in the Bournemouth Echo advertising a position for a, "Daily willing lad, 14–18, for house-work; scout-trained preferred. Apply between 11–12, 8–9 at 5 Manor Road, Bournemouth."

The willing lad who answered was the handsome but shy George Stoner. In fact, Alma found him very willing indeed: as well as his household chores, Stoner soon found very pleasant extra duties in Alma's bed. He quickly became so indispensable that his part-time position was changed to full time and he was given a

**BELOW:** A long queue of people forming outside the Old Bailey court for the trial of Alma Rattenbury and George Stoner, jointly charged with the murder of Francis Rattenbury.

**ABOVE:** Petitioners trying to persuade railway staff at Waterloo Station, London to add their names to the petition appealing to the Home Secretary to grant a reprieve George Stoner.

room in the house. Francis Rattenbury was fully aware of his wife's infidelity, but now slipping into old age he had become impotent and turned a blind eye, much preferring to share his evenings with a bottle of whiskey and let his wife have her fun.

For a while the unorthodox situation appeared to work well, but as time progressed Stoner fell ever more deeply in love with his sophisticated older mistress, and grew jealous of her elderly husband. Greedy for every moment with her, he became upset when she spent time with Rattenbury and flew into a rage when the husband and wife went away for a weekend together. Convinced that Rattenbury was finally trying to win his wife back, when they returned and Alma told him that they would also be away the following weekend, Stoner's jealousy finally got the better of him.

On the afternoon of March 24, 1935, Stoner borrowed a wooden mallet from his grandparents, telling them that he needed it to erect a screen in the garden. Later that evening, Francis Rattenbury was found seriously injured. He had been bludgeoned on the head from behind. Three days later he died from his injuries and what had previously been an assault case became a murder.

The police immediately questioned Alma, who appeared to be the worse for wear through drink or drugs. Perhaps she originally intended to take the blame, for over and over she kept repeating that she had "done him in." Nevertheless, soon after, Stoner confessed to another servant, Irene Riggs, that it was he who had dealt the killer blow that did for Rattenbury. She went to the police. Alma and Stoner were both arrested and charged with murder.

The lovers were tried together at the Old Bailey on May 27, 1935. Both pleaded not guilty with a now sober Alma passionately claiming she had nothing to do with her husband's death. Stoner was quiet in court, but his defense counsel suggested that though he had hit Rattenbury in a jealous rage, he had not intended to kill. The jury did not agree. Stoner was found guilty and sentenced to death. Alma was acquitted much to the consternation of the crowd waiting outside. In their eyes, a three-times married older woman had led an innocent young lad to kill.

A few days later, Alma took the train from Waterloo to Christchurch, not far from her Bournemouth home. She sat down on the banks of a river and wrote a handful of farewell notes. Then she plunged a knife several times into her heart, and died almost immediately. It is clear from the notes and from the words of a song she wrote while awaiting trial—subsequently published as *Mrs Rattenbury's Prison Song*—that she was deeply in love with Stoner, and took her own life out of grief for her loss and shame at what had happened. Stoner, when informed of her death, broke down and wept.

Alma was buried a few yards from her late husband, and during the ceremony signatures were collected for an appeal for mercy for George Stoner. Over the next few weeks an astonishing 320,000 people, including the local mayor and MP, signed the petition. It was handed to the Home Secretary, who commuted Stoner's sentence to penal servitude for life. A model prisoner, he was released seven years later in 1942. He died in Christchurch Hospital in 2000 aged 83 on the 65th anniversary of Francis's murder.

# John Sweeney

**Sweeney's crime of passion was a straightforward fit of selfish anger directed at a talented young actress who he had tried to love him despite the fact that he beat her. When she finished the relationship and refused to take him back, his rage was fatal.**

**Dominique Dunne was just 21 and a promising actress** with a bright future when she met 25-year-old chef John Sweeney at a Hollywood party in 1981. She had been born locally, in Santa Monica, California, but after her parents divorced had moved to New York City, before returning to Los Angeles to try for a Hollywood acting career. Within two weeks she had won her first job and the following year would land her first major movie role as Dana Freeling in the 1982 horror classic *Poltergeist*.

But while Dominique's career was doing well, her relationship was causing problems. Sweeney was the eldest son of a troubled family and had emotional difficulties. At first these manifested themselves in jealousy and attempts to control Dominique. He was suspicious of everyone she met, dominating, and would often show up at film sets, rehearsals, and Dominique's acting classes to watch over her.

However, on August 27, 1982, the couple had their first major quarrel, and Dominique got her first taste of the violence that the man she loved was capable of. Sweeney grabbed her by her hair and slammed her head on the floor so roughly that he pulled out handfuls of her hair.

A month later they had another argument and this time Sweeney threw Dominique to the floor and began to choke her. Luckily a friend was present and intervened. The next day Dominique went to work on an episode of *Hill Street Blues*. Ironically her part was that of an abuse victim. Not all of her bruises were applied by the make-up artist's brush.

By now, the actress had had enough. She finished the relationship with Sweeney and changed the locks on the doors of the house they once shared. Sweeney wasn't prepared to let his girlfriend go without a fight though. On October 30, 1982, Dominique was at the house rehearsing a scene for a television series with a fellow actor, David Parker, when her ex-boyfriend arrived. There was a fierce argument that ended with Sweeney strangling the young star, putting her in a coma. She died in hospital on November 4, aged just 22. Dominique had been working on a new TV series when she was attacked. On the credits of the second episode were the words "In loving memory of Dominique Dunne, her family and friends miss her."

**BELOW:** Restaurant chef John Sweeney sitting in a courtroom in Beverly Hills, California, during his trial for the murder of actress Dominique Dunne.

John Thomas Sweeney was charged with murder and the case came to trial in August 1983 in Santa Monica. Incredibly, Sweeney's lawyer, Michael Adelson, argued that Dominique was to blame for her own death, saying that she had provoked the violent struggle because she refused to be reconciled with Sweeney. On the witness stand Sweeney himself said he "just exploded and lunged toward her" and added that he said he had no memory of what happened next. Adelson argued it was not a real crime, but an act of despair.

The police evidence, however, told a different story. According to the officers who arrested him Sweeney seemed to be quite calm and collected—and much more interested in his own fate than in Dominique's—when they arrived at the scene. They told how, during his first interrogation, Sweeney had showed no remorse for what he had done. Medical evidence also confirmed that the duration of the strangulation was at least three minutes. If it had been an explosion of anger, there was enough time for

**RIGHT:** John Sweeney being escorted from the courthouse during his murder trial.

Sweeney to take control of himself. If he had stopped a few seconds earlier it may have saved Dominique's life.

Sweeney was convicted of the voluntary manslaughter of Dominique Dunne and only served two and a half years of a six and a half year prison sentence. Members of the jury later said they would have convicted Sweeney of murder had they been aware of his earlier history of violence against women.

Although the time he served did not seem to reflect the magnitude of his horrific crime, on his release Dominique's mother did not let him slip quietly back into Hollywood life. When Sweeney got another job as chef at a Los Angeles restaurant, Ellen Griffin founded a grievance support group called "Justice for Victims of Homicide." On the nights that John Sweeney worked, she and other group members would hand out slips of paper to the restaurant's customers that read, "The hands that will prepare your meal tonight also murdered Dominique Dunne." John Sweeney soon lost his job and was forced to move to the Pacific Northwest where he changed his name to John Maura.

# John Tanner

**The disappearance of Rachel McLean hit the headlines of the British press early in 1991, and for over a fortnight her killer fooled both the public and the police. Clever and calm, John Tanner hid his crime well and went on to make appeals for information about her whereabouts.**

**Bright and young, with a promising future ahead of her,** Rachel McLean was studying English Literature at St. Hilda's in Oxford and was just 19 years old when her 22-year-old boyfriend, John Tanner, strangled her to death. He was a British-born New Zealander, studying in Nottingham. As their relationship was deteriorating Rachel complained that Tanner was controlling and possessive. She no longer wanted to see him and started dating other students. Nevertheless, when he said that he wished to visit her, she agreed.

On the evening of April 13, 1991, Rachel waited at Oxford station for Tanner to arrive and when his train was delayed she returned to her home. He followed on by taxi, arriving at around 7.30pm. Various people later reported seeing them together around Oxford the next day, but that would be the last time that Rachel was seen alive. That night, in a fit of jealous rage, Tanner killed his ex-girlfriend.

It took him several hours to find a suitable hiding spot for her body, but when he did it was a good one. There was a closet beneath the stairs and at the back, behind piles of household junk, Tanner discovered an eight inch gap that led to a space beneath the floorboards. He dragged his girlfriend's body into it and then crawled beneath the hallway pulling Rachel to a spot under her own bedroom. Then he covered the body with old carpet and made everything look just as he found it. Tanner then left the house and made his way back to Nottingham, pausing to pen Rachel a brief love letter in which he mentioned how lucky she was that the long-haired man they had met at Oxford station had offered her a lift home.

By April 19, Rachel's friends had begun to realize that something was amiss. She had been due at a meeting with her tutor and to sit an exam in the afternoon, but had missed both. One called her parents to find out if she was okay and was told that they hadn't seen her either and that she had been in Oxford the previous weekend. By April 22, Rachel's disappearance was headline news and a massive search for her was underway. Naturally, her boyfriend wanted to help all he could and spoke movingly of how he had kissed her goodbye at the station a few days earlier. He also mentioned the fictitious long-haired man again, saying that he had joined them for coffee, and that Rachel had seemed to know him.

Police searched Rachel's house and nearby scrubland, while divers dragged the River Cherwell and Rachel's parents made a nationwide appeal at a press conference on April 24th. Still there was no sign on her. A day later a photo-fit image of the man Tanner claimed to have met at the station was released, and by April 28th police had widened the search to include the sewers around her home.

On the 29th, Tanner agreed to appear in a television reconstruction and with a female police officer playing the part of Rachel, he was filmed at Oxford station, reliving the final coffee with his girlfriend and their final kiss. As the last person to see her alive, he was already under suspicion, but said, "I did not kill her. I don't know what happened to her. In my heart of hearts I know she is still alive."

However, by agreeing to take part in the reconstruction he helped seal his own fate. Two people came forward after seeing it. Both remembered Tanner at the station, but neither saw Rachel or a long-haired man. It became even more obvious that Tanner's tale was a lie when police finally discovered her body in the cavity beneath her floorboards. He was immediately arrested at a Nottingham pub, and taken into custody where he refused to answer police questions.

The evidence against him was continuing to mount up though, and Tanner finally broke down and confessed. On May 4, 1991, he was formally charged with the murder of Rachel McLean before magistrates. He was tried for his crime in early December, convicted, and sentenced to life imprisonment. Released 12 years later in 2003, John Tanner immediately returned to his home town of Wanganui, New Zealand.

**ABOVE:** John Tanner, shown during a press conference making an appeal for information about the whereabouts of Rachel McLean.

# Marie Tarnowska

**The crime of Russian Countess Marie Tarnowska was to treat the men who adored her as puppets in her deadly games of intrigue and betrayal. Her cold appetites knew no limits and those who loved her were either ruined or died. Not by her hand, but always she was behind the scenes, pulling the strings.**

**Born in 1879**, Marie was descended from one of the aristocratic houses of Ireland and the daughter of a man who had been made Count Nicholas O'Rke by the Tsar when he emigrated to Russia. At 17 years old, and outstandingly beautiful, she married the wealthy Count Tarnowska. Together they ruled over the glittering aristocratic society of Kiev and their union was blessed with three children. But as time passed, Marie grew bored of married life and developed a taste for exercising the power she had as a countess and as a woman of boundless sexual allure.

One of her early lovers, Alexis Borzlevski, invited her to shoot him through the hand to demonstrate his devotion to her. The incident didn't go unnoticed, and the count then challenged Borzlevski to a duel. Marie's lover was shot dead. Another of her bedmates, Vladimir Stahl, killed himself rather than confront the count at a dueling ground. Yet another was shot dead by the count at a dinner party when Marie deliberately kissed him to provoke her husband. The powerful count was acquitted of the murder on the grounds of his wife's provocation.

Not surprisingly, perhaps, after this spate of incidents the marriage ended, but not before Marie had woven her lethal spell over the lawyer dealing with her divorce. After she toyed with his emotions, Maximillian Prilukoff was prepared to give up his wife and family, career, and fortune to have her. He botched a suicide attempt when she rejected him and the proceeded to follow her around wherever she went, a 19th-century stalker.

Free of her husband's jealousy, Marie traveled to Venice, Italy, and her army of lovers increased. One was young and handsome Nicolas Naumoff, who deserted his wife and children to devote himself to her. She enjoyed torturing him during sex sessions, burning his body with cigarettes. Yet another of her victims was Count Pavel Kamarovsky who insisted that she marry him. She agreed, but only after he insured his life for her benefit. He was dead within a month; shot by

**RIGHT:** Countess Tarnowska, who was found guilty of conspiring to kill her lover Count Kamarovski after persuading him to take out a life insurance policy which would pay her if he died.

**BELOW:** Count Kamarowski, who was to become the victim of his wife's heartless scheming.

Naumoff. Marie had led her masochistic lover to believe that Kamarovksy had insulted his virility and honor in various letters.

The fact that Kamarovksy had died so soon after insuring his life inevitably raised suspicion, and the Italian police arrested Marie, Naumoff, and Prilukoff (who had helped draft the fatal letters) in 1907. Their trial began on May 14, 1910, by which time the scandal of the killer countess had sparked outrage at every level of society. A lynch mob waited for her arrival at the

courthouse, and the gondola that brought Marie and her two lovers to the court was greeted by mobs shaking their fists and screaming. When she tried to step onto shore a group of women dragged Marie to the edge of the canal, shouting, "Drown her! Drown her!"

**ABOVE:** Nicholas Naumoff, who was so infatuated with Marie Tarnowska that he deserted his wife and children to be with her.

**RIGHT:** Countess Tarnowska arriving at court in Venice under a police escort for her own safety.

Guards from inside the courthouse were forced to rescue the accused!

At the hearing, Prilukoff and Naumoff blamed their actions on their infatuation with the countess, while Marie Tarnowska threw herself on the mercy of the court. She wept copiously and promised to devote the rest of her life to a convent and good works if the jury would just be lenient. The performance saved her life. Pronouncing the verdict, a spokesman for the jury said, "We reject the theory that she was mad. But we find that her mental faculties were partially destroyed." Marie was sentenced to eight years in prison; Prilukoff to 10 years in solitary confinement; Naumoff to three years in prison because he was "suffering from a partial mental collapse." One newspaper reported of Marie, "She is not yet thirty but at least six men have ruined themselves for her; two of these met tragic deaths and four of them deserted wives and children."

For a time, the prison chaplain and jail keepers in Venice treated their prisoner kindly, smuggling in

cigarettes and good food for the aristocratic prisoner. But after the chaplain found an "extremely improper" novel in her cell she was transferred to a much harsher prison in Rome to serve the remainder of her sentence. Still she used her sexual power over men, and her besotted lawyers were able to have her sentence reduced: Marie was released after five years. She later committed suicide, but before she took her own life made an announcement that became legendary, saying "I am the most unfortunate woman in the world. I am a martyr to my own beauty. For any man to behold me is for him to love me. The whole pathway of my life is strewn with the bodies of those who have loved me most."

# Michael Telling

**Although there can be never be a good excuse for killing another human being, it is difficult not to feel a pang of sympathy for Michael Telling. Already of a fragile state of mind before he married for the second time, his vicious wife did everything in her power to send him over the edge. And when he inevitably snapped, she reaped the harvest of her bitter tongue.**

**All of Michael Telling's family wealth couldn't buy him a happy childhood.** While he may have had everything he wanted in terms of material things, his violent alcoholic father and a cold, unloving mother left him emotionally scarred by the time he reached maturity. A failed marriage did nothing to help, but after he met Monika Zumsteg while on holiday in America and again fell in love his inner turmoil would reach boiling point.

He could not have picked a worse match than his second wife. Almost as soon as the wedding was over, Monika turned on her husband. Her days and nights were spent languishing around the couple's British country home in West Wycombe, Buckinghamshire, drunk and high on drugs, and for entertainment she taunted her husband. She told him that he was sexually inadequate, that she had only married him for his money, and that she had taken lovers both male and female: anything she could think of that might wound the man she had married.

For a brief period the couple seemed to realize just how destructive their problems were. Monika joined Alcoholics Anonymous, and Telling admitted himself to a psychiatric hospital, but it was to no avail. Back at home the pattern of their relationship quickly reasserted itself, and Telling was finally pushed to breaking point by the woman he both adored and detested. On March 29, 1983, as Monika sneered at him yet again, he grabbed a rifle and shot her. Telling left the body where it lay for two days before dragging it into a bedroom and then spent the next few days talking to his wife's corpse. Finally, some semblance of sanity returned and he was forced to deal with the situation. Friends were told that Monika had run off, and Telling made a long distance drive to the South West of England to dump the body after first having removed Monika's head in an attempt to stop the body being identified. Unfortunately for him, the expensive clothes that she was still wearing gave the police the vital clue they needed when the body was discovered and when they searched Telling's home Monika's decomposing head was found in the garage. "I just snapped" was all he could say.

At his trial the prosecution attempted to portray the killing as a cold-blooded, premeditated murder. They presented Telling's careful covering of his tracks as evidence that he was brutal, but sane. The case of his defense counsel, however, was stronger. Backed up by psychiatrists' reports and the testimonies of his friends and family, they showed that Telling was seriously disturbed. Even his mother took the stand to tell of her son's troubled childhood and suicide attempts and as the court heard of the verbal abuse that he had suffered from his wife, Telling gained some small measure of sympathy. When the time came to give their verdict, the jury acquitted Telling of murder but found him guilty of manslaughter on the grounds of diminished responsibility. He was sentenced to life imprisonment.

# Harry Kendall Thaw

**An obsessive, violent man of unrestrained appetites, Harry Kendall Thaw may have married the woman that he had relentlessly pursued, but he never forgave or forgot his former rival for her affections; the man who stole from her what he had wanted for himself—her virginity.**

**Thaw was the son of a wealthy Pittsburgh coal and railroad baron.** While his mother later claimed that her son had been trouble from the day he was born, Thaw's father secured him places at private schools, the University of Pittsburgh, and, later, Harvard University. Nevertheless, Thaw squandered the advantages that came with the best education that money could buy. He preferred a wild life of gambling and chasing women and was eventually dismissed from university after chasing a taxi driver with a loaded gun.

Moving to New York City, Thaw began taking drugs and hanging out with chorus girls in Broadway shows. He also became friendly with the famous architect Stanford White with whom he shared a passion for showgirls. The friendship was short-lived though; it soured when Thaw discovered White had made sarcastic remarks about him and his ability to impress women. Thaw's hatred for the architect deepened when White showed an interest in Evelyn Nesbitt, a chorus girl from the show Florodora who had also caught Thaw's eye.

Although White warned the showgirl about his former friend, Thaw continued to pursue Evelyn, presenting himself as a considerate suitor. During an illness, Evelyn was hospitalized, and Thaw visited her regularly, also taking the opportunity to ingratiate himself with her mother. Meanwhile, White's interest in her waned, leaving the way clear for Thaw to woo Evelyn (and her mother) with promises of a luxury lifestyle. Eventually, the strategy paid off and Evelyn agreed to marry him. But it was a tainted victory for Thaw. When Evelyn accepted the proposal she also confessed that her virginity had been lost to Thaw's rival, Stanford White.

Thaw's reaction was extreme. He took Evelyn to an isolated castle in Germany, raped her, and beat her mercilessly. Astonishingly, the marriage still went ahead—possibly because by now Evelyn was too scared of her fiancé to break the engagement off. The newlyweds settled in Pittsburgh with Thaw's mother.

On June, 25, 1906, they made a visit to New York City. That evening they went to Café Martin to dine. Thaw immediately spotted Stanford White and soon learned that his wife's former lover was to attend the premiere of stage show *Mam'zelle Champagne*, a show the Thaws were also planning to see that night.

Following dinner, a seething Thaw took Evelyn back to their hotel and disappeared, returning just in time to pick her up and head to the show. Curiously, he wore a large black overcoat though it was a hot evening. At the rooftop theater of Madison Square Garden, the hat check girl tried to relieve Thaw of his heavy coat but he refused to take it off. The couple were shown to their table where Thaw appeared distracted. He could not sit still but wandered through the crowd during the show, approaching White's table several times only to back away again. Then, during the show's finale song, *I Could Love A Million Girls*, Thaw walked up to Stanford White and fired three shots at close range into his face, killing him instantly.

At first, the crowd first thought the shooting was part of the show, but as realization dawned that Stanford

**LEFT:** Evelyn Thaw, whose husband's excessive jealousy led him to murder her former lover.

White was actually dead, Thaw—holding the gun aloft—walked through the crowd and met Evelyn at the elevator. When she asked what he'd done, he replied that he had "probably saved your life."

Thaw stood trial for murder twice. At the first, from January to April 1907, the jury could not reach an agreement. At the second in January 1908, Thaw pleaded insanity. In an effort to protect her son, Thaw's mother set out to corrupt the trial. She offered Evelyn a million dollars plus a quick divorce to testify that White had abused her, and Thaw had simply been trying to protect his wife from an evil man. Evelyn did just as she was asked, perjuring herself in court with the skill of a professional actress.

Thaw was found not guilty by reason of insanity and thus escaped the death penalty, though he was incarcerated at the Mattawan State Hospital for the Criminally Insane in Fishkill, New York. Here, he enjoyed almost total freedom and in 1913 Thaw took the opportunity to escape, walking out of the asylum to a waiting car that drove him over the border to Canada. He was quickly extradited back to the United States and two years later a jury judged him sane. Thaw was released after serving just seven years in a comfortable institution. Nevertheless, he soon tangled with the law again. In 1916, he was accused of sexually assaulting and horsewhipping a teenage boy. Again declared insane, Thaw was sent to another asylum where he spent seven years before regaining his freedom once more in 1924.

Thaw died of a heart attack at the age of 76 in Miami, Florida, in February 1947. He left $10,000—less than one per cent of his wealth—to his former wife for whom he had once killed. Having trusted the Thaw family, Evelyn never did receive the million dollars she had been promised for her part in helping her violent husband evade justice.

# Charles-Louis Theobald, Duc de Choiseul-Praslin

The scenario of a man growing weary of a wife and taking a younger lover is a familiar one. But while such stories usually involve heartbreak and emotional anguish, few end as tragically as that of the Duc de Choiseul-Praslin, Charles-Louis Theobald.

**ABOVE:** The Luxembourg Palace in Paris, where Charles-Louis Theobald committed suicide while awaiting trial for the murder of his wife.

**The aristocratic Duc de Choiseul-Praslin,** had married his wife Fanny when she was a dazzling young beauty of just 19. But as the years passed and Fanny gave birth to their 10 children one after another, she put on weight and her famous looks deserted her. Perhaps if her husband had loved her as he should, she would have entered a cheerful old age delighting in her family and not caring about her fading beauty, but the duke could not be content with his aging wife. He tormented her with a series of barely secret affairs. The latest in a line of young women to tumble into his bed was the family governess, and this time the duke was more in love than ever. Yearning to be free of the miserable Fanny, his thoughts turned not to divorce, but to murder.

On August 17, 1847, the Choiseul-Praslin family spent the night at their house in Paris. At 5am, servants heard screams from Fanny's room and rushed to her aid, believing burglars had broken in. They knocked at the locked door in vain. Now all was quiet. The servants ran to the garden in a bid to catch the intruder. When they returned, empty handed, Fanny's bedroom door had been opened. Inside was the duchess, dripping with blood and propped up on the bed. Her throat had been cut and her face beaten to a pulp with a blunt object.

Suspicion immediately settled on the duke, who had been nowhere to be seen during the commotion. Police searched the house and soon unearthed the blood-stained handle of a dagger, a blood-stained bathrobe that someone had tried to wash, and a leather sheath. Also discovered were pitiful letters from the duchess to her husband begging him to end his affair with Henrietta and listing his previous lovers. A loaded pistol was found by the duke's bedside. The evidence suggested that Choiseul-Praslin had first intended to shoot his wife but realizing this would be heard, attempted a silent death by cutting her throat instead. However, the incompetent killer failed to sever her windpipe with his first slash allowing Fanny to raise the alarm by screaming.

The duke's guilt was further proclaimed by blood stains found in his bedroom wash basin and bite marks on his leg that his wife had given him during her struggles. Staff also told police of the violent arguments between the couple and how, during one, she had threatened to leave her husband.

Pathetically, the duke protested that he had tried to defend his wife from the intruders, but his flimsy story fooled no one. After being held under house arrest, he was transferred to the Luxembourg Palace in Paris pending trial by the Court of Peers. However, on August 18, 1847, while in custody, he took advantage of a guard's absence to poison himself with arsenic. Even on his deathbed, the Duc de Choiseul-Praslin denied all accusations.

# Norman Thorne

**A plain woman, Elsie Emily Cameron was not used to receiving attention from men, so when Norman Thorne made advances toward her she quickly gave him her heart and her body. And when he decided that he didn't want to marry her after all, she was so distressed that she felt the only way to keep him was to lie.**

**Elsie Cameron and Norman Thorne met in 1920** while she was working as a typist in London and he was an electrical engineer. At only 18, he was nine years her junior, but he didn't seem to be put off by the difference in their ages and nor did he seem concerned about Elsie's spectacles or the fact that she wasn't a great beauty. Flattered by his attentions, Elsie fell in love. Thorne had ambitions beyond being an engineer and

**RIGHT:** Chicken farmer Norman Thorne standing amongst his birds at Crowborough, Sussex, on the exact spot where the remains of his missing fiancée Elsie Cameron were later found buried.

wanted to run his own business. Accordingly, he bought a small piece of land at Blackness, Crowborough, Sussex, and set up Wesley Poultry Farm, working hard to make it a success between rushed visits to Elsie. When he converted a farm shed into living accommodation, Elsie began traveling down to Sussex to see him and during the Christmas of 1922, Thorne proposed and was accepted.

Elsie's happiness wasn't to last though. Soon after they became engaged, Thorne's business began to fail and pleading financial difficulties he refused to set a wedding date. The situation was further complicated when he met a woman called Bessie and decided that

**ABOVE:** Norman Thorne boarding a train at Crowborough Station in Sussex, on his way to Brixton, London, for the enquiry into the murder of his fiancée, Elsie Cameron.

he preferred his new lover to his fiancée. In October 1923, Elsie traveled down to Crowborough and, as usual, stayed with neighbors. She spent a week with Thorne but her intuition told her that his feelings had changed. When she returned home to London, she wrote a letter telling her fiancé that she was pregnant in a bid to hurry the wedding. Thorne's reply was not what she expected. Cornered, he confessed that he tired of her and told her about Bessie.

Distraught, Elsie rushed to Thorne's farm and arrived unannounced on the morning of November 30, 1923. To calm her, Thorne relented and said that he would marry her and she returned to London hoping that the future she had so longed for was still just around the corner. The following week, Thorne's father visited the farm that week to discuss his son's finances and offer some advice. He warned Thorne to be cautious over Elsie's claims of being pregnant and told him to write to her and discover the truth. When she received the letter, Elsie became even more desperate than before and on Friday December 5, 1923, she again caught the train to Crowborough station from where she walked to Thorne's farm.

Five days later Elsie's father sent a telegram to Thorne asking after his daughter. Thorne replied that he had not seen her. The next day Mr Cameron informed the police of his daughter's disappearance. They found that Elsie had been seen by two flower-growers while walking toward the farm at about 5.15 pm on the last day that anyone had seen her. Thorne, however, remained adamant that Elsie had not been to the farm. By the beginning of January there was still no sign of her, and police began questioning Thorne's neighbors, one of whom said she had seen Elsie entering the farm on the day she had vanished. Sussex police requested assistance from Scotland Yard and officers decided there was enough evidence to arrest Thorne and search the farm. Elsie's watch, bracelet, and jewelry were found in a tin and the attaché case she had been carrying was later found buried near outbuildings.

Thorne denied murdering his unwanted fiancée, telling police interrogators that he and Elsie had argued over his relationship with Bessie. He had stormed off and later returned to find that Elsie had hanged herself from a beam with his washing line. Fearing that no one would believe his story, Thorne said he cut her down, chopped off her legs and head, and buried the parts under his chicken run. However, a postmortem showed no signs of rope marks and Thorne was charged with murder.

The case came before Lewes Assizes on March 4, 1925. Thorne's defence argued that the postmortem report was flawed, telling the jury that creases on Elsie's neck may have been made by a rope. The police countered this by testifying that there was no sign of a rope having been suspended from any of the farmhouse beams. Twelve days later the jury returned a guilty verdict. Thorne was hanged on April 22, 1925, the day that would have been Elsie's 27th birthday.

# Jean-Pierre Vaquier

**When British inn owner Mabel Jones took a vacation in Biarritz, France, in 1924, she wasn't the first married woman be carried away by the holiday atmosphere and the suave charm of French men. But what was for her a simple vacation romance turned into a dangerously obsessive love for the man she left behind.**

**Leaving her husband Alfred to run the Blue Anchor Inn in Byfleet, Surrey,** Mabel Jones headed for the south of France and a well-deserved break. She booked into the Hotel Victoria and soon fell in with a dapper, bearded Frenchman called Jean-Pierre Vaquier who was working there. He was a skilled technician and delighted guests at the hotel by arranging the transmission of music concerts into the hotel's salon. The debonair Frenchman was also soon delighting Mabel in different ways. The couple had a brief, but very passionate liaison.

All too soon it was time for Mabel to return home, and she bid her lover a fond farewell, thinking that would be the last of the matter. She was mistaken though. Back in England, Mabel received a telegram from Vaquier asking when it would be convenient for him to call on her. She ignored it and was startled when after she had been home a month Vaquier arrived at the

inn. While she had finished the affair with no regrets and just a few happy memories, Vaquier's love had blossomed into a driving obsession and now he wished to claim her for his own. Mabel was forced to have furtive meetings during which she tried to make it plain to the Frenchman that his attentions were unwanted, all the while looking over her shoulder to

**ABOVE:** Mabel Jones, whose vacation affair would eventually lead to the death of her husband.

make sure her husband didn't notice Vaquier ardently attempting to woo her. Feeling guilty for the lengths he had gone to out of love for her, she didn't charge him for his stay, and it was explained to Alfred Jones that Vaquier was waiting for money to arrive to pay for his "business trip."

Vaquier's love was not to be so easily turned aside and he took it into his head that if Alfred was to be taken out of the picture, Mabel would return to his embraces once more. On March 1, 1924, Vaquier went to London and bought strychnine, signing the poison register "J. Wanker." Now familiar with Alfred Jones drinking habits and noticing the fact that he habitually took indigestion salts as a hangover cure in the morning, Vaquier spiked Alfred's bottle of medicine. On the morning of March 29th, he watched as Jones swigged from the bottle and then helped carry him to his bedroom when he became ill. Alfred Jones died in agony some hours later.

The sudden death prompted a postmortem during which Alfred's body was found to contain strychnine. Both Vaquier and Mabel were questioned and a photograph of the Frenchman was published in various newspapers. The chemist who had supplied Vaquier with the poison recognized his face, and the Frenchman was arrested at a hotel in Woking, Surrey, then charged with murder. Although he maintained his innocence throughout the trial at Guildford Assizes in July 1924, Jean-Pierre Vaquier was found guilty and hanged at Wandsworth Prison, London, on August 12, 1924.

**ABOVE:** Jean Pierre Vaquier, who in 1924 poisoned Alfred Jones, proprietor of the Blue Anchor Inn in Byfleet, Surrey.

# Picture Credits

**Getty Images**
4, 7 David McNew
8, 9, 10 Topical Press Agency
11, 12, 13 Keystone/Hulton Archive
15, 16, 17 Edward Gooch
20 FPG/Hulton Archive
24 Yvonne Hemsey
25, 26 Topical Press Agency/Hulton Archive
27 E. Dean/Topical Press Agency/Hulton Archive
28 General Photographic Agency/Hulton Archive
30, 31 Leon Neal/AFP
33, 34, 41, 43 Popperfoto
44 Express Newspapers
49 William Frederick Yeames
50 Sotheby's London/AFP
51, 53 Topical Press Agency
54 STF/AFP
55 Mike Nelson/AFP
56 POO/AFP
57 Lori Shelper/AFP
58, 59 POO/AFP
60 Myungh J. Chun/AFP
61 Hector Mata/AFP
67, 69 William F. Campbell/Time Life Pictures
71 Fotos International
73 Archive Photos
75 Popperfoto
76, 82 Fox Photos
83 Topical Press Agency
84, 85, 88, 89, 91 Kirby/Topical Press Agency
92 E. Bacon/Topical Press Agency
94 Topical Press Agency/Hulton Archive
95 Firmin/Topical Press Agency/Hulton Archive

**Press Association**
21, 45, 46, 47, 63, 64, 65 (both), 68, 78, 79, 81.